20 —
(369)

D1465798

THE DEVIL TAKE THE HINDMOST

The Devil Take

The Hindmost

D. PETO-SHEPHERD

The Pentland Press
Edinburgh – Cambridge – Durham – USA

First published in 1996 by
The Pentland Press Ltd
1 Hutton Close,
South Church
Bishop Auckland
Durham

Typeset by Carnegie Publishing, 18 Maynard St, Preston
Printed and bound by Antony Rowe Ltd, Chippenham

' 'Tis myself, quoth he, I must mind most;
So the devil may take the hindmost.'

To all of my comrades who died that we might live –
and the girls who loved them.
Denis Peto-Shepherd

Contents

Illustrations

Oh! I have slipped the surly bonds of earth
And danced the skies on laughter-silvered wings,
Sunwards I've climbed and joined the trembling mirth
Of sunsplit clouds and done a hundred things
You have not dreamed of, wheeled and soared and swung
High in the sunlit silence, hovering there
I've chased the shouting wind along, and flung
My eager craft thro' footless halls of air,
Up, up the long delirious burning blue
I've topped the windswept heights with easy grace,
Where never lark, nor even eagle flew,
And while with silent lifting mind I've trod
The high untrespassed sanctity of space
Put out my hand and touched the face of God.

Pilot Officer John Gillespie Mayor R.C.A.F.,
killed on active service over Britain
in December 1941, aged 19 years

Prologue

In my early schooldays I had a close friend who was later horribly maimed flying with the R.A.F. in the Second World War, shortly after being awarded the Distinguished Flying Cross. On my first visit in those days to his home, he uneasily drew me into the shrubs beside the drive to explain hesitantly, in acute embarrassment, that I was not to take any notice of his father, who was really terribly nice but would insist on talking about his experiences in the First World War of 1914–18. He was terribly nice – and he never talked about the Great War, to my secret and most bitter disappointment.

This incident left me with some inhibitions regarding the reminiscences of ex-servicemen. They were not diminished in 1948 when, as a Squadron Leader after the close of the Second World War, deep in conversation with my fellows in the Mess Bar at R.A.F. Finningley, I noticed two unbelievably young-looking Pilot Officers (supremely uncomfortable in uniforms still creased from the tailor's packing) standing just inside the door. They were, I had guessed, fresh from the first post-war course at the Royal Air Force College Cranwell, and I made a mental note to call them over for a drink as soon as a lull in the conversation permitted. However, before this occurred I saw one turn to the other and then heard him say with an unmistakably heavy sigh: 'Ah well, the Service won't be so bad when all these old last war characters are demobilised.' It was shattering to realise that at 27 years of age I could be an 'old last war character'. To my mind I had but recently left school and now, eight years later, was apparently a doddering old bore, with one foot in the grave, who would in turn have to be magnanimously explained away.

Not having quite the restraint never to refer to it, here is some sort of account for my children, Yolande, Alexandra and Michael, as representatives of their generation – an account of how I became a doddering old bore, in case they too might secretly be interested. My excuse for so writing (and obviously I need an excuse) is not only because the experiences of the least distinguished may be of interest in forming a picture of an era, but also because many of the circumstances providing parallel opportunities for infinite good and infinite bad, only occur in war. Knowledge of this is mercifully comparatively rare, but is bound to create in many the desire to pass on such experience so dearly bought, in the hope that future generations will not continue to pay so ghastly a price for knowledge already more than once gained.

The World War of 1939–45 was a gigantic war, fiercer and more destructive than any in history. In this war it is estimated that 55,000,000 died and 3,000,000 remain missing – the domination of the world by forces of evil was at stake. I can only present events and experiences as they appeared to me, and that within the limitations of memory after the passage of many years. Of necessity I have on occasions telescoped events and combined incidents for the sake of the narrative, and hope to be forgiven for this licence. Of the rest of this account, early days and post-war years – these are included in some detail as they are particularly relevant to the years of war experienced by my generation.

D. N. P-S.
Great Durnford. 1987

BOOK I

Without
Fear or Favour

CHAPTER I

The Never-Setting Sun

We were indescribably dirty, bloody hot to the extent of being sweat-sodden and tired to the point where the demand for further effort creates an agony of mind and body. Sporadic small-arms fire ebbed and flowed over the dusty sun-dried heathland to our front, rippling suddenly and unexpectedly closer and closer from patches of cover. It was no use gulping with thirst, for water bottles had been emptied hours ago. The dust and reek of burned cordite with the ever-present smell of hot rifle oil, which had become so much a part of our lives, was no help to a parched throat.

In the din someone was saying, 'Here . . . Here . . . Here . . .' and thrusting clips of ammunition into my elbow. As I reloaded, I looked over my shoulder and past my benefactor into the large bowl-like depression over the edge of which we were firing. It was crowded with recumbent bodies, not the smart soldier-like bodies that training in military matters permitted, but dirty, dishevelled and untidy bodies in complete disarray. This was how it had been when our company, at about one hundred strong, had staggered into the depression and taken up firing positions along the far rim; too breathless to speak and running with sweat which caused the rifle sights to blur and dance. Whoever they were and however they had been put out of action they seemed almost lucky for we, more than likely, would have to move on and on and on under that remorseless blue sky, as we had done all day. Running, scrambling, crawling through shell-hole and trench, restricted by the thick canvas webbing of field equipment, desperately clutching an inordinately heavy rifle; it was terrible punishment.

Looking to our front again, I tried to drag my mind back to my responsibilities – our fellows were presumably on either flank, but one had been too breathless and exhausted to know. All day it had been on and on in that dreadful heat – take cover – forward – take cover – forward – take cover – forward – dear God, for how much longer had we to go on? Now we were halted on the rim of the depression, and had been for surprisingly long. Our officers were no longer in evidence, they seemed to have disappeared long ago; occasional orders were passed along the line. Perhaps, blessed relief, this was where we stopped.

It was where we had to stop, for facing us unseen over the deserted heathland was the enemy – in very considerable strength. All seven of my section were still present, but now part of a pathetically thin ragged line. Hours ago we had started the advance in the confidence of closely ordered thousands – how did tens of hundreds seemingly disappear? I thought of the litter of bodies in the depression behind and knew the first stirrings of a chill, paralysing sensation never encountered before, as there dawned a knowledge of the gripping fear inherent in the realisation of impending death. I looked at my once brilliantly white-blancoed, but now earth-bespattered, corporal's stripes of which I was inordinately proud, and tried to glean strength from the distant, delegated authority they represented. The intention still appeared to maintain a sufficiently heavy fire to deter the enemy on our front, and the carpet of empty cartridge cases at my elbow grew steadily. Judging from the frequent glimpses of movement the enemy was not to be deterred. What then? Presumably they would come at us – and we were there to stop them. As they were the enemy they were of course inferior, and would be repulsed. Looking across that apparently deserted, but obviously teeming, heathland I was suddenly again most terribly frightened by a sense of invisible and imminent danger.

They came at us – and they came at us with a completely unjustified confidence for an inferior enemy. The ground erupted into thousand upon thousand of uniformed figures, running steadily towards us. Our fire burst into a crescendo and in the crashing, yelling, splitting noise, the figures which had at first bobbed about the blade of my foresight began to grow rapidly. The most ghastly realisation of inevitability swept over me, and my insides seemed turned to water in the horror of the understanding that in spite of our superhuman efforts of the day, we would be completely overwhelmed. We were to be swamped and swept aside like so much useless flotsam before the tide. They were on us and steaming through us in such a multitude as I had never before seen, moving with one accord in relentless purpose. The realisation was so horrifying that I can remember it as clearly today, some forty years later. The full ghastliness of it was illustrated particularly vividly because up to that moment every figure had seemed a man engaged in a man's task. As we closed hand to hand the incongruity of bright-eyed, smooth-faced and often curly-haired boys in their early teens, wielding disproportionately large rifles with the yells and screams of victors and vanquished, could only be a disturbingly bad joke. It seemed as obscene as would-be choirboys in spotless surplices running amok in a slaughterhouse.

These events were to have a very considerable influence on my life, for the realisation in them of the fact that one could meet snickering death from a random bullet, in the golden light of a beautiful summer's day, however improbable or impossible it might seem. The realisation too that in that instant the huge human effort of upbringing and education, as well as the individual's unique blend of experience, achievement and ability, became nothing. A life unfulfilled, swept perhaps uselessly into the maw of eternity as so much litter. At eighteen years of age, my faith and fascination in the unfolding beauty of life and love was too great to accept parting from it so easily. If I was to be killed in war, then I determined that I would be killed in dealing the heaviest blow against the enemy that an ordinary man might achieve – but quite how, I did not then know.

It had all come about in this way. Redland was locked in mortal combat with Blueland, one of those interminable struggles so beloved by the military mind in 1938, only occasionally varied by Eastland at the throat of Westland. This particular action was fought over the dust bowl of the army's battle training area in Bordon, as the climax of one of the Officers' Training Corps Camps in which some 12,000 cadets were housed under canvas throughout Britain. The camps were tough, but not without their lighter moments. The day in question had been sufficiently exhausting to attain glimpses of stark realism, alternating with the periods of

unutterable confusion and the quasi-comedy inseparable from large-scale land
exercises, aggravated by lack of experience.

Too much depended on the imagination for valuable lessons to be learned. The
approach over the battlefield of an embarrassed cadet (the youngest usually being
chosen for their inability to undertake other tasks) bearing a flag representing a
squadron of imaginary tanks; accompanied by an umpire dealing out arbitrary
death and destruction to all in its path, was bound to draw reactions ranging from
polite disbelief to downright derision. What happened when an imaginary tank
met an imaginary mine, anti-tank gun or another imaginary tank, we never did
discover. And so the ludicrous charade went on, creating an unavoidable impression
of the rules and sportsmanship with which we were familiar in school life. War
was the supreme game, to which, it could not be denied, much of public school
training lent itself. It was hard to take it seriously and yet in 1938 we desperately
wanted to, and at times the reality of all we were training for broke through with
a subduing clarity.

Earlier in that day I had been delighted to place my section on the bank of a
real canal; giving imaginary covering fire to a party of imaginary sappers who
were building an imaginary pontoon bridge for our further advance. We carried
a limited supply of blank ammunition, but this was reserved for the final engagement of the day. My section's imaginations was apparently inadequate, for a
choleric and extremely dapper mounted umpire, who appeared on the scene, gazed
at us in distaste for some moments. He then, to our utter astonishment, emitted a
series of startling sounds – 'Pizzz!' – 'Wheee!' – 'Wang!' – 'Wheww!' and so
on, followed by the angry admonition, 'Get your heads down you idiots, you are
under fire.'

Angered by our lack of reaction to this performance, he suddenly stood a full
five feet four in his stirrups, and throwing his arms above his head emitted a
strangely effeminate, 'Whoomph! Whoomph! Whoomph!' Unable to contain myself
I burst into laughter at this ludicrous display, at which the umpire screamed, 'What
are you laughing for you bloody idiot? Those were howitzer shells and your guts
are hanging out.' He galloped off, his point made, for we knew only too well in
our innermost selves that war is neither a game nor a laughing matter, but perhaps
understandably we were loath to admit it.

The Bordon O.T.C. camp of 1938 ended my schooldays. The corps training was
tough and consisted largely of learning the fundamental military disciplines and
the use of small arms. The army went to considerable trouble in the support of
this training and injected much interest, sometimes however with a surprising lack
of humour. In the gathering storm of war, one did not need to be astute to realise
that the wealth of imaginary equipment we were forced to use was not in keeping
with the country's confidence in its armed might. Once we attended a demonstration
by a handful of tanks on Laffan's Plain; they were the 'I' or Infantry Tank, heavily
armoured, moving at 8 miles per hour and armed only with a machine gun. I
remember my disappointment in that not only did they not appear at all modern
or impressive, but looked and were, to say the least of it, decidedly old and battered.

On another occasion we witnessed a long demonstration of the Boyes Anti-Tank
Rifle, basically a clumsily oversized rifle firing a .5 inch solid bullet. This was

presented with an enthusiasm that left us all but speechless and with a deep-felt sympathy for any poor b—— that had to carry the thing, let alone use it. It was extremely heavy and was obviously unlikely to stop anything more than a man.

The Bordon camp of 1938 was, I believe, the last O.T.C. camp ever to be held. With the end of the 1939–45 war, the role of these school units was changed to comply with the much broader methods for the training and selection of officers evolved during the Second World War, and they became Combined Cadet Forces. I left, a hall-marked product of the public school system of the day, in which just as it was unhesitatingly assumed that one would be brave, it was assumed that one would lead. Hence the Officers' Training Corps, membership of which, far from being an automatic social privilege, was provided as a training requirement in the proof of these assumptions. Properly to view the justification for these in my own particular experience, it is necessary to go back to much earlier days – to those of my preparatory school, and even earlier.

In the year 1920, when I was born, among the notable events was the commissioning of the Royal Navy's great battle cruiser H.M.S. *Hood*. Launched in 1918, it was known as the 'Mighty *Hood*' being 860 feet long and 105 feet in the beam. It was the largest fighting ship in the world, and represented the supremacy of British sea-power and imperial might. 1920 was also the year of the first Royal Air Force air-pageant at Hendon. It was an era of heroic achievement that the average man could understand and with which he could identify himself, before the days of the fantastic technical development that was to follow and leave the populace largely dazed and uninterested. If I was too young to take note, the events of these years were, nevertheless, to have a great bearing on my life and can be seen in retrospect to have been nothing short of momentous.

In June 1919, the first east to west crossing of the Atlantic had been made in a heavier-than-air machine by Alcock and Brown; to be followed in July by the first airship (lighter-than-air) the R34, which crossed in both directions. Within two years, 1922 brought the beginning of broadcasting to the public from Transmitting Station 2LO at Marconi House, to be succeeded the next year by the B.B.C. broadcasting from Savoy Hill. Wireless Telegraphy, or Wireless as it was quaintly named, became an object of great fascination, the receiver seeming near magical in its ability to conjure sound, voices and music from the air. I can recall the receiving sets of the day, although my contact with them would have been later in their span of use. The set was not very large, something like an eight-inch cube, the controls on top usually consisting of a coil, a variable condenser and a 'catswhisker' bearing on a crystal, from which they took the name of 'crystal sets'. As the signal received was very faint it could only be heard in earphones, and as the slightest vibration could dislodge the catswhisker, 'listening' was both something of a ceremony and an ordeal – but it was regarded as well worth the effort, seeming quite miraculous.

The wavelength of the receiver was altered by changing a coil of a flat basket-weave disc of wire, three or four inches in diameter, mounted upright on a two-pin plug. Later they became a little more sophisticated, the wire being woven in a cylindrical section mounted on a similar plug. Those I knew carried on a label, with the details of the wavelength, the legend: 'What are the wild waves saying?'

The author in 1926.

which summarises rather delightfully the spirit of achievement and adventure of the day. In the later days of my time at preparatory school I built one of these receivers from discarded parts, and wound the coil myself. I doubt that anything in my life was as thrilling as the first imperfect, crackling reception of that set.

Work on something almost as exciting as wireless was begun on two great airships in 1924. The *R100* was to be built by private enterprise (Vickers Ltd) and the *R101* to be built by the government. The contrast in performance and history of these two ships proved to be astonishing. In the field of aerial achievement, the great period of record-breaking flights lay between 1919 and 1933. In 1927 the Atlantic was crossed from west to east for the first time in a non-stop solo flight, by the American Lindbergh flying a monoplane. At the time I was at my preparatory school, and the world acclaim for Lindbergh was reflected in our complete preoccupation with the topic; Lindbergh was added to our exclusive roll of heroes. It is interesting, in comparison to the present day, to recall exactly who were these heroes. While there might be some variation, names such as Raleigh, Cook, Drake, Nelson, Scott, Florence Nightingale, Grace Darling and Baden-Powell often featured, as did those of the record-breakers in the fields of exploration, and the technical development involved in the air, land and water speed records. The common factors were initiative, bravery, dedication to service and sacrifice for others.

I had entered my preparatory school at an unusually early age, too young to appreciate the stir caused by my delivery at the school gates in a variety of vehicles, including a gleaming scarlet and brass fire engine and an amphibian. This came about as my father, who had a very considerable engineering ability and was of an inventive turn of mind, was studying these vehicles. The amphibian was especially interesting as it was a beautifully and conventionally built luxury light motor launch, fitted with road wheels. This presented the extraordinary spectacle of a boat entire speeding over dry land, which never failed to create as widespread astonishment as did the sight of it cleaving the water, and then without hesitation charging up a ramp and proceeding ashore. Therein lay the snag, as it required a ramp or highly unlikely, perfectly situated and ideally inclined natural slope to get it in and out of the water.

At my preparatory school I can only think that, even allowing for the later rapid advance in educational techniques, most of the staff were peculiarly inept. It was still the era of discipline engendered by fear and learning by rote. I was not suited to these methods and, as a result, learned little but the basis of the subjects taught, and this sometimes none too clearly. There was absolutely no incentive to learn and no interest in learning for the pupils. The school was owned and run by a truly Churchillian character of imposing bulk and presence, amongst whose great interests were the classics, and who had a magnificent command of the spoken word. The general administration of the school was left to lesser mortals, the Headmaster rarely being seen by any other than the members of the sixth form whom he coached with ferocious intensity, gaining many scholarships and other distinctions. When the Headmaster did appear in public his progress was accompanied by an awe-stricken silence, the staff in particular doing their utmost not to be noticed. I remember his very fine grey spats, probably as when I first joined the school little else would have been in my line of vision, and later one hardly dared to raise one's eyes in his presence.

The increasing evidence of scientific progress was intriguing to us, but possibly disturbing to the older generations of the day in that it heralded change in a hitherto largely changeless society, and the younger generations were obviously to inherit this new order of discovery and invention. It is difficult to appreciate now that at this time the only accepted education was classical education, and that science and engineering were, in particular, quite beyond the pale and not considered to be the interests or pursuits of a gentleman. It is therefore surprising that we should have been taken as a school to see the Hendon Air Display of 1930, for there still existed much prejudice against the R.A.F. Since its formation in 1918 this had been engaged in a bitter struggle with the Army and Navy which were determined to dismember it. As it was not then generally accepted that the air had any significant part to play in either war or peace, that we were sent to Hendon on one of the rare school outings showed considerable vision. The extremely light and fragile construction of the aircraft of the day disturbed me, as I had understandably thought in earthbound terms of strength, speed and efficiency. However, a brief appearance of the airship R101 over the airfield left me spellbound, for who would not have been entirely carried away by that great silver ship, 732 feet long and 132 feet in diameter, so majestically cruising overhead in the afternoon sun – a sight never to be forgotten. With this I was totally inspired and undoubtedly in my schoolboy mind saw this 'ship of the air' as the real aircraft, and the bumping, rocking, cavorting aeroplanes, for all their breathtaking dash and manoeuvrability, as something of a far lesser order.

The total destruction of the R101 little more than three months later, on 5 October 1930, with the loss of all but six of its fifty-four passengers and crew, was both a terrible shock and a national disaster. A disaster deepened by the publicity given to the building of this great British airship by the government. For us this tragic loss only served to emphasise the glory of the conquest of the air, and the dangers against which those who built and flew aircraft pitted themselves. The R100 built by Vickers, which had been completed first and successfully flown the Atlantic and back, was as a result of this disaster taken out of service and broken up.

One factor in this surprising decision lay in the rapid development and increasing promise of heavier-than-air craft. The Schneider Trophy contest was an international airspeed competition of the time, and in 1927 this had been won by Britain with a Supermarine S5 monoplane reaching 283 m.p.h. in the competition. In 1929, the contest was again won by Britain with a Supermarine S6 monoplane, at a speed of 328 m.p.h. Great Britain then won the contest outright in 1931, with the Supermarine S6B, which eventually achieved a speed of over 400 m.p.h. This amazingly rapid technological advance was opening many new horizons. In contrast, the German airship Graf Zeppelin was between 1931–37 making regular transatlantic journeys at about 60 m.p.h., providing considerable style and comfort for its passengers.

Memorable as was the Hendon Air Display of 1930, these outings and other similar excitements were, strangely enough, not the highlight of the school year, for this was enshrined in the last day of the Christmas term. On this day, after a special Christmas supper, the school assembled for a recitation and the reading of a ghost story by the Headmaster. He would without fail begin by reciting Tennyson's 'The Charge of the Light Brigade', with so superb a delivery that as his voice 'volleyed and thundered' around us, one could sense the measured beat of that magnificent vainglorious charge. So much did his recitation impress us that we came to await it with scarcely suppressed excitement, and to applaud its completion with an enthusiasm which, though we little knew it, was as much a homage to the masterly recitation as to the Glorious Six Hundred. The recitation over, all lights were put out and by the flickering glimmer of a shielded candle the Headmaster read 'The Monkey's Paw', or some equally enthralling ghost story, while we sat spellbound and terrified – after all, what more could small boys want?

These schooldays were days of a rabbit-populated countryside, when downland was cropped to a close springy carpet-like turf, when grasshoppers abounded in the longer grass, and butterflies in beauteous myriads. They were also the days of birds' egg, butterfly and cigarette-card collecting, with all the thrill of barter in swapping to augment one's achievements. The then unspoiled heath and downland, woodland and hedgerow, permitted the minor depredations of youthful naturalists amongst the birds and butterflies without detriment. At the same time the blissful ignorance of the dangers in smoking enabled manufacturers to promote cigarettes with sets of educational, informative and often very beautiful cards. These ranged in subject from butterflies and fish to regimental uniform, railway engines, ships, aircraft and the famous 'Do you know?' series. One brand issued a magnificent set of international flags printed on silk squares. These and other pleasures of childhood were largely educational, healthy and within the bounds of the very limited pocket money of the day – many youngsters only receiving two to six pence (1–2½p) a week.

In the later years of my preparatory school life, my form master was a baby-faced graduate who had absolutely nothing whatsoever to recommend him to us. He seemed altogether as dull as his teaching – completely without enthusiasm. He never laughed that I can remember, which on reflection was strange in one so young, as he appeared to nurse some sort of grievance against the world in general and us in particular. For our part we heartily disliked him, but under his overstrict discipline could only suffer in silence. We once ventured a joke on an All Fools' Day by removing the blackboard chalk from the stone jam-jar in which he kept it, and filling the jar with ink. Sure enough, in the ensuing class he reached into the jar for a piece of chalk to illustrate a point, and withdrew a dripping blue-black hand, but we might have guessed it, he did not think it was funny – and later neither did we.

Towards the close of my last term I did achieve some small recompense during the school sports day, which was also the Open Day to parents. Early in the afternoon the parents were massed in canvas chairs, watching the athletic competitions in the heat of the sun. Hovering behind them duly bored, I noticed a large and beautifully furry dead mole lying in the grass. While reaching the conclusion that it had probably been poisoned by the groundsman in protection of his cricket pitches, I caught sight of my form master seated in the back row ahead of me and taking a surreptitious nap under a large and very magnificent panama hat. The combination of mole and hat was too much, and in a trice I had very gently laid the mole in the upcurled brim at the back of the beautiful panama. This was a good start, but the best was to come, for my form master awaking conscience-stricken from his nap decided that he should continue charming the parents, and moved into action with considerable aplomb.

It was then that I first witnessed that extraordinary facet of the British character, which leads people to extreme lengths in the avoidance of causing embarrassment. Possibly an opening gambit such as: 'Oh Mr Prior, how very nice to see you – do you know a mole has died in your hat?' creates problems. Anyway Mr Prior bobbed and oiled his way from one astonished and horrified set of parents to another, in immaculate blazer and knife-edged flannels, raising the superb panama (in the brim of which the dead mole rolled stiffly) with an impressive flourish. I was denied the eventual moment of revelation, being unable to follow indefinitely, but still like to imagine it now.

For me these were largely, but not entirely, wasted years at a critical period of my life, and I have had good cause to regret them ever since. It was not so much a shortcoming of the school as of the times, and those years left me entirely unprepared for the next stage of my education and, on reflection, with some deeply embedded and now seemingly strange ideas. Those were still the days of the British Empire and with them went the unconscious arrogance in being British. The sphere of British influence was staggering, covering a remarkable proportion of the face of the globe and ruling some 563,000,000 people, as well as the seas of the world. It would have been strange if England had not seemed to us the centre of the world (an illusion amply supported by our school atlases) and strange also if the virility of this tiny nation that had become a political and commercial Titan, had not seemed utterly unchallengeable.

In this context we were brought up and educated in the simple truths that mankind must needs live in a community; that human frailty was our greatest enemy; and that we must never cease to guard against self-interest and selfishness which are the antithesis of society. To this end we were taught to regard the Ten Commandments of Christianity as the essential common-sense rules for living in a community. While current events probably sounded many a clear warning of impending upheaval in the long-established way of things, they went unheard by the nation at large which was basking in the heart-warming influence of an empire upon which the sun never set. For our part we probably heard nothing for the drumming of the hooves of the Glorious Six Hundred.

School is punctuated by lengthy holidays, and while education can be neatly assessed in the periods of preparatory, public and university schooling, it is the product of far wider influences. The greatest of these are undoubtedly family, friends and the homes they have created, and, for its influence in my life, and sheer fascination, I would choose my holidays in Gloucestershire.

I do not know when first I visited Gloucestershire, but I can remember being driven from Surrey to friends in Gloucestershire by my father in a two-seater green Rover car of the day. I must have been very small and cars were then a considerable rarity, garages being even more so. I remember it because in those days it was an expedition to be reckoned with, requiring appropriate preparation. Not only was the distance of some hundred miles a hazard in itself, but Gloucestershire was a county of deep country, rough waterbound roads and the formidably steep gradients of the Cotswold Hills. Faced with these hills, a last resort of the time was to climb such gradients backwards in reverse gear, because not only was reverse the lowest available gear, but the fuel tank being on a higher level in this attitude, it often improved the gravity-feed flow of fuel to the engine. At some stage of the journey a radiator-hose connection burst, enveloping us in steam and immobilising the car. So few garages then existed that to venture far in a car one needed to be either a competent engineer or amazingly resourceful. My father was both and we were soon on our way again, the hose being clamped in an improvised splint of various materials and bound with my father's and my own handkerchief. I felt very important.

I had been visiting Gloucestershire from babyhood, but these are my first memories of it, memories steadily increased by holidays there which continued until the outbreak of World War 2. I had a considerable love of my home county Surrey, but was irresistibly drawn to the character of Gloucestershire, and came to love it so greatly that I completely identified myself with it, and to this day still unwarrantably consider it my real home county. Sometimes I stayed with two spinster sisters whom my parents met during the Great War. The War had been the climax of the sisters' lives, the older having definitely served in the V.A.D. as a nurse and the younger having less definitely become engaged to be married, while on war work. The First World War, or Great War as it was then termed, left in its wake an economic disaster which has been well assessed and documented; but the wake of human disaster following the huge losses in men cannot be costed or documented, for human suffering knows no bounds. There remained a host of bereaved women and children, deprived of husbands and fathers or the chance of husbands and prospects, left to live and suffer in greatly reduced circumstances and silence.

Of these the Rivers sisters were two, eking out a living by the most stringent thrift in an earthy manner possible then, but now beyond the comprehension and ability of a 'throw-away' spendthrift society. Intensely loyal to their God, their king and their country, they defied the threats of poverty in a Cotswold stone house of modest proportions. On the side of a steep rise, it was set amongst the bric-a-brac of outhouses inseparable from country living. A long-disused shed to house a trap, with stable accommodation for the pony; a wash-house containing a wood-fired copper and heavy mangle; a chicken run and dilapidated hen-house, wood-store and inevitable earth-closet. At the end of the dry-stone-walled garden was an old and half-forgotten summerhouse. Of that garden I remember most the timeless mulberry tree set in the middle of a small lawn; it was the main feature, and on to its heavily berried branches my bedroom window looked every summertime.

Water was drawn from a solitary tap over an old lead-covered sink, borne on piers in the stone-floored kitchen. This tap led from 'The Spring', a mysterious source higher up the hill with a will of its own. It ran with unpredictable intensity or frequently not at all, depending on the earlier rainfall or maybe the demands of Farmer Neale's cattle. As an alternative, a short-handled pump drew water into the same sink from a stone rainwater tank under the house. This pump, in advanced stages of dilapidation, required extensive priming (filling with water above the piston) before it would work, and emitted the most unappetising clanks, wheezes, gurgles and groans. Either of these two sources was considered fit for drinking, inasmuch as no one seemed to have suffered from so doing. Of necessity this water was carefully conserved, and for the washing of clothes or the very occasional bath, water was drawn from one or other of the huge rainwater butts that filled from the outhouse rooves. These butts fairly teemed with insect life, fraternisation with which required a strong constitution. Water could be precious in a long dust-laden Cotswold summer, and yet when it did rain it was likely to rain in torrents as only hill rain can, and the idea of scarcity seemed at the time impossible.

The rare bath was often combined with the regular clothes wash, as either required a preparatory gathering of suitable firewood, and an early start in filling the large wash-house copper from the nearby rainwater butts. This was followed by the kindling and maintaining of a fire under the copper for several hours, which was no mean task. Hot water was baled into galvanised iron baths, in which the clothes were washed with the aid of a corrugated metal scrubbing board in a wooden frame. They were then rinsed and passed through the rollers of the great cast-iron framed mangle, with a magnificent clanking, gushing of expelled water and bellowing of steam.

For a bath, the copper was kept topped up with water during the washing and the fire maintained until early evening. Then a tin hip-bath was placed before the living-room fire, and filled by means of the crank-spouted domestic water cans still in fairly common usage, especially in the country. As these held perhaps a gallon at the most, the number of journeys to the wash-house can be imagined. The labour did not end here however, as the bath still had to be emptied, cleaned and stowed away. For all the effort involved it seemed well worth while as there is little so pleasurable as bathing by lamp-light before a blazing fire.

The house was heated by wood fires augmented with carefully conserved coal, although coal was then astonishingly cheap. All cooking was done on a paraffin stove, consisting of a boiling ring and tiny oven. I remember being amazed by the appetizing meals cooked in this way. For economy bread was home-baked as were splendid cakes, buns and scones. Jams were made from garden fruits and hedgerow crops, which also provided a base for many country wines. All the food-scraps and precious little else were fed to the ducks and hens, who surprisingly provided eggs and a steady flow of poultry meat. Surplus eggs were stored against the winter in large earthenware crocks of waterglass, which stood on the stone floor of a cool semi-underground larder. Caged rabbits fed on grass also provided meat, considerably reducing the butcher's bill. The garden was cropped with the aid of the chicken and rabbit manure, to produce quantities of vegetables some part of which was, as an economy, always grown for seed. For butter and milk there was Farmer Neale's dairy, whose pastures adjoined the garden on one side and whose orchards on the other side were a continual temptation to any boy. What little else was required in such a standard of life was obtained by weekly visits to Nailsworth, some three miles over the fields.

So lived the Rivers sisters, and there I was always welcome and stayed during many a happy summer holiday, growing to love the mellow lichen-covered stone walls and buildings; the exciting hill landscape in which every turn revealed beauty tumbling upon beauty; and the beaten marl roads, bordered by hurrying runnels from roadside springs splashing into moss-encrusted stone troughs. The fabulous autumn tints of the Cotswolds have to be seen to be believed. I walked in an enchanted dream as I drank in these scenes wandering far and wide and once through the fields, valleys and woods between Nailsworth and Cirencester, a distance of some twelve miles each way. On that occasion I lunched at a wayside inn on Cotswold cheese and strong local draught-cider at a few old pence a pint. Tea in Cirencester consisted of as much bread, butter, jam, scones, cream and cakes as I could eat for ten pence (4p).

Farmer Neale, the Rivers' neighbour, loomed large in their lives perhaps not only owing to his proximity, but also to his membership of a brutal and licentious sex with which they had lost contact without ever discovering the facts of its reputed depravity. I was once treated to an extremely sympathetic account of Farmer Neale's problems, which embraced nearly every disaster that can befall a family. It included the severe illness of several members, the penultimate disaster being the loss of his wife; but the ultimate and crowning disaster was in the statement '– and then he lost his hay,' uttered in the tones of a catastrophe almost too terrible for words – which led me to ponder for quite a while on the priorities of country life.

These delightful sisters were, towards the end of a life of continual labour and frugality, to receive some reward upon earth which was indeed a glimpse of the heaven that sustained them. A bequest which coincided with the arrival of mains services in the area enabled them to instal mains water, a bath, hot water system and waterborne sanitation. At almost the same time, greatest wonder of all, the house was wired for electric light. After lengthy deliberation Hilda announced with the satisfaction of one to whom has been revealed a great and obscure truth, that the wonder of electricity was easily understandable when one realised that it was God's breath. Not for her were the technical complexities of conductors in the form of low impedance copper wire – they were, she realised, simply pipes leading from a supply of benevolence as distant, mystical and wonderful as heaven itself. In consequence, each light switch was painstakingly labelled with 'on' and 'off' positions (regardless of the fact that the light indicated the situation with much greater clarity) in recognition of the respectful handling of so precious a commodity. A supply of well-fitting corks was also always to hand, and whenever for any reason a bulb had to be removed from its socket a cork was immediately substituted, presumably not only for fear of lack of consideration in causing the Almighty possible breathlessness, but because waste was abhorrent. Although a privilege to pay for it, there was always the reckoning of the meter ticking away in a cupboard to be considered.

If electricity was beyond the comprehension of such people, it has firstly to be remembered that after a lifetime of candle and paraffin-lamp light, with all its cleaning, filling. lighting, trimming and constant carrying from one point in the house to another, then so brilliant a light at the touch of a button was wonder and luxury beyond belief. Secondly, since time immemorial the fundamental human necessities of warmth and light have appeared to be divine gifts in the natural cycle, and perhaps so childlike a gratitude for the receiving of these necessities was by far more worthy than today's technologically sophisticated indifference to life's bounty.

The stream in the bottom of the valley meandered for miles through unspoiled country, every now and again bestraddled by a flour or woollen mill which in many cases still used the water for power. These mills, mill ponds, races and sluices, now mellowed with age, added greatly to the interest of an otherwise insignificant stream, and stood testimony to the one-time-great Cotswold wool industry which made Gloucestershire a rich and fascinating county.

Downstream lay Nailsworth (the nail being an old-time wool-measure) and upstream nothing much until you came to the small manor house and little estate, owned by a wonderful character and his delightful wife, Commander and Mrs Nevis. I knew them to be wonderful (although many may not have shared this view) and they were my friends. They did not have many friends (as grown-ups judge others by strange and unimportant things) or perhaps any need of them. Years later I was to read *The Little Prince* by Antoine de Saint-Exupery, and to understand so well the Little Prince's explanation that 'It is only with the heart that one can see rightly; what is essential is invisible to the eye'. Commander Nevis was a retired Engineer Commander of the Royal Naval Reserve, who had sailed before the mast in his early days and retained undiminished a rolling gait, foghorn voice and generally salty tang. The son of a Gloucestershire parson, he had retired to a small, solid, Cotswold-stone country house of indeterminate date and style, and proceeded to invest it with an even greater and battleship-like solidity.

The surrounding fields belonged to the property, which lay in the valley astride this typical Cotswold stream, and complete with its barns, stabling, outhouses, orchards and cottages, it made an attractive miniature estate. Although there was a man or two to help at times, most of the work of the estate was done, with considerable enjoyment, by the Commander himself, who left the house after breakfast only to return briefly for lunch and again finally at dusk. In the intervening hours he could be found turning his hand, with the greatest of ability, to every conceivable job and what could have intrigued a boy more? There were always the hens to be fed and watered, and buckets full of both brown and white eggs to be gathered, graded and packed or sometimes preserved in waterglass. Cattle to be fed, dry-stone walls to be repaired, pot-holes in the unsurfaced road to be filled with stone and Gloucestershire 'marl' and then rammed down by hand, as did the professional roadmen. Doors and gates to be rebuilt or replaced, and endless woodwork to be painted bright. As the years went by I must have watched and assisted in nearly every job that arises on a small country property, and these are legion. In this way I became permanently fascinated by the wide general skills called for in working an estate, and the appeal of the reality of this relationship with nature and the pride of its largely self-supporting independence.

The Commander had no children, and as his knowledge of them was minimal he either ignored them completely or considered them much as equals, which for the fortunate made him the most marvellous company. As he worked, be it on the spring, well water supply, drainage, electrical systems, woodwork, car or whatever else, he painstakingly described and discussed in minute detail exactly what he was doing. I only realised long after his death how much of my fund of general knowledge I owed to him. I still wonder at the fact that he gave me a clear understanding of the principles and working systems of the pre-selector gearbox fitted to his car, a forerunner to the automatic gearbox of today and little less complicated.

He never showed the slightest emotion in my presence and had I been older and wiser, I might have felt much pathos in this. At the end of my holidays when the dreaded moment of parting came he appeared completely unconcerned, and like as not never paused in his work to say goodbye. I can remember with absolute clarity on my arrival in the locality after a year's absence, speeding on foot down the dry-stone-walled road towards his house, with my heart pounding in joy at the familiar Gloucestershire scene and the anticipation of a renewed association. Over the orchard walls I caught sight of the Commander with his back to me, atop a tall splayed-base ladder, in a heavily laden apple tree. I climbed the gate and crossed the grass in absolute silence to the foot of the ladder, where I stood overcome. After many minutes of quiet, but for the rustling and snapping of twigs inseparable from apple-picking, a familiar voice from above bellowed, 'Just bring me that skip (basket) behind you, up here, m'boy.' The orchards were considerable, and apple-picking a major operation lasting several weeks. The apples were picked-over to exclude damaged fruit and the bulk of the remaining packed into the attractive, standard, round woven-osier, bushel baskets of the day, for transport to market.

Mrs Nevis was a good-looking, gentle, delicate woman who must have been very beautiful in her youth. She kept a spotless house and a bright, warm, delicious-smelling kitchen, into which I would be admitted at mid-morning for a large piece of superb home-made cake, often still warm from the oven. It would have been hard to feel anything but inadequate in the shadow of a man such as her husband and I think that sometimes she, in consequence, longed to talk to me – but having absolutely no idea of how to set about it, we usually sat in silence which was a pity as I became very fond of her. On occasions I was invited to tea in a cosy little room with a charming view down the valley, seated around an elegant table bearing a silver teapot and jugs, delicate flowered porcelain tea-service, and for my benefit, a profusion of sandwiches, biscuits and cakes, Mrs Nevis, always so daintily dressed, presided and I have never forgotten that once she of a sudden appealed to her husband for help as the teapot would not pour properly. 'Wha's that dear?' he bellowed. 'Teapot won't pour – blow down the spout then – blow down the spout.' I don't think that I had ever heard, then or now, a more incongruous suggestion!

It was the Commander's belief that every self-respecting boy's idea of heaven was to eat himself sick. There was at least a germ of truth in this, and it was certainly heaven when of a summer's evening he would push me into the gooseberry cage, lowering the net after me with the admonition: 'Make yourself sick, boy – make yourself sick.' I am not sure if I ever did, but might well have done for the gooseberries were red, as large as small hen's eggs, sunwarmed and they burst in one's mouth in a delicious and addicting sweetness.

As soon as the cattle were fat a visit was planned to the Gloucester Cattle Market for their sale, and at the same time to purchase new stock. I was thrilled to be invited. The Commander's car, a large Armstrong Siddely saloon, was beautifully built but generally considered to be over-bodied. The preparations for taking to the road in this were protracted, quite astonishing and very much like the upheaval of a battleship about to leave harbour. Once under way he did not so much 'drive' anywhere as 'proceed' and on arrival the car was not parked, but positively docked after considerable slow and carefully calculated manoeuvre. The cattle market was fascinating, although much of it went over my head. In between lots the Commander told me the story of the farmer at a cattle sale who, while an expert on cattle, could neither read nor write and was not too good on figures either. He was bargaining with a friend who eventually offered him his price of one hundred and forty pounds, less two per cent for cash. Unwilling to display his ignorance he agreed to consider it over a drink, and rushing into a nearby public house confidentially drew the Irish barmaid into a corner explaining, 'Look Mary, if I was to offer you one hundred and forty pounds – less two percent for cash, how much would you take off?' 'Oh George,' she said with sudden warmth, 'Everything!' I thought this very funny and was hugely proud to be included in this man's world, but I suspect that the Commander must have had to search his repertoire from end to end to find anything so innocuous!

The business of the day over we adjourned to Gloucester's smartest hotel for tea, and properly headed for the cloakroom to make ourselves 'ship-shape'. There the problems began, for the diminutive tablets of soap provided by this hotel disappeared in the Commander's massive hands and defied the anything but nimble gropings of his large, strong fingers. This deficiency somewhat vociferously over-come, we re-entered the crowded lounge, at which point the Commander, clapping his hands to his nose, roared in his finest gale-penetrating voice: 'My God, after all that I smell like a harlot – like a damned harlot!' The horrified silence was arctic and only broken by the disapproving rustle of newspapers. Undeterred, he proceeded to order large plates of jam doughnuts, cream puffs, sugar buns and so on and when all this was assembled, with undisguised joy, ordered the 'carry on' with a stentorian: 'There you are m'boy – make yourself sick – make yourself sick.'

The Commander rarely spoke of his experiences in war, but at some time or other he told me of an incident in Weymouth Harbour during the Great War. He was in his cabin shaving when a nearby paddle-steamer, which had been converted into a minelayer, blew up as the result of an accident. When his ship righted itself after listing in the blast, he rushed to a porthole which he described as looking like a screen showing a damaged and dirty film, while falling debris streamed past it. The casualties were appalling and in his own words: 'In due course I found myself detailed for the funeral party, and so I lashed on m'gaiters and lashed on m'sword and went ashore, to give them a proper send-off.'

I last saw the Commander in December 1938, when he took me to an A.R.P. (Air Raid Precautions) display in Stroud. The Home Office was then urgently setting up an organisation, which the general public was loath to take very seriously. The Commander was most worried about this and he, who knew more than many of war, took it very seriously indeed in spite of his general depression at the idea. He was deeply concerned for me and all youngsters, a thought with which I then felt he was unnecessarily preoccupied. As it happened, Germany forced Great

Britain to declare war in September 1939, and almost exactly a year later, the Commander died whilst building a sandbag blast-wall to protect the windows of the room in which we had so often sat at tea. Anywhere less likely to suffer aerial attack than that remote Cotswold valley is hard to imagine, and this he certainly knew, but as reassurance to his wife it was no doubt built as massively and superbly as anything else to which he had turned his hand. A valiant man who died as he had lived, facing the problems and threats of life four square and pitting himself unhesitatingly against them – defeated only in death. I like to think that when he lashed on his gaiters, lashed on his sword and went ashore in that final harbour, he found a special place there in spite of his intimate knowledge of what a harlot smells like!

In my years at preparatory school I made a number of friends, with the closest of whom I used to spend much time, and we were so frequently in or around each other's houses that we became honorary members of one another's families. My friend had two brothers and a sister, Catherine, who would have been about four years old when I first became aware of her in 1930; I being about ten at the time. She inhabited a remote and closely regulated world of nurseries and nannies, and even as the years went by I don't suppose that we ever had cause to exchange a single word. Instead, on our rare encounters we gazed at each other in silence and with that completely open childhood curiosity which combines both a touch of challenge and disdain. Catherine was golden-haired and hazel-eyed, and gradually I became aware of a compelling interest in her for no reason that I could understand. As the years went by, during holidays which I spent with this family on the South coast and later in the Isle of Wight, I saw much more of her – but she remained in an aloof and distant world of her own, additionally isolated in an apparent deep serenity. Had I been older, I might have recognised in it something of the complete equanimity of that truly great rarity, the guileless child of nature. Such latent beauty – for this it is – is a rare privilege to see, especially as it seldom survives adolescence.

As it happened it did survive adolescence, and Catherine's near-nordic beauty began to acquire much of the classical ideal, with an almost iridescent purity which would not have been out of place clad in a classical white tunic amongst the columns of a temple. At this later stage much of my fascination was no longer a mystery, but there remained unexplained the fact that I had been so strangely drawn to this girl at a remarkably early age – unexplained as it could hardly be accounted for by discernment: and so we continued to gaze upon each other in diffident silence.

Returning to the last terms at my preparatory school, my guardian Admiral Sir John Kelly* arranged for me to see a submarine in Fort Blockhouse, the submarine base. He was known as 'Kelly of Invergordon', for the fearless part he played in openly criticising the Lords of the Admiralty in his finding on the causes of the Invergordon mutiny. My arrival at the gates caused a flurry of activity such as a thirteen-year-old boy seldom experiences, and this coupled with the awe-inspiring

---

* At this time, 1934, Commander-in-Chief Portsmouth.

atmosphere of a naval base caused me some secret distress. In a remarkably short time an immaculate Lieutenant Commander arrived, who introduced himself as Officer of the Day and proceeded to thrill me with the most fascinating tour of a big ocean-going submarine.

The electric and diesel engines were, to me, of particular interest. After explaining their roles the Officer of the Day completely intrigued me with the announcement that while running on the surface under diesel engines, should a crash dive be ordered and the conning tower hatch be closed before the diesel engines had been stopped, such was these powerful engines' consumption of air that the eardrums of the crew would burst and their eyes pop out in the ensuing vacuum. This enthralling situation was left for me to ponder over in a meaningful silence, which I eventually broke by stuttering in awe, 'But suppose somebody makes a mistake?' The officer looked down at me in pained astonishment and explained gently, 'In the Navy, no one makes mistakes.' I was hugely impressed at the time, and have been hugely impressed ever since by this magnificent example of spirited arrogance, which plays an essential part in the achievement and maintenance of standards second to none.

The tour at length completed, my escort took me ashore to the Ward Room for a drink. My choice was a ginger beer, and my host in mistaken generosity ordered a large pint glass. I was by then completely overawed, and so muffed taking my glass from his hand that I shot the lot over his uniform, gold braid and all. Absolutely aghast at what I had done I burst into frantic apologies, only to be quite charmingly assured by my host that it really didn't matter in the slightest, and anyway he had another uniform. I was not then to realise that such is the might, majesty and aura of a Commander-in-Chief.

CHAPTER 2

The Clouding Horizon

M y guardian cherished the hope that I would enter the Royal Navy, but this thought I turned down as I did not feel drawn to the sea or that it was in any way my element. For me, it was then to be a public school, and to this I was despatched with the admonition of my guardian ringing in my ears. I would, he hoped, make the most of this opportunity to equip myself to play a praiseworthy part as a true English gentleman, without fear or favour, in the life that lay ahead of me. A simple yet all-embracing admonition which I have never forgotten, typical of such a grand old seadog and containing the challenge, inspiration and encouragement that every boy on the threshold of adult life desperately needs.

At that time Europe was in a state of great unease, for after the subjugation of Germany in 1918 (a bitter and bloody struggle in which the losses in human life were terrible) the allies sought by the imposition of conditions set down in the Treaty of Versailles to ensure that Germany never again threatened Europe. Then had begun the rise to power of two tyrannical dictators. Mussolini, whose Fascist Party seized power in Italy in 1922, and Hitler, whose Nazi party (hardly less ruthlessly) gained a position of dominance in which Hitler was offered the Chancellorship of Germany in 1933. A year later, on the death of the German president Hindenburg, Hitler created himself Head of State and Supreme Commander-in-Chief of the Armed Forces of the Reich. Hitler was convinced that the Germans as a master race were destined to lead and dominate the rest of mankind; in the face of which any thinking person could only have the gravest of misgivings for the future.

It was against this background that I entered my public school in 1935 and the situation was, some months later, greatly worsened when Hitler repudiated the Treaty of Versailles by re-introducing conscription and launching a rearmament programme. Not to be outdone, towards the end of the year Mussolini invaded Abyssinia with the aim of annexing that country.

A study of my public school could well have caused much disquiet even in those days, for it was in many ways the closest thing to the Rugby of *Tom Brown's Schooldays* of which I have ever heard. Based on a tradition of its old boys' remarkable achievements in numerous walks of life, it embodied many of the conventions of the upper class and aristocratic English family. In spite of what the school authorities would undoubtedly have seen as radical changes and progressive innovations, the fact remained that, regardless of a rapidly changing social structure and declining international role of Britain, we were schooled to take our place in the male-orientated world of 'the Empire on which the sun never set'. A magnificent and inspired achievement that had carried British influence, from its diminutive source, across the face of the world. It might well have been intended that every one of us would lead a 'Charge of the Light Brigade' as magnificently, if futilely, as on that immortal day in 1854. While today this may well seem inconceivable it was the prevailing attitude of the time; which must in all fairness be judged in the light of the enormous and dizzily accelerating change that has since occurred, and which could not then be even remotely imagined.

There in the isolation of the English public school system our characters were formed by a basic Christian faith, a strong tradition of leadership, and an involved and meticulous network of social mores. A brilliant games coach, an ex-Regimental Sergeant Major of the Coldstream Guards, and a permanently bemused teaching staff, who fought a not altogether successful campaign to establish that education included scholastic achievement. The atmosphere was one of adventure, achievement, and imperialistic glory, in which courage was considered to be the essential quality and was very much held to be a virtue required of the upper classes.

It was assumed that the social qualifications of admission to such a school, and the years of intensive training that followed, gave one the right to lead those less fortunate. This assumption was largely carried into practice by the influence of the old school tie and grossly over-emphasised merit of prowess in games; both of which remained deeply entrenched in society. Few saw to be ludicrously inept the widely accepted philosophy of cold showers and a healthy interest in games as an antidote to undesirable preoccupations. Our own version, 'A healthy interest in sex avoids an undesirable preoccupation with games' we found amusing, but we would have been surprised to have known how much sane truth lay in this inadvertent gem.

To us war in the guise of valour was the supreme adventure, and our local heroes the R.S.M., the games coach and those selected as prefects or for the award of school colours in games, loomed large in life. Curiously in such an atmosphere I do not remember any thought of war in offensive terms. We thought of war purely in defensive terms and hoped ardently that our country would never be faced with it. If it should be we were well aware of who would be called upon to defend it, and accepted as right and proper that we should be trained so to do. We unconsciously saw war as the ultimate game, and it would have been hard to see it any other way, as we were brought up on the orthodox tactics and gentlemanly procedures of warfare, as the British believed that they waged it.

Such was our tiny blinkered world. As it happened the immediate developments in world affairs were to prove that we could not have been better prepared for the role we were shortly to be called upon to play; not only in the defence of our country, but in the threat to the very fundamentals of all in which we believed. I, of many, should remain ever grateful to those school authorities for the earnest sincerity of their time-worn values, for if not adequate citizens of the future, we were at least to be the answer to the National Service Selection Board's prayers.

At this school, although largely unconscious of it at the time, I learned something of a mighty tough discipline, intense loyalty, self-reliance, a tremendous spirit of unity and imperturbability in the face of adversity, the conviction that nothing was impossible if approached with determination, and the complete unacceptability of failure and defeat. I learned much more besides, including in some miraculous way an enduring love of beauty, and an interest in English and also scientific subjects, in which I excelled. In these days of destructive criticism such an experience of education would evoke ridicule, and certainly its partisan imbalance is obvious, but a comparison with the characteristics and qualities of today's 'enlightened' school-leaver would be interesting.

On leaving I was undoubtedly much of the typical English public schoolboy, attributed with being horribly physically fit and schooled in clean living; by which was meant the avoidance of excesses in food, smoking, alcohol, sex and inactivity. Conscious of a respect for, and duty to, one's physical and mental self, and above all 'decent' and prizing integrity with the virginal intensity of guarding against a fate worse than death. Mercifully I was blissfully unaware that these very hard-won, sterling qualities would prove first to be my making, and then my undoing; although this obviously inescapable consequence of changing values was being foretold by, amongst others, the far-seeing educationalists of the time.

Be that as it may, how the values that I learned were inculcated is of interest, as on the face of it our 'tiny blinkered world' contained nothing like the breadth or depth of human experience necessary to produce all of these qualities. The fact was that many of them were the by-products of irregularities springing from the basic school organisation, which would have appalled the school authorities had they had been in the least aware of them. Of the authorities and staff, at no time in my years at public school did I meet with anything but extreme kindness and selfless devotion to their calling. Strangely, their many efforts to improve contact with changing values were largely balked by the boys themselves, and it was in the hands of these self-same boys that I was first to meet many of the brutalities of life.

The school had been founded as a small school of limited numbers, in the belief that in this way individual attention could be given to the education and character-development of each boy. This was undoubtedly so, and this David amongst the Goliaths of its brother schools was indeed something of a giant-killer. With the intense spirit of the united few in the face of overwhelming odds, its achievements were in many ways outstanding and often beyond the comprehension of the experts. The generation of this great spirit of loyalty and pride came from within the body of its boys, who would accept from each other nothing but the highest attainable of general standards and the utmost individual contribution to community effort. It was a living example of the superiority of a dedicated few.

If limited number led to valuable advantages, it also led to serious disadvantages. In a small community it is possible for a group of like-minded and ruthless individuals to gain far-reaching influence, if not absolute power, which in a larger community would be overborne by sheer weight of numbers. This was the situation existing at the time of my joining the school, and which obtained during the greater part of my public school days. Unbelievable though it may seem, the boys of the school presented so powerful and unbreakable a united front that to a very large extent 'the tail wagged the dog', and the school authorities and staff (who can, after all, only function with the co-operation of the boys) were seriously limited in certain fields. How this can have come about is difficult to imagine. It was probably due to the preponderantly benign attitude of the authorities and staff who were loath to think ill of the school, it being based on strong religious principles. There was in addition their complete underestimation of the ingenuity of the boys, and a boy's latent potential for evil as well as good.

The boys were divided into an Upper and Lower School, the head boy and prefects being drawn from the Upper School. The Lower School was composed entirely of fags who served in this capacity for two years from arrival. In common with most such schools there existed a system of privileges designed to level every boy, however exalted in birth and background, initially to that of something approaching a servant. As a member of the Lower School one did not have any privileges, but many duties, and was at the continual beck and call of any prefect or house prefect who felt the need to be waited upon. This most salutary experience was invaluable to any who were in later life to be in positions of authority and who, as a result, rarely failed to show consideration to subordinates. It was one of the distinguishing marks of a gentleman, and an almost infallible indicator of the type of man under whom one was serving. Those years of fagging were unmitigated hell, and as such were also a harsh grounding in elementary discipline.

Privileges had to be earned by time, promotion, or ability and although often only petty, were most welcome relaxations of discipline. Amongst many others were the privilege of putting hands in pockets. As a fag and member of the Lower School, being the lowest form of animal life, it was not allowed to put hands in pockets at all. On passing into the Upper School it was allowed to put hands in pockets, but the jacket had to be buttoned. As a prefect, house prefect or member of the Sixth Form, it was allowed to put hands in pockets and truly to swagger with unbuttoned jacket. Other privileges were to do with the time of 'lights out', regulations regarding 'leave out' of school and so on.

The basic punishment by teaching staff was that of 'lines', which while a bore caused no problems, but in addition they could fall back on 'extra drills' which were not so easily disposed of. An extra drill involved parading in the gymnasium during spare time, changed into physical training kit of thin cotton shorts and vest. Offenders were there given a wooden bar of about the same dimensions as a Service rifle and weighing about half as much – perhaps some four pounds. The Sergeant Major was in charge and used loudly to proclaim during this parade, 'I give no sugar,' for it was a punishment and he intended to make it one. The offenders were doubled around the gymnasium in a large circle and at a fast trot, with bars held at arms' length or full arms' stretch above the head. Any slackening of pace or effort drew a smart cut across the buttocks from the Sergeant Major, standing in the centre of the trotting circle wielding a fencing foil. This cut on thin cotton shorts stung nastily and was worth avoiding.

The procedure was a variation of an army punishment where, instead of a wooden bar, a rifle was used and the offenders might be in full marching order. Even the school version was not funny to experience and would tax a young boy near to the limit of his endurance, and older boys to a painful effort – brief halts with arms lowered being few and far between. I never remember extra drills being given unfairly, but they could easily be awarded as a result of bullying, and even if the staff suspected this they had no choice but to punish an offence. In my later years at school this punishment was abolished and replaced with detention, which consisted of extra school work in free time and which was probably more constructive. Unfortunately I had by then done more than my fair share of extra drills.

Prefects and house prefects were authorised to operate a system of fines for a host of minor offences such as dirty shoes, unpunctuality, walking on certain prohibited areas of grass, and so on. If in any week an individual's fines totalled more than a stipulated amount – about half a crown (12½p) in the Lower School, and five shillings (25p) in the Upper School – the punishment was a beating, and, as can be imagined, this system was a real problem. The school was probably well ahead of its time in that discipline and a good deal of day-to-day administration was in the hands of the prefects, who had very considerable authority. This essential delegation of authority in training leaders poses a dilemma, as the proper use of authority can only be learned with experience, and in the learning there must be freedom of action, allowing ample opportunity for mistakes or even misuse. To supervise to the extent of ensuring neither mistakes nor misuse would make the original delegation meaningless, and so there exists an essential situation of trust which makes or breaks the trainee leader and it can only remain a situation of considerable risk. The hard fact was, that for the reasons which later follow, the staff never heard the slightest murmur of the misuse of authority by the school prefects, whether such misuse was by intent or default. The school authorities must have prided themselves on so apparently effective and easily supervised a system.

So much for the official organisation of the school, but in my time (and there seemed every reason to believe also throughout the past) there was in the Lower School a clique of boys whose warped personalities and sadistic inclinations united them inseparably. By instituting a reign of terror they became the undisputed masters of the Lower School, where they were more feared than the most officious of the prefects or teaching staff. It may be wondered how such a situation could thrive unchecked, but there were many reasons, a number of which will become evident later. Probably the most far-reaching of all was that as with the delegation of authority, in creating the necessary freedom to engender the qualities sought in character education, there was scope for individuals not only to go wrong but indeed very wrong. Every school has its quota of such individuals, but as a percentage of the whole they are insignificant, and it is perhaps the essence of this type of education that this is accepted as a justifiable risk.

The power of this clique, then numbering four, was absolute in the Lower School where they maintained their own discipline by illegal fines and illegal beatings, or just intense bullying. That neither the prefects nor Upper School intervened in these goings-on was firstly because they did not know of the full extent of this terrorism. It was traditional that juniors should be given 'hell' as an important part of their training, and what was known of the situation was accepted as such. Secondly, prefects for their part seemed to admire what they saw as forceful junior leaders, whom they tolerated as long as these paid due allegiance to the prefectorial body, and left them with the internal affairs of the Lower School entirely in their hands. Of the Upper School's yet few privileges, probably the greatest was that they had escaped from the Lower School and to emphasise this they maintained a complete aloofness. In the Upper School were some who had themselves been members of factions that once dominated the Lower School, and if anything these would have encouraged rather than discouraged the situation in the Lower School, which considerably strengthened the position of the terrorist clique.

The underlying memory of my early public school days is one of the fearful bleakness of the great, gaunt rooms. The oppressive darkness in the huge windows after nightfall was barely held at bay by lighting limited to the sparse wiring of a 110 volt system, once no doubt the pride and wonder of the locality, but in my time painfully inadequate. The self-same sash windows rattled persistently, in a hollow booming melancholy throughout the building, particularly in the blustering winter winds which ripped over the downs to buffet the gaunt, rambling mansion mercilessly. This sound would still chill me if I were to hear it today. Above all in those first few terms there was the acute sense of loneliness, of isolation from friends and family and the sense of malevolence lying ahead, causing one to dread the next day.

The new boy was allowed a fortnight in which to learn the rules and customs of the school. During that time, should he fall foul of either, he was immune from punishment. This seemed less reasonable when one discovered the huge amount of knowledge which one was expected to acquire; as while the rules were comparatively simple, the customs of the school were many and devious. It was during this time that two vital things were borne in on one. The beginnings of an intense loyalty to the school, and within this loyalty the sanctity of the unbreakable custom that one never in any circumstances gave adverse information on anyone, or in other words 'told'. To transgress in either of these matters was to place oneself irrevocably beyond the pale and to risk instant and savage retribution. Nothing evoked so unanimous a fury in the school, and it was tantamount to the expelling of an undesirable from the community.

The penalty was somewhat medieval in that apart from the instant placing 'in Coventry' of the offender, he was at the first opportunity dragged in secrecy by the entire division of the school to which he belonged down to the nearby lake, stripped, and hurled in regardless of season or temperature. As the opportunity might not occur for some considerable time, the offender would meanwhile suffer agonies of anticipation which enormously increased the punishment. Once in the lake he was pelted with sticks, mud and possibly even stones; at the same time he was prevented from landing until exhausted by physical effort, or cold, or both. Eventually on crawling up the bank he was in the summer liable to be seized and dragged naked, wet and mud-covered, through the nearest nettle patch for good measure. I can recollect this procedure being carried out two or three times during my years at school, but as far as I remember it was in every case a punishment for conduct deemed to have 'let the school down' and not for 'telling'.

Such mob savagery cannot be defended in a civilised community, but it denoted a great pride in 'belonging', and the rigid safeguarding of the standards of those entitled to belong. Unfortunately it did at the same time provide perfect cover for the operations of the bullying cliques in the school, who could flourish with impunity by so ensuring absolute security from the escape of information to authority. This was why the school authorities and staff were totally unaware of anything undesirable that went on within the school, and why even the prefects and Upper School were only partially aware of the actual state of affairs in the Lower School.

At the end of the new boy's fortnight of grace he began 'fagging' and found himself at the beck and call of any prefect or house prefect, in spite of the school rules on the subject, to carry out whatever tasks they might require. Fags ran to the fag call (the last to arrive received the task) and fags ran in the execution of the task; the penalty for failing to run was a beating for slack fagging. The tasks involved in fagging were limitless, and in my two years as a fag I quickly learned to take anything in my stride with the impassiveness of the perfect servant. Amongst our tasks one was frequently detailed to take shoes for cleaning to Fred, the odd-job man. Should one fail to mark them correctly, confuse them with other pairs, or fail to return them at the correct time, all of which eventualities were more than possible, then the penalty was a beating for slack fagging.

Almost as frequently one was instructed to wash up a collection of plates, cups, saucers, jugs and saucepans, heavily encrusted with congealed grease and beverages from the day before. There were no facilities or materials for doing this, but one never enquired as to how a job was to be done as this would be impertinence, for one was expected to find out, and impertinence was punishable by a beating. The washing up was done in the handbasins of the games changing rooms, washed laboriously with hot water, block soap and loo paper, and then dried on the roller towels.

The fagging system greatly simplified life for the prefects, for whatever they might at the time require this was obtained simply by instructing a fag to get it, or to do it. Once instructed in a task one never returned without having executed it, as to do so would mean a beating for slack fagging. As a result one developed very considerable initiative, and learned that truly little is impossible to the ingenious and determined. The prefects were merciless in their fagging, for it was traditional to give the fags hell as part of their initiation and training. Fagging was indeed hell – absorbing most of one's free time and imposing a considerable strain in avoiding punishment.

Besides fagging, every junior was liable for a 'duty' on a roster basis. These duties consisted of the responsibility for keeping an area of the school or grounds clean and free of litter for a week at a time. Again this might seem easy enough, but the detection of the slightest scrap of litter by a prefect constituted a warning, and three warnings meant a beating. The prefects themselves were not averse to dropping litter 'to keep the fags on their toes'. Neither were the Upper School, who though not privileged to use fags could obtain instant attendance in this way, and so emphasise their superiority – and then of course the senior fags could by dropping litter 'give the juniors hell'. It was necessary virtually to live on the area for which one was responsible, in order to remove any litter immediately that it appeared. Even if one sat there during every moment of free time there were always periods when one was fagging, at meals or in class and so on, when one could be caught out. The state of mind of a fag who had received two warnings relating to his duty can be imagined.

There were habitual offenders, as there are in any community, who seemed unable to avoid frequently exceeding the limits which qualified for a beating. It was also extremely easy for an officious prefect to pick upon some poor fag who displeased him, and simply persecute him until the Fine limit was exceeded, and this quite often occurred. Similarly it was very easy, by systematic bullying in the Lower School, to ensure that an individual exceeded a limit and received a beating.

The prefects were primarily responsible for school discipline, and were empowered to beat any offender below their own rank. Before administering a beating, the Captain of the School had to obtain the Headmaster's permission. It was not possible to know how freely this was given and there was, we realised, no knowing that permission was requested on the actual grounds of the case. The occasions when an offender was summoned to appear before the prefects and then dismissed with a warning were extremely rare. It always seemed most likely that in these cases permission had been withheld.

The prefects were an elite within the school by virtue of their seniority and age, and were physically almost fully grown young men. Their privileges were many, including beer served with the evening meal and the freedom to smoke in their studies. As befitted 'young bloods' such as themselves they maintained a distant aloofness from the rest of the school, and developed such presence and style that the teaching staff were often somewhat in awe and showed them considerable respect. It was the power to administer beatings that greatly enhanced their status, and this they well knew, introducing a ritual into the process that made it a doubly terrifying ordeal. The offender was sent for by the captain of the school, or a school prefect, informed of his offence and asked if he had anything to say. Once he had been sent for in these circumstances, it was extremely unlikely that anything he might have to say would make the slightest difference. The outcome was almost certainly a warning that he would be required to appear before the prefects, which amounted to the sentence of a beating. Once so informed, the sentence would be carried out after the evening meal at the prefects' convenience.

If there was any rule in this matter it was never discernible, and the torment of fear undergone by the offender in the intervening days had to be experienced to be believed. As each evening meal ended, he would steel himself for the ordeal. Normally the Captain of the School led the prefects from their table, through the dining hall, while the school stood behind their chairs. If there was to be a beating, then the junior prefect led and in the ensuing absolute silence would stop opposite the offender and inform him that he was to appear before the prefects. It was perhaps this moment which was the most terrible, for there was no reprieve, no escape, no help, no support, and no relief in the situation; he was appallingly alone. After sweating it out for several interminable days the strain of apparent imperturbability, and keeping a 'stiff upper lip' demanded by convention, could be becoming insupportable. As the summons reduced the victim's knees to jelly, he could well be on the verge of abject terror. On leaving the dining room and crossing the assembly hall to the prefects' quarters, the victim was met by the junior prefect at the communicating door with the hall, and this was then closed behind him as he passed through. The closing of this door was in itself most disturbing for it was only closed when a beating was in progress, and cast a markedly deep depression over the whole school until it was opened again.

Waiting in the passage outside the prefects' common room (while inside they discussed the business in hand and practised a few cuts on a cushion) created a tension in which the offender, sick with apprehension, would probably not have minded if the world had come to an end, and more than likely actively prayed for it. Called into the common room, charged with the offence by the Captain of the School at the head of his prefects and informed that the punishment was to be a beating, there could rarely if ever be any point in the offender availing himself of the invitation, 'Have you anything to say?' Placed in a corner grasping his ankles the beating began. The prefects were at a peak of fitness and could, by running the diagonal of the room, deliver a stunning blow with the cane, and as they vied with each other to achieve the best possible 'strike', the results were vicious. Each blow would almost knock the victim off his feet, and yet if he flinched in any way he was liable to receive an extra stroke. The impact of the cane caused a numbing faintness, and after six such strokes he would have very little idea of what was happening. To survive any more, which was essential, was a considerable feat of endurance. The weals that such a beating left were frightful to behold, and would not wholly have disappeared after several weeks, leaving a nasty discoloration for very much longer.

This process certainly taught one 'to take punishment like a man', for men do not cry, neither do they whine in adversity. Sometimes it was justified but more often it was not, and I have seen very great bravery in the face of such brutal injustice. In the form in which the authorities intended it had something to recommend it, but in the actual form practised it was completely unacceptable and entirely inexcusable.

The clique mentioned earlier, whose power in the Lower School when I joined it was absolute, numbered basically some four; with of course a collection of hangers-on. Of those forming this clique the indisputable leader (King Rat) was good-looking, well built and very strong. His constant companion (Brother Rat) was a really mean-looking individual, but also well built and strong. The third member (Slob Rat) was the school fat boy, who overcame this disability with a cruel aggressiveness. The most inventive and merciless of the four (Weasel Rat) was a weedy and vicious character in whom it was impossible to see the slightest trace of the redeeming features that one might grudgingly have had to admit in the others. As might be imagined all four were academically impotent but, from what I remember, while the first two achieved distinction in games and sports, and Slob Rat held his own, the Weasel was a non-starter in this sphere also. These four were inseparably united, although it often seemed that Weasel was in a position of having continually to prove his right to such notoriety and their common bond of sadistic cruelty. Their reign of terror was based in the tradition of 'giving hell to the juniors' adhered to throughout the school.

This tradition existed to a degree in most, if not all, public schools and training organisations, probably reaching a peak in the Dartmouth and Sandhurst Navy and Army colleges of those days. Some form of reasonably harsh treatment is necessary in the weaning away from pre-adolescent standards and influences, in preparation for the vicissitudes of life as a red-blooded male, and especially for crown service in war or Empire. It was such walks of life for which we were being trained, and not a commuting nine-to-five existence in the city; which was by no means considered to be 'a man's occupation'. In our sophisticated society the basis of this tradition has long persisted, and it seems likely that when society no longer recognises the need to wean a boy from pre-adolescent standards, it is in effect entering a general state of arrested adolescence. The system at school was aimed at eliminating any traces of effeminacy in a boy, generally toughening him up and creating a 'man'. Although they may have been, to some extent, complementary to each other, there was a great difference between the desirable traditional toughening, and the largely undesirable bullying. There were four main recognised 'toughening' processes and these were the game of rugby, associated training runs, the Officers Training Corps and physical training.

The training runs varied from four to eight miles across country and the penalty for stopping, walking or taking short cuts was a beating for slackness. Eventually these runs came easily within our capacity and one acquired a considerable pride in this ability. However, to this day I can remember as a junior the agonies of extreme exertion, battling for breath and dragging foot after foot to eventually stagger into the safety of the changing rooms, in a state of exhaustion. Rugby is a war game and, as war, has to be played all out; which was the way it was played at school. A thirteen-year-old boy, being normally both small and light of build, might be forgiven some apprehension in hurling himself under the pounding boots of considerably bigger, heavier and older boys. Any such apprehension was totally unacceptable, and failure to get right in after the ball (regardless of consequences) would draw vicious wallops from seniors on the field, or even lead later to unofficial beatings for wet behaviour. Many of the practice games were supervised by one of the prefects, often armed for this duty with a cane which he used liberally on laggards in the scrum. One did learn, if somewhat painfully, not only that hurling oneself into the heart of a mêlée is not as dangerous as it might appear, but that to give way to timidity is indeed dangerous, as in hesitation the risk of being hurt is considerably greater. I was fairly fast and while I had to serve a gruelling apprenticeship in the forward pack, during which I broke my nose and permanently damaged a knee, in my later years at school I played in the three-quarter-back line of the 1st XV.

Rugby was played to positive rules, and although it was common practice to rough up the juniors at every opportunity these were limited. This was not the case during physical training, although well supervised by the Sergeant Major. He was aware of the totalitarian control within the Lower School and also how this control was exercised, but he was above all a soldier and a very fine one. He had, no doubt, experienced intensive bullying as a youth in the army, and considered it to be the natural way of things. His position was a difficult one for he enjoyed a special relationship with the boys, to whom he was a considerable hero and ready friend without the aloof authority of other members of the staff. His sole recourse to punishment was by reporting an offender, which would probably lead to a beating by the prefects. This was far too akin to 'telling', by which he would run the risk of not only losing his special relationship with the boys but also their co-operation, making his work insufferable. Once when faced with this predicament during a P.T. class, the Sergeant Major (whose many qualities and abilities did not extend to an understanding of elementary logic) called us to a halt, and glowering in suppressed fury came out with the prize statement: 'There are two members of this class who are not pulling their weight

– I will not have it – mentioning no names, one of them is O'Mara and the other O'Brien!'

So it was that while he never lost the whip hand, he acknowledged the unofficial leaders of the Lower School and allowed considerable leeway, turning a blind eye to many of their activities. In the same spirit he occasionally allowed them, with some reluctance, a game of 'King' for which they repeatedly clamoured during P.T. periods. This game was in effect nothing other than a mass beating-up of the juniors, and a 'game' which perhaps understandably we juniors dreaded. Somehow the nominated king was always one of the bullying clique, who promptly chose as his bodyguard the remainder and hangers-on. This group took up a position against the wall, and it was the part of the rest of the class to attack the bodyguard and prise away the king. The juniors were so much lighter and less strong than the king's group that it was much akin to hurling oneself into a mincer; and we suffered accordingly. Should the juniors not display enough enthusiasm, one of the toughest of the king's guard would detach himself and stand on the fringes of the mêlée, bodily hurling in any junior who hesitated. It might be wondered why this was not a glorious opportunity for the levelling of scores, but had any group of juniors contrived to badly hurt one of the clique, their lives would have ceased to be worth living.

The Sergeant Major came into his own in the Officers' Training Corps, which as in all training for school representation was taken very seriously. On the one side of him, so as to speak, stood the Corps Commander who was a member of the teaching staff, and a particularly bloody-minded no-nonsense old boy of the school. On the other side were the Company and Platoon commanders who were prefects or House prefects, and who were more than ready to stamp on any real or imagined indiscipline. In all military matters the Sergeant Major was a fire-eater of no mean order, with whom one took no liberties and we learned to 'jump' and to jump efficiently. As might be imagined one of his basic demands was steadiness on parade, and his withering bellow of 'Stand still – *stand still* – STAND STILL – no matter if the world falls down – STAND STILL!' reached a petrifying crescendo. This seemed ridiculously over-played, and reminiscent of lines of rigid redcoats facing a hail of grape-shot and bounding cannon balls, only moving momentarily to close ranks as they were decimated. In fact he wanted the imperturbability that can only be achieved in the turmoil of action by absolute discipline, and I for one have good cause to be eternally grateful to him for implanting the seeds of such discipline in my own early life.

As all such excellent men he appeared to be devoid of heart, soul and feeling of any kind, which had been replaced by an intense and all-pervading steel-hard efficiency. We were sure that were he stuck with a bayonet, he would bleed pure rifle oil. We were immensely proud of this man whom we believed as a Sergeant Major to be second to none, and in this we were more than likely right. He was devoted to his work, and took no count of the endless hours he gave to maintain the highest of standards in his responsibilities; his armoury and small bore range were a sight for the gods, as were his stores and the school shop.

Looking back, I can see that the Sergeant Major's wooden inflexibility in his oft-quoted policy of: 'I give no suga—ar,' was to convey to us a great principle.

It was a sharp reminder that all of us had an inescapable moral obligation to humanity and society, and within that to the school, the corps and one another. This he expected us to fulfil to the best of our ability without any sort of prompting and least of all reward. The reward, of course, lies in the many benefits of society which we inherit in return for the duty of our support. Any rejection of this moral obligation can only lead, in due course, first to the receipt of benefits to which no contribution has been made, and therefore at the cost of others, then to a declining level of the same benefits and rapid impoverishment of society.

This in his own peculiar way our Sergeant Major clearly understood, having no doubt witnessed the principle in the barrack-room. Throughout our training at school it was borne in one us, in many ways, that it was as despicable to seek praise for fulfilling one's moral obligations as to shirk them, and one imagined that in the face of such obvious logic all would be like-minded in the matter. However, encouragement and reward for service apart, I was to be continually taken aback in later years by the ever-growing number of individuals who not only expected to be recognised and thanked for fulfilling the least of their moral obligations, but began positively to demand it. It is a small step from there to bargaining for reward in the matter, from which the logical progression is to hold society to ransom for fulfilling moral obligations. On account of its obvious evil dangers, I was never able to accept this reprehensible conduct, which I was amazed to find presented no bar to such individuals achieving positions of authority and responsibility.

Shortage of time and the conservation of equipment led to our normally parading in old everyday school clothes of grey flannels and sports jacket. Over this we fastened the regulation belt supporting a sword-bayonet, and a khaki shoulder patch to ward off the grease of the D.P. (Drill Purposes) Service rifle. The webbing of this belt had to be perfectly blancoed and brass polished brilliant bright, which in the time available was a considerable imposition, but this was nothing compared to the work involved in preparation for Field Days or the annual General's Inspection.

The field equipment worn by the O.T.C.s of those days was a fearsome thing of 1914 or earlier vintage, and basically consisted of a canvas webbing belt supported by shoulder straps on which were mounted graduated tiers of canvas ammunition pouches, covering one's chest from shoulder to waist. The webbing framework was littered with brass slides, clips and tabs to which could be attached the most astonishing miscellany of accoutrements. Mercifully we were only concerned with a bayonet (the long sword-bayonet, the laboriously polished black leather scabbard of which was covered with a canvas sheath by way of protection), a water bottle and haversack, the last two of which also possessing a fair share of slides, clips and tabs.

As we were to experience there is no end to the inventiveness of the evil mind, and no way of avoiding bullying except possibly by hiding, but this was dangerous, for anyone whose absence was noticed would be selected for special attention. Each one of the Rats had his own specialities, but none equalled the Weasel in the scope of the ruthlessness of his activities. They hunted sometimes in a pack, but such was their power that they were individually completely immune from attack and able to wreak havoc at will. There was a great deal of physical torture on trumped-up excuses, and much forced indignity. It was not uncommon to be trapped outside the school shop and made either to hand over money, or to purchase some specified article for one's tormentor.

Another entertainment was to order the youngest and most innocent-looking member of a class to ask the luckless master in charge sordid or embarrassing questions. There was one master whose tactic in these circumstances was to come up in silence behind the offender, and bring the flat of his hand down on his victim's head with an awful thump. At least that was his tactic until the Rats chose a cherubic junior with a mop of curly hair as the provocateur, and filled his hair with drawing pins carefully arranged point up. The result was extremely funny, and the master concerned was quite unable to make any sort of case of it without a public admission that he had struck the boy; filling one's hair with drawing pins may be eccentric but there can be, after all, no rule or law against it!

It was a routine pastime to force juniors to visit the dispensary to propose marriage to the Matron, an ascetic shrew. This required considerable nerve, and the performance had to be both entertaining and convincing – or else! The Matron knew full well what was going on, but must have been surprised by the lengthy and impassioned pleas for her hand by youngsters who looked as if they had not yet left their mother's apron strings. What she did not know was the terror that lay behind these performances – but in spite of her never-failing anger, as far as I remember, she did not report anyone for these incidents as well she might. A favourite with the Rats, as soon as a class became boring or one of them was in danger of being found deficient in subject preparation, was to order a junior to faint. The ensuing pandemonium put an end to the class although the Matron, with twenty-six years of school experience behind her, was never fooled and the offender was inevitably punished.

Even night did not bring relief to the juniors, for amongst the entertainments devised by our tormentors to fill the boring hours before sleep, were two in particular. One was the Aunt Sally, where a junior was made to stand immobile in the centre of the dormitory, while his tormentors hurled slippers at him with the sole edge-on and with great force; until they wearied of the sport. The slightest flinch protracted the agony, and should anyone imagine it is a torment easily borne, he should try it. The other was the demand: 'Tell me a story and if you stop before I say so, you will be beaten.' An already tired-out thirteen-year-old, whose repertoire of stories was bound to be severely limited, embarked upon hour after hour of desperate concoction, while unbeknown his tormentor slept; eventually the terrified junior would be overcome by exhaustion.

The academically inclined boys, as is so often the way, were in some cases physically deficient to the point of being apparent oddities. These were specially selected by the Rats for sport, and were subjected to endless indignities. One of these unfortunates was found to have a curious ability, and was frequently stood on a table and ordered to be some inanimate object, such as a teapot or sponge, and this he did with surprising conviction. The superb endurance and bravery of these clever but physically helpless boys was an inspiration, and to those few we owed a very considerable debt, for they attracted much of the attention that would otherwise have fallen upon ourselves. They were lone souls by virtue of their oddities, and because anyone who openly sympathised with or befriended them would only have provided additional sport. While in the realm of bullying absolutely no hold seemed to be barred, contrary to popular belief I never knew of any case where bullying was used to sexual advantage.

Fiction satisfyingly provides a just retribution for those who offend against the decencies of life, but as far as we were to know our tormentors eventually moved on to fresh fields entirely unmolested. There was, however, one gratifying incident that I remember. Although there were a number of well-equipped bathrooms to each dormitory floor, such was the pecking order that a junior had little hope of a bath at night. A number of us therefore used to get up in the unpopular early hours of the morning, before the 'Rising Bell', when with luck one could find an empty bathroom. On occasions King Rat would decide to take a morning bath and should all the bathrooms prove to be occupied, he resorted to the simple expedient of beating on each door, demanding the name of the occupant and then ejecting the most junior, naked and dripping, into the corridor. One day it happened that his demand for identification remained unanswered, and livid at such unbelievable temerity, he pounded on the door again blaspheming volubly and bellowing dire threats. Again there was no answer and, in a flash, he was into an adjoining bathroom and with one great bound leapt up and over the dividing partition, to mete out a violent retribution.

There was the most awful commotion, for unwittingly a new assistant matron had decided to avail herself of what, at the time, had seemed a row of unused bathrooms, to find herself in a completely unimagined mêlée with a six-foot rugger-playing egotist. From this she emerged not only somewhat ruffled but, no doubt, a good deal older and wiser. For this exhibition King Rat was beaten by the Headmaster, which if infantile compared to a beating by the prefects, was nonetheless a great indignity. Even this was mitigated by the fact that the assistant matron was an outstandingly pretty blonde, which left King Rat with some priceless and dazzling information.

Although such a reign of terror could never be advocated, I learned much of great value from it. I was left with no illusions as to the true nature of mankind, and the knowledge of a positive need for a controlling philosophy in life. For one thing I had learned 'to take it', and for another I had realised how easily a small evil-minded group could, by the use of violence, hold a community to ransom. This and much else I had learned, but overall it left me with an unutterable loathing of the bully, and a great awareness of the need to guard against the circumstances in which such behaviour, in any form, could take root; as its pernicious effects in a civilised community are out of all proportion to its origin.

The six terms which constituted my two years in the Lower School were the longest two years of my life. However, I was fortunate for I made three firm friends, in company with two of whom I was to acquire a growing reputation in the school, which eventually did much to screen us from the worst of the bullying.

The other, Horace, springs to mind first as a fellow new boy with a most delightful, if sometimes tortuous, sense of humour. Horace was not his name, or at least so we had imagined, but was the name of a popular Walt Disney cartoon character of the day in the form of Horace Horsecollar, and we could not conceive a more ghastly name with which metaphorically to saddle him. It was however one of the names he was given at his christening, but he managed to conceal this dark secret until shortly before he left.

Once in later days at school when commenting on his early and somewhat horrific experience as a new boy, Horace mentioned that perhaps they all paled to insignificance in comparison to the episode of his arrival with his parents. Horace, personally speechless and overwhelmed by the ominous strangeness of it all, was with his parents received by the appropriate house master, who led them to his own quarters. After the house master's effusive greeting he never looked at Horace again, but sat them all down and proceeded to impress the parents with what he, no doubt, imagined to be a dazzling personality. During this process the house master, never taking his eyes off the parents, with considerable dexterity opened a cupboard, withdrew a tin, extracted a biscuit and moving over to Horace (who was all but lost in the depths of a most comfortable armchair) held the biscuit out in his direction. Horace took it and began determinedly to demolish it, which proved to be a lengthy task and created considerable foreboding as to school food.

Some time later, when Horace was about halfway through this task, his house master suddenly looked at him in disbelieving astonishment and said, 'Great heavens boy, that was for the dog,' – which Horace then realised was balefully eyeing him from a basket in the corner. He was never sure whether his house master or the dog was left with the lowest impression of his intelligence, but inevitably the very sight of the dog induced a marked inferiority complex in Horace, and he came to loathe it.

Horace was a fascinating character of an apparently laconic, easy-going and lethargic nature, whose approach to most things was decidedly novel. He insisted, for instance, that there was no reason to hurry when catching a train or bus as one was never late, but early for the next one. He once decided that it was a physical possibility to balance three billiard balls one upon the other, and when I heaped ridicule on the idea, the points of contact being infinitesimal, he spent weeks attempting to do it, and do it he did. Later he announced that he could cut down any tree that I cared to name, with a pocket knife, and I hastily acquiesced to the theory before he began to prove his point. He was wonderful company and we spent long hours together, amongst which was a lazy afternoon lying in the tall grass beside the lake; watching the summer sky and listening to the larksong. The heat was enervating, and after a long silence Horace suddenly asked apropos of nothing:

'I say, can you dye the sails of a boat brown?'

I gave this lengthy consideration before answering, 'I suppose so; the Thames barges used to have brown sails.' To this there was no answer, and eventually, curiosity getting the better of me, I asked: 'Why? Have you got a boat?'

'No,' he replied, 'but I have some brown dye.'

Horace and I shared one most salutary experience together, which came about in the following manner. The Rats, to demonstrate their absolute power over all things at all times, had taken to evicting the occupant of any W.C., or bog, as it was termed, that happened to take their fancy. Any real or imagined delay in obeying such an eviction order resulted in an immediate battering open of the door to the detriment of the lock. The walls of these cubicles neither reached the floor nor the ceiling, but nevertheless it was not always easy to see if they were occupied; a problem the Rats overcame by posting a junior on guard outside the lockless cubicle, while they took up residence at their leisure.

On one occasion I came into the deserted changing rooms having left a class, to make use of a bog. While dubiously studying the locks in turn to find a serviceable one, to my delight Horace arrived from another classroom and asked whatever I was doing. I explained, and with an air of superior intelligence he offered to let me into the secret of how one could use a penny piece to jam the door. Thrilled at the prospect of this invaluable information I stepped into the nearest bog with Horace, and sure enough he jammed the door closed with a penny piece. It was then that two things happened, one was that the penny piece refused to come unjammed, and the other that (as luck would have it) multiple footsteps could be heard approaching the changing room door. Whatever our fertile minds might have got up to, homosexuality was definitely not included; chiefly as in our eyes it was completely unmanly. The situation could not however have been worse, for we heard the door open and the Headmaster usher in what was known in school parlance as 'prospective parents', with a flowery spiel on games, clothing lockers, and so on. This suddenly came to a jarring halt – obviously as he caught sight of two pairs of feet behind the one bog door.

The rapidity with which he reversed the direction of his conducted tour, and accompanying patter, was remarkable. In the ensuing interlude we managed to remove the penny and were slinking out when the Headmaster, who had abandoned his parents to the nearby view over the downs, burst in on us scarlet with fury and demanding an explanation of what we were doing. Here I made an awful mistake in hurriedly breaking the convicting silence that followed with the prize statement: 'Nothing, Sir, nothing at all – he (Horace) was just showing me something . . .' and then realising the chasm opening at my feet, lapsed into a weak giggle. This taught me for all time to watch for the potential bottomless pit situation, which one can only dig deeper by frantic efforts to escape from it. It perhaps says something for the both of us that the Headmaster did accept our perfectly true, but most improbable explanation: a much greater good fortune than we could have had any right to hope for.

My friendship with the two others was based fundamentally on a common interest in scientific subjects, electricity and mechanics in particular. R. de B., or de B. as we usually called him, was a slight, extremely intelligent, quick-witted and quick-moving individual, of substantial academic ability. He was a good linguist and, like all of us, had considerable mechanical skill. Of a bizarre turn of mind, his sense of humour was astute and lively. His leading characteristic was perhaps a charming, if aggressive, arrogance – probably a legacy of an aristocratic background. This led him to attempt with great aplomb virtually anything, regardless of whether it was within his capabilities or not – a spirit which surprisingly often meets with success. Always an interesting and amusing companion, de B. was nothing if not highly enterprising and adventurous.

Last but by no means least was 'Bladder', not so named on account of an unfortunate intestinal weakness, but because we were at the time wrestling with

Shakespeare in our English studies, and were struck by the aptness of the comment 'A plague of sighing and grief! It blows a man up like a bladder!' (1 Henry IV.II.IV). Bladder he became with the usual derogatory directness of boys, and he bore this inelegant nickname with a tolerant indifference. Something of a mother's darling, on the weighty side, ponderous in manner and with an amusing turn of quiet humour, Bladder kept a large and well-stocked tuck box. From this he would withdraw, amongst other succulent items, jars of home-made jams the taut paper-covered tops of which he would burst under his nose so as not to miss the scent of home air! He was something of a mechanical and electrical genius, and from the entirely spurious but highly effective burglar alarm on his tuck box, to the junk-like collections of condensers, coils of wire, Leclanche cells, spark gaps and switches that he managed to cram into his lockers, the single-mindedness of his interests became obvious. He was not himself an adventurous individual, but certainly an inventive one, and his role in our association was chiefly that of the technical specialist.

The three of us, de B., Bladder and myself, were a widely assorted trio, but perhaps this very fact was our strength as between us we were enterprising, adventurous, resourceful and inventive; few opportunities passing us by unnoticed. Early in our association the more acceptable of our activities became known throughout the school, and the three of us were named the Unholy Trinity. Unholy on account of our known and suspected activities, and Trinity because we were three but reputedly indivisible. Our unofficial activities were legion, and ranged from lock-picking, to the feeding of current into the school automatic electric bell system used to mark the beginning and end of classes, time of assemblies and so on. This was operated from a master clock which was kept locked, but our 'modification' enabled us to operate it at will, to the complete mystification of authority and regular disruption of the routine.

We had systematically located the extensive labyrinths of attics and cavities that exist in any large building, and which are often unknown or completely overlooked. To these we gained entry by making or obtaining keys, or creating concealed entrances by removing and refitting wall or ceiling panels. This gave us access to many out-of-bounds areas, and also enabled us to move from one area to another unobserved or to disappear almost at will.

Our official achievements were many, and the taming of the Bursar's car was one of these. It was a big and ageing Morris, weighed the best part of a ton, and was almost impossible to start by normal means. When he intended to use this venerable machine we were informed, and set about it with the precision of a trained crew. The radiator was drained and filled with hot water from the boiler house, the engine unstuck by vigorous turning by hand, and petrol circulated. We then pushed it down a selected incline – banged it into gear – and hey presto! – it was going! Understandably when the Bursar was out in his car he never dared to stop the engine, for fear of being unable to find anyone gifted with the necessary magic touch and this led, we learned, to some amusing if hair-raising incidents.

One winter term we were given an unusual task, as the weather had been so wet that large pools of water, some three to four inches deep, had formed on the rugger pitches. The groundsmen were secretly delighted, and held that the ground would be unplayable for several weeks. The games coach asked the Unholy Trinity to come to his aid, but quite how he had not the vaguest suggestion. We drained it in seven hours by looking for a fall in ground level, and then commandeering and connecting every length of hosepipe that we could find. To the horror of the coach we laid the hose from the pools to the area of lower level, and began pumping water from a wheeled carrier into the pools via the hose. Once the hose was filled with water we reversed the flow, so beginning a syphon which ran steadily until the last drop of the pools had been drained away. The ground was in play again two days later, and the solving of this comparatively simple problem further enhanced our reputation and mystique, which we were at some pains to foster.

During the time that I had progressed from first term fag to second term fag and so on up the ladder of seniority, the Rats had moved into the Upper School. With the exception of the Weasel, who now found himself a junior in the Upper School and with no 'legitimate' mode of proving his right to belong to the brotherhood, they left us alone. The Weasel, now only barely tolerated by his own kind, surreptitiously continued to vent his frustrations on the Lower School. In our time of supremacy in the Lower School, although we maintained the basic traditions, we were in comparison to the Rats extremely moderate and almost totally preoccupied with our own interests. However for all of that we remained fags, exposed to the problems and vicissitudes inherent in this status however senior.

By the end of my sixth and last term in the Lower School we had become increasingly aware of the outside world, where some major events had occurred. Although 'Current Affairs' was not then recognised as a schools educational subject, it was assumed that the well-educated would keep themselves fully informed as a matter of general intelligence. We were able to study the newspapers in the school library although the information that these carried, however momentous, could only seem disconnected and remote from our isolated and engrossing life. However, a far-seeing senior English master managed to include, in an overcrowded curriculum, many commentaries on national and international affairs.

These were indeed momentous times, for in May 1935 the Silver Jubilee of King George V and Queen Mary was celebrated; the last truly great national celebration of its kind. Every city, town, village and hamlet was involved in a programme of festivities. Most enthralling of all was the state procession I was fortunate to watch in London, a panorama of pageantry and magnificence, in which endless colourful and spectacular contingents of troops from throughout the Empire paraded in their full dress uniforms. Only some six months later in January 1936, King George V was to die, and the country mourned in a state funeral. The popular Prince of Wales became King Edward VIII, but almost immediately the nation was involved in the trauma of his entanglement with Mrs Simpson, and he was forced to abdicate in favour of his brother King George VI.

In Europe, Hitler had continued his avowed intentions by reoccupying the Rhineland in March, and later beginning to fortify it in further defiance of the Versailles treaty. This was problem enough, but in July a rebellion against the Spanish socialist government broke out, which developed into a full-scale and horrifying civil war of fascist versus communist. This Germany openly used for battle experience by supporting the fascists with men and material. November 1936 saw a most sinister move by Hitler in the completion of a German-Italian–Japanese treaty.

These were some of the events occurring during my first two years at public school, the most significant being the growing threat of war in Europe and the launching of a rearmament programme in Great Britain, but to this the nation seemed all but numbed. The attitude of the time was a mixture of arrogant conceit in the impregnable wealth and might of Britain, and the general disbelief that any nation would actually launch another war, the horrors and suffering of 1914–1918 still being deeply embedded in living memory. While Sir Winston Churchill has so aptly termed this period 'The Gathering Storm', our youth with its engrossing pursuits had at first limited comprehension of the omens to a clouding horizon. Now we were to become increasingly aware of the menace and apprehension in the great brooding, precariously leashed, destructive energy threatening Europe.

CHAPTER 3

The Gathering Storm

My promotion to the Upper School in January 1937 was a moment of superb achievement, for to be freed from the shackles of fagging was, as can be imagined, the most colossal relief, as too the fact that one no longer was of the lowest form of animal life even if only a junior in the Upper School. In our new-found and gratifying status, we embarked upon the increasing tempo of our last twelve to eighteen months of study before sitting for the School Certificate examination. At the same time we were working for Certificate 'A', the Officers' Training Corps proficiency certificate; developing our abilities in sports and games, while unconsciously acquiring the enterprise, audacity and élan considered essential in an educated and trained leader.

In this particular context, as an Indian brave, it was necessary to prove manhood not only in games and competition, but in everyday life. The obvious field for such activity was in flaunting authority, be it that of the prefects, teaching staff, or even the law itself. There was absolutely no antagonism to authority or discipline in this attitude, but purely the running of calculated risk. For failure the penalties could be harsh indeed, to the extent of expulsion from the school with the ignominy and debarring from all public schools that this could mean – but herein lay the very challenge. Many masters who were actually popular found themselves the perpetual target of this activity, and an unpopular master was in for a thin time indeed.

Naturally the first objective was the school rules, of which the prohibition on smoking was an obvious target. To be caught smoking, or 'weeding' as it was termed, automatically elicited a beating and to be caught with cigarettes on one involved the same penalty. In consequence, to acquire any merit in the matter, it was de rigueur to carry a filled cigarette case frequently flaunted, however little one used it. We formed the Chimneys Club, whose members met in selected hideouts when no alternative illegality seemed readily attainable, and partook of the forbidden weed with the exaggerated, casual ceremony that the occasion demanded. These hideouts were code-named for security and I remember one in particular, a deserted summerhouse in a densely wooded area of the grounds, which was named The Weeders' Arms. I doubt that any fearful addiction led from this bravado, as I for one gave up cigarette smoking on leaving school; a comment that was never believed in later life but attributed, quite incorrectly, to a droll sense of humour.

Such group activity was but a background to the business of weeding as a whole, in which individuals lost few opportunities to score. Typical of this was the astonishing autumn and winter sight of a lone figure strolling across the mist-wreathed North Front and openly smoking. However, smoking at just a distance from the windows of the masters' common room, and Head Boy's study, that it was not quite possible in the limited visibility for an observer to be completely certain of the fact; or to identify the offender.

The executive authorities of the school fell into three categories: the first and most to be feared being the prefects, next the teaching staff, and then the auxiliary staff such as the school Sergeant Major, the Matron, the Games Coach and the Headmaster's Secretary. All of these last held a difficult position owing to their close relationship, often amounting to friendship, with the boys. None of them completely escaped our activities, although the auxiliary staff were less often involved.

The Matron, who was no chicken and had in our opinion been a superannuated boiler for some time, ran with great competence a highly efficient domestic section, which did her much credit. The three floors of dormitories were entirely her responsibility, and their gleaming orderliness gave the impression that they could never be used. This was particularly so in the washrooms in which the rows of shining mirrors, glistening basins and brilliant brass taps were set off by the glass-like finish of the polished linoleum floors. All of which was lost every twenty-four hours in the maelstrom of enthusiastic and soapy splashing, inseparable from boys at their ablutions – yet would be duly restored to a pristine splendour in the course of each morning.

Our beds were made up with a superb uniform precision, and our clothes lockers, of which the shelves were stacked with beautifully folded and ordered clothes, were always impeccable. This was all achieved by a team of young girls, the dormitory maids, little if anything older than ourselves; and about the only knowledge it was intended we should have of them was the disembodied and rhythmical thumping of the floor-polishing 'bumpers', to be heard throughout the day. This was the intention, but with considerable difficulty we managed to contact one or two of these girls, who smuggled in such essentials as air pistol pellets, cigarettes and other banned articles. Several of the dormitory maids were decidedly pretty; a blonde by the name of Bella in particular, who contrived to evade the Matron's draconian restrictions and appear, fleetingly and vision-like, on the landing galleries when numbers of us were passing through the hall below between classes. In consequence we all idolised Bella!

The Matron, or 'Hag' as she was traditionally termed, previously not unfairly described as an ascetic shrew, operated with her large black cat Richard from a dispensary-cum-office, and we naturally assumed the rest of her equipment to be concealed in the broom cupboard. Richard was a hefty and peculiarly inactive cat, very well aware of his privileged position, conducting himself with an idle and loutish indifference to all but his mistress. The dispensary opened every morning after breakfast for those reporting sick, and was characteristically run on strictly hospital lines; the baize-covered table bearing a precisely ordered array of medicines, hygienically prepared medical equipment, and of course, Richard. The Hag had a penchant for ether, of which a bottle was kept handy and used liberally for many purposes, probably largely because its all-pervading reek created a satisfying authentic hospital atmosphere. How we discovered it I cannot imagine, but Richard was partial to ether of all things, and we delighted in distracting the Hag while Richard was fed a teaspoonful of his elixir. He would then stagger around the table cross-legged and with a stupid leer, impervious to the Hag's dismayed endearments, and she never could fathom these inexplicable personality changes in her hitherto faithful companion.

If the auxiliary staff were largely immune to our activities, the teaching staff were most certainly not so favoured, and were involved in an incessant battle of wits. It was, for instance, a school rule that only school, house, or games-colour ties could be worn, a rule the staff supported by wearing some club, university or school tie to which they were entitled. One junior master, fresh from a militantly political red-brick university, chose to appear regularly in a red tie. This we considered to be unacceptably aggressive, and lacking in the consideration for others which we were so painstakingly taught to exercise. Our displeasure was conveyed to him, but he chose to dismiss it out of hand as of complete inconsequence. He had yet to learn that this was far from wise, and was fortunate in our mild reaction. Within a couple of days this master was taken aback to find that the boys of every class he took were, every one of them, wearing a red tie. It did not long escape the notice of the Headmaster, who, alarmed at the apparent infiltration of subversive political views into his educational liability, whether in fact or fun, hastily interviewed the master responsible and the offending tie was never seen again. It was, we felt, well worth our investment with the local branch of Messrs. Woolworths, and the behind-scenes quick-change act in the hurried swopping of ties between classes.

Less fortunate was the senior history master, whose almost ruthless discipline was a severe challenge to our activities. However, one day he overstepped the mark in causing a prefect considerable loss of face before the members of an entire class. Retribution was swift, for at the close of the next late afternoon history period the class left the ground-floor room in which it had been held, with no particular haste but more promptly than was usual; the last out closing the door while the master was collecting his books. When he came to open the door, he found it locked and no amount of dignified calling or gesticulating through the huge and insurmountable sash windows could gain any response. Classes were finished for the day, those masters who lived out were making for home and the rest were repairing to their rooms while the school was enjoying free time until supper and preparation. It was soon obvious to the master that most of the school was drifting in twos and threes past the classroom window, but at such a distance as to be able to peer at him with ill-concealed interest, and yet maintain the impression that the windows had suddenly become completely soundproof.

After a considerable period he succeeded (he thought) in attracting the attention of one of the most junior boys, although it was in reality pre-arranged. The boy approached the window and, maintaining the pretence of its soundproof qualities, extracted a superb performance in a bellowing and ire-permeated pantomime. This was intended to convey an instruction to the apparently imbecile boy to fetch a fellow master; all of which was hugely enjoyed by a large part of the school, watching from a safe distance. Needless to say, after a long interval it was explained by the boy that the fellow master in question could not be found and neither, it seemed after lengthy searches, could anyone else the imprisoned master cared to name, including the school carpenter, or that invaluable substitute, a screwdriver.

By then some hours had passed, and the master was in no doubt of his predicament or of in whose hands he was being held. He was beginning to lose all composure, and on the eventual approach of a school prefect was relieved that release, or at least some sort of understanding in the matter, could now be achieved. Unfortunately the prefect had apparently become as uncomprehending and hard of hearing as the earlier fag. To demonstrate the prefect's concern and consideration for the master's plight, he sent for a plate of buns (saved from the earlier tea) and with a number of his fellows began proffering these on sticks through the limited aperture at the top of the window, to the huge delight of the watching boys.

When the prefects could no longer justifiably delay the matter, they reported to authority that this master had been discovered after somehow shutting himself into a classroom, and rescue operations were begun. For a long time these turned out to be fruitless, for the lock was mysteriously jammed, and even the school carpenter (who was sent for from home) was unable to effect an entry and release the prisoner until late at night. During this time a large number of boys found one reason or another for being in the vicinity, and proffering far from helpful advice. Our senior history master, if later outwardly unconcerned by this experience, developed a somewhat undignified complex over never being the last to leave a classroom and he did become far more circumspect in his dealings with the boys.

It was Bladder's tireless researches into the mysteries of electrical equipment which led to a series of other incidents. At the time he had dismantled a radio transformer revealing the primary winding and soft iron core, and leaving him with a massive quantity of extremely fine and all-but-invisible black enamelled wire, from the secondary winding. This seemed too good to waste, but his first essay into making use of its near invisible properties ended in disaster. The senior house master, tall, angular and of an aristocratic appearance, had been at the school for as long as anyone could remember, and was a perfect embodiment of the legendary Mr Chips. His chief subject was Latin, of which he had a complete mastery, and his relish for his subject often led him into a monologue study of the piece in question, entirely forgetful of his class. One of his idiosyncrasies was that he could not abide litter and as he taught, striding around the classroom, he had developed an eagle eye for any offending paper. This he would stoop and collect in his free hand, faltering neither in stride nor superb Latin oratory.

Now having a suitable means available, Bladder had the temerity to decide to call this master's bluff. To this end he attached a large and tantalising piece of scrap paper to a considerable length of invisible wire, the paper being placed in sufficiently obscure a situation as to arouse no suspicion. The invisible wire was painstakingly laid through the labyrinth of desks, to give Bladder (in the security of the back row) complete control. The class began and in no time the bait was sighted and pounced upon. But at the very moment of triumph the paper jumped just beyond the master's grasp. A rapid further swoop led to a similar result and the paper, seemingly endowed with an astonishing ability of self-preservation, evaded one skilled grasp after another – but the flow of Latin translation never ceased. The chase was becoming somewhat heated and the master, in black flapping gown, was floundering amongst the desks like a huge jackdaw – still the translation never stopped, if slowed by a growing shortage of breath.

Bladder's manipulation was faultless, and the paper jumped and danced over the floor, from desk to desk, in split-second timing. In the thrill of the chase Bladder had forgotten one thing – the wire was shortening and too late he realised this, to find himself face to face with a frantic and purple-countenanced housemaster still spouting Latin, if somewhat laboriously. Bladder's punishment was summary, for the master, raising his volume of Roman History, brought it down on Bladder's head with a most dreadful thwack – and Roman History never had been light reading.

The extreme fineness of this wire added a further property to its invisibility, in that it was all but weightless in moderate lengths, and this led to thought on its use for overhead control. Someone came up with the idea of the nuisance possibilities of a controlled wasp, and this was investigated with enthusiasm. As it turned out wasps proved unsatisfactory, but bumble bees were superb. With a tweezer-tied loop around the waist they could carry an amazing length of wire; the greater the load the greater the effort required by the bumble bee, and correspondingly the greater the droning buzz, which could be fearsome in itself. The idea behind these controlled bumble bees was, so to speak, to dive-bomb our masters at their desk and then capitalize on the ensuing pandemonium. In practice, owing to singularly uncooperative bumble bees, this was rarely achieved. These captive bees were for a period often flown during classes, and on account of their impartiality in target selection, the pandemonium throughout the class was real and exceeded our wildest expectations.

The staff eventually tumbled to the explanation for this sudden plague of peculiarly aggressive bumble bees, but knowing how it was done was one thing, and to detect who was doing it quite another. Some members of the desperately frustrated staff, determined not to be outwitted, made the dreadful mistake of attempting to intercept and grasp the invisible wire in order to identify the operator. This led to the extraordinary sight of a master frenziedly grabbing in all directions at thin air, mumbling such statements as: 'I know what you are doing – you can't fool me.' We at once rose to the occasion with much sympathy, commiseration on overwork, offers of fetching medical aid and expressions of complete mystification as to whatever he could be talking about. For the staff the situation was not improved by one of our number, who insisted on regularly complaining to the master in charge about these dreaded 'arselbees', as he called them. The first time he did this the outraged master sharply rebuked him, saying, 'They are bumble bees, and please refer to them by that name.' The boy created a neat deadlock by saying loftily, 'My mother said I was never to say bum – it's rude,' and he continued to call them arselbees, to our huge delight.

More often than not, our activities relied on the impossibility of detecting or proving the guilt of the perpetrator in these incidents, and our insistence that they had never happened, or only existed in the imagination of the victim. This last, demanding impeccable team spirit, was surprisingly effective, and was best demonstrated in two particular pranks. I don't think that the ethics of the thing worried us much although we had a considerable conscience in the matter, for these were agreed group attitudes, or if anything culpable, white lies which though mischievous were of no evil intent. At the white variety we drew the line, as anything else was, in our code, entirely unacceptable. We knew that above all no master wished to appear unfair in the eyes of the boys, and on this we played ruthlessly.

One of these pranks was performed by a boy who was capable of the most disturbingly lewd and wicked laugh, with a perfectly straight face. He would laugh loudly in this way as soon as the master's back was turned at the board, but when the master swung round and demanded who was laughing the class would show distress and concern, quietly insisting that there had been no laughter. Curiously, for a master to persevere in these circumstances and insist that there had been laughter began to sound sillier and sillier, and was liable to leave him looking perilously like a babbling idiot; few tried it. Similarly with much practice we perfected, as a class, a very well orchestrated hum swelling from a distance slowly into a powerful crescendo, and then fading slowly away again. This we could effect while to all intent and purposes engrossed in our work, and would on questioning strenuously deny that there was any hum, although this might still be very much in evidence.

New masters, or masters with a bad memory, were invariably subjected to the 'mass response' technique, which we had perfected with considerable care. The master, on summoning an offender with: 'Come here, you', would be appalled to find the entire class rising with ballet-like precision and advancing upon him. On hastily attempting to stem this threatening mob with: 'No, not you – *you*', the entire class would about turn and resume their seats, leaving the situation precisely where it had begun.

Without doubt, the most sophisticated of these activities were those which relied on putting the master in a pseudo-morally intimidated situation. One of these played by Charlie B., a colourful boy of considerable charm, presence and astonishing *sang-froid*, had much of the Grand Guignol about it, and was a joy to watch. About ten minutes after the beginning of the class, Charlie B. with superb composure opening the doors from inside, stepped out of a cupboard in the classroom, engrossed in a book held before him and silently mouthing the text. Looking up surprised and slightly pained in the complete silence at his entry, with great deference and politeness he said, 'Oh, am I late Sir? I am most extremely sorry.' The master's response was obvious, and calling the boy sharply by name demanded, 'What do you think that you are doing?'

'Doing, Sir? Revising. I always revise before your classes, you have me so completely in the grip of your subject.'

An incoherent and rapidly colouring master made a final attempt to regain control, with: 'I will not have this!'

'What, Sir? Do you not wish me to revise your subject?'

The master was lost, and he should not have persevered. 'Yes of course I do, but not in the cupboard.'

'But Sir, no one ever told me that I could not revise your subject in a cupboard.' And so it went on, Charlie B. eventually taking his place in the class, none the worse for a masterly and audacious piece of calculated insolence.

It was also Charlie B. who burst into a class late, laden with books and without his trousers. This was heaven to watch as initially the outraged master could only point a quivering finger at the region of the missing clothing. To this Charlie B.

seemed oblivious, happily expressing much regret for being late, and stressing how he hurried so as not to miss a moment of this particular master's period; which was so interesting. At this point the dialogue became standard, for the master recovered his composure sufficiently to demand, 'What do you think you are doing?'

'Doing, Sir? Hurrying to be sure not to miss a minute of your class. I am so anxious to do well in your subject this term –'

'Boy, where are your trousers?'

'My what, Sir?'

'Trousers, boy!'

'My trousers?' said Charlie B. with amazement, and then looking aghast at his legs: 'Good Lord – I knew I had forgotten something but I could not remember what it was, I was so anxious not to let you down by being late,' – and so on.

Of course the master knew exactly what the true situation was but, as most, he hesitated to act in the face of such professed good intentions, however improbable, and he who hesitates is indeed lost. There was too added pressure in the knowledge that disciplinary action would evoke an artificial wave of protest from the class at such 'injustice'. With this would be dark hints of shaken confidence and damaged morale, and an exaggerated show of sympathy for the unfortunate sufferer 'who was trying so hard to do his best' for the very hand which had, so to speak, struck him. In all probability, whatever course of action the master chose to take, he could only appear to lose.

These long-suffering masters were greatly to be admired for they were never diverted from their task, nor did they weaken in their efforts to impart knowledge, understanding and the many qualities of education to us. They possibly recognised our adolescent 'muscle flexing' and certainly never lost faith in our fundamental worth although, had they been lesser mortals, well they might. Our judgement of these men was harsh, unsophisticated and unforgiving. We, of course, judged them in relation to our world and our life, with no allowance for the world or life at large. In this way they fell into an order of precedence which might well have been expected, and somewhere near the bottom of which came our French master Monsieur Bodell.

Bodell was the typical Frenchman, small, quick-moving and to our so very English minds, hopelessly demonstrative. His threadbare and ill-fitting clothes never varied in my five years at this school, and I strongly suspect that they were the same garments throughout. He was a kindly man, but to us he seemed soft as he would not readily punish anyone. Nature endows the most defenceless of creatures with some compensating form of protection, and Monsieur Bodell was no exception. He possessed the ability to move absolutely soundlessly and had an uncanny perception which would detect almost any sort of trap or dangerous situation. However cunningly one might, for instance, devise a loaded door he would avoid it by entering silently through another one, or once even through a window. This left us in the uncomfortable position of spending a class with the evidence of our perfidy plainly visible, stacked above the booby-trapped door, and this he would completely ignore. One might wonder that we repeated such experiments, but we often did, and with great ingenuity as we were not used to failure and were as determined to catch him as he was never to be caught.

Bodell had no presence, and only a most conscientious and earnest desire to teach his subject. In this he met with little success, but his efforts to capture our interest never ceased. One day he embarked on the story of the Valse Triste with such feeling and involvement that, as he concluded a French-English translation of this tragic piece of music, tears were streaming down his cheeks and he openly wept. We were of course acutely embarrassed by this dreadful exhibition; the chap had actually cried in front of the whole class, and over a somewhat sloppy story at that – but then of course he was French. It did not occur to us that he was a musician, a violinist, and a violinist of some considerable ability. Teaching French must have been a terrible but unavoidable chore as the only way he could find to earn a meagre living. For myself, I was not then to know that by the most extraordinary turn of fate, within little more than two years, I should find myself in all but bitter tears of sympathy for Monsieur Bodell.

If we were merciless with the staff we were little less so amongst ourselves, and our activities in this region were ceaseless. The three upper floors of dormitories were equipped with uniform and almost indestructible iron truckle beds, beside each of which was a chair. A highly entertaining dodge was to wait until the occupant of a bed was asleep, and then gently to raise it on to four chairs, one under each leg. Few of us awoke before the rising bell, at which point it was necessary to get out of bed rapidly in order to make the early morning roll call. On awaking, the victim was unlikely to notice anything amiss owing to the considerable height of the dormitory ceilings; the ensuing totally unexpected and uncontrolled crash to the floor on leaping out of bed was spectacular in the extreme, if alarming and brutally uncomfortable for the unsuspecting victim.

We had to be in bed at night by the end of the last bell for lights out, which rang for one minute. A member of my dormitory had perfected an impressive display whereby he could time a casual appearance at the dormitory door, followed by a run across the dormitory at increasing speed, taking off and hurtling horizontally over the last couple of yards to land face down on his bed as the bell stopped. There he would be safely ensconced when the house master, or prefect, looked in to wish us goodnight, and turn off the lights. This ritual became monotonous in its perfection, and we decided to introduce a variation. The heavy gauge wire mesh base of the beds, which supported a mattress, was secured by a number of hooks anchored in the frame. These we removed, except for one at each corner which we gravely weakened. The bed looked exactly as usual, but this time when its occupant came hurtling face down through the air, exulting in a sort of Olympic swallow-dive, instead of being brought comfortably to rest on his bedding there was a horrible twang. In a plethora of sheets, pillows and blankets, he went straight through the frame to land with a soggy thump on the floor. Our bemused victim had recovered sufficiently to be sitting upright amongst the wreckage and peering over the frame, when the house master entered. To the inevitable question of 'What do you think you are doing?', his quite genuine explanation of 'Getting into bed, Sir,' was worse than inadequate, and he suffered accordingly.

It would be misleading to imagine that our entire time was spent much in this way for obviously it was not. These are incidents drawn from a considerable period, but it is true that they formed a continuous background to our other activities. Amongst these an important factor in the doings of the Unholy Trinity was our relationship with the various members of the school maintenance staff, for they were not in any position of authority and could be most useful links with the outside world. In addition they had ready access to many parts of the school buildings which were out of bounds and therefore interesting to us.

Of the maintenance staff the head groundsman, Gray, with his watery eyes, drooping walrus moustache and completely uncompromising personality, considered himself the doyen. He always wore a cloth cap and green baize apron, and moved in a strange stooping shuffle which the more unkind of us attributed to the fact that he was rarely out of the seat of one of the heavy motor mowers – but Gray was probably older than we realised. Certainly the view from the windows of the North Front seemed always to include Gray on his motor mower, hour by hour, day in and day out. He seemed to find some fascination in the monotony of the endless task of keeping the great games field close cropped, and utterly lost in the reverberating roar of his machine he passed to and fro throughout the day, in a hypnotic obsession. We might well have been excused if, like the Incas on their first sight of horses in the invading Spanish cavalry, we had assumed that the mount and the mounted were one strange beast.

The head gardener was known to us as 'Pudden', heaven only knows why. He had been a coachman in the days of the private house and stayed on as a gardener when the school took over. A rotund figure, in his traditional green baize apron and felt hat he was the essence of jollity, with one major shortcoming in that it was almost impossible to understand anything he said. This was due to a combination of circumstances involving a congenital inability to communicate, a broad country accent, and a complete lack of teeth. It never deterred him, and we were treated to vociferous streams of what sounded pure 'gobbledygook'. We tried answering in kind, and Pudden didn't seem to notice this in the slightest. Perhaps on this account he was a lonely figure, and was to be seen in odd places at odd times scrabbling away with his barrow and tools, regardless of the weather.

Kelly, an ex-long-service stoker R.N., inhabited the boiler room which was half below ground, and seemed to extend interminably into a labyrinth of dark and extremely dusty passages and cellars, endowed with the ever-present possibilities of the unknown. Stocky, bullet-headed and retaining a rolling nautical gait, he was to be seen wearing a freshly laundered boiler suit standing in the entrance of his boiler room, tattooed arms akimbo as though looking over empty heaving seas. He appeared to spend the greater part of his time shovelling mountains of coal into the Lancashire central heating boiler, and most of the rest of it tending the large circulation pumps in a back room, with the air and devoted attention of a nurse in an intensive-care ward. It was as if all depended on keeping alive and well this sole remaining mechanical responsibility of a once extensive machine-tending career. He was devoted to his responsibility, and could be seen at times flitting furtively through remote corridors and fastnesses of the school, feeling the supply pipes and radiators rather as a doctor takes a pulse. He had to be continually restrained from shovelling an uneconomic stream of fuel into his boiler for fear that someone somewhere might feel he was failing. Kelly ran his boiler room very efficiently, somehow finding time for endless and scattered plumbing jobs, and not only to face his huge coal stacks with ordered blocks and lumps built into retaining walls with mason-like craftsmanship, but also neatly to whitewash any corners of these stacks that might conceivably prove dangerous in the dark.

Beyond the park wall, and strangely isolated in the fields, was a long, low, patched and tattered wooden army hut of 1914–1918 vintage, which had been divided into two sections each heated by a potbellied iron stove. One of these rooms was the carpentry shop and the other a paint shop, both hopelessly littered with the accumulated junk and paraphernalia of their respective trades. Mike, a large-hearted bog Irishman, presided over the carpentry shop in a powerful aroma of glue, wood shavings, sweat and coarse tobacco. Tall, gangling and with his completely uncontrolled mop of hair invariably full of sawdust, Mike was seldom without a large cherry-wood pipe clamped, mostly unlit, in his teeth. He always had time for us, and I was once sufficiently incautious to offer him my tobacco pouch. This he took with a practised hand, placed his pipe on the open flap and began scooping and compressing the tobacco into the bowl with a horny powerful thumb. Only when every shred in the pouch had been painstakingly gathered and miraculously compressed into the bowl, did he return my pouch. He would never have been able to draw the slightest breath of air through it, and must have had to drill it out with a brace and bit after we had left.

The paint shop was the jealously guarded preserve of a truly remarkable character, whose appearance never differed. A cloth cap only partially covered a thin, tired profusion of grey curls, and behind his steel-rimmed glasses darted lively enquiring eyes. He always wore a shapeless jacket over his painter's apron, with the inevitable paint-smeared cloth hanging from the heavily laden apron pouch. A craftsman of the old school, he still painted primer, undercoat, colourcoat and varnish whenever possible, and considered gloss paint to be a cheap-jack expedient. He made up his own paints from raw materials and a miscellany of strong-smelling size, resins, oil, turpentine and other ingredients stored in the most unexpected multi-coloured and gummy-looking containers. These he presided over with that half-mysterious air of a chef about to produce a masterpiece.

He loved nothing more than to reminisce at length on major projects, and the craftsmanship involved. There was apparently no work in his calling beyond him, and for all his stories he might well have lain on his back, through those long years, painting the ceiling of the Sistine Chapel with Michelangelo. He would, no doubt, have made an expert antique restorer, but somewhere along the line something had miscarried and as a result he wore in the main the sad and defiant air of the unrecognised artist. Always in the accounts of the intricacies of his art, he returned to descriptions of his 'scraffitta work', which, unintelligible to us at the time, earned him the nickname of 'Old Scrafitta'. Although his craft was his passion, Scrafitta would often talk most interestingly on many subjects, and frequently left us wondering as to his vague and mysterious origins, and the possibility that there was more truth in all he told us than ever we imagined.

With the exception of Gray, these men were our good friends. They managed somehow to cope with the Unholy Trinity, which was no mean feat. We were however beyond Gray, whose long experience of boys led him, most understandably, to avoid them like the very devil himself.

How exactly we hit upon the idea of our next venture I no longer remember, but perhaps it was a natural development of our intense mechanical interest, and apparently boundless initiative. The idea was fundamentally to obtain a car, but as the three of us were in the sixteen-to-seventeen-year-old age bracket; none of us could drive; and school rules specifically forbade 'the hiring or driving of motor cars'; this required a cautious approach. It was not long before we had devised what we calculated to be an irresistible proposition to the school authorities, based on their policy of establishing facilities for hobbies and handicrafts. We asked for the allocation of a garage space in the staff garages for use as a workshop, and permission to obtain and install an old and defunct car for stripping and examination. To the authorities the idea of boys happily engaged in irretrievably dismantling a car seemed both educational, desirable and almost too good to be true. It was – for we had an ulterior motive; with certain stipulation, permission was granted and the garage allocated.

The car of our choice was a Rover 10 h.p. fabric-covered coupé, with Viking-head radiator cap and what was charmingly described as a 'boot' at the back, an attached box no longer for the accommodation of the long and heavy footwear of coaching days, but intended for light luggage. This car, ex the local scrap dump, cost us three pounds including delivery or rather depositing in our garage space. With this we were well pleased, as the Rover was a soundly built car assembled from quality components which would ease our task of renovation. The state of the bodywork was beyond repair and we solved this problem by removing every scrap of it behind the line of the windscreen, retaining only the two front bucket seats, running boards and rear mudguards. We then set to work painstakingly dismantling, cleaning and refurbishing every piece of the suspension, transmission, engine and ancillary systems which was not sound, and this was all but a few fundamentals. We did it by careful study, the drawing-up of copious notes and diagrams for reassembly, a basic mechanical flair, much poring over technical reference books, and extensive advice from the local garage where they always found time for our latest problem. We had none of the specialist tools required but between us we extemporised, borrowed and begged, Bladder in particular proving not only a master in these arts but a surprisingly knowledgeable and ingenious motor mechanic.

The Rover steadily dissolved into a frightening spread of dismantled components, on the face of it far beyond recovery and totally beyond the abilities of three unskilled teenagers. The school authorities no doubt felt gratified in their judgement of this situation, and a stream of visitors to the garage began to include not only house prefects, school prefects and the occasional master, but also parents conducted around the school by the Headmaster.

Undeterred, we toiled on and on in a perpetual aroma of petrol, which clung to us as closely as the remnants of the aged black grease with which our hands were permanently stained. We had our periods of depression, frustration, near-disaster and apparent stalemate. By dint of devoting every spare moment to the task for the better part of a year we reassembled this car, in the process fitting to the engine new main, big and small end bearings as well as new piston rings; a formidable task in itself. The ignition timing defeated us for a while, but eventually the engine would start and run, if somewhat erratically, and we set about tuning it. It was fortunate that at this stage interest in our activities had waned, and we rarely had a visitor. As we neared the finishing touches, it was obvious that our once defunct wreck was already in so vigorous a state of health as to be unlikely to remain confined to its garage for much longer.

We began road trials in the grounds with great secrecy, selecting times when we were least likely to be detected. At first covering only a distance of twenty yards or so at a time, partly on account of the need for continual adjustments and corrections and partly as none of us could yet drive. This was the ulterior motive; we all three intended to learn to drive. These secret road trials extended further and further into the grounds, as our driving ability and the mechanical reliability of the car improved, until there came a time when the limitations of secrecy were frustrating our progress. At this point we risked approaching the Headmaster for permission to carry out road tests by driving the car on a mile-long stretch of unsurfaced road within the grounds. After lengthy consideration, no doubt influenced by the immense amount of work that we had put into the project, he agreed provided that we were on all occasions accompanied by a member of the staff.

Although our mechanical achievements in this renovation were remarkable and we had great confidence in our creation, on reflection I would not like to have guaranteed the reliability of our workmanship. Apart from anything else our limited funds had not stretched to replacement parts for more than bare essentials, and we had scoured the local scrap dumps for many of our 'spares'. As a result the steering, for instance, retained a fascinating lag between the movement of the steering wheel and the response of the road wheels. The brakes also displayed an exciting inconsistency in performance. The Headmaster's stipulation appeared to solve our problems, but perhaps not surprisingly we found an acute shortage of staff willing to face the dual hazards of our driving and the unproven performance of our machine. The staff, apparently, being of the unanimous opinion that mutilation or sudden death were no part of the teaching contract. This led us to an evaluation of the various members of the staff on the grounds of their likely susceptibility to persuasion to ride with us; from which we reached the sad conclusion that the only possibility was the music master. A most kind-hearted and inoffensive little man who as with all musicians had his head permanently in the clouds and would, we supposed, be less likely to imagine his feet following.

On the chosen day we approached the music master who readily agreed to accompany us, losing his nerve at the very moment of climbing into his seat. However success was within our grasp, and we were not to be trifled with. Uttering honeyed words we literally press-ganged him into the seat and virtually held him there while our 'ace' driver, Bladder, got under way. It must have taken years off that poor little man's life, but in the process Bladder achieved a speed of just over 60 m.p.h., nothing like so commonplace a speed for a car then as it is now, and a considerable achievement. Much elated by our success we christened the car the 'Flying Bedstead', a name immediately adopted by the whole school. The development of the Flying Bedstead continued apace, and while the music master would make off in horror at the mere sight of any of us, for fear of an 'encore', his very survival seemed to shame other members of the staff into occasionally coming forward, and between legal and illegal runs our driving experience steadily mounted.

If I remember rightly, a good quality petrol then cost one shilling and threepence a gallon, or in decimal coinage about seven pence. A cheap grade such as R.O.P. (Russian Oil Petrol) cost tenpence halfpenny in old currency, but in spite of this we were perpetually without petrol on which to run the Bedstead. It was not long before our fertile minds lighted on the senior science master's Super Sports Riley car, with its twin carburettors and large petrol tank. We were all three uncomfortably aware that 'Thou shalt not covet thy senior science master's petrol', but as mild inoffensive Bladder said, we did not need to look upon the idea as dishonest but Robin Hood-like, as a contribution to a worthy cause. This drew the inevitable observation that, in that case, Bladder had better do the Robin Hood stuff – and to our utter amazement he did.

Armed with a two gallon can and a suitable length of rubber pipe, he waited until after dark and then crept to the rear of the senior science master's car, which was standing outside the common room window, close to a side entrance of the building. We secreted ourselves at a safe distance and soon judged by the spluttering and spitting in the dark that the siphon was underway, for Bladder had to start the flow by sucking petrol through the pipe. An unforeseen development was the all-pervading reek which could not fail to draw attention, and the can was a fearful time in filling from the small-bore tube. In the middle of the operation the side door opened, and the unmistakable figure of the assistant science master emerged. The two science masters were close friends and Bladder's discovery, caught in the act, seemed inevitable with consequences that were a foregone conclusion and which did not bear contemplation. MacPherson, the assistant science master, turned to the figure huddled over the petrol tank at the rear of the car and called, 'Goodnight, Partridge.' This was the moment of revelation and we could not bear to be so helplessly witnessing it. Bladder could cut and run but the equipment would be discovered and would lead inescapably to us, bringing personal disaster to Bladder and the end of the Bedstead project. Our darkest fears were suddenly cut short by the unhesitating and unmistakable tones of the senior science master in a brisk 'Goodnight MacPherson,' and MacPherson strode into the darkness. From this I learned not only that Bladder was an admirable mimic, but that the ability for quick thinking and courage can be found in the most unexpected personalities.

Meanwhile we negotiated with Mike, the school carpenter, for the fitting of a wooden truck body to the Bedstead chassis; and with Scrafitta, the school painter, for an overall coat of glossy paint. The result was a smart and handy little estate type of truck, which achieved semi-official recognition when it was adopted by the O.T.C. to take part in field exercises. While we never parted with the Bedstead during our schooldays it had served its purpose, and our interest in it lessened as we became involved in other activities.

Of all the Unholy Trinity's exploits the most remarkable was probably the incident of the Great Crib. It originated in the prefects approaching the Trinity with the statement that one of them, due to sit the Oxford and Cambridge School Certificate examination, had to pass, and we were to submit a plan to ensure that he did. The prefect in question, T.B., was an invaluable member of the school games teams and excelled in almost all activities, other than academic. Threatened by his guardian with a crammer if he failed the exam, the school was certain to lose his services and this seemed clearly a needless disaster. So great was our corporate spirit and our pride in the record and achievements of the school that we were completely blind to the moral issues involved, but I have no doubt that had they been considered they would in such dire circumstances have been relegated to secondary importance.

The School Certificate papers lasted on an average two hours each, and covered a week or ten days in mid-July. As far as I remember the minimum number of subjects to be sat was six, and a pass in all six subjects in the same exam was necessary for the award of the certificate. Some subjects consisted of several papers and while we had expert crib manufacturers, who could write in a microscopic but clearly legible hand, the information necessary for a pass was nonetheless so voluminous that we would never get it in or out of the examination room. Even if we did the crib could never be referred to unobserved. It looked as if there was no way of getting our 'client' through, and it took us four days to formulate and develop perhaps the most ingenious and audacious plan for cribbing in an examination ever attempted.

Our solution hinged on obtaining the seating plan for the examination in advance, and also a copy of each relevant paper. In all much more than this had to be achieved but it was enough for the prefects to veto the scheme as too big an undertaking. For our part we were confident of success, and were only concerned by the limited time in which to complete the arrangements. True that if discovered the plan could only lead to disaster for all involved, but we had no intention of allowing discovery. In the end the prefects gave way to our insistence, agreed to the plan, and work began upon the arrangements.

Fortunately the examination had always been held in the same classroom, No. 4, and this ground-level room faced onto a large yard. It was kept locked when not in use and one of our first tasks was to obtain a key to this and the adjoining room No. 8. It is not generally known how quickly a plasticine or putty impression of a key can be taken, and certainly no one was ever aware that these keys had fleetingly been used for this purpose. The next move was to find an easily accessible, but totally secure, hideout and this was difficult, but in the end we struck on the near ideal. Perhaps only twenty-five yards away in the edge of a wooded area was a cluster of half-forgotten out-buildings, in one of which was stored games equipment such as goalposts, nets and other clutter. This would not be required for use until the next term, and was most unlikely to be disturbed over the critical period of several weeks in which we would need the hideout. With great care we created a large concealed cavity at the back of the shed, underneath the mass of netting and equipment, and made it completely undetectable by casual observation.

This completed, the next task was to link No. 4 classroom to the hideout by a single-line insulated wire every inch of which had to be effectively concealed. It was carried under the floor from No. 4 classroom into the adjoining classroom No. 8, and through the door to the edge of the drive lying between this classroom and the hideout. From the hideout, the line was run back from branch to branch of the surrounding trees, and down the trunk of one at the side of the drive opposite to No. 8. All of this was completed undetected, and camouflaged to perfection.

If it was nerve-wracking it was nothing compared to the actual crossing of the drive which could only be achieved by burying the cable, and this in turn could only be done unobserved at night.

We were fairly adept at breaking out of the dormitories but it was no easy task, the first of two major hazards being traversing the long flights of stairs, effected by hugging the outside edge of each tread (which is not so likely to squeak) in stockinged feet, for absolute silence, meanwhile leaning heavily on the handrail to reduce one's weight. The second was getting out of the locked main building. This we were in the habit of doing through the Upper School library windows, which opened on to a narrow grass verge and the wide gravel drive of the South Front. The windows were of a huge and heavy sash type, which seemed to rumble thunderously however careful we were in raising them inch by inch, just enough to squeeze through the gap at the bottom. Once through and on the grass it needed considerable nerve to gently close the window to avoid detection, and in so doing cutting off our retreat. Traversing the South Front and penetrating the buildings to No. 4, was a question of keeping off the gravel and knowing the ground in the dark. While it was easier in the moonlight we needed for this task, it increased the chances of detection and left one feeling far more exposed than was the fact.

Our first objective was the groundsman's shed where we collected a pickaxe, with other tools, and then repaired to the site planned for the crossing of the drive. None of us had expected the ringing thud of the pick in the still night air; it was petrifying but unavoidable, and we chipped away at the channel to cross the drive, in complete suspense. The technique was to strike two or three times with the pick, and then to listen in silence for sounds of detection. This way progress was slow and the increasing tension awful. We had cut a three- or four-inch channel across half the drive when the lights of an approaching car sent us scuttling for cover, tools and all. It turned out to be the junior English master, and we noted that it was shortly after two o'clock when he locked the nearby garage door on his little sports car. We were horrified, and agreed that our parents would be most disapproving of such goings-on. To make it worse he was sufficiently inspired by the lingering aura of his girlfriend, and the brilliant moon, to decide on a stroll along the South Front, passing right by us and heedlessly over the scene of our activities on the way.

It was some long time before we dared to begin work again, and had hardly started when we detected a hesitant rustling in the wood behind us. This was an unexpected and dangerous development as we were relying upon the woods for cover if surprised, and were left with no feasible alternative. It was, we realised, a brilliant move to work around and close in behind us, leaving no escape but to break into the open and certain recognition. Our tortured imaginations worked at desperate speed until the rustling changed to the rattle of gravel, and into the moonlight waddled a large hedgehog, happily oblivious of the pounding hearts for which it was responsible.

Time was passing fast, marked by the sudden, slow, deliberate striking of the nearby stable clock – alarming at such close quarters in the night silence. It was well into the early hours of the morning before the channel was dug, a length of lead-covered cable carefully laid into it, the channel filled with gravel and rammed home as silently as possible. While the connections to the line were made at each end, the recent excavation was obscured and the camouflage completed. All traces of our activities removed, we returned via the library window. It was never so good to be safely back in bed – and with the knowledge of a difficult and demanding task achieved.

During this time work had been going ahead by day on the conversion and installation of a multivalve amplifier, to be operated from the hideout. This was to feed transmissions from a microphone through the line laid to No. 4 classroom, the other side of the circuit being completed with an earth return. By inserting a milliammeter in the circuit it was possible to know exactly when the circuit was complete, and when it was broken.

So far so good, but the plan depended on knowing exactly where our 'client' was to sit, and this information was a closely guarded secret until the first day of the examination. The prefects did know as soon as the seating plan was drawn up, and they also knew that it was locked in a drawer of the desk in the Headmaster's study. Time was getting short and we needed to move fast. Access to this office was possible by devious means, but we had no way of opening the desk drawer undetected. However we soon found one, and in the dead of night the entire top of the Headmaster's desk was unscrewed, the seating plan copied, and the desk top replaced without a trace of interference. We found that T.B. was not to be sitting in the best of positions, however the scene now shifted back to No. 4 classroom. There, by dint of removing and replacing skirting and a certain number of floorboards, we picked up our line from the hideout and ran it with another (earthed to the central heating system) below the floor to a point beneath the crucial desk. Here we drove two woodscrews through the floor about one foot apart, then cut off the heads and filed the shanks down to protrude unnoticeably but just above the floor level. Our two lines were connected to these screws from underneath.

The stage was now set, but while we were rigging out T.B. with a metal plate on each of a selected pair of shoes, and wiring these via his trouser legs and left-hand sleeve to a tiny deaf-aid receiver, disaster struck. The line to the hideout went dead – there was no easy way of finding the fault and time was desperately short. We eventually deduced that there was a break under the drive, and this proved so. At some time Gray had trundled a heavy motor-mower over the cable, and a stone had been driven through the cable cover and severed it. It meant a repetition of the earlier night's work, with no choice of timing, and on this we embarked digging up the cable; replacing it and burying it considerably deeper. It only remained to assemble in the hideout a complete reference library on the necessary subjects, and all was ready.

The examination started. Only the prefects, ourselves and one or two of the 'brains' of the school had the slightest idea of what was afoot. However, the candidates between T.B. and the window did know that they had to pass his paper to the window and drop it out unobserved. Outside the window was waiting Pudden, whose aid we had enlisted – but alas, Pudden was no actor, and his interpretation of casual weeding below the window was horribly lacking in conviction. However, Pudden was so much accepted as part of the school scene that nobody seemed to notice what he was, or was not doing. In this way he retrieved the paper for us on a number of occasions, and on the others we used a variety of individuals. The precious paper was then hurried to the hideout, where the best brains of the school in the subject rapidly set to work. This recurring period was the most worrying, for T.B. was in the examination room not only without a paper, but until we began to dictate the answers to him, without a genuine task, either of which might well have attracted the invigilator's attention. However he satisfactorily played his part casually supporting his head with his left arm, elbow on the desk, which enabled him to press the diminutive deaf aid receiver (concealed in his left hand) to his ear. Nothing had been left to chance, and to hide the wire at his wrist he was wearing a broad leather athlete's wrist support of a pattern commonly worn by tennis and squash players.

When T.B.'s feet were on the studs in the floor the circuit was complete, and this the milliammeter indicated in the hideout. He could communicate with us in a simple code, two disconnections meaning yes, three no, and so on. As soon as disconnection was indicated we stopped transmitting until he was connected again. In this way we conveyed the answers to paper after paper with never a problem. T.B. later described his greatest worry as the still small voice of guidance in the absolute silence of the examination room, which seemed to him as though it must be clearly audible to the invigilator. T.B. broke contact on his approach rather than run the risk of detection, for while entirely mysterious it was after all unlikely to be accepted as either the voice of conscience, or heavenly inspiration.

On one or two occasions the invigilator leant over T.B.'s shoulder to see how he was getting on, but nothing was suspected – until the results were published many weeks later and T.B., who was one of the school plodders, was found to have passed the examination with several credits. The school authorities must have spent endless hours attempting to divine how on earth it had been done, but by that time every trace of our operation was removed, and the mystery remained completely unsolved.

So passed 1937, during which I gained the O.T.C. certificate 'A', and possibly more important, there was a major disaster at Lakenhurst naval air station U.S.A., where the German airship Hindenburg was destroyed by fire. The Hindenburg, carrying up to 72 passengers, could make the westward Atlantic crossing in 52 hours, as opposed to the four to five days of the Queen Mary. The 803-foot airship was landing after such a flight when, as it approached the mooring mast, an unexplained explosion in the stern ignited the huge hydrogen-filled lifting bags, and the ship was rapidly and completely destroyed by a great, roaring ball of flame in which thirty-six passengers died. Although these were the first passenger casualties in the history of commercial airship operations, this disaster spelled the end of commercial airships, their role being taken over by aeroplanes.

Later in that same month, in a great national celebration at home, King George VI and Queen Elizabeth were crowned. In retrospect this was something of a sobering occasion not only because of the abdication of King Edward VIII which had preceded it, but because there were already indications that King George VI was to be our king throughout times of the greatest trial, tribulation and triumph that the nation had ever known. In consequence many of us were to feel a special relationship with this monarch, in spite of his comparatively short-lived reign of fifteen years.

In March 1938, Germany invaded Austria and proclaimed it part of the German Reich. It was then barely possible to imagine that Europe was not heading for war, and we boys were at the same time reaching an age when our careers would be decided and our destinies set. In this the School Certificate examinations in mid-July would be critical, and our reaction was to work hard and to play hard in the hope of making the best of whatever time remained to us.

Bladder had produced from home an old, blue, four-seater Morris which, in spite of the multitudinous imperfections inherent in the passage of the years, still ran determinedly in response to Bladder's expert coaxing. Better still, Bladder having recently passed his driving test held a road driving licence; the only one of the Unholy Trinity in this happy position. The car was euphemistically named the Bluebird after Malcolm Campbell's land-speed record-holding car of this name; and was garaged in complete secrecy in a nearby village. At this time fewer than one in twenty of the population owned a car, and this acquisition opened up many new fields of opportunities to us, of which we were not slow to take advantage within the bounds of our funds. These only allowed for sporadic licensing and a limited supply of the cheapest obtainable petrol and oil, both of which the car consumed in large quantities.

One of our earlier expeditions was into the local town to see a film. The fact that the town was out of bounds and the car unlicensed and in dubious mechanical condition anyway, did not deter us in the slightest. However we can hardly have looked a law-abiding trio, for our friend the garage owner on seeing our approach surveyed us thoughtfully and uttered feelingly, 'My God – if the devil were to cast his net now!' Fortunately he did not, and we embarked in the Bluebird and took to the road. All went reasonably well until we neared the centre of the town and encountered a traffic light, which as it hove in sight changed to amber. This was more than the Bluebird's aged braking system would stand and although Bladder literally stood on the brake pedal our stately progress was only diminished, and to our horror we rolled very gently through the crossing against the red light, miraculously missing the busy cross traffic. The rest of the journey was executed on the handbrake, which was rather more effective.

It seemed wiser to park down a side street than in the cinema car park, to avoid possible recognition, and this we did. The film was good and as all good films should, completely transported us from our existing circumstances. We left the cinema in a glow of enjoyment, and still only partially aware of our surroundings. However we were brought very swiftly to earth on turning into our side street to see a policeman leaning on the roof of the Bluebird, and waiting. We were back round the corner in a flash, and held a council of war. The obvious course was to cut away undetected and to travel back to the school by bus, but the Bluebird could be traced. We would then not only face legal action for the lack of a road-fund licence and insurance, but also the penalty for possessing or driving a car during the school term and being out of bounds in the local town; all of which added up to very much more than enough for certain expulsion. The only alternative was to throw ourselves on the mercy of the police constable in the hope that he would overlook the matter, but this was hardly likely. We realised 'we had had it' as the expression so aptly went, and were devastated by such bad luck so early in our new venture. In an attempt to weigh up our constable, and assess his susceptibility to possible persuasion, we peered around the corner again just in time to see him straighten himself up, dust himself down and walk off! He had apparently only been resting, and we were into the Bluebird and away as fast as our legs and four venerable wheels would carry us.

Across some very lovely country lay Henley on the river Thames, and during our earlier years we had in the summer bicycled to this then unspoiled riverside town. The hot and exhausting journey we considered well worth while although there were few in the school who thought so, and thereby it had the added advantage of a secluded corner outside our school world. With the advent of the Bluebird and seniority which gave us, student-wise, considerable freedom in our study programme, we often made for this heavenly and so very English stretch of river. There we basked in the sun, letting the beautiful tranquillity take complete possession of us, and bathed intermittently or took a skiff or motor boat and idled on the slow-moving water.

It was just such a summer's day, on which we had cut lectures and been bathing and sunbathing all afternoon, that we were drifting downriver in a skiff as the sun acquired the mellow and wistful quality of early evening. We paddled heedlessly watching the shadows lengthen, until suddenly we realised their portent – it was late evening and we had to be in school by the roll call for evening chapel, or our illegal absence would be detected and we would face an extremely nasty situation. The water flew from the sculls as we drove our skiff to the distant boathouse, leaping out on arrival, stopping only to grab our belongings, and then racing barefoot and still clad in brief swimming slips for the Bluebird. The Bluebird was rapidly cranked up and headed for home, but as we passed through the streets of Henley we were conscious of a sudden stir, for passers-by were stopping and pointing or even gesticulating and shouting, and faces were appearing at gates, doors and windows. Something was seriously amiss and we ran the gamut of guesses from flat tyres, trailing silencers and wobbling wheels, to leaking petrol, but it was some time before the truth occurred to us.

We were wearing only bathing slips, concealed by the window level; to all outside appearances four naked boys in an old car were disturbing the peace, and violating the susceptibilities of the good people of Henley. This was before the days of mass semi-nudity, the streaker, or even the bikini the very idea of which was heavily frowned upon. It was an era when to many nakedness was indecent, a sin in the eyes of God and irrevocably linked with the fall of mankind from grace in the Garden of Eden. This attitude was the result of a sustained effort by society, led by the churches, to shed the animal aspect of mankind. Possibly little better than the present swing to the animal with a regrettable shedding of the spiritual aspect of mankind, and ensuing life of futility and vulgarity. Be that as it may, these feelings of the day played a large part in the ideas and attitudes of the life of the time.

We began pulling on our clothes as soon as we realised the situation and modestly draped Bladder, at the wheel, with his shirt. The disturbance we had caused was a nuisance as it was possible that the police had been alerted ahead of us. Bladder coaxed every scrap of sedate speed from the Bluebird, but the result did not reduce our apprehension. We arrived at our village garage-hideout unmolested, and after dumping the car tore over the fields, through the school grounds to scramble into the assembly hall completely breathless, and still adjusting the last items of clothing, at the very moment that the roll-call began.

Throughout my schooldays rugger was my game, and in the 1st XV I gained my games tie and later house blazer. In cricket I had one stroke, which if it coincided with the bowling was extremely stylish and effective. However, owing to the law of averages this was a rare occurrence, and I spent most of my cricketing time either buckling or unbuckling pads, and as long stop or some other innocuous position in the field. This stroke at one time led our games coach (who was an ex-Yorkshire captain of considerable repute) to believe that he had unearthed a potential discovery, but he was completely blind to the fact that to me the tedium of cricket was the most appalling waste of time, as there were so many exciting and interesting things waiting to be done. When he became aware of it this unpardonable heresy left me, in the eyes of the coach, an irredeemable Philistine. After playing sporadically for the Colts XI as a last resort stand-in, when I became too old for this I achieved the distinction of the Stragglers XI, which consisted of the eleven worst cricket players in the school.

Far from the disgrace with which some would have wished the Stragglers XI to be viewed, it attracted considerable interest and its members, if denied the glory of famous team fixtures and the glamour of Lords, had a great deal of interesting fun. Fixtures of much charm were arranged for the Stragglers, mainly with village or private teams, and typical of these was a match we played against Lady X.'s eleven at her country house.

On arrival we were led across acres of immaculate lawns and garden, which boded well until we realised that we were heading towards a field in the distance. There a small marquee had been erected as a pavilion. We took the field first, 'field' being something of an euphemism as it was an area of cattle pasture, potholes, tussocks, thistles, cowpats and all. In the centre of this was the wicket at which the grass had been shortened over the necessary square chain, but it remained a daunting hazard to batsman and bowler alike. We assumed that as neither of these could have any idea of how the ball would pitch, fair play if not the character of the game would be retained in this contest of chance. So it seemed – but the local team were well practised in all the vagaries of their ground and we were not, with the result that to the great jubilation of its supporters the home team did surprisingly well.

The first men to bat were the village baker's boy and the captain, eighteen year old Lord X. Lord X. disposed of, the next man was the head footman, a grey-haired old fellow with a magnificent and slightly disdainful bearing. He was bowled first ball, and took it absolutely without a change of expression. At this stage our bowler was sufficiently confident to pointedly mark the start of his run by balancing several cowpats one upon the other, and we had time to observe the village church in the distance; which every now and again provided a practice peal of bells, punctuated by a farmer in the next field shooting rats. The contest was the centre of keen interest, and villagers could be seen converging from all sides as the game continued.

The rest of the team was composed of gardeners, gamekeepers, farmers (complete in leggings) and tradesmen. It was not the village blacksmith who smote the ball most spectacularly and effectively, although indeed 'a mighty man was he'. It was the cowman, a lanky youth with apparently fully castoring joints, who burst into the most fantastic of gyrations on the approach of the ball, or frequently when the ball was out of play, in a sort of intimidating shadow-boxing. This would have been farcical if it had not proved amazingly effective. Without fail, somewhere in his gyrations the madly threshing bat connected with the ball and it was driven in a huge parabola over the boundary. He did all too well before scattering his own wicket to the winds, which presumably was an ever-present hazard in his game.

Each successive batsman's calling was identifiable in his clothing, and with it went a highly individual style. None however was as superb as that of the butler who unbent sufficiently to remove his jacket, but at this drew the line. Then positioning himself at the wicket as though encased rigidly in his stiff shirt, winged collar and tie, he proceeded to 'stone-wall' inexcusably; no doubt to avoid any display of presumption before his watching mistress. The home team amassed a tidy score before we managed to dispose of them, but we were by no means downhearted for brains, we felt, would undoubtedly triumph over brawn, native cunning or whatever.

Here we were again completely wrong, for our neatly flannelled professional turnout did nothing to aid the inadequacy of our strictly conventional and stylized batting. No match for the unorthodox pitch and bowling, we were dismissed for a pitiful score, the most of which were extras donated by our jubilantly enthusiastic opponents. We were of course magnanimous in defeat – with the silent reservation that 'it simply wasn't cricket'. Some of us experienced unease over this situation, for it *was* cricket, but not as our narrow-minded and completely rigid conventional ideas accepted it. Had we been more flexible, we might well have won the match. Our failure was not a matter of our superiority, but sadly one of a conceited inadequacy. While I probably did not see this so clearly at the time, the thought was later to come back to me frequently in the realisation that as a nation much of our thinking seemed unbelievably to be based on this conception of 'cricket', as though international affairs were played according to a rigid set of rules and customs applied by an umpire whose decision was final, and which could not conceivably be questioned or ignored by an adversary.

Our rapid dismissal had the advantage of deciding the match before tea, which left us free to get down to the important work of the fixture unimpeded by further play. Lady X., a well known stage personality, had never given less than a superb performance and our entertainment was in the same category. In the role of the fellow conspirator she provided in the great, imposingly furnished drawing room, the most magnificent spread including every sickmaking jam and cream confection dear to the heart of a boy. To cap it all there was tray upon tray of bottled beer; an offering to our vanity as young men. Lady X. basked in our adoration and unconcealed fascination in her theatrical poise. She was of course in complete command of the situation, showering her largesse and contraband upon us with exaggerated gestures and exhortations to have a good time and safely break the rules under her protection. We needed little encouragement, the party throve as Lady X. swung amongst us from one theatrical pose to another – until of a sudden she froze, the gaiety falling like a mask from her features to leave a totally unguarded expression of grey horror-stricken panic.

What had happened was that one of our number, entering into the spirit of the thing, had decided that illicit beer would be improved by an illicit cigarette, and was at that moment wrestling with a large ornate silver box removed from the mantelpiece. The box, it seemed, contained the ashes of the late Lord X., and goodness knows what the situation would have been if our 'bon viveur' had succeeded in getting it open. The casket restored, the party continued; but in the disembodied presence of our host it lost much of its sparkle.

I sat and gained School Certificate during the summer term of 1938,* with several credits and a distinction in Science; the term closing with the Officers' Training Corps camp at Bordon with which this narrative began. It was at this camp I had been led to resolve that if I was to be killed in war, it should be only after striking the heaviest individual blow against the enemy that was normally possible. Quite how this was to be achieved I was still not sure, but it was frequently in my thoughts and my ideas on the subject were slowly resolving themselves. A bitter blow at the close of this term was the loss of Horace, who left for a crammer to ensure his gaining the Royal Military College entrance examination for the regular army. At the same time Bladder also left for a crammer, seriously depleting the Unholy Trinity. However, it was so deeply established in the school that its presence remained undiminished, R. de B. and myself merely closing ranks and continuing undeterred.

On August 12 1938 Germany mobilized its armed forces and in this sombre atmosphere we returned to school for the winter term. Hardly had we returned than the Royal Navy was mobilized on 27 September; virtually all reasonable hope for lasting peace was gone.

Both R. de B. and myself had been promoted to house prefect, and with other privileges were entitled to a shared study. This we set about decorating, furnishing and equipping making it second to none, and the object of some interest and envy. It was an unwritten rule that no member of the staff entered a study without asking permission, ensuring that there was always time to remove and conceal illicit items, such as pin-up magazines, cooking equipment and so on. Amongst these, R. de B. and I possessed Winchester .22″ rifles, which we greatly enjoyed using for grey squirrel, rabbit and hare shooting. R. de B. was an extremely good shot and together we spent many a long hour stalking our prey while evading authority; doubly exhilarating! From various carefully organised clandestine sources we were able to borrow a twelve bore and also a .410″ shotgun to add to our armoury.

The possession of any firearm, or shooting other than the Corps small arms training, was completely against school rules. While there was a certain amount

---

* Without any assistance!

of sport to be had within the school grounds (and this carried the added hazard and challenge of evasion in an easily supervised area) by far the best shooting lay in the country surrounding the school boundaries. This was before the days of myxomatosis and the rabbit was a serious pest. Woodpigeon and ring dove were in much the same category and it was these, and the occasional hare, in which our interest lay. We were, outside the school grounds, both trespassing and poaching but as we would not have dreamed of touching partridge, pheasant or any game, we felt it to be only technically poaching. This provided the necessary degree of danger and risk without breaking our moral code or doing any harm.

The surrounding land belonged to a retired General of an old country family and was keepered for him by one we had named Cronje, for what reason I cannot imagine unless he was a veteran of the Boer War. Cronje was a great tactician and would lie in wait for poachers sometimes on his own, but often with a posse of estate workers which he controlled with whistle blasts, rather as the beaters of a shoot. There was something of an unspoken vendetta between us and Cronje for we were a perpetual affront to his professional ability, and as a result he lived for the day when he would catch us red-handed. Our superb fitness and employment of numerous stratagems, often so audacious that they were totally unsuspected, made Cronje's task an unenviable one, and while we were often the quarry of Cronje, and sometimes his posse too, we always easily evaded capture.

Sometimes I shot with a companion but more often than not would take a gun and a pocket of cartridges and walk out on my own. It was in this way that I first succumbed to the wonder of the early morning. So entranced was I by this daily revelation that it was my delight to be up as early as a quarter past four of a midsummer's dawn, in order not to miss the miracle of sunrise.

Leaving the dormitory was difficult and more complicated than might be imagined, as to leave fully clothed at that hour left absolutely no hope of evasion if detected. The technique was to leave in one's dressing gown, and once in the hall, it was a question of flitting from cover to cover down to the east wing and the studies. There, one dressed in previously prepared shooting clothes, pocketed some shot and taking a gun (often by choice a .410″ on account of the lesser noise on discharge), left by the study window. Crossing the open from the window to the cover of the woods was a critical stage, as there could be little subterfuge in heading for the woods carrying a gun at that time of the morning.

In this way I could clear the school grounds before sunrise and begin a long brisk walk with the chance of a shot, exulting in the still of the early morning; the heavenly scent of dew-soaked grass, fern and undergrowth; the dull muffled movement and occasional snort of cattle, and above all the ever novel glory of the rising sun. Life in these moments held a rare and exquisite quality in which the cool and delicious air was intoxicating. Re-entering the school buildings in time for the early morning roll-call and chapel felt more hazardous than leaving, on account of the number of people about. Mingling inconspicuously with one's yawning and sleep-ridden companions seemed impossible, as borne high on a wave of exhilaration one must surely have glowed almost with the incandescence of a rising sun!

My particular strength was the marksmanship possible with a .22" rifle, and the pursuit of this I greatly enjoyed. I could more often than not hit a sitting rabbit in the head at a range of one hundred and twenty yards over open sights, at which distance the blade foresight of the rifle more than covered this target. A shotgun is limited in range and is designed for fast-moving, close targets against which a rifle is all but useless. When alone I would sometimes carry both, but with two of us we would take turn and turn about with the two weapons. On occasions I took a fag as a gun bearer, but most of all I enjoyed shooting on my own for the communion it allowed with the wild. So I came to know much of the wonder of the seasons and their changes, and in consequence have never been able to elect any one of them the most beautiful.

One winter, snow had been falling fitfully for two days and the gently undulating downland was blanketed in white. Underfoot it lay a good six inches of dry powdery snow, and yet still from a leaden grey sky, in deathly silence and complete tranquillity, it drifted softly to the ground, or driven by occasional feeble gusts eddied and whirled, pattering gently against the gaunt trees and leafless undergrowth. During a lull in the snowfall the lure of this fascinating beauty drew me inescapably, and after extensive padding against the cold I took a rifle and set out. My tracks were readily detectable, but this could be offset against the knowledge that few if any would be about and I would almost certainly have this remote, unsullied and silent white world entirely to myself. I strode in a little cloud of steaming breath through familiar yet totally transformed scenes; in which every now and again, with a dull thump, an over-loaded branch incapable of bearing more would bend, depositing its load in a silvery white cascade. From the scattered trees and shrubs an occasional bird winged its way into the shelter of the woods, woebegone and silent, for the days of song were for the while gone by. Not so for me, my heart sang in joy at each turn and wondrous scene. A joy so great that at times my being seemed unable to encompass the immensity of it.

In the open rising ground of a great and spotless field of white I crossed the freshly made track of a hare and turned to follow it. There ensued a chase so memorable that I still recall it clearly. After more than an hour of stalking and concentrated fieldcraft, in which the trail led past several huddled coveys of partridge, I knew that I was very close. On topping a rise I came upon the hare some eighty yards away and standing upright in an attempt to sight me. He hesitated to determine my course, and the whipcrack of the high velocity bullet shattered the silence to be instantaneously muffled by the blanket of snow. The hare fell dead on the spot, shot clean through the shoulders, and I knew the primeval thrill of the chase. With it the exultation at the skill of my success and admiration for the courage and ability of my quarry, which has ennobled hunting in this common process of nature throughout the ages of man.

In much the same way passed the winter term of 1938, and spring term of 1939, during which in mid-March Germany moved into Prague and occupied Czecho-slovakia. At the end of the same month, after some two years and eight months of particularly bloody fighting, the Spanish Civil War ended in the surrender of Madrid by the Communists to General Franco. Hardly had the school broken up for the Easter holidays than conscription was introduced in the United Kingdom for men in the 20–21 year age group.

The following summer term of 1939 was scheduled to end schooling for de B. and myself. Now all but fully fledged young men, we carried on as ever, making the most of these golden days of school life. Although we were acutely aware of the sense of destiny in the times, we nonetheless refused to allow this to curb our exuberance. The staff, on the other hand, must have been greatly distressed by the inevitability of war and the losses it would mean amongst the boys; on this account turning a blind eye to many of our excesses. It was a time of uncertainty, anxiety and great unrest. The hitherto impregnable seclusion of school life was shattered by the immensity of developments outside, and the community drew together as all communities in the face of danger. The lowering of conventional barriers of seniority between the prefects, house prefects and older members of the Upper School was most noticeable, and there developed a moving camaraderie. We had all undergone a tough and arduous apprenticeship and not been found lacking. In the testing times to come we would be closely bound by common ideas, ideals, understanding and experience. For the time being our only defence against the threat of war was an attempt to minimise it drastically by an exaggeration of our natural, youthful light-heartedness; perhaps a little after the fashion of children's naive attempts to stave off the terrors of the dark.

One of the advantages of elevation to a study was the freedom to prepare snacks whenever the mood might take one. School meals were plentiful and adequate if not inspiring, but teenage boys are liable to develop insatiable appetites, particularly for those items of home food never met in the simplicity of institutional catering. R. de B. and myself had equipped our study with an electric kettle, cooking ring, small saucepans and coffee-making equipment. In the main we concentrated on percolating coffee, of which we were both very fond, and on toast laden with various spreads. Perfectly made coffee has an irresistible aroma, and our percolating activities seldom passed unnoticed.

We continued to shoot, to drive and to break bounds. Our escapades sometimes brought us back into school long after lights out. My house master's room was at the head of the stairs, and in the summer he was in the habit of leaving the door open while he listened to music, wrote or read late into the night. The only way of overcoming this hazard required considerable nerve; to lie face down on the floor, and wriggle slowly and in absolute silence across the doorway, getting to one's feet when clear of the other side and silently making off to the dormitories. This had never failed, or so we thought, until the occasion when Michael B., halfway across the doorway, was petrified to hear his name called by the house master followed by the comment, 'If you can't come in at the correct time, I shall write to your parents and ask them to find you another hotel!'

In our travels we occasionally visited a smart hotel on the banks of the river, in a delightful village not many miles from the school. There were not only strawberry and cream teas served in the fragrant sunshine of the riverside rose garden, but also Sonia. Sonia, a dark-haired beauty of little more than our age, was the hotel receptionist and she smiled upon us. Truly she seemed one of the loveliest and most wildly exciting of girls, which in such a setting was the very stuff of which dreams are made. We never missed an opportunity of seeing adorable, warm-hearted, sparkling Sonia, who spoiled us unashamedly if occasion allowed and even contrived for us to drink our illicit beer in semi-privacy. So Sonia became an almost fairy-tale symbol of desirability, and indeed our princess.

By mid-term the international situation was so desperate that nothing would restrain R. de B., and he inveigled his mother into withdrawing him from the school, to personally press his application for entry to the R.A.F. under the Short Service Commission scheme. Thus ended the Unholy Trinity, laid to rest with a list of 'battle honours' that was in later years to surprise even ourselves.

The Royal Air Force was coming into considerable prominence on account of the predictions of the Italian General Douhet, in his thesis *The Command of the Air*. In this he saw aerial bombardment as a weapon that could destroy cities in rapid hammer-blows, causing the collapse of the social structure and disintegration of a nation. This coupled to the experience of the German air raids of the First World War, and the bombing of Guernica during the Spanish Civil War, led to an expectation of horror almost unlimited; in which war could develop into a slogging match between rival bomber forces. It indicated a war of fast-moving action in the air, which de B. had not been slow to detect. For my part I realised that in aerial attack or defence the individual was going to play a larger part than in any other form of conventional warfare, and wondered if this was the heaviest possible individual blow against the enemy which I had sought since the Bordon O.T.C. camp of 1938.

Before many weeks were out de B. was back in his new-found car, a Morris two-seater with a dicky (boot convertible to two unenclosed seats) at the rear. He stayed a couple of days, during which we visited Henley for as enjoyable and perfect an afternoon as ever. The next morning, prior to his leaving, we were up before six o'clock and drove to a stretch of river above Shiplake, for a memorable bathe in the early morning sun.

There was to be no O.T.C. camp that year as it had been cancelled on account of the international situation. This resulted in an earlier close to the term and during the last few weeks, amongst the traditional school social events, we organised a secret bottle party as a farewell to all our friends. It was to be held in the shower-room, of all places, on account of easy unobserved access and its isolation allowing for considerable undetected noise. The party was organised with great care and in much detail, a quantity of whisky, gin and beer being imported via our friends of the maintenance staff. In the event it was highly successful, and being run on an open house basis we were visited by many of the prefects, the Sergeant Major, most of the maintenance staff and a number of juniors. The night watchman, an ex-soldier, truly entered into the spirit of the thing and had eventually to be guided to his place of duty. There were casualties amongst ourselves, and getting them to the dormitories undetected, smelling like Christmas puddings, proved no easy task.

The summer term always ended in a spate of events including the speech day, old boys' match and so on, in which one was borne aloft on a general wave of celebration, exuberance and anticipation of the glorious weeks of carefree holiday to come. In this euphoria I had not experienced any particular feelings at the close of my schooldays, even in the pandemonium of loading cars, harassed parents and shouted farewells that marked the end of speech day and the last day of term.

I had stayed on overnight with the usual handful of long-distance travellers and others whose parents had not borne them away, and now in the first day of the holidays fully savoured walking down the main staircase (normally reserved for masters and school prefects) into the hall, on my way to breakfast. Everything was strangely quiet, and the marble mosaic of the hall floor was littered with trunks happily abandoned by their departed owners to the mercies of the staff and carrier. There were no familiar figures to be seen, and the scattered trunks were strangely eloquent. I picked my way through them to the refectory. It was empty, the long lines of tables were empty and the assembly hall below was empty. The tables were all bare, but one short one set with a handful of places for breakfast.

I was considering this scene somewhat nonplussed, when the doors at the far end of the hall burst open and two diminutive fags hurtled through into the dining room, to come to an over-awed half before me. Owing to their size they were known in the school as the Mighty Molecule when they were together, which they habitually were, or separately as the Mighty Atoms. I realised that I had never said a word to these two bar the giving of instructions, and struggled without success for an appropriate and friendly greeting. My eventual 'Good morning,' sounded patronisingly ridiculous, but I was saved acute embarrassment by their simultaneous ready smiles and very correct greeting. The arrival of a handful of others was the signal for breakfast to begin, a breakfast designed by the cook to delight any boy's heart, and it passed almost without incident in a satisfied silence, but for the fags who communed in happy and cryptic undertones. It was the removal of the last piece of toast, which I had secretly been coveting, from under my very grasp by a small ink-stained hand, which first shook me. The hand proved to belong to a Mighty Atom, who was unconcernedly carrying on a work of destruction aided by huge helpings of marmalade – this I realised abruptly was the rising school generation, to whom I was already an old boy and thereby no longer in any position of authority.

I left the dining room and descended the steps into the deserted assembly hall, suffering a growing and inexorable sadness that permeated to the very roots of my being and which I was only to experience in such a degree twice again in my lifetime. I realised that I needed to be alone in this hour of the passing of a fundamental period in my life. Reluctantly I wandered for the last time through the corridors and halls, into the grey stone courtyards and passages, out onto the terraced front, down beside the lake and into the woods. Every pillar, every arch, every doorway, window and even every stone of that building held a deep personal familiarity and attachment from years of incident, of experience, of study; of a dawning realisation in the possibilities, the joys, the agonies, the beauties and the brutalities of life – of endeavour, of failure, of success. Above all in the achievement of a growing aptitude to recognise, extract and nurture the good and desirable in an informed and logical reasoning, which is education. Those walls had afforded me such knowledge and experience in the desperately short span of time allowed – a whole life premier.

It was all so much part of me it seemed incredible that I could be separated from it, and survive. It was here in the cool leafy tunnels of oft-trodden footpaths, interconnecting familiar vistas, that I first came to realise the sad consolation of a great truth. It is that whatever time or circumstances may decree, one can never be completely parted from a great love, for as at least some part of it will always remain enshrined in one's being, so in turn some part of one must remain for always similarly enshrined in the object of one's devotion.

CHAPTER 4

Twilight and Darkness

As soon as we beat England, we shall make an end of you Englishmen once and for all. Able-bodied men and women will be exported as slaves to the continent. The old and the weak will be exterminated. All men remaining in Britain as slaves will be sterilized; a million or two of the young women of the Nordic type will be segregated in a number of stud farms where, with the assistance of picked German sires, during a period of ten or twelve years, they will produce annually a series of Nordic infants to be brought up in every way as Germans. These infants will form the future population of Britain . . . Thus in a generation or two, the British will disappear.

Walter Darre, German Minister of Agriculture.
April 1942

In its preparations to put the nation on a war footing, much thought had been given by the government to mobilising national resources for Civil Defence. This form of defence was a comparatively new conception in war and therefore there was little precedent for use as a guide. Thinking was based on the Douhet theory mentioned earlier, which had led the Committee of Imperial Defence to certain conclusions, based on statistics from the German bombing of England during the First World War, and the bombing of Guernica during the Spanish Civil War. The committee warned in 1937 that a German air attack on London, lasting sixty days, would kill 600,000 people with a further 1,200,000 wounded, requiring between 1,000,000 and 2,800,000 hospital beds. Material damage to property and public services was calculated on the same scale.

With this warning in mind the Observer Corps, formed in 1925 and transferred to Air Ministry control in 1929, was greatly strengthened to assist in the detection and reporting of enemy air attack. An Air Raid Precautions (A.R.P.) organisation had been set up, and by the end of 1938 much general information had been circulated to the public, with the first priority met in the issue of 38,000,000 civilian gas masks. Meanwhile, the Auxiliary Fire Service had bene expanded and equipped with a handy two-wheeled trailer carrying a petrol-motor-driven pump. Amongst others, plans were prepared for the strengthening of the police force with War Reserve Constables, and also to co-ordinate and strengthen the existing voluntary services. Not surprisingly in these arrangements there was a preoccupation with the disposal of casualties, and preparations were made by the conversion of a number of trains to hospital use and a large number of road coaches into ambulances. A huge store of collapsible cardboard coffins was assembled and held in readiness, in the stark realisation that already hard-pressed timber stocks would be inadequate to meet such a demand.

At home, life during August 1939 was disrupted and of a curious twilight nature; in some moments one carried on as before but in others there was an acute sense of restraint and impending disaster. A popular attempt at light-heartedness was a resurgence of the old-fashioned D.V. (*Deo volente* – God willing) once piously used at the close of all mundane arrangements, but now amended to H.V. – Hitler willing! I heard at this time from Robert de B. who had reported to R.A.F. Yatesbury and was beginning a concentrated flying training with much enthusiasm; news which left me with an increased sense of the apparently aimless drift of the nation at large.

In mid-August we received at home a surprise visit from my uncle, Gerald Shepherd, who had been appointed in 1938 as British Consul-General in Danzig. He had in 1913 entered the Consular Service in preference to the Diplomatic Corps, my grandfather's fortune by then being considerably diminished, and had since held a number of colourful and interesting posts. My uncle was alert, observant and a man of great charm with a quiet and subtle sense of humour. Both his memory and his capacity for work were prodigious, and his account of the most trivial of events would be fascinating in the profusion and accuracy of detail. Fifty-three years old at the time, he was of the old school in his fierce patriotism, devotion to duty and desire to serve. A more upright man I cannot imagine, and his exceedingly handsome presence befitted his transparent honesty.

His visit was a surprise, as Poland was at the time the centre of world concern over the German dispute with its demands on Danzig and the Polish Corridor. The carefully guarded story that he had to tell was disturbing enough at the time, but much more so in later years when the full story became known. To quote from an article in the *Sunday Times* Magazine of 30 August 1964:

> The British Consul-General in Danzig, Gerald Shepherd, realised that more was at stake than the fate of a single city. He was 53 years old – experienced and without illusions about German aggressive intentions. He begged Lord Halifax, the Foreign Secretary, not to contemplate handing Danzig back to Germany.
>
> But Halifax hoped to avert war by making timely concessions. He saw Danzig as a sacrifice worth making, if, by persuading the Poles to allow its return to Germany, Hitler would be satisfied. Halifax still thought it possible to satisfy Hitler. Shepherd disagreed violently. To give Danzig to Germany, he argued, would only stimulate Hitler's appetite. Such a sacrifice, he insisted in a despatch to the Foreign Office, would 'unquestionably be followed . . . by the absorption of most, if not all, of the remainder of Poland.'
>
> Halifax resented this realism and ordered Shepherd to leave Danzig at once. He was replaced by a man of the same name, with the result that few people outside the Foreign Office knew that anything unusual or discreditable had occurred.

My uncle had observed and reported the systematic and increasingly rapid Nazification of the Free City of Danzig, and its conversion into an armed camp with tank traps, machine gun nests, anti-aircraft guns, coastal artillery and no fewer than 30,000 German troops where not a single soldier of any nationality had any right to be.

It was during the visit by my uncle that a good friend of my mother's called, and seizing the opportunity for an opinion by our man on the spot, with its priceless gossip value, asked him what he thought of the situation. My uncle replied, 'It regrettably seems that war is most likely,' to which, completely aghast, she countered, 'But Hitler would never dare – think of the British Navy.' There spoke the voice of Britain 1939, and I have never forgotten my uncle's agonized silence.

On 23 August the Russians signed a non-aggression pact with Germany, taking the British Cabinet and diplomatic service unawares, and astonishing the British people who had been led to believe that an Anglo-Russian pact was under negotiation. The next day the Emergency Powers Bill was approved by Parliament, and on 25 August the Anglo-Polish Mutual Assistance Treaty was signed.

As often happens in periods of great import, time itself appears to slow and all but to stand still. In my diary for 28 August I noted: 'We have nearly completed plans for sand-bagging the house, as it seems that delay will be dangerous. There is feverish activity, but paradoxically an unusual quiet in the towns. It has been a wonderful day, very hot, real summer weather and the promise of more.' And then on 30 August: 'It is late in the evening now, it has been a fine day and in the clear cool air a full moon is turning night almost into day – but it is dark, very dark in the shadows where the silver light does not fall. International negotiations seem to be on the verge of breaking down and war is very close indeed.' On the last day of August the evacuation from London of women and children began, and the country waited.

The Germans invaded Poland on 1 September 1939, and began the destruction of the Polish armed forces in a blitzkrieg (lightning war) – a closely combined action by the army and air force, including a violent air bombardment of communications and centres of population, with rapid thrusts by great masses of armour. In the United Kingdom general mobilisation and a blackout was ordered. In keeping with our treaty obligations to Poland, Great Britain declared war on Germany on 3 September 1939. The next day the British Expeditionary Force began to move into France.

Within the range of emotions experienced at the fateful moment of actual commitment to war, there was undoubtedly a general sense of relief that the die was cast, and that after the shameful period of appeasement in which Czechoslovakia had been sacrificed by the 'Peace in our time' Munich agreement, signed on 30 September 1938 (nearly a year before) we were now, if tardily, acting with honour and fulfilling our treaty obligations. It was, however, painfully obvious that to save our ally Poland, or in fact to provide military assistance of any sort was a physical impossibility.

Douhet's theory that aerial bombardment could destroy cities in rapid hammer-blows, cause the collapse of the social structure and disintegration of a nation, was by no means irresponsible thinking. However, the entirely unestablished factor was the scale of bombardment necessary to achieve such a chaotic situation.* While

---

* This was to prove far greater than had been realised and was never within the capacity of the German air force during the whole of the 1939–45 war.

the government had been careful not to publicise the expected casualty figures, the extensive preparations had been obvious and the populace was thinking in Douhet terms of an attempt by the Germans at an immediate knockout blow from the air; almost certainly in an attack on London. The civil defence measures included a total blackout, the limitation of the B.B.C. to one programme of recorded music, bulletins and announcements, and the closing of all cinemas, dance halls and places of public entertainment. With the blackout came a darkness literal and meta-phorical, which was to enshroud the nation for the next six years. Fear, anxiety, and new-found authority in the Emergency Power measures on the part of many little people now suddenly elevated to petty officialdom, led to a loss of perspective at times exceeding the ridiculous and verging on insanity, which much increased the irksome restraint of the endless new restrictions.

Following the declaration of war, there ensued a totally unexpected situation in which instead of the holocaust of 'Blitzkrieg', with the attendant chaos and wholesale destruction that had been generally imagined, there reigned a com-parative calm broken only by minor and often isolated actions on the part of either side. In these circumstances the immediate civil defence restrictions which had been imposed were too drastic by far. The almost complete blackout was causing distressing road casualties, great irritation, endless difficulties and a sharp increase in crime. No more successful was the very British idea of painting white stripes on the New Forest ponies, in the hope of avoiding blackout collisions with our animal friends. Not surprisingly scores of ponies continued to become road accident victims, and worse the foals wanted no part of this tomfoolery and refused to know their clowning mothers. Similarly, the ban on entertainment was lowering morale. These restrictions were all eased in January 1940, the B.B.C. improving its programmes and later opening a new Forces Channel. By this time most civilians had ceased to carry their gas masks or to retain them within reach, as the govern-ment had instructed on the outbreak of war.

This extraordinary period, ultimately lasting some eight months, became known as the 'Phoney War' on account of the disparaging attitude of the Americans to the war in Europe. Such was the unpreparedness of the Allies for war that this time was essential to the mobilisation of the war effort; and incredible though it be, it was allowed to them. The decision to stand on the defensive while gathering strength, entailed avoiding provocative action which certainly led to 'phoney' situations. Looking back on it later, it was easy to see that the complete military and civil requirement in putting a peace-seeking nation on a war footing is a task of such magnitude as to be beyond normal comprehension. As it can only be a chain reaction in which each link is forged onto the previous links, all emanating from so small a nucleus of knowledge and experience in matters of war, the initial stages are bound to be painfully slow.

In 1939, it was possible to form only the haziest conception of what contem-porary war would mean, or to imagine to what extent the civilian would be involved; other than to realise the need for urgency and a massive national effort. As the days and weeks of the Phoney War slipped away the sense of gathering and intensifying danger was ever present; the initial stages of educating and equipping the nation for war made even more apparent the frightening general state of unpreparedness – yet still, on the face of it, there was little sign of a general sense of urgency or a massive national effort.

Following the declaration of war my elder brother Allan had been placed on full-time service as a Special Police Constable, in London. This was a volunteer organisation he had previously chosen in the rising threat of war, in the conviction that he would so be of maximum help in the instant chaos resulting from the aerial attack that the outbreak of war would precipitate. It was brave and extremely sound thinking, but the fates were unkind to him in the completely illogical development of the Phoney War, and he found himself committed to the anti-climax of endless absolutely uneventful spells on the beat.

A curious aspect of this period was that it became virtually impossible to volunteer for service in the armed forces, and considerable influence was needed to enlist. The problem was probably an administrative one, as the Services had neither the accommodation, equipment nor instructors immediately available for large numbers of recruits, and were already fully extended in handling the conscription of all men aged 20 years, introduced on 27 April 1939. In the circumstances it seemed an unbelievable situation and one which caused much criticism, anger and recourse to devious methods of enlistment.

Petrol rationing was introduced on 16 September, allowing a small basic ration to all car owners and limiting the supply to one medium-octane blend, named Pool Petrol. To avoid misuse, petrol for commercial vehicles was dyed red. These were restrictions to which the motoring public did not take kindly, especially as Pool Petrol varied greatly in quality (possibly due in some cases to illegal adulteration) and it was referred to in derision as being named Pool because of the tadpoles and other pond life it supported!

Three days later, on 19 September, the aircraft carrier H.M.S. *Courageous* (it was later announced) had been torpedoed and sunk in the Bristol Channel. This, to the public, could only seem a disturbingly questionable loss. On 14 October the battleship H.M.S. *Royal Oak* was torpedoed and sunk by a U-boat, in the fastness of our great naval base at Scapa Flow. The public shock and consternation was immense, the more so for the lack of other warlike activity at the time. The war at sea was far from phoney for there was considerable action by German surface raiders, U-boats and aircraft, against our shipping. The losses in these attacks, although minimised, could not be concealed from the public who were aware of the sensitivity of our sea supply lines and that, in the First World War, the German U-boat campaign had brought the country to within three weeks of starvation.

Immediately after the outbreak of war, the mining of British estuaries and coastal waters with the first of the German secret weapons, the magnetic mine, destroyed over a quarter of a million tons of shipping in three months. While at the time the public were not aware of the full facts, the danger of the obviously heavy shipping losses, suffered without any opportunity of retaliation, was deeply disturbing and brought the existing frustrations to a pitch of exasperation. Fortunately, once one of these mines had fallen into British hands on 22 November 1939, they were speedily mastered.

Towards the end of October, my eldest brother Neville was ordered to report to the 3rd Battalion London Scottish, for which he had volunteered earlier; and on the last day of the month I became nineteen years old. During the month I had heard from Robert de B. who had completed his elementary flying training at R.A.F. Yatesbury, and was accordingly commissioned as an Acting Pilot Officer. These schools were then civilian-operated, and he was posted in November to the Service Flying Training School at R.A.F. Little Rissington in Gloucestershire. The satisfactory completion of the S.F.T.S. course brought the award of the coveted pilot's wings, and the confirmation of the substantive rank of Pilot Officer. However, the numbers who failed to reach the necessary standard at each of these stages were considerable.

In this strange contrast of war and peacetime conditions much of life was going on as before, with the increasing application of War Emergency regulations and restrictions creating an embarrassing incongruity. There were parties, picnics and dinners; the digging of shelters; the extended search for sandbags and blackout materials in extremely short supply. There was the covering of windows with paper tape to minimise splintering; the making of blackout curtains and shutters, and the obscuring of many windows with thick blackout paint. There was the issue of identity cards, and official vandalism in the painting of a three-inch white line around all cars at bumper level. There was a spate of camouflage painting, many factory buildings being daubed in irregular patches of sand, green and brown, with a fervour born of a belief that this made them invisible from the air. It made them little less noticeable and clearly indicated buildings of importance! There was too the ceaseless 'Digging for Victory' food growing campaign, which in time reduced pre-war food imports first to a half and later to one-third. There was endless talk of the war, of friends who had been called up and who in this much-envied state were quite unjustifiably credited with extensive inside knowledge – and still an almost complete ignorance of the might of the German armed forces, and our pitiful unpreparedness. Most of all there was a desire for information on any and every aspect of the bewildering situation with which the nation was faced, and a deep sense of frustration at the lack of opportunity to give one's all in what must surely be the nation's hour of need.

November ended with a Russian attack on Finland, against which the hopelessly outnumbered Finns put up a most heroic resistance inflicting many defeats on the invading Russians, but the outcome was never in doubt and the Finns surrendered on 11 March 1940. Allied help for the Finns having been balked by Norway and Sweden, the sense of once again 'fiddling while Rome burned' became acute and added greatly to the general frustration.

Early in December I was given my first job, by a friend of the family, Sir Robert Davis, as a junior in the offices of his firm Siebe Gorman Ltd. Sir Robert was an expert in safety equipment and the inventor of the Davis Submarine Escape Apparatus. At the time that I joined the company, in keeping with the large-scale evacuation from London, the office staff had been moved into Sir Robert's own house in Surrey where it was deemed to be safe. As it happened this area received very considerable bomb damage during the Battle of Britain and later. It was there, in the unbelievable scrum of a general office packed into the dining-room of a private house, that I received my first weekly pay packet of £1 10s. 0d. (thirty shillings – now £1.50) less the standard deductions. For the kindness I experienced in this start, I remain most grateful to Sir Robert and the members of his staff.

In the period 13–17 December the German Atlantic raider the *Admiral Graf Spee*, an eleven-inch gun pocket-battleship, was brought to action by the *Exeter* (eight-inch) and the light six-inch gun cruisers the *Ajax* and *Achilles*. The *Graf Spee* withdrew to the river Plate to dock at Montevideo, after crippling the *Exeter* and severely damaging *Ajax* and *Achilles*. Seventy-two hours later (the time limit allowed to belligerents in neutral waters) the *Graf Spee* sailed and, believing superior forces to be in the vicinity, was scuttled by her crew in deep water. This brilliant action was in the true traditions of the Royal Navy, and greatly enheartened us all after the country's earlier losses.

It was during November and December that some of the first Canadian, Australian and New Zealand troops arrived in the United Kingdom.* Initially there was a degree of secrecy regarding their presence, and our attitude towards them was one of uneasy aloofness which must have been disappointing and hard to understand. These early arrivals included some of the toughest and roughest elements of their countries, and were not always representative of their people. They too were looking for action, having travelled a long way to support the mother country, and they did not take kindly to the enforced boredom of the Phoney War. Life for them in wartime Britain was hard and cheerless, many of them at this time living under canvas. In early January butter, bacon and sugar were rationed, which with growing shortages of many commodities greatly limited the nation's capacity for hospitality.

The winter of 1940 brought some of the most appalling weather in living memory, almost as if this too was involved in the cataclysmic European upheaval. There occurred towards the end of January exceptional conditions, which created a prolonged fall of super-cooled rain over much of the country. Super-cooled rain is a phenomenon with which aircrew are familiar as it occurs at height, but hardly ever at ground level. In those conditions each droplet of rain, although liquid, is at a temperature below freezing and remains liquid until it suffers a shock, at which moment it spreads turning to clear glass-like ice.

We awoke to find the entire countryside turned to ice in this way, every blade of grass, twig, branch and stone encased in clear ice, sometimes of as much as one-and-a-half to two inches in thickness. The effect was one of incredible beauty, and the creation of a frozen crystal fairyland. I walked out to explore this wonder, made my way over the glassy ground to a nearby copse and entered a familiar, partially sunken lane. The spectacle was absolutely breathtaking, and I was halted in my tracks by a long vista of fantastically intricate glass-like tracery, where the frozen hazel and hawthorn bushes met overhead in a glittering translucent and light-spangled tunnel. Such a mass of ice represented a great weight, and many branches and limbs of trees had been torn from the trunks. Most strange of all were probably the telephone lines, which had assumed the appearance of sagging

---

* The first detachment of 7,449 officers and men, representing the 1st Canadian Division, disembarked in Great Britain on 13 November 1939.

glass rods of some one to two inches in diameter, in the centre of which could clearly be seen the wire. These lines had collapsed in masses, and lay like a giant shattered glass spaghetti in tangled heaps on the ground. I later heard from Robert de B. who had experienced as severe or worse an ice accretion in the Cotswolds. True to style he had brought out his skates and begun by skating over the parade ground at R.A.F. Little Rissington, and then taken to the communicating roads, and finally skated into the open country for miles.

For much of this winter my brother Neville, serving with the 3rd Battalion London Scottish, was living under canvas in unbelievable conditions. Not surprisingly he succumbed to pneumonia from which, owing to the rigours of the general shortages of equipment, facilities and knowledge of life under field-service conditions, he was lucky to survive. That never-to-be-forgotten winter was a winter of appalling hardship for many ill-sheltered units, and a cruel introduction to Service life for the country's growing 'civilian army'. It both seriously hampered the mobilisation of the nation's war effort, and highlighted our desperate unpreparedness. The full severity of this winter was never realised by most of the public, owing to the ban on publication of all weather forecasts and reports of local weather conditions as information of value to the enemy.

With the occupation of Norway by the Germans in early April 1940, the war was brought uncomfortably closer. However this seemed an obvious opportunity for the British land and sea forces to put an end to the Germans' limitless aggression. In mid-April a British expeditionary force landed in Norway where fighting brought an end to the Phoney War. At last we were getting to grips with the enemy and as though fortune smiled on our efforts, after a winter of near-arctic conditions we began drifting into the finest summer in living memory, this glorious weather lasting from May to September. The demands of security limited news of the British landings but the lack of information, which in time could only be interpreted as a lack of success, was disturbing. The campaign proved to be a costly misadventure, due primarily to lack of superiority or even any significant strength in the air; the lack of guns for defence against air attack; a general lack of essential equipment and most serious of all, a complete lack of the knowledge and experience necessary for operating in Scandinavian conditions.

Meanwhile, in early May the German armies attacked through Holland, Belgium and Luxembourg which move began the blitzkrieg in the West. At home we were astonished to read in the *Daily Mail* of 15 May 1940, the following despatch from Reuters' Special Correspondent:

Sir – May one of the 600 British subjects evacuated from Holland yesterday have space to make the following three points, based on personal experience of the past days:

1. Universal admiration was felt by all of us for the work done on our behalf by Mr. E. H. G. Shepherd, our Consul-General in Amsterdam, and Mr. P. L. Carter, vice-Consul, who was in charge of the evacuated party.

The sight of the immaculate figure of Mr. Shepherd coolly sitting on the wharf at Amsterdam, his legs dangling over the water, while an air raid was in progress, and the evacuees were going on board, was in the best tradition

Sir Gerald Shepherd K.C.M.G., who, with his guardian Admiral of the Fleet
Sir John Kelly G.C.B., G.C.V.O., was the author's great inspiration.

of British coolness and efficiency.

We were also deeply grateful to the British Navy for escorting us, and to the Dutch military who, with a war going on in the very region through which we were passing, gave us every care and help.

2. – etc.

My uncle Gerald would have been wearing a grey pin-stripe suit, pearl tie pin, grey Homburg hat, and looking, as always, magnificent. During the four days after the invasion of Holland, he had arranged the evacuation of some 1,500 British subjects in three ships from Rotterdam. In the last, a tramp steamer with accommodation for twelve, he packed 500 people, including 60 teenage girls from the Sadlers Wells Ballet who were in Holland on a goodwill tour. When the last evacuee had left, as effective Dutch resistance had ceased and all normal escape routes were closed, my uncle embarked on a twenty-mile cross-country flight, at times crawling on his stomach amongst the long grass, in an attempt to avoid the German strafing aircraft. Finally he boarded one of several small boats at Ymuiden, and set out for England. German planes machine-gunned the boats, and there were many casualties. Crushed with 70 others in a drifter designed for eight people, my uncle watched the tracer bullets pass him like fire-flies and later confessed that he was really frightened.

In 1939 my uncle was made a Companion of the Order of St. Michael and St. George for his services in Danzig, and was later the first to be transferred from the Consular Service to the Diplomatic Service. In 1946 he was knighted – he was indeed a knight in the truest sense. He believed implicitly in his country and his duty to serve it giving his everything, including his personal fortune to War Bonds, sadly a government-sponsored confidence trick that cost him and millions of other their savings.

It was not in my uncle's nature to conceal the facts or the truth, although this might not be acceptable to a Minister of the Government who, in the maintenance of disastrously illogical policies, did not want to know what was going on. In considering my uncle there comes to mind the sense of duty of my guardian, 'Kelly of Invergordon', in his direct criticism of the Lords of the Admiralty and his admonition to me 'to play a praiseworthy part, without fear or favour, as a true English gentleman' in the life that lay ahead of me.

There were by then in this country a number of Czechs and Poles, who had escaped from the invading Germans. The first contingents of Canadian, Australian and New Zealand troops, to which had been added Norwegians who fled their country on the German occupation and now, as the Germans advanced into the Low Countries, Dutch and Belgian refugees. London became almost colourful with this cosmopolitan influx, bringing a realism to the Allied concept, but their presence also evoked considerable dismay and some confused feeling of failure and treachery.

Ever since we had parted at school Horace had been writing charming and informative letters, and it was at this time that I learned from one of them that he was under training at an army Officer Cadet Training Unit, in Chichester. Some seven months later in mid-December 1940, he was commissioned in the Rifle Brigade.

My eldest brother Neville, serving in the London Scottish, was manning a battery of 3.7″ anti-aircraft guns mounted in a desolate site on Dartford Heath. I visited him there, and was somewhat shaken by the primitive conditions under which they were living. These were considerably aggravated by a high security fence surrounding the site, and within which they were virtually confined. It was their good fortune (or misfortune) to be equipped with one of the first anti-aircraft fire control predictors, which equipment was highly secret. For all this sophisticated weaponry they had no small arms or any means of protecting the site at all, and had been given an afternoon off to manufacture personal weapons. Advice on how to make an effective club had actually been published in orders – should the mind boggle now at such memories, however can it have seemed in the dire predicament of the time? Neville was later selected for officer training, and posted in mid-July 1940 to the 124th Officer Cadet Training Unit (Royal Artillery) at Llandrindod Wells, near Cardigan in Wales.

It was as the Germans began their attack through the Low Countries on 10th May that the Prime Minister of Britain, Mr Chamberlain, resigned and the King sent for Mr Churchill to form a government. From the first it was obvious that all was not well with the Allies' efforts to halt the German advance, and that we were in fact being forced into a headlong retreat. What was happening appeared inconceivable, and was made no more credible by the superb early summer weather. In the Surrey fields larks sang under blue skies, and the warm sun created a sense of natural well-being in which the ceaseless rumble of guns from France seemed completely unreal. The full gravity of the situation was brought home to us by Mr Churchill's magnificent and inspiring address to the House of Commons on 13 May.

> I would say to the House, as I said to those who joined this government: 'I have nothing to offer but blood, toil, tears and sweat.' We have before us an ordeal of the most grievous kind. We have before us many, many long months of struggle and suffering. You ask: 'What is our policy?' I will say: 'It is to wage war by sea, land and air with all our might, and with the strength that God can give us: to wage war against a monstrous tyranny, never surpassed in the dark lamentable catalogue of human crime. That is our policy. You ask: 'What is our aim?' I can answer in one word: 'Victory!' Victory at all costs, victory in spite of all terror, however long and hard the road may be, for without victory there is no survival.

The next day, 14 May 1940, only a few hours after the Dutch army had surrendered to the Germans, Mr Anthony Eden, the Secretary of State for War, broadcast on the B.B.C. Home Service announcing the formation of a new part-time force of men between the ages of seventeen and sixty-five, to be known as the Local Defence Volunteers. The role of this force would be mainly anti-parachutist, and recruiting was to start the next day at all police stations. First thing next morning I was at our local station, only to find that men had been arriving at many police stations to register for service within half an hour of the broadcast. The police were taken completely by surprise, as they knew nothing about it. However my name was taken, and I later heard that it was one of about 500 taken locally in the first few days. Within a fortnight we were allocated to units, and I found myself in 'A' Company of the 6th Battalion 1st Surrey L.D.V. My commanding officer, a local man, was a captain who had been awarded a Military Cross in the Great War and was, as were many such men, eminently suited to the initial formation of this force. Within a month we had loose-fitting khaki denim overalls to add to the initial issue of caps, L.D.V. armband, .300 inch Canadian rifles of 1914 vintage, bayonets and ammunition.

However, before this equipment arrived the country was involved in the crushing military defeat of the British withdrawal from France. The evacuation of the Expeditionary Force from Dunkirk by the Royal Navy and an armada of small boats was a national epic. We had lost 30,000 men and the equipment of an army but between 26 May and 4 June, in nine desperate days, 335,000 British and French troops were saved. A considerable administrative feat was the dispersal of these men by rail and road, some of whom were amazed to find their king at the dockside barrier as they passed through to board the waiting trains. At midnight on the day that Dunkirk fell, Hitler ordered bells should be rung throughout the Reich for three days, to celebrate the victorious end of the greatest battle in world history.

In the midst of the Dunkirk evacuation, on 31 May, a government order was published for the immediate removal throughout the British Isles of signposts, milestones and any notice that could guide or inform an invader.* There could then be no doubt as to what lay in store for the nation, and on 4 June, Mr Churchill spoke to parliament in the following terms:

> We shall not flag nor fail. We shall go on to the end. We shall fight in France, we shall fight on the seas and the oceans, we shall fight with growing confidence and growing strength in the air. We shall defend our island, whatever the cost may be. We shall fight on the beaches, we shall fight on the landing grounds, we shall fight in the fields and in the streets, we shall fight in the hills. We shall never surrender: and even if, which I do not for a moment believe, this island or a large part of it were subjugated and starving, then our Empire beyond the seas armed and guarded by the British Fleet, would carry on the struggle, until in God's good time, the New World, with all its power and might steps forth to the rescue and liberation of the old.

The nation's chapter of disasters did not even temporarily end here, as in the final British evacuation from Norway, the aircraft carrier H.M.S. *Glorious* was sunk on 8 June.

By 10 June the French armies were broken and Italy declared war on France and Britain, acting in the popular conception of the Italian character. The French government under Marshal Pétain then sued for an armistice, and Britain stood alone in the face of a triumphantly victorious Germany, which had swept through the allied countries of Europe almost without hindrance. Churchill broadcast the following message to the nation on 18 June:

---

* This order was not rescinded until October 1942

Hitler knows that he will have to break us in this island or lose the war; if we can stand up to him, all Europe may be free and the life of the world may move forward into broad, sunlit uplands. But if we fail, then the whole world, including the United States, including all that we have known and cared for, will sink into the abyss of a new Dark Age made more sinister, and perhaps more protracted, by the lights of perverted science. Let us therefore brace ourselves to our duties, and so bear ourselves that, if the British Empire and its Commonwealth last for a thousand years, men will say: 'This was their finest hour.'

The nation had by then been at war for some ten months, and the Allied cause in this time suffered the most catastrophic of reverses in the events of the German blitzkrieg in Europe, with the invasion, conquest and occupation of Poland, Denmark, Norway, Holland, Belgium, Luxembourg and France. From this emerged an outstanding lesson in the devastating effect of the ruthless use of air power and that the deciding factor in the waging of this war was to be superiority in the air. Here was the medium for 'the heaviest possible individual blow against the enemy', which I had sought since that O.T.C. camp of 1938, and I determined to pilot a heavy bombing aircraft.

So it was that on 2 July 1940, at the age of nineteen years and eight months, impatient to throw my personal effort into the now most desperate fray, I applied to the R.A.F. Area Recruiting Headquarters in Kingsway, London for enlistment as Aircraft Hand/Aircrew in the Royal Air Force Volunteer Reserve (RAFVR). My family's reaction to my declared intention varied from incredulity to pained indifference, which at the time I put down to pure conservatism. Later I was better to understand these disturbed feelings, for traditionally the Navy and the Army were acceptable, and indeed many of my relatives had served in them with some distinction, but the idea of the R.A.F., so junior, unconventional and ill-established a Service, was met with uneasy silence. There was too, the uncomfortable fact that aviation was a largely technical operation, and that was still considered by many to be 'hardly the sphere for a gentleman'.

My application was acknowledged on 8 July, and I was invited to attend at Croydon Combined Recruiting Centre on 15 July, for preliminary documentation and medical examination. As bidden, I presented myself at the drill hall in Croydon which was as cold, cavernous, gaunt and gloomy as only a drill hall can be. I was aware of the long-established belief that to cross the threshold of a Service recruiting office was to sell one's soul, and to sell it for a pittance. There certainly was an air of finality in crossing the drill hall entrance, and I mused on the memory of my clandestine reading at school, which had led me to believe that if selling one's soul was an irrevocable step, it was a wildly pleasurable and possibly lucrative transaction. As things stood I was to lose all influence over my fate, to become a number, to be at the beck and call of all but the lowliest, and to enter a future that held nothing for me but mystery and dark horror. Yet I was determined to sell my soul in this way and mine was to be a very poor bargain, no music, no wealth, no wine, women or song – it was cold, drab, gloomy – and it echoed.

Documentation, as I learned it was termed, was a novel and brief experience. I had not then discovered that however much personal information is given to the Services, it disappears into some fathomless pit, or so it would seem, for it is apparently never heard of again. Next came the medical inspection. Such was the pressure of work presented by the rush of volunteers that the Service authorities had eased the problem by setting up, on the floor of the drill hall, little cubicles composed of loosely assembled screens. In each of these was seated a doctor who, on the production line principle, concentrated on one particular aspect of the inspection. The system was that one removed all one's clothes and then stood stark naked in a long queue, slowly filing through each of what seemed an interminable succession of open-topped cubicles. However at ease one may be without clothes, it is hard to retain the composure possible in normal circumstances. A brief appearance in one's birthday suit might be carried off to some advantage, but several hours of standing around stark naked on the floor of a drill hall, even in summer temperatures, is liable to leave one feeling strangely foolish. Here and there was placed a paraffin heater, but I defy anyone in these circumstances to remove the gripping psychological chill by warming their hands. It was dawning on me that I had indeed sold my soul for I was already suffering the torment of the damned, and much as in one of Blakes's drawings illustrating Dante's Inferno, the floor of the hall was criss-crossed by a long trail of hundreds of naked men shivering in miserable apprehension.

At length the ordeal ended with something of an anti-climax, for back in my clothes I was instructed to return home and await details of the Aviation Candidates Selection Board, which would be held at R.A.F. Uxbridge. I had passed the preliminary medical and was over the first hurdle, but being unaware of the nation's general standard of health, was amazed by the very large number of aspiring aircrew in the shuffling queue who had not.

The L.D.V. (newly formed Local Defence Volunteers) was claimed with wry humour to stand for Last Desperate Venture. In many senses it obviously was and particularly in one, for knowing the extreme care, rigid discipline and control normally considered essential in the training of the use of small arms, and even the handling of a drawn bayonet, I realised that the acceptance of the situation in which totally untrained personnel were readily provided with these weapons must be desperate indeed. They were likely to be almost as dangerous to friend as to foe. On 23 July 1940 the L.D.V. was officially renamed the Home Guard, a title suggested by Churchill. It was at about this time that the Germans began an anticipated period of air-reconnaissance attacks. The government had assumed that if the Germans conquered the Low Countries the ensuing attack upon Britain from the air would be crushing, and would precede a German invasion. This once highly confidential thinking was now so obvious as to be common knowledge, and for this attack we waited tensely.

Life began to be dominated by the eerie and spine-chilling wailing of the air-raid warning, and the following dolorous all-clear siren; which sounds were to become a symbol of the war on the Home Front. Surrey, lying between the German airfields now established in occupied France and many of the Luftwaffe targets in England, was to see much aerial action. This became increasingly intense, and my home area suffered bombing both by day and night, much of which may have been due to bomb loads jettisoned by German aircraft to improve their manoeuvrability when attacked. It was a gruelling and at times a frightening experience, but I can remember being perpetually more terrified of the ten rounds of live ammunition carried by each Home Guard than I was of the tons of steel and high explosive dropped during such raids.

Service in the Home Guard was not without its excitements, but nonetheless it was for me a life tinged with impatience, for while I was to witness plenty of action on the Home Front in the incessant air raids, it was galling to be hit again and again and perforce to rely on others more fortunate to hit back. Others whom I longed to join, and every day's delay in my summons to the R.A.F. seemed both desperate and interminable. I was certainly the youngest member of my platoon if not the youngest member of the unit, yet oddly enough, while it did not amount to much, my O.T.C. training gave me a military knowledge by far superior to the majority. It also gave me an insight into the fate that lay in store for us if we were called upon to use our Ross rifles, Molotov cocktails (a bottle filled with inflammable liquid with a rag fuse in the neck, for use against tanks) and Stokes 'drain-pipe' gun – a knowledge spared most of my companions.

The L.D.V., or later Home Guard, had been formed as a counter to massive parachute landing and its function was to observe and report parachute attack, to obstruct and hamper the enemy from the moment of landing, and to protect vulnerable spots. Ideally this force would have been guerilla trained, and its whole conception lent itself to this type of warfare, but in keeping with much of the hopelessly outmoded thought of the time it was set up and developed on strictly conventional, static defence lines modelled on the army, or more often the army of yesteryear. Guards were carried out standing in the open in traditional style, and even the suggestion that sentries should be concealed was brushed aside. The slaughter of such innocents would have been horrible in the hands of a professional army. The idea of guerilla tactics did eventually percolate to a minor degree, but was never wholeheartedly accepted or implemented. Unbelievable though it is I suspect that this was largely if not entirely due to the belief that guerilla fighting, and all it implied, just simply was not cricket – we British fought clean, we liked to think, and this was far from clean fighting. The belief that it was better to die 'fighting clean' than to live by using highly effective guerilla methods was to prevail for a long time.

The collapse of France was so inconceivable that it was at the time attributed to two myths: a massive airborne invasion, and fifth columnists dropped by parachute in various disguises. We now know that France was defeated by conventional uniformed land and air forces. Some airborne troops were used, but in legitimate military units. However it is necessary to dismiss this from mind if a true picture of the time is to be achieved, for it had not then been realised and an insidious fear of the two mythical threats was very real indeed. The definition of Fifth Column was: 'An underground organisation of enemy spies, agents, sympathizers and saboteurs. The hidden enemy within the walls, a concept most likely to strike panic and unbounded suspicion into the very heart of a nation, particularly in the confusion of adverse circumstances.' The imagined size, omniscience and all-pervading nature of the Fifth Column indeed rapidly exceeded all bounds of reason and possibility.

With this we were familiar, for in the Phoney War there had been only the Fifth Column with which to do battle, and it resulted in the most ludicrous shadow-boxing on a huge scale – although at the time it seemed necessary and was all in deadly earnest. Now the threat of the Fifth Column received a powerful new impetus, and yet to what extent it existed is debatable. There are those who have suggested that it was purely a figment of the imagination, a product of invasion hysteria. The idea that enemy troops had been dropped behind the lines disguised as postmen, police-men, nuns and so on was complete fantasy, but again in the apprehension and anxieties of the time, all of this was believed with a fervent intensity.

At about the time of the formation of the L.D.V., legislation introduced addi-tional powers which amongst other things enabled road blocks and observation posts to be set up at any point of vantage. A rash of these appeared at first of such flimsy construction as to be only of great nuisance value to the civilian and Service population alike, but later they were replaced by heavy concrete obstruc-tions which were often most cunningly contrived and defended. The fall of France triggered a frenzy of digging in Southern England in the excavation of air-raid shelters, trenches, earthworks and anti-tank ditches. Church bells were banned except as an invasion signal,* the construction of pill boxes and concrete 'dragon's teeth' continued, mines were laid in thousands, and open spaces obstructed to deter glider landings. Everywhere – sandbags. Entwining all appeared thousands of miles of barbed wire. The effort involved in all of this was prodigious and ceaseless.

The complexity and extent of some of these desperately contrived defensive works is worth examining in detail as a measure of the nation's plight. Owing to rigorous security little was generally known of them at the time, and little more is known now on account of hasty and limited contemporary records and the steady erosion and demolition of these defences (an overlooked national monument) since 1945. When the fall of France became inevitable the Commander-in-Chief Home Forces, General Ironside, called for the creation of a coastal defence belt of Britain reinforced with a network of inland stop-lines, to prevent German mobile-columns breaking through from the coast and running riot, as they had on the continent. This belt and the stop-lines were composed of many obstructions, some natural and some artificial such as barbed wire, minefields, anti-tank ditches and so on, but the lines were based on a number of different types of small fortified strongpoint or pillbox, erected at intervals.

The pillboxes of the coastal defence belt were numerous, covering the entire coastline from Scotland down the east coast, along the south coast and up the west coast as far as the Solway Firth. Of the inland defence lines the G.H.Q., or Ironside Line, was the major work and would have been virtually the last line of national defence. In late 1940 General Alan Brooke succeeded Ironside and revised the defence policy. As a result, defence lines were left unfinished and a series of anti-tank islands created instead.

---

* Not until April/May 1943 were church bells again rung as a summons to worship.

In all some 10,188 pillboxes were built inland, and a further 3,972 on the coast. During a hectic summer of construction by local builders, there were many variations. Most common were concrete hexagons found along defence lines and around airfields, military establishments and factories. They had a loophole, for rifles or the Bren light machine-gun, in each of the five walls. In the sixth wall was an entrance flanked by two smaller loopholes. The walls varied in thickness from six inches to two feet nine inches, the thinner being bullet-proof, and the thicker intended to withstand shell fire.

On the surrender of the French, Churchill had observed '. . . The Battle of France is over. I expect that the Battle of Britain is about to begin.' For a time invasion was expected hourly, and with a wholesale roundup of aliens, the Government distributed to every home a leaflet titled *If the Invader Comes: What to Do – and How to Do it.* This cosy, if totally inadequate, leaflet astonishingly urged the population not to be taken by surprise, and confronted the British public with the stark realisation that the invader could burst into their homes at any moment, whether or not they were expecting it. Our position was unenviable for the army needed time to reform and re-equip, and the navy was fully preoccupied in the war at sea, protecting vital merchant shipping, blockading Germany and shadowing the pocket battleships. The only means of striking the enemy and the enemy's homeland at that time lay in the R.A.F.

To invade Britain the Germans would need total control of the air for the defence of a vulnerable sea and airlift, ferrying troops, equipment and stores. During this extended period no British ship could be allowed to operate in the English Channel. In keeping with the thinking of the day Hermann Goering, the head of the Luftwaffe, wishing to demonstrate the power of this formidable and much-vaunted air army, promoted the belief in the German High Command that the Luftwaffe could alone force Britain to capitulate.

The inland activities of the Luftwaffe in the pre-invasion reconnaissance-attacks became known as nuisance raids, for although carried out by comparatively small numbers of aircraft they were widely scattered and strung out over long periods, causing disruption out of all proportion to the weight of the attack. My first involvement in this activity is recorded in my diary:

'The local air raid warning was sounded at about 21.30 hours, and from the roof of the house the fluctuating wailing of these sirens could be heard from miles around (they were later synchronised in districts) it is an ominous and eerie sound. The searchlights are awe-inspiring, a forest of beams sweeping the sky, on a clear starry night for as far as can be seen. Overhead lone German planes pass continuously, recognisable by the unmistakable and malevolent reverberation of their engines.

'Midnight – still very quiet but for German planes overhead ceaselessly – occasionally the distant rumble of bombing, and banging of anti-aircraft fire.

'02.00 hours – terrific explosions approaching at very great speed. The whistle and roar of the falling bombs was nerve-wracking – it was possible to count to about six while the whistle increased in volume until it seemed to be directly overhead – and then the explosions, much closer than were comfortable. We were shaken by ground shocks and the noise was overwhelming – lasting about two minutes – twenty-one bombs were dropped – went back to bed.'

During this time I heard from R. de B. who had been awarded his wings, and posted to No. 2 School of Army Co-operation at Andover. There he was flying the twin-engined Bristol Blenheim, a fighter/bomber aircraft. He spoke of the heavy losses the R.A.F. was experiencing in Norway and France, and also the relentless toll taken by accidents to his fellow course-members, particularly at night. He wrote to express his delight at my application for enlistment in the R.A.F., included much useful information on the Service and ended, 'It would be marvellous if we fetched up together somewhere – I don't mean in the same grave!' On 6 August R. de B. crashed on take-off, his gunner was killed and he was badly injured, suffering a smashed arm and severe burns to his feet and legs. He continued to write (with the aid of a typewriter) from Tidworth Military Hospital, and sent a graphic description of an air attack on Tidworth a fortnight later, in which there were eighteen casualties. 'A regular procession,' he wrote, 'to the stiffs' hideout,' by which was meant the mortuary!

The German pre-invasion air attacks and reconnaissance of Britain had begun in July with a view, it was later known, to a main attack on 12 August. Our defence against these attacks developed into an air battle reaching a peak on 15 September, and ending on 30 September. Although it was not so named at the time, this was later recognised as the Battle of Britain. The assault was primarily an attempt by Germany to destroy R.A.F. Fighter Command as a prelude to Operation Sea Lion, the invasion to be launched in mid-September. Operation Sea Lion, issued as directive No. 16 by Hitler, was to take the form of a feint in the North and a massive thrust against London from landings in Essex, Kent, and Sussex, with slightly later landings in Dorset and Hampshire. The German plans for a conquered England were concise, and circulated in outline orders. They included drastic martial law, the surrender of anything the occupying forces might require, and the internment of all able-bodied males between the ages of 17 and 45 years, for the earliest despatch to slave labour camps on the continent. The population of Britain was to be reduced to 30,000,000 and the country plundered industrially and stripped bare. The fate of the Jews, exiles and other 'marked' peoples in Britain can be imagined. There was no mention in these orders of the fate of British women, but there can be no doubt that many would have been used for slave labour or concubines, as was the case in the countries that had suffered Nazi invasion.

The details of these orders could not be known to the British nation at the time, and the full extent of the Nazi atrocities had yet to be revealed; but we were well aware of the nature of the Nazis and of much that had already occurred in occupied Europe. The continuing threat of invasion was very real and coloured all thinking, resulting in a strange uplift in morale. According to a Gallup Poll taken when France fell, only three per cent of the population thought that Britain might lose the war. It is hard to know whether this was akin to the trembling bravado of the child faced with impossible odds; a gross conceit and complete disconnection from reality; or a magnificent unity and determination in the face of dire peril. I had leaned at school that difficulty and disaster must be turned to stiffen resolve and not allowed to weaken it, and that there are in every group, community or nation, waverers whose influence can spread with disastrous rapidity unless checked instantly by firm and decisive leadership. Churchill's magnificent statements and exhortations of the time were my language, our language, the nation's language, and the waverers were swept up in the powerful forward-moving inspiration of great leadership, from which point onward the nation barely looked back.

The Battle of Britain was fought chiefly over southern and south-eastern England, usually in the clear blue skies of the most beautiful summer weather. Skies that were repeatedly torn into a tangle of vapour trails, as the opposing forces met in a struggle witnessed helplessly from below by apprehensive millions. This battle developed in three stages. In the first the attack was delivered against the south coast, coastal radar stations and some airfields. The next stage was directed against R.A.F. Fighter Command and its airfields, and the last stage an unexpected switch to an attack against the great cities, ports and industrial centres. So, day after day the perilous struggle continued, a small and numerically inferior force of R.A.F. fighter pilots repeatedly hurling themselves against the German air armadas, a feat to which Churchill paid tribute in a speech to the House of Commons on 24 August:

> The gratitude of every home in our island, in our Empire and indeed through-out the world except in the abodes of the guilty goes out to the British airmen who, undaunted by odds, unwearied in their constant challenge and mortal danger, are turning the tide of the world war by their prowess and their devotion. Never in the field of human conflict was so much owed by so many to so few.

Not nearly so well remembered is that this speech also included a tribute to R.A.F. Bomber Command, as follows:

> All hearts go out to the fighter pilots, whose brilliant actions we see with our own eyes day after day; but we must never forget that all the time, night after night, month after month, our bomber squadrons travel far into Germany, find their targets in the darkness by the highest navigational skill, aim their attacks, often under the heaviest fire, often with serious loss, with deliberate careful discrimination, and inflict shattering blows upon the whole of the technical and war-making structure of Nazi power.

Within the Battle of Britain developed a German air offensive on London, opening with an all-night raid on 23/24 August, which was to herald the beginning of the London 'Blitz'.

The Battle of Britain raged day by day unabated and frequently anti-aircraft shells burst over our house, in the wake of enemy aircraft, with a sudden ear-splitting and hollow detonation. On 29 August the house was damaged by bomb splinters and the majority of its windows shattered by blast, during a raid in which some forty-eight bombs fell nearby, twelve of which were within a three-hundred-yard circle centred on the house. The nearest, mercifully a D/A (Delayed Action) was only some ten yards away. Earlier in the week a stick of twenty-four bombs had fallen about 150 yards away, which had then seemed uncomfortably close.

At first we were detailed for nine-hour L.D.V. shifts, that is to say all night once or twice a week, which amounted to thirty-six hours with little or no sleep – a day's work, a night on duty and then another day's work. These periods were initially guard or 'watch' duties but later, as the Home Guard became established, included trench-digging and training. At the time in question, I was undertaking three all-night duties a week in which, owing to the ominously increasing tempo of enemy activity, we rarely got any sleep at all. Being (as the German bomber flew) so close to London, the area came in for much scattered bombing which took a steady toll of life and buildings.

September 7 saw the heaviest daylight raid of the war, aimed at the London docks and causing extensive damage and enormous fires. That night a similar attack gravely hampered rescue and fire-fighting activities, and seriously extended the damage and conflagration. The scale of this raid caused the Chiefs of Staff to issue the code word 'Cromwell', which denoted invasion imminent, and led to the premature ringing of some church bells – the invasion signal. Over London the night sky was a terrifying sight, the enormous, pulsating, lurid glow was all too eloquent and one could only fear the worst. Perhaps most distressing of all was the scattered and sporadic anti-aircraft fire, which in the face of what was happening seemed utterly futile.

From this date London was bombed for fifty-seven consecutive nights, and often by day as well, followed by further attacks ending only on the night of 10/11 May 1941. Returning to the following night of 10/11 September, we were amazed to see the first raiders of the attack met by the most terrific A.A. barrage. The immensity of it was staggering, the night sky over London being made light not only by bursting shells, which at a distance twinkled incessantly in myriads, but also sweeping searchlights. Down below fluctuated a great glow, as London burned. The guns defending London had been increased, and were firing every possible round on approximate bearings and elevation. The expenditure of ammunition was colossal and London and its environs were subjected to a hail of shell splinters, with many faulty A.A. shells which burst on impact with the ground adding considerably to the air raid casualties. Just such a shell burst in the road close to a girl I knew, who was at the time returning in the blackout to her home. A splinter struck her in the thigh, knocking her down and causing such copious bleeding that she realised some vital artery had been severed. Her cries brought an air raid warden to the scene, to whom she explained that she had been hit in the thigh and urged him to do something quickly, or she would bleed to death. After some thought he announced that he had better fetch a 'lady' warden, and disappeared on this errand of idiotic propriety. Such was the curious unreality of the Home Front, and its bewildering situations of war sporadically imposed upon civilian peacetime conditions.

The sight of the barrage was awe-inspiring, and at last it was possible to feel that we were hitting back. Fortunately, we were only later to know that other than as a deterrent it was almost completely ineffective, and at best averaged 20,000 rounds per enemy aircraft destroyed. However this magnificent gesture of defiance was most effective in maintaining the essential civilian morale. The air battle continued by night and day. The Government's concern over the likelihood of invasion was reflected on 13 September in a request to Home Guard volunteers for additional hours of duty, creating a situation in which they were virtually either at work or on guard. September 15 saw the repulse, with heavy losses, of the greatest Germany daylight air raid, and due to the insupportable losses suffered by the Luftwaffe this proved a turning point in the daylight air battles. Of more immediate importance to myself was the receipt on 27 September of my long-awaited instructions to report to R.A.F. Uxbridge, on 4 October.

The last heavy daylight raid took place on 30 September, which signalled the close of the Battle of Britain, although this could not have been known at the time. Neither was it known that on 17 September Hitler had given orders to postpone Operation Sea Lion indefinitely. The initial assault was to have been made by four divisions of the German 16th Army, embarking at Rotterdam, Antwerp, Ostend, Dunkirk and Calais. These were to land in the Folkestone, St. Leonards area. Two division of the German 9th Army were to embark at Boulogne and land in the Bexhill, Eastbourne area. A further three divisions of the 9th Army were to embark at Le Havre, and land between Beachy Head and Brighton. The invasion plan included the rapid capture of the high ground north and north-west of Folkestone. It was to be facilitated by the dropping of the 7th Flieger (Parachutist) Division; and a Luftlande (Air Landing) Division, to be set down near Folkestone. Other airborne troops were to be dropped on the downs behind Brighton. Giant cargo-gliders capable of transporting a fifteen-ton tank or an eight-ton 88mm gun, had been specifically developed for these operations. In this area my brother Allan was waiting on the coast, with the 1st Battalion London Scottish, often standing-to and even sleeping in full infantry battle order. His regiment formed part of the Terri-torial Division grouped into the inadequately armed, equipped and supplied XII Corps defending Kent, Sussex and an area of Surrey. This Corps then consisted of one Territorial Division, one theoretically motorised brigade, 5,000 stevedores armed with rifles, a District H.Q., and a number of minor units. There was little artillery and hardly any ammunition.

From the German bridgeheads a breakout was to be made by the two armies, to secure the objective of a line Portsmouth-Petersfield-Guildford-Reigate-Gravesend. The German 6th Army landing in Lyme Bay, Dorset, was then to have swept around to the North of London. Had this plan gone through, whatever its ultimate outcome, my brother's chance of survival in the 1st Battalion London Scottish, or my own in the 6th Battalion 1st Surrey Home Guard, were extremely remote. However, I have no doubt that as Churchill had exhorted the nation, we would each have done our best to 'take one with us'. Supremacy in the air was a prerequisite for invasion, and failure to achieve it in the skies over southern England was the first check that Hitler had suffered. The public could sense what a near thing the air battle had been and there was no complacency, but only an added awareness of the continuing threat of invasion.

The night attacks on London continued unabated, during which in the early hours of 2 October I was on patrol with a fellow Home Guard. We had watched, through the long hours of the night, the London A.A. barrage which rumbled and flashed in the night sky some twenty miles away. It was still raging fitfully when we reached the limit of our mile-long 'beat', on rising ground at the eastern end of the village; a vantage point marked by a stone memorial-fountain alongside the main road. After looking down into the sleeping village, from beside the fountain, I turned to search the night sky to the east and at once became aware of the shadowy shape of a parachute, silhouetted against the flickering light of the London barrage and descending towards us from approximately the north-east. The Home Guard's prime function was an 'on the spot' anti parachute-troop defence, and we immediately loaded our rifles. The parachute was indistinct, dropping silently towards us and the shadow suspended below it was inert. As far as we could see it was a lone parachute and as we sighted our rifles on the dark mass below the canopy, it crossed our minds that it could be one of our own night fighter crews, or a German airman. We hesitated, and as we hesitated it passed right over our heads not more than twenty feet above us. In that moment it was possible to see that it was no human silhouette, but a metal cylinder about 8′ long and 1½′ in diameter; at once we knew what it was. It drifted rapidly into the village and was lost to sight amongst the buildings. To be helplessly watching this instrument of many sleeping villagers' approaching death, without any means of even raising an alarm, was agonizing. I shouted with all the power of my lungs, and as I shouted there was a blinding flash, a fearful roar and we were thrown rifles and all onto the steps of the fountain.

The German parachute mine was a sea mine, the magnetic mine of earlier mention, containing about 1,500 lbs of high explosive creating a considerable blast effect. It was utterly impossible to aim or guide this weapon, which was therefore entirely random in its destruction and nothing other than a terror weapon. In this instance it landed in a densely built-up area by pure chance, as it could well have landed ineffectually in the open country surrounding the village. Shortly after dawn I returned home to find that for the second time we had lost our windows, this time to the blast of the mine.

Two days later on the night of 3/4 October, the house of my preparatory school friend, which lay on the other side of the village and in which I had spent so much time throughout the years, received a direct hit. The bomb pierced the roof and dropped through three stories into the hall where it exploded, blowing the four walls of the house outwards, completely demolishing it. At the time there were eleven people asleep in the house, amongst them thirteen-year-old fair-haired Catherine who was sleeping on the first floor. She was catapulted into the wreckage of the hall and there pinned under a beam, from which she was eventually rescued badly concussed and seriously bruised, but otherwise miraculously unhurt.

With daylight I had to prepare to report, as instructed, to the Aircrew Selection Centre at Uxbridge, and on this two-day series of tests and interviews depended the achievement of my chosen role in war – on which I was more than ever determined. The instructions were to report to the guard-room at R.A.F. Uxbridge; but in those days having no idea whatsoever as to what this constituted, once inside the gates I looked around for a likely guide. I found it in a little gnome of a man, with a tanned and wrinkled face that had no doubt weathered many a desert storm; in his smartly pressed, but nearly threadbare uniform, he gave the impression of being altogether dehydrated. It was the lively twinkling eyes dancing under a flattened and shapeless sidecap (bearing an R.A.F. badge polished to a detail-less wafer-thin remnant of glistening brass) that held my attention. I halted my eager stride and looked at him questioningly.

'Son,' he said, 'where are you going?'

'To join up,' I answered with the pride and unshakeable confidence of my nineteen years.

'To join up?' he croaked in exaggerated disbelief, and glancing rapidly over his shoulder as though some omnipotent power was crouching behind every white-washed kerbstone, beckoned me closer and then pointed, whispering hoarsely, 'There's the gate, son – get out while you can – don't volunteer, they'll break you soon enough.' With an air of remarkable finality, and the art of an old sweat, he then disappeared.

I continued on my way, thoughtful if undeterred by this hardly unqualified welcome, and a little way inside the main gate, found with some comfort, a small group of fellow civilians standing outside what was presumably the guardroom. This then was the great moment, and I reported importantly to the Service Police-man at the window. After a cursory inspection of my instructions he told me to wait with the others, and I joined them in the uncomfortable detachment of English strangers forced into proximity, and we waited as we were so often to wait in the months to come. It was something of an anti-climax, but then so was to be much of the months to come, during which the conviction that my country had urgent need of me as a pilot in the Royal Air Force at times seemed increasingly to be only my own, and there is no impatience as that of youth.

The entire first day was taken up with protracted administrative detail, such as once again the tedious mass documentation, and then the issue of bedding, knife, fork, spoon and an inordinately large earthenware mug. The business of 'attesta-tion' was taken very seriously, being explained step by step, and with others I then signed on for service in the Royal Air Force Volunteer Reserve, 'for the duration of the present Emergency'. We were taken afterwards, about twenty at a time, into another room to swear an oath of allegiance, a formality which I believe was later dispensed with. Much ado was made of handing around bibles, rather as hymn books, no doubt in the belief that this added solemnity and an unbreakable strength to the bond of the oath – but had they known some of my fellows, as I was later to come to know them, they would have realised this to be the most futile of wishful thinking!

Together we swore the following oath on our bibles:

I swear by Almighty God that I will be faithful and bear true allegiance to His Majesty King George the Sixth, His Heirs and Successors, in Person, Crown and Dignity against all enemies, and will observe and obey all orders of His Majesty, His Heirs and Successors, and of the Air Officers and Officers set over me. So help me God.

I welcomed this opportunity to swear allegiance to my monarch, who represented my country. It was clear that more than adequate provision had been made for His Majesty, His Heirs and Successors, and that somehow the Air Officers and Officers had (one suspected surreptitiously) acquired quasi-royal status, and with a bit of a whimper after so magnificent a royal roar; but I was left with growing misgivings as to what provision was intended for myself, heirs and successors. Misgivings in no way alleviated by experience of the long drawn-out and mass administrative procedures, barrack rooms and Service meal arrangements, which I was meeting for the first time.

After an eventful night wrestling with the vagaries of a telescopic truckle-bed and mattress in three uniform sections, known as biscuits, we embarked on the crucial day of examinations, tests and interviews. The day was long, involved and eventually, in turn, I found myself in Station Sick Quarters facing the dreaded medical examination.

The medical was followed by a series of examinations and tests in various subjects, in which I judged I fell far short of the required standards. Worst of all was an intelligence test, for these tests required a technique I had never met. Much of it was of the 'If your mother's brother is your father's uncle, who the hell are you?' type of question and these, and all party games, are anathema to me – I did dreadfully badly. My heart slowly sank in misery as I realised how far short I was of my long-cherished aim to fly with the R.A.F. Finally came the interview before a board of officers, and I think that I muffed every single question.

Following this debâcle, my papers with the confidential results of all the exams, tests and interviews were sealed into a large envelope which I was instructed to take to a distant Orderly Room. I set out through the complexity of barrack blocks, parade grounds and so on knowing that all was lost. In this knowledge it occurred to me that there was nothing more to lose, and sidetracked into the nearest W.C. There I locked myself in, prised open the envelope and began spreading out the contents on the floor. The first sheet to catch my eye was a summary of many of the tests and there, as I had feared, entered against 'Intelligence Test' was 'Below Average' – but stamped across this sheet in large red letters, and embracing this damning statement was – RECOMMENDED FOR COMMISSION. This was enough, I thrust the papers back into their envelope and carefully re-sealed it, for I realised that mine 'was not to reason why' over such Gilbertian comic opera material, and that I could hardly have been recommended for a commission had I failed selection. In the Orderly Room, as 1268464 Aircraftsman Second Class, I was granted seven days' leave in which to settle my civilian affairs, and returned home hotfoot and wildly elated.

It was just over a year since I had left school, during which time I had started on my first job, served nearly six months in the Home Guard, and gained entry to the R.A.F. for pilot training. For the nation, an eventful, momentous, fateful, historic and epic year – a year which no combination of such terms could adequately describe – a year in which Britain had known its darkest and also its finest hours – to some part of which I had been witness – a year in which the unrelieved gloom of the blackout was appropriate to the nation's misfortunes and the brutal, marauding malevolence of war.

CHAPTER 5

Per Ardua ad Astra

By Trial to the Stars –
the motto of the R.A.F.

If my acceptance by the R.A.F. left me highly elated, it also left me acutely aware that I had surmounted only the first of many hurdles, of which the greatest was learning to fly. Flying required numerous qualities, amongst them aptitudes of temperament, dexterity of mind and a co-ordination far less common then than was to develop with the increasing technicalities of life later. Something of this I had realised, and my anxiety was far from allayed by the common knowledge that of those who were accepted for flying training, large numbers failed to qualify. There was a widely held belief that barely anyone but the occasional superman ever gained the R.A.F.'s coveted 'wings' – a belief those who had so qualified were naturally at some pains to perpetuate!

At the end of my leave I reported back to Uxbridge with a number of others, and there learned that we would be sent to a Receiving Wing. This turned out to be in the delightful seaside resort of Babbacombe, alongside Torquay, and for some unexplained reason we were despatched on the journey independently. Little could have been more exciting than that rail journey on the Devon Express from Paddington to Torquay, but although an aircraftsman (albeit 2nd Class!) I was still disappointingly in civilian clothes.

There could hardly have been anywhere more pleasant than Babbacombe and adjoining Torquay in which to start Service training. Perhaps there was some such intent in this, but primarily it was probably considered that the area was unlikely to draw enemy attack, and offered ideal accommodation in the form of empty hotels. Babbacombe reached precariously to a 280-foot clifftop, from whence were magnificent views of sheer, wooded rock-drops to the superb bays, coves and inlets of the locality. In spite of the semi-dereliction that blights coastal resorts out of season and the restrictions of the Emergency Regulations, it was possible to appreciate the reputation of which Torquay boasted, as the English Riviera. In the almost Mediterranean atmosphere of the palm-scattered parks, cliff gardens, streams, waterfalls and the sheltered climate, little could have seemed further removed from the tensions and eruptions of war, with the taste of dirt and sting of blast that I had left behind in south-eastern England.

From the moment of our arrival we were swept into an intensive system of conversion from 'idle and ill-disciplined civilians', to R.A.F. recruits. This process was for us a twelve-hour day (paid at 2/6d. or now 17½p) starting at six o'clock in the morning. The work although intensive was not continuous, probably owing to administrative difficulties, and often there were intervals of an hour or two. In these most welcome breaks we strolled along the front in the sun, dropped into one of the dozens of popular cafés, or sat in gardens or on the beaches.

Shortly after arrival we were issued with uniform and a comprehensive kit of clothing and equipment, including a mysterious item officially designated a 'hussif' (housewife) which proved to be a complete sewing and repair outfit. All of this, we were assured, could be packed into the accompanying kit bag, although quite how this could be done took us many days and much frustration to discover, to the amusement of our instructors. Amongst our other issues were a knife, fork, spoon and white earthenware mug. These became something of a perpetual night-mare as without them one was unable to take a meal, and it was not possible to carry them around all the time. As a result one was forever fetching them from one's bed space or returning and concealing them, for they were 'attractive' and easily stolen items. We drank tea in vast quantities from these half-pint mugs, and it was here that I first met the age-old legend that 'they' put 'something' into this tea, to cool our supposedly wild and insatiable sexual ardours. This patently impossible myth was widely believed and is to this very day – quite why I cannot imagine, and it would surely make a most interesting study. For myself I greatly like the story of the two venerable Chelsea Pensioners, who having laboriously installed themselves on a park bench in the sun, were resting after their exertions and watching the passers-by. Eventually one called toothlessly to his friend, 'George?' to be answered after some delay, 'Ay, Ben?'

'George – does'ee remember the stuff they did put in our tea?'

'Ay, Ben?'

'Well, George – I do believe its a-beginning to work!'

Caring for our new kit in faultless order initiated the relentless background to Service life, with the ceaseless cleaning that this involved. Life became a perpetual round of boot and button cleaning, in a fruitless search to satisfy our N.C.O.s. We were distinguished, since signing-on, by the official appellation of UT/P (Pilot Under Training) after our names, and were addressed as cadets by the officers. This was a 'red rag' to our N.C.O. instructors, to whom we were 'sprogs' (recruits) the lowest form of Service life, and woe betide anyone who thought that he was a cadet.

Almost as soon as we arrived, four of us drifted together, obviously on account of similar interests, experiences and characteristics. Of the three others, one was a delightful, quiet, deep-thinking and humorous ex-schoolmaster by the name of Woodhouse. He seemed to be considerably older than ourselves but as the age limits for pilot training were then 18–28 years, old was purely relative! Of the others Brockman, ex-Cheltenham College, was the fair-haired, blue-eyed, charming and typically extrovert, enthusiastic public schoolboy, complete with (to my more crudely Service-orientated mind) the somewhat puerile school slang of the day. Gaynor was ex-Ampleforth, and something of a dark horse. We four spent most of our free time together and much enjoyed each other's company.

We were accommodated in requisitioned hotels, from which the furniture had been removed and replaced with Service issue. Somehow, against great odds and by close co-operation, Brockman, Gaynor and myself managed to secure one of the best rooms in the Oswalds Hotel, which slept three only and was complete with a washbasin and mirror. Better still, our dining hall was in the same hotel, and our Flight parade ground in the car park. Some of the others had a walk of as much as twenty minutes to either of these focal points. The Oswalds Hotel had previously been R.A.C. recommended, and even in its transformed state was very pleasant.

Our training consisted of an intense knocking into shape, with squad drill by the hour, route marches, physical training for two hours every day, and endless lectures covering elementary maths, elementary theory of flight, Service organisation, gas warfare, hygiene and so on. For a number of us the transition from school life to the Service was extraordinarily easy, partially because public schools were designed to prepare boys for this type of life, and partially because of much the same discipline, loyalties, sportsmanship, competition and so on. However there were many who resented the discipline and training, even in these early stages finding it unacceptably tough. This was a complete surprise to me, as was their homesickness and astonishing dependence on 'Mum'. It was to these individuals that the course was geared, with many breaks throughout the day of which we had no need, but which were naturally always welcome.

The knocking into shape continued, amounting at times to a considerable battering. We were subjected to all the maddening extremes of discipline including the polishing of soles, heels and insteps of boots, and being kept on parade for up to an hour at a time in pouring rain. A greatcoat would absorb rain for about this time before letting it through (becoming incredibly heavy in the process) but it then took many hours at the right temperature to dry out, and getting back into a wet greatcoat was an appalling experience.

In spite of it all, we were for the only time in our training without the background pressure of continual study for examination, and we made the most of this last brief period of freedom. All hotels were out of bounds to us, as the lowest form of Service life, these being reserved for officers. The most senior officers used the Rosetor, a large country house hotel in Georgian style standing back impressively from the sea front, on the rising ground of Torquay. This hotel, it seemed, belonged to Brockman's aunt (or was it cousin?) and there we were frequently entertained in her private flat where, after fortification with much sherry, we descended into the hotel dining room to feast royally. There the officers had to be content with the services of one waiter or waitress, and to suffer the astonishing spectacle of four AC2's being waited on like kings. After one such sumptuous repast we were approached by the head waiter, and attendant assistant, with the query, 'Do you wish for anything further, gentlemen?' To this Woodhouse was unable to resist the reply, 'Well no, unless you could serve some metal polish and a few thinly sliced dusters!' Technically we were breaking bounds and were open to severe disciplinary action, but the matter was never raised and I suspect that this too we owed to Brockman's aunt (or was it cousin?) and her kindness to four 'sprog' airmen meant far more than she probably ever realised.

All those accepted for pilot training at this time passed through No. 1 Receiving Wing, and being volunteers; in the lower age bracket; extremely fit and desperately keen to fly; we had much in common which made for tremendous morale. We were acutely aware of our embarrassing lack of knowledge and experience of the air, and attempted to alleviate the situation by constant mention and discussion of all things aeronautical; including a rather desperate form of humour. This ranged through the quotation of a notice allegedly displayed in a parachute section reading: 'Should your parachute fail to open, it will be exchanged at once on return to the section', to a number of the Little Audrey series of jokes. The best of these found Little Audrey being given a flight, during which the engine caught fire. The pilot bellowed to the observer: 'Jump!' but the observer remonstrated: 'What about little Audrey? There are only two parachutes.' Whereupon the pilot yelled: 'Oh, f—k little Audrey,' and jumped – but little Audrey laughed and laughed, because she knew that there wasn't time!

Our aeronautical ardour was somewhat dampened by the astonishing policy of returning to the Receiving Wing, as our seniors, pilots u/t who had failed the flying courses. These disgruntled and discomfited individuals, now stripped of the slightest shred of glamorous potential, naturally excused themselves by piling on the difficulties and dangers of flying, leaving us with the impression that those who escaped death would almost certainly meet disaster in failing the course.

The next stage in our training would be a posting to an Initial Training Wing (I.T.W.) of which there were a number, the most sought-after being in Cambridge. Amongst other there were two I.T.W.s in Torquay, and one in Newquay. At the close of our course we awaited our posting with great impatience. After many false rumours it transpired that Woodhouse and Brockman were posted to Cambridge and Gaynor with myself to Newquay on 2nd November 1940. This was the eagerly awaited official moment at which we sprouted the white flash in our forage caps, indicating to all that we were Aircrew Cadets. By way of leave-taking and a fitting end to the course, Woodhouse gave a farewell dinner for the four of us in a Torquay hotel, which we hugely enjoyed and returned to our billet that night in most decidedly high spirits! Our first three weeks in the Service had certainly proved a promising overture.

No. 7 Initial Training Wing was, at the time of my posting, in the process of establishment at Newquay on the north coast of Cornwall. Considerations in the geographical situation of this choice may again have been the availability of accommodation in requisitioned hotels, and comparative freedom from air raids as an area of low population and agricultural nature. Whatever the reasons for this selection it made sense and was, for me, a fortunate one in many ways.

The remote beauty of the Cornish coastline never ceased to fascinate me, and I could have watched indefinitely the Atlantic rollers spreading themselves on the superb sands, or beating against the rugged cliffs and boiling in a seething foam up rock-strewn inlets. We were to experience this coast, under the sea in many moods, from blue-skied sunlit tranquillity to the crashing fury of full gales, when wind-driven spray and rain could sting horribly. For good measure, the rare event of steady snow swirling and eddying fiercely in the almost ever-present winds.

Understandably the people of Cornwall did not relish any sort of Service 'occupation', and the ten or eleven thousand inhabitants of Newquay were no exception. The traditionally isolationist attitude of the county was augmented by the always limited, but now additionally restricted communications; highlighted in the arrival of the national daily newspapers by rail from London, at about lunchtime. Our home for the next five months was to be the St Brannocks Hotel, situated on the cliff-top front and overlooking magnificent sands.

There were in Newquay several other R.A.F. units, and an airfield at St Eval, some four miles to the east. One of these units was a W.A.A.F. unit in which was serving Marian Ainsworth, well known to radio audiences of the time as a pianist of considerable note. I remember the anguish of a music-loving friend of mine, who one day found her scrubbing floors in her billet. There was too an appreciable amount of other talent, such as Cyril Fletcher's and Vic Oliver's (leading B.B.C. comedians of the day) script writer, and between them all they produced and put on a revue in early December, entitled 'St Brannocks – and the same to you!' This was extremely good but must have confirmed the residents' worst fears regarding the brutal and licentious soldiery in their midst!

It was in the initial mêlée that I met Mortimer, an ex-medical student. Bent on enlisting in the R.A.F. to fly, he had presented himself at a recruiting centre only to be summarily rejected on disclosing his studies; the medical profession was a reserved occupation from which it was only permitted to join the medical branches of the fighting services. Undaunted, he retired to the back of the queue and at his next appearance stated that he was a bricklayer, to be accepted without question! Mortimer was an interesting, quiet and amusing personality, with a considerable knowledge of ornithology, and I learned much about the birds we encountered later in our long walks along the sands and cliffs of the coastline, which added greatly to my enjoyment of Cornwall.

A most interesting experience was the way in which from a nebulous milling mass on arrival, extraordinarily like the apparent confusion of a scattered ants' nest, there at once began to form an orderly and organised community. Unofficial leaders emerged, specialist abilities found demand, while groups and cliques proliferated. The automatic and popular choice as Flight elder was an ex-tea planter who had returned to this country to volunteer for service in the R.A.F. He was of course one of the few older and comparatively experienced men amongst a Flight of 18–19 year olds. Although Young by name, I never heard him referred to as anything other than 'Bugger-me-Young' on account of his pet expletive. Young gathered around him one or two like souls, such as an ex-Palestine Policeman who rejoiced in the name of Courtenay-Cox, with a moustache to match, and they operated from their room which they named 'Gen Corner'.

'Gen' is R.A.F. slang for information, being an abbreviation of 'genuine information'. Gen is a vital commodity in Service life and falls into the two self-explanatory categories of Pukka Gen and Duff Gen. In the ranks, because the men are isolated from even the lowest policy-making levels, and there is little call to inform them of plans and decisions (other than a bare minimum when orders are issued) there is a continual demand for information of every sort. In such circumstances rumour is rife, hence the need to determine what is 'pukka gen' and what is 'duff gen'. The inhabitants of 'Gen Corner' very soon established a most effective intelligence network, and were able to produce much gen. However, with the time came sophistication and they were not averse to trading or issuing duff gen either for entertainment value or 'political' motives.

The I.T.W. course was a tough one, and scheduled to be completed, under very high pressure, in six weeks. The working day lasted from six o'clock in the morning until six o'clock at night, which included two hours of preparation for the next day's subjects. Against a background of fierce discipline, standards of drill and turnout, we covered two hours physical training a day with studies in Maths, Aerial Navigation, Meteorology, Signals, Armament, Aircraft Recognition, Civil and R.A.F. Law, and minor subjects such as Gas Warfare and Hygiene. Our instructors were a mixture of officers of the Education Branch, and N.C.O.s of the trades involved. So far these were our closest links with the R.A.F. proper, to which we so ardently aspired, and we observed them minutely. We were, all of us, volunteers and our enthusiasm and determination to succeed was boundless, creating a superb but dangerously hypnotic spirit. While only some 5% of the applicants for aircrew training passed the medical, selection tests and interviews, this was but the beginning, and of this 5% some would fail their first hurdle in the I.T.W. course.

Classes and lectures were held in various requisitioned premises throughout the town, and many excellent instructional films were shown in the Newquay cinema. This arrangement involved considerable movement and we forever seemed to be marching in the town, with the regulation white hurricane lamp carried by the first file of the Flight and red hurricane lamp by the rear file, for safety during the hours of winter darkness.

For I.T.W. purposes a Flight numbered fifty men, and was in the charge of a Sergeant or Flight Sergeant, aided by a couple of Corporals. A Squadron, consisting of a variable number of Flights, was commanded by a Flight Lieutenant, assisted by two Pilot or Flying Officers. The Wing, again composed of a variable number of Squadrons, was commanded by a Squadron Leader. Officers were thin on the ground at this time and we saw little of them. Each group of N.C.O.s vied with the others in turning out the smartest and most efficient Flight. We were Sprogs (recruits) and the N.C.O.s knew that many of us would receive rapid promotion to ranks of which they could only dream. Having considerable power within their limited sphere they instituted, with relish, a regime of absolute hell. An enormous amount of time had to be devoted to the care and preparation of one's uniform and equipment, seldom if ever to the satisfaction of the N.C.O.s. All this had to be done in 'spare' time, when in addition it was necessary to work on the subjects we were studying for the forthcoming exams.

The N.C.O.s' object was to make the Sprogs sweat, and in this they undoubtedly succeeded but there was in the Flight, to their consternation, a group of us who were well used to this and could take it and more, apparently without the resentment upon which they thrived. This confused them and created suspicions that, in some way they did not understand, we were getting the better of them. In consequence they tended either to leave us largely alone, or to react with unreasonable severity as in one typical incident. We had been instructed that the proper time to assemble for a parade was five minutes before the time specified. Once, by mischance, I arrived a good six minutes before the specified time and was promptly informed by the N.C.O. that I was late. Automatically I glanced at my watch in surprise which evoked a furious outburst of: 'If I say you are f——ing late, you are f——ing late,' and I was in consequence awarded several extra guard duties for dumb insolence. The wearing of a wristwatch was in those days by no means almost universal, as it is now, and was a rare sight in the ranks being automatically associated with 'education' and the high income brackets. Very few of our N.C.O.s sported a watch, although some carried a pocket watch. The wearing of a wristwatch was likely to be considered effete by such company and to engender antagonism.

Part of the unrelenting pressure to achieve an atmosphere of smartness and to make the Sprogs sweat was the ruling that all marching, other than route marches, would be carried out at 160 paces to the minute. This was a very brisk pace indeed compared to the standard 120 paces to the minute, and was correspondingly difficult and exhausting to execute.

If we learned to be wary of our N.C.O.s, we learned to be doubly so of the Station Warrant Officer, who was the equivalent of the Army Sergeant Major and was similarly responsible for overall discipline. Invariably a fearsome individual, this rare and most senior of N.C.O.s created an illusion of being behind every door, tree, lamp post and around every corner – in fact nowhere did one seem safe from his eagle eye or baleful influence. Quite how this omnipresence is achieved I never discovered; it must be a closely guarded professional secret. However it is extremely effective, and we lesser mortals avoided this S.W.O's piercing gaze as the evil eye. To be fixed by it was almost certain doom, as even in the unlikely event of all about one's person being perfection, one was automatically a slovenly or idle airman, and suffered accordingly. In time I came to realise that, just as in our meteorology lessons we learned the advance indications of impending changes in the weather, there were infallible indications of the approach of the S.W.O., one of which was the sudden and complete disappearance of every airman and junior N.C.O. free to move from his path.

The standard of physical fitness in the armed forces is of necessity high, and considerable time is devoted to maintaining it, but over and above this the standard demanded of aircrew under training was the highest that could be achieved. I found myself playing rugger, or taking part in long runs over beautifully desolate Cornish country with splashes through some glorious streams, sometimes in the most atrocious weather, and with the same sort of frequency as at school. For some of us this was easily taken in our stride and could even be enjoyable, but for others it was an agonizing innovation contrary to their experience, mode of life and way of thinking, which they resented accordingly. I was learning that the public school training in discipline and physical fitness was considered by most to be near barbaric. Whether or not this view was justified I could see clearly enough that it would seem so, viewed from the standards of schools where such training was by far less severe and lacking the elements of self-discipline, determination and resilience surely essential in a virile nation. The antipathy, or in fact marked resistance to any form of physical exercise was something of a shock to me and I could never become accustomed to it, although I was to meet it repeatedly in later years.

One of our Physical Training Instructors (P.T.I.s) was a Corporal Berg or Kid Berg, the ex-lightweight world boxing champion. He expressed his joy in physical fitness by stripping his classes to the waist, regardless of weather conditions, and putting them through it in no mean manner. Those of the populace sufficiently hardy to brave the elements would watch in some awe as, bare to the waist and clad only in thin cotton shorts, we were put on our backs or chests in the snow to execute arm and leg exercises, for all the world as though in the comfort of a centrally-heated gymnasium. I enjoyed it and was not only proud of my physical fitness, but well aware that qualification and survival as a pilot might depend upon it.

Route marches were frequent, and in this way we saw much of the surrounding countryside. As the winter weather hardened we marched in greatcoats, which while welcome in the early stages of a march became intolerable heavy and hot as the miles went by, but we were being broken in gently. The Drill Instructors' delight was to double us up the long Cornish hills, and then to blow on a whistle the gas alarm. This meant fitting respirators on the march without breaking step, and then struggling for breath as the eye-pieces misted over in a Turkish bath atmosphere of heat and perspiration.

Therein lies a tale, for the R.A.F. respirator was fitted with a long corrugated rubber breathing tube to enable the haversack, canister, filters etc. to be worn on the back. This arrangement was to keep these clear of work, such as that on engines etc., that might have to be undertaken during a gas attack. In greatcoat-order without packs the respirator was worn on the back, and on one such occasion when approaching the inevitable hill our instructor, seeing his chance 'to make us sweat', doubled us up the hill and then blew the gas alarm. The drill was to reach behind, open the respirator haversack, pull out the facepiece, clap it on securing it in double quick time, without slackening pace or losing the dressing of the ranks. Breathing inside the mask was considerably restricted, and in these circumstances it was a battle with semi-suffocation, but woe betide he who attempted to ease the situation by lifting the edge of the facepiece. The N.C.O.s moved up and down the column to make sure that no one did, or if they did – that they were unlikely to do it again.

A companion of mine was on this occasion doubling in the file behind me, and had obviously come fully prepared, for he leaned forward and clamped a clothes peg on the breathing tube just above the canister at my back. I was already near asphyxiation in my mask, and the sudden inexplicable cutting of the meagre air supply produced immediate suffocation. I whipped two fingers under the edge of the facepiece to admit desperately needed air, only to find myself the object of a furious tirade by an apoplectic N.C.O., and in addition the recipient of several extra guard duties. I found the peg.

On the next route march I contrived to get into the file behind this joker, and to await the turn of events. It came. A likely hill, the order to double-march and then the gas alarm. All went perfectly, for the three N.C.O.s converged on my companion and delivered a multiple tirade to end all tirades. It seemed they felt that he was trying to take it out of them, and on this point they were very sensitive. The reason? Tied in a magnificent bow around his breathing tube, just above the canister on his back, was revealed a large and beautiful pink ribbon of finest chocolate box proportions. Of this he was totally unaware – as of my painstaking efforts to fold it into his respirator haversack the night before. The score was evened!

In due course we graduated to full marching order, which consisted of greatcoats over which was strapped heavy webbing, carrying two packs and rolled gas cape on the back, a haversack on one side and water bottle on the other. Respirators were worn on the chest. Marching in this could be heavy and hot work in any weather, and the N.C.O.s' uphill gas drill at the double a truly nasty experience.

These marches were the occasion for the singing of time-honoured Service songs, to break the monotony, cheer us on our way, and finally to spur us into continued effort as fatigue took its toll of our spirits and strength. These songs were all of them bawdy, most bemoaning our communal fate as airmen, and some shamelessly nostalgic. There is something very inspiring in the spirited singing of men en masse, and such was our spirit that we sang mightily at every opportunity whether on the march or not. Even when dragging our weary feet home, when each pace was becoming agonizing, we chanted to the time of the step that traditional and mournful dirge: 'Left – left – bloody good home that I left – right – right – it serves me bloody well right!'

During these early days we were issued with flying kit, an exciting and long-awaited event, being the first proof (in a welter of theory) of our elected destiny. We were thrilled and immensely proud to accept the responsibility of this expensive equipment, if a little apprehensive of a complexity which warned of hazards yet completely unknown.

Compared to the strictly functional, low-cost equipment we had so far received as airmen, this was carefully designed, scientifically thought out, and expensive. The leather helmet was accurately fitted and the position for earpieces marked individually, to be built in by leather workers of the equipment section. Over this fitted well-padded goggles constructed of optical flats for wide and accurate vision. The flying boots, of canvas and leather reaching to about mid-calf, were fleece-lined and enticingly comfortable to wear, which allied to the fact that they had become the completely unofficial badge of aircrew off duty, led to a widespread flouting of authority in the matter. To protect one's hands, there were four pairs of gloves worn one over the other. First a pair in white silk, then chamois leather, next a woollen mixture, and finally large leather gauntlets. Body protection was provided by the issue of special woollen vests and long combinations, of a quality not to be seen again in Britain for at least a decade. An antique if effective style, and surely the original 'Passion Preventors'!

Over these monstrosities, one wore personal clothing and uniform followed by a single-piece, thickly quilted lining, the Inner Sidcot. Over this again a single-piece, fur-trimmed outer covering of canvas closed by lengthy zips, the Outer Sidcot. It was protective clothing evolved for the flying of open cockpit aircraft and was seriously outdated. Had we been capable of realising this we might well have wondered quite what lay in store for us, but perhaps mercifully we were not, and it all seemed very wonderful. Encased in the lot, one bore a striking resemblance to the Michelin Tyre advertisement of a man formed from tubes, inflated to an unhappy rotundity and apparently eternally about to float helplessly away. It was a shock to realise that contact with the aeroplane was going to be remote, as almost every sense would be masked by enclosure in this way, and this would not make learning to fly any easier.

The issue of flying clothing (which necessitated a distinctive second kitbag in which to carry it) was supervised somewhat sourly by our Flight N.C.O., who resented this indication of the coming reversal in our roles. For us the thrill of the issue was somewhat diminished when one of our number, holding his stiff canvas Outer Sidcot at arms' length, queried: 'I wonder why ever they make this thing in one piece?' In a flash the N.C.O., with the air of one who has seen it all, answered: 'Son, it's to make it easier to pour you into your coffin through one sleeve – after the accident.'

Initially, while we were working from reveille to lights out, there had been no time for any sort of diversion – or so I had thought, but in this I was undoubtedly wrong. There was a N.A.A.F.I. canteen for our use in Newquay, and it was the then usual highly institutional, soulless and bleak affair. The main stock in trade was squares of a vivid yellow block cake, absolutely plain and looking for all the world as though it had been cut from a thick and evil-coloured plank – it certainly could well have contained a high percentage of sawdust. This was the 'N.A.A.F.I. Wad' of great renown, and with it went heavy cups of newspaper-flavoured grey tea, or 'char'. Sometimes, as a great treat, there were available little individual jam tarts, consisting of a grey cloying pastry filled with violently coloured, sickly sweet and tasteless 'jam'. The N.A.A.F.I girls who served these horrors were traditionally and individually referred to as 'the original N.A.A.F.I. tart', not to be confused with the jam variety, although there were some amazing similarities and in the deprivation of wartime shortages both were considerably sought-after. In the evenings, fried meals were sometimes available with the inevitable chips, and a choice of a 'coffee-type' drink or quite unspeakable beer.

Many of our lectures were in the form of instructional films shown for us in the comparatively luxurious comfort of the Newquay cinema. An entire morning spent in a cinema seat can become uncomfortable, and we much looked forward to the ten-minute mid-morning break. At this point there was always a rush by the nicotine addicts for the exits, as no smoking was allowed in the cinema. This seemed at least undignified and never ceased to surprise me. However, it was nothing compared to my utter astonishment one morning when a fellow aircrafts-man, who had been sitting next to me, came dashing back to ask if I had a F.L. (French Letter or condom). I did not, but someone else obliged, and while it was being produced I asked whatever he wanted it for. 'Oh,' he said, 'I have got one of the usherettes set up in a broom cupboard down the corridor.' He was back, with an unmistakably self-satisfied smirk, in good time and I reckoned that he could have given the usherette no more than four minutes at the best. This, I consoled myself, was a startling measure of the pressure and urgency of our course – but I was wrong, for such continuing experience brought me to doubt that pressure necessarily had any bearing on the duration of the matter at all.

We slept in the former bedrooms of St Brannocks Hotel, the movable furniture, floor-coverings and curtains having been stripped out and replaced with truckle beds and the other limited utilitarian impedimenta of military life, contrasting strangely with the residual fixtures of fitted cupboards and pastel-shaded wash basins. This was luxury indeed, but perhaps a greater luxury was that no amount of ingenuity, or even brute force, could cram more than three or possibly four men into a room; an improvement on life with the twenty or so widely varied companions of a barrack room. However inured one may become to communal living (and boarding schools are an intensive training in the art) one is bound in a strange relationship with one's room-mates, whether they be few or many. Regardless of difference in intelligence, temperament, interests and all that goes to make personality and character, one is forced to share many of the intimate details of life by virtue of sheer proximity. This situation is not eased by a reduction in room size or number of occupants, but becomes more acute. At the time I automatically accepted my room-mates without demur, although we probably could not have been more oddly assorted.

There were three of us and of the other two one was a ruddy-complexioned, somewhat stocky individual who began life as an agricultural worker but aspired to better things and, to his credit, studied the hard way. However, *en route* he had 'found the Lord' or 'got religion' as it was aptly described by his fellows, and as a result seemed incapable of talking of anything else. The ranks of a fighting service being hardly conducive to any brand of religious discussion, he seldom talked but maintained instead a mildly aggressive, martyred silence. Although I had not by his standards 'been Saved', for some obscure reason he considered me to be more promising material than my fellows, and I was treated to many patronising dissertations, of the most elementary tub-thumping variety in which spiritual cleanliness figures prominently. He carried this zeal for cleanliness into his physical life, and seemed forever to be cleaning himself or his equipment. His gyrations before the basin were fascinating and highly involved, demanding a considerable contortional ability. It more than once occurred to me that a bath would have been a very much simpler operation, but it was some long time before I realised that he was unfamiliar with a bath, and was probably not willing to risk displaying his ignorance.

My other room-mate, Stewkley, was one of the least likeable men that I have ever met, being one of those whose mind seldom, if ever, rises above a woman's navel; a man of great cunning and absolutely no morals of any sort whatsoever. His utter lewdness and crudity were openly apparent in watery eyes, a large and prying nose and a loose and at times almost slavering mouth. I was reluctantly fascinated by his undoubted success with the opposite sex and had particularly noted his current girl companion of the time, with whom I had seen him walking in an off-duty moment, having been struck by her general attraction and charm.

Judging from Stewkley's frequent absences between the last lecture of the day and lights out, which was a period in which we lesser mortals studied and cleaned our kit, Stewkley was pressing his attentions on this girl with his complete single-mindedness.

Inevitably there came the day when at 'lights out' Stewkley was absent and, although it was no concern of mine, I could not help feeling some sadness. In this frame of mind I fell asleep, to be awakened much later by dragging footsteps on the stair accompanied by stifled groaning. Jumping out of bed, I pulled open the door through which staggered Stewkley clutching his groin and groaning wretchedly. It being no time to ask questions, I sank on to my bed and watched an astonishing performance. Stewkley, leaning heavily on the basin, filled it with cold water, dunked a towel in it and then dropping his trousers tenderly wrapped the wet towel, in a large bandage, around what he described as his f——ing pulverised prick. Between groans, exclamations of self-pity and the problem of a somewhat inelegant treatment, which necessitated carrying a large and wet bandage before him, Stewkley, with the complete lack of sensitivity of his ilk, explained his predicament.

Unfortunately it is impossible to record Stewkley's descriptive, if crude and colourful English, but it seemed that the turn of events was more or less as follows. Stewkley had contrived a walk with his girl on the moonlit sands, which were in themselves at the least romantic if not staggeringly beautiful, and judging the time and place to be ripe suggested, 'after a bit of the old turning-on process', that they should make love. The girl's response was that she had tried that once, and did not like it. Stewkley (he felt) took the very logical line that this was only because she had set about it the wrong way. Such were his powers of persuasion that in the seclusion of a rocky, sand-floored inlet, he expertly coaxed her out of her stockings, belt and panties, discovering in the process such perfection that he could hardly contain himself.

Naked to the waist under her skirt, the girl submitted to his suggestion that she should bend over a nearby rock, and Stewkley unable to believe his luck, 'bared the old quivering prick', and seizing the girl's delectable buttocks, apparently clamped her to the rock and with a complete disregard for her safety, thrust violently between her thighs – however before he could achieve the urgent business of the moment, his 'prick' was caught in a paralysing and vice-like grip from which he was unable to withdraw, and locked together in this way he was forced to undergo a lengthy and excruciating agony. How the problem was resolved at length was never clear, but it must have led to a fascinating if not incongruous 'pas de deux' in the beauty of the silver-lit sands.

Perhaps most astonishing in the whole event was the resentment that Stewkley harboured against the girl for 'so dirty a trick', although, apart from anything else, he was fully aware that this not unknown situation is an involuntary reaction to fear. Stewkley's uncomplicated and graphic description of the incident left our now awakened religious enthusiast in grim and triumphant silence. For me, the spectacle of Stewkley's 'injured pride' was so excruciatingly funny that I collapsed in helpless laughter, which puzzled Stewkley completely and he temporarily lost much of his bombast. However his chagrin was soon forgotten in the pursuit of another girl.

He was later killed with his instructor, in a flying accident, at the Elementary Flying School to which we were both posted. As a member of the funeral party, I found myself at one stage 'Resting on Arms Reversed' as the coffins passed. The coffin of the flying instructor, an officer, traditionally bore his Service cap and medals – that of Leading Aircraftsman Stewkley UT/P, bare of such achievement, unmistakably bore in my mind's eye a wet towel bound into a large bandage.

In marked contrast, after lunch one day as I passed from the dining hall through the clatter of heavy china and hubbub of voices, I heard the soft notes of a piano played with great sensitivity and feeling. The piano stood in the bare, pillared room that had once been the hotel lounge, but was now used as a common room for the Flights quartered in the hotel. I knew the room and piano well for night after night, in the crowded atmosphere of thick tobacco smoke, the strident notes of that piano led boisterous, high-spirited drinking song after drinking song far into the night. One no longer wondered at the expression 'raising the roof', for just that very thing always seemed imminent. The repertoire invariably included the R.A.F. trooping song 'Bless 'em all', with 'Three German Officers Crossed the Rhine', and 'There was an Old Monk of Great Renown' who was indeed the monk with a dirty habit. But this was different – the wistful music drew me into the room, which was deserted save for the solitary figure now absolutely lost in the gentle sound flowing from schoolboy hands. I stood beside the piano in silent delight as the haunting music flowed on, and gone were the bare boards, scarred pillars and dirty paintwork, gone in a soft flood of gentle beauty.

I do not know for how long I stood there, but it was when I leaned forward and said, 'John, that's wonderful,' that I realised he was not aware of me. Was he, I wondered, perhaps in a far-away summer garden in which a mother pottered amongst the flowers, a sister lazed reading in the sun and a younger brother played with a pet? I could not know, but wherever he might be I knew well that I was intruding in something too personal to ever know, something that had no place in barrack life, something that was greater than the calamities of war, perhaps than life itself, for I realised that schoolboy John did not want to die, and this was his agonizingly wistful cry to destiny and eternity. The impact of this realisation was a chill draught of reality – I had to escape or be lost. I turned and ran from the hotel, over the road and down the cliff path, in amongst the rocks. I ran along the sands of the sea's edge until I could run no more – yet I had not escaped, for that music was still with me and I was afraid for John – but perhaps most of all, afraid for myself.

Fortunately the pressure of events allowed little time for reflection, or in fact anything other than the course syllabus. The twelve-hour-a-day programme of our course did not include either the time spent in individual study, or in cleaning and preparing our kit. Saturday and Sunday were full working days as was Christmas Day, which fell at the end of the course. If this was tough, we expected no less, and were so dedicated to achieving the aim of success in flying that most of us were aware of little other than the immediate task. In late November we sat an examination in Maths and War Gases. On 9 December 1940 the first British offensive in the North African desert began under General Auchinleck, but it is doubtful if this meant much to us other than to increase our sense of urgency. We then sat examinations in Air Force and Civil Law, Aircraft Recognition, Signals, Navigation, and an examination in Armaments on Christmas Day!

Christmas Day did not pass entirely unnoticed, and it is to the credit of the R.A.F. that the menu for lunch included tomato soup, roast pork and stuffing, roast potatoes, brussels sprouts and apple sauce. This was followed by Christmas pudding, cheese and nuts. For each of us there was a glass of sherry and a pint of beer. Not bad for an airman's lunch and served, as is customary, by our officers. In the beleaguered Britain of 1940 this meal must have taken considerable thought and effort to achieve; it was greatly appreciated.

The 29 December ended our examinations and I.T.W. course – with the inevitable failures. Life for these was bleak, as apart from the bitter disappointment of failing to achieve a cherished aim, there was the ignominy in taking farewell of their successful companions. Perhaps worse was returning on leave to their once-admiring family and friends, shorn of the considerable aura that had surrounded every R.A.F. pilot and pilot under training since the Battle of Britain, to be left looking the complete charlatan. It was not then possible to see such failure in perspective, as the German conquest of Europe, the threat of invasion and the aerial attack on England created a tension and sense of urgency that is now difficult to imagine. Also the spirit of the course, from which the failures were now excluded, was headily inspiring; then too they were young enough for this early frustration and its comparatively bleak alternatives to seem the end of the world. There were three suicides during my time with No. 7 I.T.W., and while it seems hardly likely that course failures were the direct reason for these, it is possible that they were a contribution to them.

The successful completion of this course brought me promotion on 4 January 1941 to Leading Aircraftsman, and an increase in pay to five shillings and sixpence a day (27½ pence). This was welcome and with great pride we received the L.A.Cs.' cloth badge, of an embroidered two-bladed propeller, to be sewn onto our sleeves by the next parade.

The night of 29/30 December saw a great fire-raid on the City of London, and in this devastating attack huge areas around St Paul's were destroyed. On the 29th, we had learned from Daily Routine Orders that my Flight (no. 5 Flight) was to proceed on seven days' leave, with effect from Monday 6 January. Naturally those who lived in London were relieved at this opportunity to see conditions in London for themselves. However, many of us whose journey home would be across London were understandably concerned at the loss of precious leave arising from problems in travel through the city and other damaged areas.

In the event, my journey by rail from Newquay home took some fifteen hours, about twice the normal time required, and in addition was fraught with complications and uncertainties. Wartime rail travel was optimistically limited to a maximum speed of 60 m.p.h., but this was rarely approached owning to longer and heavier trains, poor fuel (an important consideration in coal-fired locomotives), air raid warnings and interminable delays due to the passage of special trains, re-routing and so on. The trains themselves had little or no heating, no restaurant or refreshment cars, suffered from chronic overcrowding, and poor ventilation after dark caused by the blackout requirements of drawn blinds.

Little relief was to be found in the corridors, as these were crowded with seatless passengers, kitbags and equipment, to traverse which was a struggle by daylight, let alone at night when the sole illumination was a very dim and eerie blue corridor light.

My train eventually crept into London after dark and during an air raid. No sooner had we thankfully escaped into the blacked-out vaults of Paddington Station, than we were herded into shelters by steel-helmeted Air Raid Wardens who appeared in the gloom like so many will o' the wisps. Herded, not altogether unwillingly I admit, for the flash and noise of the anti-aircraft barrage and bursting bombs was disquieting, as was the reflected flicker of nearby fires.

I made for the Underground, knowing these stations had been opened to the public as shelters in addition to their normal function, and I was hoping for a train to Waterloo. Such station shelters were a remarkable sight, and Paddington was no exception. They were the deepest and therefore the safest shelters generally available, and at night became mass dormitories, a process which began in the late afternoon with the occupying and reserving of pitches. Every available space would be taken before the night was out, even to the major part of the platform, barely leaving room for the movement of passengers who were obliged to step over and among sleeping bodies to reach the trains. The platforms had been marked with two white lines, one painted eight feet from the platform edge and one four feet from the edge. It was intended that the eight-foot line should not be crossed by those sheltering, before 1930 hours daily, and that the four-foot line should not be crossed before the trains stopped running at 2230. At this time the trains service was discontinued and the station lighting was dimmed.

The teeming compressed mass became completely inured to these conditions, and insensible to observation with few concessions to propriety. The main impression was one of extreme weariness, due to long hours of work, long hours of duty, shortage of food, lack of sleep and the multitudinous strains and problems of life under bombardment. Men, women, girls, boys and children, with their strangely contrasting choice of minimum requirements, were abandoned to sleep in all postures and stages of dress and undress. Passengers clambered over bodies completely dead to the crashing rumble and roar of trains, screeching of brakes, explosive hiss of compressed air, slamming doors and drumming compressors. Old couples in the careless proximity of familiarity, or tender proximity of care and affection. Young couples pressed in the fierce, rebellious and urgent embrace of snatched hours in a gnawing frustrated love. The unattached often lying together in fear, common hardship, or exhaustion; and over all the hot electric smell of forced ventilation.

I wandered for sometime in this fantastic, packed but almost lifeless underworld until it was obvious that with the closing of the flood gates in the rail tunnels running under the river Thames, there would be no trains to Waterloo that night. My emergence from the underground unfortunately coincided with a prolonged hail of bombs on the area; an inauspicious start to my plan to end the loss of precious leave, by ignoring the cost and taking a taxi from Paddington to Waterloo Station. This was altogether easier planned than executed, for back in the blacked-out station and its environs there was not only a complete absence of life, but an air of stalking doom. With understandable discretion, the buses and taxis had long ago deserted the street, leaving no alternative but to begin a three-mile walk in the direction of the river and Waterloo. It was only possible to head roughly to the south-east, on account of the fires and frequent barricaded roads denoting damage or unexploded bombs. Progress was painfully slow in the maelstrom of noise and flashing, flickering light, because of the repeated need to take cover when the terminal roar of falling bombs came uncomfortably close.

To feel acutely and strangely alone was contradictory in so great and populous a city, but a sensation enhanced by the continuous, malevolent and pulsating drone of the German aircraft overhead. There was rarely a sign of life in the streets and yet on one occasion, when slow in identifying the roar of a falling bomb as almost directly overhead, I hurled myself into the roadside gutter and was instantaneously buried under considerable weight. The blast and noise of the burst over, the weight diminished and turned out to be the hardier remnants of a bus queue, which had been sheltering against the buildings, and the members of which made for the gutter at the same moment as did I. Up to this point I had been walking on the footpaths for the cover afforded by the walls from the sporadic hail of shell fragments, which rattled over the roofs and into the road. So many were the undetectable obstructions that I decided to walk in the centre of the road, which was more likely to be clear – or so I imagined.

When eventually I arrived at Waterloo station the scene was quite extraordinary. Superimposed on the almost continual flash of the guns, blaze of bursting bombs and flickering light of fires, were brilliant points of intense blue-white light all over the platforms, track, stationary train roofs; and in the steel girder-work of the vast glass roof as showers of incendiary bombs fell and ignited on impact. The noise of shattering and falling glass was continuous, and I think I was more concerned about this than anything else, as for a start I had no 'tin hat'.

Silhouetted against the glare were scattered a number of figures, desperately working at extinguishing incendiary bombs and the minor fires they were starting. I approached one fire-fighter to see if I could be of help and to my astonishment found it to be an aged and bewhiskered porter, a veritable grand-daddy of all porters. In spite of his frail bent frame, he was nipping about with extraordinary agility from one blazing incendiary to the next, fearlessly extinguishing them by shovelling sand from a bucket, and mumbling toothlessly, 'One hundred and forty-two – one hundred and forty-three – one hundred and forty-four,' and so on. So engrossed was he in his task that he was oblivious of my offers to assist, and after unsuccessfully searching for further supplies of sand, I lost contact. He had moved on to pastures new and I realised that he knew the station and its fire equipment, and I did not.

At about this time the weight of the full marching order I was carrying began to make itself felt. In those days this was obligatory on leave, in case of detachment from one's unit or the dislocation that would result from intense aerial bombardment, or invasion. As there were no trains running, and feeling extraordinarily useless, I sought a shelter. On entering I found to my delight that it contained a canteen, which was luxury indeed, and with the reaction of the trained opportunist joined the queue at the counter.

The unheard-of situation of going on leave from I.T.W. in full kit, was due to the German threat of sudden invasion, expected on the south and east coasts of Britain, with the disruption and dislocation that this would cause.

The canteen was run by one of the voluntary organisations to which all Servicemen are eternally indebted, but it was under great pressure, and all that was
available so late in the night were dry and thick tinned-salmon sandwiches, and
stewed tea made with powdered milk. I retired into a corner triumphant with a
large sandwich, which I attacked with the aid of the tea, and then as no trains
were running tried to snatch what sleep was possible propped upright in my
equipment. The raid dragged on above and finally petered out with the dawn.
Daylight brought the resumption of some train services, and I was able to reach
my home in Surrey for a late breakfast. There followed, joy of joys, a long
uninterrupted bath, and undisturbed sleep in a real bed; in my own room; with
six more days of leave to which to look forward.

It was a short-lived joy, for I awakened feeling unaccountably ill; and ill enough
to report officially sick. As my nearest R.A.F. doctor was ten to twelve miles away
a Canadian military doctor, stationed locally with the concentration of Canadian
troops in Surrey, offered to see me. As a result of his examination, he called an
ambulance, and arranged for me to be admitted to the 4th Canadian Casualty
Clearing Station, situated in a large requisitioned private house, below Box Hill
in Dorking. There they diagnosed a vicious attack of food poisoning, without
doubt caused by the tinned salmon sandwich which I had considered myself so
fortunate to come by in the Waterloo air raid shelter.

I was at the time too ill to be much concerned by this or my surroundings, but
forty-eight hours later, as I began to recover, it dawned upon me with growing
horror that I was in an officers' ward. Of my fellow patients two turned out to
be Colonels and two Majors. When the Colonel in Command visited the ward I
drew this ghastly error to his attention, explaining in acute embarrassment that I
was only a Leading Aircraftsman (perhaps equivalent to a Lance Corporal in the
Army) Pilot Under Training. He looked at me solemnly and said, 'Oh yes, we
know – but it is the least that we can do for the R.A.F.' This, and the ceaseless
kindness and care that I experienced there, left me particularly conscious of our
debt to the Canadians. They not only stood by us in our hour of need, but endured
long months of waiting and training in England, a country renowned for its
aloofness to visitors, and anyway too preoccupied to be conscious of the niceties
of hospitality.

It was pretty below Box Hill, especially as the Surrey countryside was then
under snow, and while the flakes drifted against the windows, I learned much
about Canada from my fellow patients who were marvellous. Time was punctuated
with strange, and in wartime-rationed England, exotic Canadian meals. It was
during one of these I learned that the Major in the bed nearest to me was a
Commissioner in the Royal Canadian Mounted Police. The 'Mounties' numbering
amongst every British boy's major heroes, I pressed him for any and every bit of
information about his life as a Mounted Policeman, but he was very quiet and
seemed to think the whole thing quite unnoteworthy. Over a period of time, he
did recount the bare details of a series of incidents which could have filled a small
library of first-class adventure books. It gave me an insight into a life, much nearer
to nature than we could easily imagine, in great unexplored tracts of country, and
the fascinating characters and individuality of the isolated trappers and people of

the scattered settlements. His matter-of-fact accounts of some of the gunfights in which he had been involved were fascinating, especially that in which he and his quarry ended behind boulders only about ten yards apart. There they cracked away at each other for three days with .45″ revolvers. When I asked who got the best of that one, he replied somewhat pained: 'Me of course, I am still here!'

After a stay of five days, I was discharged with pressing invitations to visit their Mess when next I was in the locality, but this was not to be for a considerable time, by when they had moved. At home, I just had time to pack my kit before setting out on my way back to Newquay and my unit; so ending my first seven days' leave.

The bad weather we were experiencing was general throughout the country, and while this was to some extent foreseen, its effect on flying training was not. All flying was seriously curtailed, especially in our next stage at the Elementary Flying Training Schools (E.F.T.S.), where reasonably good weather conditions were essential for the pupil pilot. This led to a situation in which courses that had finished I.T.W. training were piling up, unable to get into E.F.T.S. Our I.T.W. course at Newquay had been designed to be covered under very high pressure in some six weeks, and was completed on time by Christmas. Owing to the delay, those of us detained for E.F.T.S. in the U.K. were held ultimately for a further ten weeks at I.T.W. Little of this time was wasted, as we could and did benefit from continued study of the subjects covered in the course, with an introduction to additional subjects which we could cover at E.F.T.S. Worked into this programme were firing courses on the .38″ revolver, the pilot's personal weapon; the service rifle; Vickers 'K' gas-operated machine-gun, and a considerable amount of clay-pigeon shooting as a co-ordination training.

The pressure remained high, with continued emphasis on physical fitness, but there were officially recognised free periods and we were not averse to adding unofficially to these if nothing of importance would be missed. Thereby arose many fascinating conflicts of intention between authority and ourselves, which became a considerable sport. Perhaps the first of these was the day when L.A.C. Allen (an ex-schoolmaster) had decided that he wanted the afternoon off to pursue his own interests, the R.A.F. having decided that he was to spend this on a route march with his Flight. The Flight was paraded after lunch, the roll called and then while the N.C.O.s were conferring, Allen about-turned and marched straight out of the ranks and away down the road out of sight. It was an amazing exhibition of nerve, but unnoticed he got clean away with it. A technique we perfected was inspired by the N.C.O.s' rigid adherence to the drill book, which laid down that when a Flight is ordered to turn before moving off, then the N.C.O.s also turn in the same direction and in time with it. This made it perfectly possible for the rear file, or even two, to turn in the opposite direction on the command, unobserved. On the order quick march, they marched away, the tread of their boots being completely masked by that of the Flight, and made for the nearest cover undetected.

The risks we ran in this game of 'beat the N.C.O.' were considerable. Apart from the official punishment and consequences involved in the serious charges of disobeying an order, and being absent from one's place of duty, the N.C.O.s were united in never forgiving anyone who got the better of them. I was nearly caught, on one such occasion, when the R.A.F. had decided that the Flight was to spend the afternoon watching a football match, but several of us (namely L.A.C.s Gaynor, Duncan and myself) had other plans. We decided to form the rear file, and to use the 'dropping off' procedure. This involved dropping off the rear file one by one, when suitable cover presented itself at the roadside as the Flight marched to the football ground. Gaynor dropped off almost immediately, and Duncan followed shortly after. I was about to go next but at that moment Sergeant Gardner, the senior N.C.O. in charge of the Flight, appeared on a bicycle and proceeded to bring up the rear. My heart sank, for it looked as though I was going to watch a football match, and I could see the other two (now safely mingled in the roadside bustle of pedestrians) gleefully laughing at me. However, to my delight, nearer to the football ground an army convoy of armoured cars drew level with us and, seizing the first opportunity, I made off under the cover of one of these.

As there is always so much going on in any military establishment, it is not possible for authority to know if every individual is going about an authorised activity. However, an airman who appears to be doing nothing is the immediate target of every N.C.O. or officer he may encounter, and every Serviceman knows the answer is always to appear to be doing something. I made use of this principle most happily one afternoon, when the film Waterloo Bridge was being shown at the New Theatre in Newquay. The cast of Vivian Leigh, Robert Taylor and Aubrey Smith was too good to be missed, but the R.A.F. had decreed other plans for me. At the appropriate moment I seized a broom, sloped it smartly over my shoulder and marched out of our billet at a sharp pace, heading for the New Theatre. Arriving there unhindered I 'ordered brooms' smartly, stowed it in the cashier's office for collection on my return, and bought a ticket. It was a very good film.

On 22 January 1941, the Allies took Tobruk in the continuing desert offensive of the North African Campaign, which further increased our anxiety to get training behind us and to take part in operational work. The war was then brought sharply closer by the bombing of R.A.F. St Eval on 26 January. This airfield, some four miles to the east of Newquay, was attacked in the late afternoon without any warning. Other than the heavy explosions of the bursting bombs and pall of smoke, which told its own story, we knew nothing about it until a heavy truck, driven by a desperate airman, careered to a stop on the cliff-top road near our hotel. The driver yelled to me for directions to Station Sick Quarters, and when he careered off there remained a small pool of blood in the road where the truck had stood – the truck was piled with dead and injured.

In the first week of February the weather excelled itself with a heavy gale from due north, lasting for three days. The roaring seas were initially obscured by cutting rain driving horizontally, and then by driven snow. Our only protection against water was the issue groundsheet/cape, which in these conditions we wore over our greatcoats, and was far from adequate. It was 4 February before my posting came through, to No. 9 E.F.T.S. Ansty, near Coventry. This news was somewhat blunted by the weather, as it was obvious that the current courses would be delayed and, sure enough, before long my posting was postponed to 21 February. The weather began to improve, and in astonishing contrast was at times quite warm and sunny. With the improvement in the weather came other good news; of the first E.F.T.S.

course from No. 7 I.T.W., numbering thirty, only eight failed the course and only two had been killed in flying accidents. Those of us who were to train in the U.K. had now been told of our postings, which left the bulk of the Squadron scheduled for training overseas. The Squadron overseas draft left for leave on 11 February, amidst extensive celebration. At least they were positively on the move, with the excitement of life in a new country where they would benefit from better weather conditions. On the other hand they were faced with the possibility of six weeks at sea in each direction, no joke in war, and also loss of contact with conditions in the U.K. However, none of this seemed of much import at the time, and St Brannocks rang with singing and laughter as scores of men struggled into and strapped on their packs and equipment. There was an exaggerated end-of-term atmosphere, and much fooling in which the place became smothered in confetti. Anything went as long as nobody had to say anything that might have sounded like goodbye. Each one of us knew that the others knew that it was laughter that wasn't felt, and jokes that were lies, to cover the knowledge that very few of us would live to 'knock into each other again one day'.

The weather, although improved by day, remained bitterly cold at night, an overriding problem during the guard duties that came our way. I was several times in charge of a guard of four men, posted at night on the R.A.F. warehouse by the railway station. Strictly speaking I did not have to do a turn on guard myself but I always did, and contrived earlier in the day to hide my flying boots on the guard beat, retrieving and exchanging these for my uniform boots when my turn of duty began. Incredibly I got away with this, which was pure luck. Nonetheless, in that weather these duties were hell. To bolster our spirits, on two occasions when going on duty I marched my little guard at the 'slope' down the road from St Brannocks to the station, halting outside the bar door of a hotel on the way. There I fell-out the members of the guard, to conceal their rifles behind the door blackout screens, and pile into the bar for a double rum all round. As all Servicemen on or off duty were in uniform, we were unlikely to be noticed. Suitably fortified by the rum we collected our rifles, fell-in again outside, and marched glowing and in surprisingly high spirits to our duty. It seemed well worth the risk, but of course it wasn't, because the penalties for leaving rifles unguarded, drinking on duty etc. would have been frightful – but then we were after all being trained in taking calculated risks!

If the delay enforced by the weather was tedious, it provided a less intense period in which to gain knowledge and experience of the wider aspects of Service life. There is probably no better opportunity for learning about one's fellows than living and working with them in the close proximity of a billet or barrack room. It was here that I was, for the first time, brought face to face with individuals who did not contribute to a disciplined community (other than under acute duress) and who would accept all the benefits, while acting against the ordered society which created them. In the kaleidoscope of personalities forming the ranks of aircrew under training, the existence of certain groups quickly became evident. For instance there was drawn to flying a small number of individuals of merit, to whom the Service organisation, methods and discipline were distasteful, and they had not the temperament or inclination to suffer easily the lowest common factor approach in mass training. In this their attitudes were legitimate and usually moderate. Their numbers were, however, greatly swollen by a multitude of hangers-on, self-styled intellectuals, writers, actors, producers, socialites, games professionals and others whose attitudes were rarely legitimate or moderate. Amongst these figured prominently the pub-orientated beer-swilling fraternity.

This group of hangers-on developed a technique of vociferously knocking the system, in which they were always assured of popular appeal, and were loudly applauded. The telling question was, how would they have managed the task of turning men so widely differing in education, background and experience, into fighting pilots of the R.A.F.; in the minimum of time; with the facilities available; and then used them with maximum effectiveness in this role? A question to which the answer would have been as inadequate as these individuals themselves. The truth was that in the past they had studiously avoided both responsibility, and accepting or developing self or any other form of essential discipline, and had no intention of so doing now.

At first the influence of these individuals was minimal, being irritating rather than dangerous, but I was later to realise again and again that promotion and responsibility seldom modified the technique of knocking the system in the individual, but rather strengthened it either as a need to cover their shortcomings or in the purchase of cheap popularity – or both. This self-styled 'gifted band of amateurs' was able to criticise and act totally irresponsibly to great acclaim, for they were completely divorced from any real knowledge of using men and materials for the optimum physical achievement, which is what war is about. They never did see the crux of military flying, or that the appalling accident rate and many losses in the R.A.F. were largely due to a direct and indirect lack of application, conscience and discipline.

In later years there was every indication that the R.A.F authorities were hypnotised by these individuals, and many surprising appointments and promotions were made from their ranks. Once in power, the thinking (if it can be so called) became self-propagating, and there arose in the wartime R.A.F. a considerable body of amateur uniformed civilians, rather than the professionally minded uniformed ex-civilians which were so desperately needed. This body was disastrously undermining and destructive to the Service, the moral damage it did being in a deeper sense damage to the very nation, for every man under such supervision or command was ultimately a citizen. However, although all of this was to become increasingly apparent in the future, for the time being it was only thought-provoking and had little bearing on the matter of the moment: our progress towards qualifying as pilots.

Only days before I was due to leave, as is so often the case, some kind friend of my mother's sent me an introduction to a family in Newquay. The letter was spiced with the comment that she felt sure I would like Janine, but this was quite superfluous. The prospect of the luxury in a fleeting return to home living and home cooking, with the chance of a proper bath; or just the peace and freedom from harassment of Service life, was in itself an irresistible draw to which Janine, surprisingly, took second place.

They were very kind to me, and I did like Janine who was perfectly sweet. To take the initiative in seeing Janine again was all but impossible, for returning hospitality, or cutting any sort of a dash on five shillings and sixpence (28p) a day, was beyond the greatest ingenuity. One thing civilians did appreciate was that Servicemen were paid a pittance,and any return of hospitality was mercifully not expected of them. Eventually I braced myself to take the plunge in asking Janine if she would like to accompany me on one of my walks along the clifftops, and far from scorning so mundane a suggestion she willingly agreed.

She was a joy, and such a direct contrast to my life of that time, that I found her companionship refreshingly reassuring and enjoyed every moment of her. Walking the clifftops with the sea breeze swirling her dirndl skirt and streaming her hair, I was enthralled by this glimpse of how beauty enhances beauty. The blue of the sky, the boisterous breeze, the thundering Atlantic rollers below, the tumbled rock, golden sand and Janine, all seemed part of a joyous, urgent and vital message of the profound value of the glories of life; eternally threatened on every side by man's destructive cupidity.

Arm in arm we strode over the springy clifftop turf along the sea edge of the Newquay golf course – and then I caught sight of it. Only a little way ahead, and right beside our path, in the bottom of a bunker was a couple locked together in a tangle of semi-discarded R.A.F. uniform and feminine underwear. The taut buttocks questing urgently into white semi-protesting thighs were crudely eloquent, and with a crash I was back in the barrack room – the sun seemed gone and the birds no longer singing. All of this I had observed in a flash, and with great presence of mind swung my gaze out to sea and pointing urgently began a competent, if anxious dissertation on the tumbled cloud formation building on the horizon. The sky was my element, and I was proud to be beginning to know something about it. After some moments of desperate effort, it was borne in on me that I had no audience, and halting in mid-sky, so as to speak, I turned to Janine to find her wide eyes fixed in fascination on the bunker, her golden head swivelling slowly as we passed.

At length, tightening her hold on my arm and turning an angelically pretty face to mine she said confidingly, 'You know, I couldn't do that.' In the flood of relief I experienced, the sun suddenly returned and the bird song burst on my ears again. 'I couldn't do that,' she repeated. 'Just think of the sand!' Quite what to make of this I never decided, in spite of pondering over it often since. I still do now.

The further postponement of my posting to E.F.T.S. was hardly unexpected, but did nothing to diminish our acute frustration in the realisation that the war was developing without us. The country remained threatened by invasion and, in our own sphere of aerial warfare, the continuing London Blitz (begun on 7 September 1940) and devastating attack on Coventry on 14 November, if nothing like the cataclysm that had been forecast, threatened to be extremely serious – and we were kicking our heels in the remote security of the Cornish coast.

We could not then know the government's highly confidential forecasts of the likely effect of aerial attack, but there was much in the resulting preparations that could not be concealed. I, for one, had been considerably disturbed by the number of First Aid posts established in London, the movement of buses and coaches converted to ambulances, and the long ambulance trains of converted passenger coaches assembled in the rail sidings. Here and there also became evident the government's plans for burials on a massive scale. The basis for estimating casualties was the German bombing of Britain in the Great War, and the experience of the Spanish Civil War. From this it was calculated there would be some fifty casualties per ton of bombs dropped. On an estimation of a German ability to drop 1,000 tons of bombs a day by early 1940, it is now known that the Ministry of Health forecast 600,000 killed and 1,200,000 wounded in the first six months. With this was expected the total destruction of some 500,000 houses, and the severe damaging of between one and two million others. In those circumstances public services were expected to break down, and wide-scale panic was feared. In the event this was a considerable over-estimate, but the general opinion of the likely effects of enemy bombing was on much the same scale, and this, with the lingering possibility of invasion, formed the background atmosphere of the day.

At the end of February my posting to E.F.T.S. was again postponed, but with the weather steadily improving it seemed that we must soon get away. Other than those posted in England, the rest of the Squadron was on embarkation leave having been split into several drafts for various overseas destinations, as yet undisclosed. However, we had been wasting no time, and 'gen' at moments such as this being at a greater premium than ever, we were sparing no efforts to get it. The leading question on passing out of I.T.W. became whether or not one had been recommended for a commission. Each one of us had been interviewed by the Squadron and Wing Commander, which august personages would obviously be the recommending authority. The results of these interviews were confidential, and we would have no way of knowing our progress, if any, until the completion of our Service Flying Training Course (yet some considerable time and many trials ahead) when some of us would be commissioned.

Although I did not aspire to a commission, my ambition being to qualify as a pilot in any form, I was perfectly willing to lend my experience (!) to a scheme to obtain this much-sought-after information. By cautiously pressing various instructors and N.C.O.s on the subject, it was possible to piece together indications that the information was probably kept locked in the Squadron Commander's desk. It was not difficult to 'borrow' the key to the O.C.'s office, on a carefully selected occasion, as this was held overnight in the guard room. The guard being drawn from one of our Flights and in the charge of an N.C.O.; we had only to avoid the N.C.O. Neither, as it turned out, was it difficult to remove the top of the O.C.'s desk by withdrawing the screws securing it, although it took four of us to do this silently; and there in the top locked drawer was our prize. The most nerve-wracking part of the whole business was the delay, while the list of recommendations was copied by the light of a drastically shielded torch. As the curtainless office windows faced on to the road and seafront, the slightest glimmer of light would almost certainly have attracted attention. It was especially nerve-wracking because the various lookouts were very jumpy, and we had many false alarms. Had we been caught, literally stocking-footed if not red-handed, at this stage it was unlikely that even 'Bugger-me-Young' could have talked his way out of it. However, all was with great care safely restored to normal, and no one was the wiser but ourselves! I doubt that the Air Ministry had reckoned on this sort of thing when they advertised so widely for 'Men of Courage, Cool Calm Nerve and Initiative, for training as aircrew!'

To my astonishment I had again been recommended for a commission, and fortified with this information I was not as abashed as I might have been by the announcement that we were to take part in a series of psychological tests, formulated to assist in aircrew selection. We were assured that these would have no bearing on our own progress. Nonetheless we all harboured a secret fear that some genuine or imagined incapacitating discovery would come to light, in the mumbo-jumbo of the headshrinkers' experiments.

To most of us psychiatrists were of the 'odd socks and adenoids' variety, and so it was surprising to find firstly that the team was composed entirely of girls, and secondly that they seemed to be quite normal. The tests were partly mechanical co-ordination tests, partly written and partly questions in the form of a conversational interview. My final test, for which fifteen minutes had been allocated, was conducted by a very attractive red-haired W.A.A.F. sergeant, a species with which I was completely unfamiliar. The situation was not eased when, after looking at me thoughtfully for a moment, she laid down her pencil, leaned back and began an animated discussion. When we came to earth again (which was nearly an hour later) we could have been the closest of friends; she was late for lunch, and I had not begun the test that she was supposed to have given me. Her parting comment was an expression of gratitude for an unusually interesting conversation, but that the disciplines, values and qualities in which I obviously believed were, in a far from altruistically minded world, hard and even dangerous to live up to. Then most prophetically she stated: '. . . And in all probability you will hang yourself in your old school tie,' – which was exactly what eventually I was to do.

CHAPTER 6

Wings

'Only birds and fools fly – and birds don't fly at night'

A draft of fifteen cadets, which included myself, left Newquay on 25 March decked out in full marching order, looking something like overgrown Christmas trees and with two kit bags each to complete the effect. After twenty-two hours of hard wartime rail travel we accomplished the 200 miles, as the crow flies, between Newquay and Coventry, to be joined at Ansty by a similar draft from Cambridge, forming No. 33 Course at No. 9 Elementary Flying Training School. The village of Ansty, from which the airfield took its name, is five or six miles to the east of Coventry in the midst of some lovely Warwickshire country. We were taken aback when, in the usual reception procedure at R.A.F. Ansty, we were allocated to a billet at Newbold Revel. This great house, based on a fine Queen Anne mansion, stood in open country some four to five miles from Ansty, again to the east and lying to the north west of Rugby.

The Air Ministry obviously considered us too valuable a commodity to be risked in air raids, and the German attack on Coventry of 14 November 1940 had threatened the airfield at Ansty. In this night attack, which lasted ten hours, about 495 tons of high explosive and incendiary bombs were dropped with 130 parachute mines. The concentration was the first of a devastating intensity, killing a total of 554 people, seriously injuring some 800 more, causing great disruption and perhaps the worst damage of any single raid on a British city.

The billet at Newbold Revel was a village hall close to the house, to which we were conveyed in trucks each evening – to our shame leaving the ground crews, staff and others on the airfield. We were then collected the next morning and driven back in time for breakfast. Our accommodation in the hall was over the boiler-room, where copious fumes seeped from a large and archaic coke-burning central-heating boiler. These fumes caused a choking cough, left us with sore throats by morning, and turned the brightest brass buttons a dull and evil bluish-tinged orange colour overnight. We assumed that the R.A.F. authorities knew what they were doing, but there can be little doubt that this billet was deadly dangerous. Fortunately there were no serious consequences during our tenancy – possibly as we spent the minimum of time there, and advancing spring weather encouraged ventilation. How it came about that this accommodation was ever accepted by the R.A.F. is hard to understand. Newbold Revel was at the time occupied by a community of Seventh-Day Adventists, who being conscientious objectors did not enjoy the best of relations with the local residents, and contact with the R.A.F. authorities (to whom little of these conditions was known, supervision being minimal) may have been considerably strained.

On arrival that first evening we had yet to discover this problem and, after happily establishing myself in a bed space, I walked into the park to explore the lakes, home farm and nearby village. In the park were two cadets standing on the bank of a pool watching a small waterfall. Curiosity drew me to join them, and as I approached I recognised with surprise and delight the familiar figures of Brockman and Woodhouse, who had arrived with the Cambridge draft. This was a remarkable coincidence, as there were so many E.F.T.S.s up and down the country amongst which we might well have been dispersed. We made our way to the White Lion, in the tiny village of Easenhall, there to celebrate our reunion and excitedly exchange information, news and most important of all urgently to review the progress of the war, which to our dismay showed every sign of developing rapidly without us.

The situation was fraught, for Britain remained standing alone and in the face of possible invasion. The material help of the United States was invaluable, but a pitiful substitute for the massive force that full participation would add to the Allied effort. Yet in spite of the tragic destruction of Europe, the United States showed little sign of declaring war on Germany, a situation which, not only in Easenhall, seemed incomprehensible. At this time, apart from the continuing battle of the Atlantic and its frightening shipping losses, our forces were involved in two other campaigns: North Africa and Abyssinia. In the North African campaign (opened by the Italians in September 1940) British forces had launched an offensive in December, after the crippling of the Italian navy by the Fleet Air Arm on 11 November 1940 at the battle of Tarranto. The offensive progressed to a resounding defeat of the Italians on 7 February 1941, at Bedafon, and the Italian resistance in North Africa was broken. On 7 March British troops had invaded Abyssinia, occupied by the Italians since October 1935, and once again the fighting went consistently in favour of the British. The tide of war seemed at last to be turning in our favour, and we discussed at length our anxiety to throw our individual weight behind the Allied impetus, for the might of Germany had yet to be dislodged and defeated.

No. 9 E.F.T.S. was initially a confounding experience, for these schools had, until the outbreak of war, been civilian schools working under contract to the R.A.F. That at Ansty was operated by Air Service Training, and was (in company with many such others) taken over entire by the R.A.F. At first this meant little more than some members of the staff donning an unfamiliar uniform, the actual

R.A.F. presence being very small, and the bulk of the ground crews and many other staff remaining civilians – even at the time of my course it was still generally known as the A.S.T. Flying Club. This situation engendered a strange attitude amongst the instructors and school administration, partly an innate dislike of the Service intrusion into their hitherto comfortably ordered life, and partly a lack of confidence springing from their new involuntarily found status, with ignorance of Service matters and methods.

For us it was difficult to adjust to the sudden change from the rigours of Service discipline, in force at the I.T.W.s, to an indeterminate level in the business of learning to fly and operate aircraft at an E.F.T.S. A discipline designed to meet the needs of an infantry task in war, and the lowest levels of intelligence and initiative involved, could obviously not be appropriate to the individual (or small group character) of fighting in the air. Neither could it be appropriate to the higher levels of intelligence and initiative called for in the skills of flying. I could clearly see the need for a different discipline, and was intrigued by the form and mode of transition through which it would be achieved. However, it later became apparent that this transition depended upon a far wider degree of general discipline than was imparted at an I.T.W., and assumed a background level of social discipline by no means achieved, or accepted, by all the cadets selected for aircrew training. As the course developed it became apparent that the entire emphasis was to be put on learning to fly, in the shortest possible time, to the detriment of all else, discipline included. I could only wonder as to whether this was a policy born of ignorance, a truly desperate gamble in the cause of expediency, or something of both; and wonder too at the outcome.

At Ansty we had our own mess containing a bar, lounge and billiard room, all part of the original club facilities. The food was good, with no signs of the civilian shortage of sugar, jam,* butter, bacon, eggs and cheese. It was served by waiters at small tables, complete with tablecloths, cutlery and crockery. Although enlisted aircrew cadets, we were still regarded much as had been the pre-war, R.A.F.-sponsored, civilian aircrew candidates – temporary members of a civilian club. There was no drill, P.T. or parades, and the standard of turnout was left very much as a matter of personal pride. The course was extremely intensive and specialised, in as much as it was limited to subjects with a direct bearing on flying, largely to the exclusion of general Service studies. We worked ten hours a day for six or seven days a week, alternately attending lectures in the morning and flying in the afternoon, or vice versa.

On the flying side, the De Havilland D.H. 82 Tiger Moth had been the standard elementary trainer since 1933, and in all 9,000 of these superb little open-cockpit biplanes were built by Britain, Canada and Australia. It was powered with a 122 horsepower De Havilland Gypsy Moth Major 1 engine of amazing reliability, which gave it a climbing and landing speed of about 65 m.p.h. and a cruising speed

---

* Wartime issue jam, which owing to its unidentifiable red and pulpy nature was always known in the Services as Rear Gunner Jam. This was a reference to the state in which many rear gunners were hosed out of their turrets after aerial combat.

of about 95 m.p.h. From the earliest moment after our arrival, we gazed fascinated at these 'Tigers' as they taxied or were manoeuvered about the airfield, and were taken off and landed by a very superior senior course. Disappointingly, for safety reasons, we were at this stage not allowed to approach the aircraft unless accompanied by an instructor, but were lectured extensively about them, and were shown over one, *en masse*. We were not to be kept in suspense for long, being detailed, within forty-eight hours of our arrival, for flying in 'B' Flight.

It seemed hardly possible that at long last we were to begin our flying training, and our excitement was unbridled. However, the situation concealed an obvious hook, for in the elementary flying course there also began our first major trial, in which on the average some 30% of the selected cadets failed to reach the necessary standard and were returned to ground duties. Even worse; this school had a reputation for a particularly high standard, of which it was very proud, and the failure rate was reputed to be above the average, sometimes as high as 50%

March weather is fickle, and we had been warned that the air temperature fell about one degree fahrenheit in three hundred feet of altitude (average lapse rate) which causes a drop of 17°–20°F in 5,000 feet, a height at which we were likely to be flying. The purpose of the seemingly multitudinous layers of flying clothing with which we had been issued now became evident. As each instructor had two or three pupils, we waited our turn to fly accoutred in boots, Inner and Outer Sidcot, helmet, goggles and multi-layer gloves under heavy leather gauntlets. In this we were supremely awkward, having gained neither the familiarity nor the confidence of experience. One could only feel as ridiculous as must a deep sea diver, in weighted canvas suit and domed metal helmet, floundering around out of water. To cap it all, each one of us had his own seat-type parachute drawn from the parachute section before flight, where it was stored and maintained with great care. This parachute had a heavy webbing harness, making it a big and cumbersome affair with flailing metal-lugged harness ends. There are neat and competent methods of handling this, in keeping with the professional nonchalance of the daredevil aviator, but until these had been learned by considerable bitter experience, it remained akin to a most inexpert wrestling with an oversize webbing octopus.

The final indignity lay in the fitting of the parachute, carried out by experts, for one pair of webbing harness straps passed over the shoulders and then locked into a quick-release box on a broad waist belt, and another pair passed between the legs, also to lock into the box. The jolt of an opening parachute is severe and to avoid undignified, not to mention excessively painful and dangerous injury, the harness had to be so tight as to preclude standing completely upright. Thus having got into the thing, anyway difficult unaided to the inexpert, one was committed to a sort of semi-anthropoid shuffle, which was completely devastating to what little ego one may have succeeded in retaining. So was one ordered by one's instructor to mount the wing and swing into the cockpit – having forgotten the preceding rapid and deft instruction in the mechanics of the operation, knowing only that there is precious little in the aircraft structure strong enough by which to haul oneself up, and that one false step meant putting a foot through the fabric covering.

The De Havilland Tiger Moth DH82 in flight.

The pupil pilot occupied the rear cockpit, the bucket seat of which was designed to take a parachute. Into this one was strapped tightly by the four further diagonal webbing straps of a Sutton Harness, secured with a quick-release pin. Had I not been schooled to take anything in my stride, I might well have resented the restriction of being so 'tied up'. As it was, the realisation that encased within all this equipment the senses of sight, sound and touch were heavily insulated, was a sobering thought. It was a tenable situation provided one was not required to *do* anything. Fortunately, initially this was the case and my instructor, the comforting back of whose head I could see in the cockpit in front of me, started up and began to taxi.

For power and weight considerations aircraft engines are unsilenced, and in spite of a close-fitting leather helmet with thick sponge rubber insulated ear-pieces, in close proximity to the engine the noise was considerable. Above this racket came the thin reedy voice of my instructor, conveyed by a system of Gosport Tubes (a speaking tube) to which my ear-pieces were connected. As in taxiing he was doing at least four things at once, as well as speaking to me, his concentration on the tube mouthpiece was limited with the result that his disembodied voice came and went with varying intensity and much interference, like distant and extremely

"Nice to be in harness again."

John Melville   1940

bad radio reception. This was to be the case throughout the whole of my elementary dual flying instruction, a period of struggling to learn against unfamiliar and heavily stacked odds.

The view from the aircraft, restricted anyway by flying goggles, was additionally limited by the length of the fuselage ahead and the biplane wings. So began a

complex process, involved in all flying, of learning to assess one's position in
relation to the ground with complete accuracy, by indirect vision. It was perhaps
this essential ability that proved the greatest problem to many would-be pilots in
landing. An ability they were either too slow or totally unable to acquire.

The Tiger, in common with many light aircraft of the day, had no brakes and
was taxied by sharp burst of engine to provide traction and create an airflow over
the rudder, which was then used coarsely to change direction. A truly Heath-
Robinson process in which considerable skill could be acquired but, nevertheless,
in confined spaces or windy conditions one or two men were essential at the
wingtips to guide the aircraft. This sort of taxiing was, I realised, likely to be more
than ungainly with a novice at the controls, as even in the hands of a master the
aircraft rocked and bumped over the grass of the airfield as we made our way to
the take-off point. On the way I began to accustom myself to the unfinished
appearance of the inside of the aircraft and the rudimentary design of many of the
controls, instruments and fittings. There was little, if any, finesse in the weight-
saving, brute-primitive construction of the Tiger Moth. One sat in a fragile canvas-
covered wooden framework in which ran a medley of cables, rods, pulleys, wires
and stops, interspersed with occasional pipes and tubes. My initial astonishment
at this was never to be completely dispelled, and in later years I was forced to the
conclusion that as a nation, while we were amongst the leaders in aircraft design,
our lack of imagination, style, ingenuity and finesse in the fittings and instruments,
was more akin to the ruggedness of railway engineering than the sophisticated
fragility of an aviation industry.

All of these thoughts were swept, with everything else, clean out of my mind
as my instructor turned into wind and began the take-off run. The noise and
vibration of the engine as it was opened up to full power was overwhelming,
and with the propeller at maximum revolutions the slipstream became a chill,
buffeting hurricane of wind beating mercilessly in my face, gravely impeding
breathing. The tail of the aircraft came up, as we bumped and lurched over the
field in ever-increasing speed, and suddenly we were airborne. We left the ground
at what seemed to be a horrifyingly steep angle, all the familiar landmarks had
disappeared and we were boring upward into the sky, seemingly suspended from
the propeller – surely in all logic an appallingly ill-advised procedure. The noise,
vibration, cold buffeting slipstream and unfamiliar attitudes combined to be
completely faculty-snatching, and I was considerably relieved when at last we
levelled out and cruised at reduced power. Here curiosity got the better of me
and I took a cautious look over the side at the ground below – only to realise
that I was suspended at a suicidal height, on the frailest of woodframe and canvas
platforms, in a strange and hostile element; a sensation that was only to leave
me slowly, as with increasing experience I identified myself with my aircraft, until
in complete unity I was to become as at home in the air as on the ground.

This however was yet to be, and while pondering over it the horizon began to
tilt as though in some sudden cataclysmic happening. The natural points of reference were, in my immediate surroundings, the nose and wings of the aircraft, and
distantly the horizon. Earthbound one moves in the horizontal or vertical plane,
in which the relation to the horizon remains constant and is taken for granted; I

don't suppose that I had ever before moved in the rolling plane, which I was now experiencing, and which was causing the horizon to appear to tilt. I realised that the aircraft was banking in a turn, and had to make a conscious effort to regard the horizon, and not the aircraft wings, as the static reference point. This discipline was almost immediately replaced by another in that as the turn tightened and the bank increased, the natural sensation was that just as a boat heeled over beyond a certain point would lose the support of the water and capsize, or plummet to the depths, an aircraft would suffer likewise. This was once again 'horizon' thinking, for an aircraft gains the same lift from the air in whatever plane it is moving, and of this I had at first to constantly remind myself.

We turned and climbed for something like twenty minutes, every moment of which was a fascinating challenge. At height, Warwickshire lay below in a chequered pattern of engrossing detail, stretching away into county after county and on into a distant blue haze on all horizons. Braving the blast, I hung first over one side of the aircraft and then the other, in a hopeless effort to absorb it all. Coventry and Rugby were plainly visible, as were the masts of Rugby wireless station, the railways, and Roman roads of Fosse Way and Watling Street. To me, most enthralling of all was the spreading three-dimensional detail of the open country below, and the opportunity to see so many of the beauties of the English countryside in one great panorama.

Gliding back to the distant and toy-like airfield, with the engine throttled back, the only sound was the rush of air through wires and struts, giving an increased and invigorating sense of flight. At first the steady loss of height was not obvious, but in later stages the ground rose towards us at an alarming rate. At one thousand feet we levelled out, and my instructor made a copy-book circuit of the airfield and turned in to land. The approach to land took me completely unawares, for it appeared that we hurtled steeply towards the grass of the airfield at a fearful speed, and when it seemed that all was lost and my so-brief flying career was to be ended in an inevitable and appalling crash, we mystically rounded out and held-off just above the ground, to make a perfect three-point touchdown.

My reactions contrasted strangely between intense relief at being safely back on the ground, after so fantastic a series of experiences, and a wild desire to get into the air again. Amongst my fellows later (with the absurdity of being airmen who had never flown safely removed) we, the initiated, eagerly discussed our experiences. I was anxiously asked how sick I had felt, a question upon which I had to reflect for I had never felt the slightest bit airsick, and was never to do so in any circumstances. I flew again that day, and for two forty-five-minute flights every day on which the weather was considered flyable. By virtue of the concentration involved this was intensive and tiring dual instruction, but that was not the least of it. Owing to the extreme need of pilots in the squadrons, much of our dual instruction was given in weather and conditions of visibility which in peace-time would have been considered completely unsuitable, and which added immeasurably to the difficulties of learning in the air.

Learning at such a pace and in such conditions did have compensation in enabling us to acquire a rapid familiarity with, and experience of flying, as we worked through the syllabus to solo standard. This syllabus was comprehensive and included spinning and the recovery from a spin. The aircraft was spun from a stall, at a safe height, and left in the spin for several turns before recovery. The stall is the point at which the airflow over the wings has fallen so low that it no longer supports the weight of the aircraft, and the aircraft drops out of control. Needless to say, in normal flight a constant guard has to be kept against the approach of this easily overlooked speed, especially during the approach and landing. There is probably nothing so disorientating as the spin in which the aircraft, out of control, rotates around its own axis in a nose-down attitude, rapidly losing height. Some aircraft pitch in the spin, the nose rising and falling to a degree, as it rotates. To the pilot, it is the ground below which appears to spin, and if the nose bucks he may in addition be treated to brief glimpses of a rotating horizon. The method of recovery is comparatively simple, but this was not known in the early days of flying when the dreaded spin claimed many victims.

The average flying time to solo was eight hours, but I passed this point without reaching the necessary proficiency, and became most desperately worried as hour piled on hour and I had not reliably mastered the approach and landing. Here lay the crucial test in which so many failed to reach the R.A.F. standard, and I was about to number amongst them. My instructor was changed for an older and more experienced man with unending patience, and we battled on.

At this time of the most acute and engrossing personal concern, I somehow contrived to miss the early morning transport from Newbold Revel to Ansty. Undaunted, I was walking the three miles or so of inter-connecting road, almost enjoying the April weather and wondering how to escape the dire penalties awaiting me, when a car approached from behind and stopped alongside. The window was lowered and a voice said: 'Get in.' This I did, climbing into the seat beside an aristocratic and battered pork-pie behatted, middle-aged Scot, of obvious character. He never said a word, but without question drove me to the main gate at R.A.F. Ansty where he deposited me (now in good time) with the brusque instruction: 'Telephone me anytime,' as he handed me a card and drove off. Overcome by my good fortune, I pocketed the card and scuttled through the main gate to my place of duty.

The battle to get off solo dragged on day after day, taking precedence over all else, and almost obliterating the depressing turn of events in the war. Hard on the British defeat of the Italians in North Africa, the Germans had entered the campaign in aid of their Italian allies, launching a formidable counter-offensive on 31st March. It was precisely at this time that the Greeks (who had been resisting an Italian invasion since October 1940), fearing German intervention, requested British aid which could only be drawn from North Africa. A British force landed in Greece on 5 April, and the very next day German forces invaded Greece and Yugoslavia. There followed the now familiar ominous silence as to what was happening. A British withdrawal was begun on 22nd April, to be completed on 2nd May. Meanwhile in North Africa the British evacuated Benghazi, and began falling back before the Germans.

The war on the home front erupted in our midst in a series of air attacks on Coventry, only five or six miles from Ansty, the last of which, on 11th April, was severe. Some R.A.F. personnel were called upon by the weary army A.A. gun crews to help in bringing up ammunition, and were surprised by the number of shells fired and the exhausting work involved. We were most envious of those so able to take a small part in these actions, and fumed at our compulsory exclusion in the safety of Newbold Revel. Coventry had suffered the most devastating raid which the country had experienced on the night of 14th November 1940. Such were the sombre memories of this attack that, even some five months later during the attacks we witnessed on Coventry, we were to see a daily trek of refugees from the city beginning in the early evening. This completely foreign sight of civilians on foot and in every available form of transport, streaming into the countryside carrying their treasures and bare necessities, was deeply disturbing.

The thirteenth of April brought the depressing news from North Africa that the Germans had recaptured Bardia, and encircled our troops in Tobruk. I was completely involved in my own perilous position, working desperately day after day to achieve the necessary constancy of performance in my flying. Such inexplicably slow progress, after so promising a start, was difficult to understand and I did not then know it was a recognised, if infrequent, development in the early stages of learning to fly, and anyway such knowledge would have been cold comfort in the circumstances. I remember being wryly amused by my instructor who once I had lined up the aircraft on the approach to land would, with mathematical exactitude, indicate in the pocket handkerchief-sized airfield ahead on precisely which narrow strip of grass he wished me to land. The demands of the approach and landing so engrossed me that I considered myself fortunate to achieve a touchdown anywhere on the airfield at all!

Day by day I battled on until having amassed the rarely permitted total of fourteen hours dual, without flying solo, the fateful moment arrived when I was put forward for a test by my Flight Commander, in whom was vested the authority to suspend pupils from further flying training. This august personage said very little, and after only twenty minutes flying, instructed me to taxi back to dispersal. It was all over – and in the numbing void of a final realisation beyond which one has considered nothing, I shrank into the cockpit and stared sightlessly between my feet. The engine was still running and after a while, as nothing seemed to be happening, I roused myself to peer out of the cockpit. There met my gaze the inelegant vision of a flying overall-encased backside and pair of legs, hanging from the front cockpit, as the Flight Commander braced and locked the Sutton Harness clear of the controls. Stepping down from the wing he bellowed, 'Off you go – one circuit and landing and then back to dispersal.'

It was difficult to grasp this momentous portent, and I don't think I even tried. In case my Flight Commander should think better of his decision I hastened to taxi out, dismissing the airmen at the wingtips as soon as possible, and making for the take-off point with controlled haste. From there I soared into the air, exulting in this supreme moment, for I was at last flying solely by my own judgement and ability. Once airborne and clear of the airfield came the sobering realisation that I had to land again, and was not at all sure of my ability to do this. Whether I or my Flight Commander was the more surprised by my safe arrival back in dispersal I shall never know, but the far-sighted decision to send

me on my first solo flight was fortunately one which the R.A.F. never had cause
to regret.

That night the peace of the little villages of Monks Kirby, and later Easenhall,
almost in the grounds of Newbold Revel, was shattered by our rafter-raising
celebrations. There in the White Lion amongst a collection of deer heads, fox
brushes and crossed fowling pieces, we caroused to the confusion of the locals.
Again and again we sang the Song of the First Solo, a neat parody of the hymn
Nearer my God to Thee, retaining the refrain and last verse:

> Or if on joyful wing
>   cleaving the sky,
> Sun, moon, and stars forgot,
>   Upwards I fly,
> Still my song shall be,
>   'Nearer my God to thee,
>   Nearer to thee!'

It was a time of great happiness, excitement and achievement – but we had no
illusions.

Only the next day did I remember my benefactor, who had saved me from
trouble with a timely lift, and searched my pockets for the visiting card he had
given me on parting. Studying the card in conjunction with the telephone directory,
I learned he was Major T. S. Dick D.S.O. (retired) and that he lived in Stretton-
under-Fosse, perhaps a mile from Newbold Revel. After work I telephoned, in
some trepidation, from a call box outside the airfield to the now charmingly
quaint-sounding number of Pailton 78. My call was answered by the Major himself
with a curt 'Yes?'

'I wonder,' I ventured, 'if you remember the airman to whom you gave a lift
about a week ago?'

'I do,' he said. 'Why haven't you telephoned before?' – and so began a lifelong
friendship with Richard and Dora Dick, whom I came to love very dearly.

I was instructed to present myself for supper, and this I did, taking the Service
transport to Newbold Revel and then walking to Street Ashton Lodge. The Dicks
could not have been kinder or more hospitable, and I learned that they had a son
Ian (whom I was later to meet) perhaps a year or two older than myself, training
in the R.A.F. as a navigator. Before leaving I had been given the key of a car (there
were, I think, seven garaged around the yard), allocated a delightful bedroom and
bathroom to match, and issued with an open invitation to come and go as I pleased,
using the car, and to take a bath or stay overnight at any time. In later years I
was once scolded for using the front doorbell, and told in Major Dick's inimitable
humour, that it meant his wife had to sit in the kitchen listening for it! It was the
only house in my life (other than my home) into which I walked unannounced,
and this came to have very great meaning to me. I visited the house frequently,
sometimes staying overnight and often, luxury of luxuries, taking a leisurely bath.
On arrival in the evening at Newbold Revel I used to clean my kit, make up my
bed-space for the next morning, and then take a short-cut through the fields below
Street Ashton Lodge to be with the Dicks (who could see me coming from quite

a distance) within half an hour. The next morning Major Dick would drop me at Ansty on his way to work. This was hardly 'soldiering', but it was heaven!

In spite of Major Dick's terse, efficient and to-the-point manner, he had a tremendous sense of humour. Mrs Dick had an amusing and interesting turn of mind and together they were two of the gentlest, most thoughtful and kindest people that I have ever known. Major Dick played a leading part in the formation of the Coventry Home Guard, and characteristically during the air raids on Coventry (and long after) their house and outbuildings were filled with refugees. The Major was later to receive the Order of the British Empire for his war services and it was undoubtedly more than merited, but their worth as people was inestimable and the eventual passing of such, mourned or unmourned, can only be a sad loss to humanity.

My solo flying went on apace, interspersed with periods of dual in which I learned the various forms of landing, aerobatics, instrument flying and cross-country flying. I thrilled to a growing understanding of flight and the strange 'being' of my aircraft beginning, to my surprise, to be able to make it do much of what I wanted. Most incredible of all was that aerobatics were no longer the petrifying experience of hanging upside down, suspended in the straining shoulder straps of the Sutton Harness, or fighting with the grey mists and momentary loss of consciousness induced by centrifugal force, while the horizon came and went, lurching, spinning and inverting itself until all sense of balance, order and direction was gone. Instead, as part of my aircraft I began to exult in its mastery of the air and the uninhibited joy of cavorting in space, freed from the trammels of mankind.

By now more that 30% of my fellow cadets had been suspended from flying duties, and the remainder had in turn become the senior course. The aim was to achieve fifty hours in flying time and to do this we rushed into the air at every opportunity.

An almost perpetual hazard was the poor, and sometimes extremely poor, visibility of the Midlands. In those conditions it was necessary to have your wits very much about you in order not to become lost, and to keep clear of both the Coventry balloon barrage, and great circle of aerial masts at Rugby wireless station which rose to some 1,180 feet above sea level. During my course at least one pupil struck a balloon cable to his detriment and another, in some astonishing way, contrived to get inside the ring of wireless masts at Rugby and could not get out again!

With increasing confidence, my natural curiosity led me to ask my instructor about the curious fittings on the underside of each lower wing of the Tiger Moth. He explained with the hesitance of one imparting an embarrassing truth, that these were bomb racks, and went on to brief me on how they were to be used. It seemed that in the event of invasion, the instructors would at once join the fighting squadrons to which they were already allocated. The bombs the Tiger Moth could carry were simply tiny, and for this purposes, of the anti-personnel variety. Armed with these it would be our task to fly to the invasion beachheads and bomb the enemy. To my astonished comment of: 'But we will never even get there,' he said with chilling candour, 'Well, you may if you hedge-hop to the perimeter of the beachhead, and then pull up to drop your bombs into it.' Pulling up from ground level, at a speed rapidly reducing to something like 60 m.p.h., into the intensely concentrated fire of a beachhead could obviously have only one result. And then, if by any chance one survived this 'attack', one would be left a sitting target making a slow turn, at point-blank range, in an attempt to get the hell out of it – all in the best traditions of the Charge of the Light Brigade, and just about as futile. There seemed very little point in pursuing the matter further.

During the course there were a number of minor and not so minor flying accidents, and then our casualties occurred in quick succession, two aircraft crashing one shortly after the other, in each case killing an instructor and pupil. The unit was not large enough to mount a Service funeral without interfering with the training programme, and flying was stopped for seventy-two hours while we rapidly trained in the foot and arms drill involved. A tall order, as three bearer parties, an escort party and firing party had to be found and rehearsed in this brief time. The funeral was held at the quiet little church in the fields, and there we stood on a spring afternoon, drawn up under the trees, the smell of newly dug earth strong in the air. After the farewell salute of three volleys, and the sounding of the Last Post by two R.A.F. trumpeters, we marched off. The fathers, mothers, wives, sons and daughters were left bemused in the silence of the churchyard, beside the crumpled Union Jacks that had draped the coffins, laid aside on the upturned clay.

The close of the course brought examinations in ground subjects, in which I managed to do quite well. I last flew at R.A.F. Ansty on 9 May, to complete the E.F.T.S. syllabus and 56 flying hours in 52 days. A reduction in the time allowed for this course to between one-third and one-quarter of its peace-time duration, and a training intensity which, only shortly before, had been thought utterly impossible. On this day I was granted four days' leave before reporting to No. 6 Service Flying Training School, R.A.F. Little Rissington, in my beloved Gloucestershire; the very school where R. de B. had gained his wings. On the next night (10 May) the House of Commons was destroyed in London's heaviest air raid, which caused much damage by fire. The London 'Blitz' ended with the attack on 11/12 May, although this could not be known at the time. The disruption and the travelling time involved gave me little more than forty-eight of my ninety-six hours at home.

On the platform at Bourton-on-the-Water, we were met by a group of N.C.O.s from R.A.F. Rissington headed by an aircrew Warrant Officer. We had not met anyone of this category before and were somewhat apprehensive, least of all expecting the friendly weariness with which we were rounded up and packed into American crew buses, also completely strange to us. Our arrival at Rissington was of twofold significance, for firstly we had never experienced a major R.A.F. station as Servicemen before, and secondly we were embarking on the next stage of our flying training where those of us who survived the course would be awarded the much-prized 'Wings', in the form of the R.A.F. Pilot's Flying Badge, with which went the rank of Sergeant or Pilot Officer.

R.A.F. Little Rissington is perched in the Cotswold Hills 750' above sea level, making it one of the highest airfields in England. The ground on the southern boundary falls away sharply in a complexity of ravine-like valleys, a feature which I noted did not seem conducive to happy landings or even take-offs, for the inexperienced. Close by this isolated Cotswold fastness lay the beautiful and unspoiled villages of Little Rissington, Great Rissington and Great Barrington, each one a rural poem in weathered stone. Hard by Great Barrington, on the river Windrush, is the village of this name and to the south of this, five miles as the aircraft flies from Little Rissington, was a relief landing ground pressed into round-the-clock service to relieve the flying pressure on the parent airfield. There was always a sense of isolation from higher authority at these R.L.G.s, which made them pleasant to work from. Initially the facilities were most rudimentary, often consisting of converted aircraft packing-cases for use as shelter, offices, stores and so on, calling for much improvisation. As time went on the facilities were expanded and became more permanent in nature, sometimes growing into satellite airfields with a resident staff. Windrush was then no more than a relief landing ground to which ground staff and pupil pilots, with fire tenders, petrol tankers and so on, travelled by road daily. The aircraft were flown in from Rissington.

The local gem was Bourton-on-the-Water, below and perhaps three miles to the north-west, of Little Rissington, chiefly of note to us for its village shops, public houses and hotel the Old New Inn. It is probably the most beautiful village of the Cotswolds, through the centre of which flows the river Windrush in the most delightful setting. The Old New Inn was the site of a fascinating curiosity, for behind the Inn, in a one-time vegetable garden, had been built between 1936 and 1939 a miniature replica of the village, in most exquisite detail. No one could have failed to have been charmed by this beautiful place and its miniature, for at this time it was all but entirely unspoiled and uncommercialised, retaining a peaceful and remote atmosphere.

The height of the airfield, and its consequent exposure, brought some extremes of weather in the ten weeks of May, June and July of 1941 during which I was stationed there. If there was any low cloud about, at that height we were in it which considerably curtailed flying. Similarly, if there was any rain in the vicinity it fell in torrents – rain in the Cotswolds can be astonishing, briefly equalling monsoon intensity, and this was certainly our lot at Rissington. In addition it could be very cold, especially at night, and conversely by day it could be roasting hot in the sunshine we often experienced. Rissington was one of the purpose-built airfields of the R.A.F., completed in the early thirties. In 1941 it was suffering the imposition of an ever-increasing proliferation of temporary hutments and buildings of many descriptions, run up to accommodate the equipment and personnel of a rapidly increased wartime task. In spite of this the impressive, imaginative, efficient and generally attractive layout and building of the permanent station was most evident, and I came to know my way about with an increasing sense of pride.

We were to constitute No. 34 (War) Course, the insertion of the category 'War' seemed a denigration, and probably sprang from the intense solidarity of the regular R.A.F. in the face of an overwhelming invasion of civilians in uniform. It certainly denoted an essential, but unfortunate, reduction in the syllabus and flying hours. Because of the pressure on the station's accommodation we were housed in former airmen's married quarters, a little village of semi-detached houses within the camp. Each house had three rooms, and we were allocated six to each house, or two to a room. It was by far the best accommodation we had so far experienced, especially as we were able to scrounge fuel for a roaring fire in the kitchen range to counter the cold evenings. On this my companion and I often heated cocoa, or baked potatoes in the oven, which strange combination was, at times, augmented with large chunks of a gruyère cheese washed down with flagons of Gloucestershire cider. From our windows we looked onto miles of typical, peaceful and remote Cotswold country, and tried to ally this serene, beautiful and strangely contrasting rural world to our future.

For meals we used the Junior N.C.O.s' section of the Airmen's Mess. Both the accommodation and the food this provided were well below the standards of our Mess at Ansty, but undoubtedly we had been spoiled there, and as Service food went that at Rissington was better than average. For all our privileges as cadets we were most anxious to learn of the general tenor of the station; how we would be affected by it and what sort of impact the Station Warrant Officer, Adjutant and Commanding Officer would have upon us. To a large extent we need not have worried, for in the atmosphere of preoccupied bustle, we seemed hardly to have been noticed. The Station Warrant Officer was, with massive determination, fighting a hopeless battle in the preservation of standards and discipline, against a rising tide of disguised civilians woefully ignorant in such essentials. The Adjutant, a most distant individual, shot himself in front of the guardroom for personal reasons, which seemed a little melodramatic. The Commanding Officer, an even more distant individual, was obviously working under tremendous pressure to meet the demands of the continuing expansion. The way seemed clear for us to concentrate on the real business of learning to fly.

Once again the course was divided into two, one half being engaged in flying and the other half on ground instruction, the change being made over the lunch hour. The chief subjects with which we were concerned in ground instruction were Navigation, Meteorology, Aero Engines, Armament and Airmanship, around which were packed a number of lesser subjects. To all of this we applied ourselves with great determination, for on ground as well as on flying examinations would depend not only our success or failure but, more likely at some future date, our very lives. The working day was up to twelve hours long, and longer if we were night flying. In this way an astonishing amount of training was packed into a frighteningly short course, and the desperate urgency of the arming of Britain was brought fully home to us. A natural consequence was cumulative tiredness, barely offset by a forty-eight-hour stand down every fortnight. In the later stages of the course I noted that I had, over the period of a fortnight, averaged four hours sleep a night and no free time. This was probably justified in the circumstances but such fatigue is extremely destructive to learning, particularly learning in the air where a pupil is under considerable tension and strain. In addition fatigue is a major contribution to flying accidents. Very little of this was known or recognised in those days, and the fearful responsibility for instituting such a policy may not have been realised, although even if it had it might have been felt necessary to take the same dangerous decisions.

Navigation was a subject which I enjoyed and in which I was reasonably proficient, but to my dismay my end-of-course report stated: 'This cadet could reach a high standard in Navigation, if he did not fall asleep at the beginning of the class and only wake up at the end.' After a morning's flying, and the sort of lunch an active twenty-year-old is capable of stowing away without batting an eyelid, the sizzling summer heat we often experienced was indeed too much for me, and nothing would stave off the inevitable outcome of accumulated weariness. I did reach a stage, in company with others of my course, where I was so tired as to have lost interest in most of the normalities of life, which was unusual at my age.

To return to the earlier days of the course, there was much to learn about the advanced twin-engine trainer, the Airspeed Oxford, before we flew it, and this was largely covered in our Airmanship studies. The Oxford, a twin-engined monoplane developed from the Airspeed Envoy (1934) was of wooden construction with a plywood covering, powered by two Armstrong Siddely Cheetah X engines, driving wooden airscrews. Equipped with hydraulically operated flaps, a retractable undercarriage, and capable of a speed approaching 200 m.p.h. in straight and level flight, it was a modern, efficient and good-looking aircraft introduced into the R.A.F. in December 1937 to replace the Avro Anson. Its looks however concealed some pretty wicked characteristics, for it was firstly aerodynamically extremely sensitive and damage, dents, or ice on the leading edge in particular drastically changed its performance and could make it very difficult or impossible to handle. Secondly, it flicked at the point of stall into the first stages of a spin, which if not immediately arrested reached a stage from which there was no recovery. Thirdly, it could develop a disastrous swing on take-off or landing if allowed the slightest latitude, and was anyhow extremely difficult to land well. To add to this, its performance on one engine varied from fair to very poor. This might have seemed a dangerous and unsuitable training aircraft, but that it had to be flown and flown well (for neither of these things would it do for itself as would the Avro Anson) and many of the operational aircraft that we were to fly possessed similar, or worse, tendencies than the Oxford.

Naturally these characteristics were minimised for presentation to us, but we inevitably became aware of them in the course of time. However, nothing would have detracted from the thrill and excitement of beginning to train on an advanced aircraft. Thirty-four feet from nose to tail, it seemed vast when first entered through the cabin door. One climbed over the main spar into the cockpit, where the instructor and pupil sat side by side. Seated under the sectionally moulded perspex (clear plastic) cockpit roof, the view to either side was over a large engine nacelle to what, after the Tiger, appeared huge tapering wings although the total span was little more than fifty-three feet. The idea that I should ever be able to control this huge thing on the ground, let alone in the air, seemed utterly impossible.

For all of the Oxford's advanced design, when I first flew it there were speaking tubes for inter-communication which were, in later years, replaced with a primitive 'intercom' and R/T (Radio Telephony) set. It also relied on hand starting which, the engines being too big to be started by swinging the propeller by hand, was operated by a crank inserted in the upper side of the engine nacelle.

My instructor was a New Zealander, and it is doubtful whether he had very much instructional experience. He was conscientious and kind, but largely at a loss in dealing with myself as for one thing he did not understand what made me 'tick'. For another his knowledge of flying and teaching flying was limited, with the result that if I struck any particular difficulty, or asked a searching question, he more than likely retreated behind a formal aloofness. This was not difficult for, being a Flying Officer, the difference between our ranks was very great.

As already mentioned, the Oxford could develop a wicked swing on take-off, which was likely to end in a collapsed undercarriage and shattered airscrews if nothing worse. This led to an incident which totally changed the relationship between my instructor and myself, introducing a considerably greater personal interest. As the cockpit seats were side by side, the instructor's (right hand seat) was lowered and run back by an attached lever, to facilitate entry. Once in the seats, the instructor brought his into the flying position by this lever, and he could then reach the dual controls. On his first demonstration take-off the aircraft had gained speed with its tail well off the ground, when with a crash the instructor's seat collapsed into the retracted position, from which the controls were completely out of reach. I had time for only the most fleeting glimpse of a face white with horror as my instructor disappeared, before I had to take control and apply myself to the urgent business of making my first completely untutored take-off in an Oxford. We became airborne in reasonably good order, and I climbed the aircraft while my instructor clawed his way back into the flying position, locked his seat and took over the controls. He was extremely shaken, and exhibited the over-enthusiastic relief of one who had narrowly escaped disaster. From then on he was at times surprisingly friendly and this seemed strange to me, for if he thought me remarkably unshakable and steady, it was no more than expected in my world, just as it was expected as a matter of course that however terrified one might be, one never showed fear.

Steady I may have been, but I was slow to learn for I needed fully to understand all that I was doing. In addition, never having had a very good memory I found the greatest of difficulty in learning the various mnemonics. The vital actions before take-off were, for instance, covered by T.M.P.F.F.S. as follows:

T.   – Trim; rudder trim neutral, elevator trim slightly tail-heavy
M.   – Mixture; rich, carburettor air intakes cold, air-filters in
P.   – Pitch; to fine (fixed pitch on the Oxford)
F.   – Fuel; cocks on, reserve cocks off, check tank contents on fuel gauges
F.   – Flaps; check in up position, or set as required
S.   – Sperry; check setting of Sperry giro direction-indicator with
        magnetic compass

Time and again this defeated me prior to take-off for I frequently forgot or misplaced something or other in the mnemonic until the day my instructor being away, a Flight Sergeant of pre-war vintage and virtually no instructional technique or inhibitions, took me up on a brief dual check. Rapidly discovering my weakness he explained, 'Look, remember it this way:

T.   – Try
M.   – My
P.   – Prick
F.   – For
F.   – Full
S.   – Satisfaction.'

Human nature being what it is, I never again found any difficulty in remembering the vital actions before take-off. On the same flight I learned a remarkable number of new swear-words – and these I did not seem to forget either.

At 9.00 p.m. on 24 May, the B.B.C. broadcast an Admiralty communique, announcing the loss of H.M.S. *Hood* (15" gun battle cruiser) in action with German naval forces, which included the battleship *Bismarck*. This news was absolutely stunning, for the 'Mighty *Hood*' was not only well known to the nation but to the world at large and had become a symbol of British sea power and imperial might. Launched in 1918 and commissioned in 1920, I had seen her sail from Portsmouth in 1934 and experienced the same involuntary surge of overwhelming pride and awed respect at the sight of this beautiful and mighty ship, as did most who saw her. This news coming after a succession of British reverses was a national disaster, in no way mitigated by the facts as they became known later. In an eight-minute action, the *Hood* had been struck and set on fire by a hit in the third German salvo, and then destroyed in a huge explosion by a hit in the fifth German salvo – while her own fourth salvo was in the air. Of her 94 officers and 1,321 ratings, there were only three survivors. The sinking of the *Bismark* by a British force on 27th May, while some recompense, did little to alleviate the grievous loss of the *Hood*.

It was no time for the faint-hearted, and we were fortunate to be able to throw ourselves, with added determination, into our training. After eight flying hours experience of the Oxford, and a fortnight after our arrival, my instructor sent me solo, and unbelievably I found myself alone and in flight in this awesome machine. The fabulous sense of triumph was wildly exhilarating and my heart sang in one of those rare moments of a lifetime. There followed days of intensive dual and solo flying during which my ability on type steadily improved, to the point where I began on the advanced exercises of a reduced safety margin, demanding additional skills and judgement. By mid-June the weather had been set fair for some time and the heat during the day in the open was considerable; but this was nothing compared to the heat in the cockpit on the ground, which was quite terrible. Even in shirt-sleeves it was gruelling and in the air, at low level, only better for the hot airflow one could direct into the cabin from the windows. Owing to the need for maximum unobstructed visibility from the cockpit and a constant lookout in the air or on the ground, it was impossible to fit any sort of blind or screen. There was no alternative but to stew, none too gently, in the close confines of the cockpit with the transparent cover acting much as a burning glass in the blazing sun.

In this period my instructor embarked on teaching me precautionary landings. This landing is made into the shortest possible space, normally in an emergency such as bad weather forcing an aircraft below a safe altitude. A landing in these circumstances was not likely to be made on a familiar airfield, but into the nearest suitable field to hand. The principle was to lower the aircraft just over the boundary at a speed slightly above stalling speed, so that on cutting the power, the aircraft sank immediately to the ground in the three-point (two main wheels and tail wheel touching together) attitude. It was then possible to brake strongly at once and, in a reasonable wind, the Oxford could be put down in a remarkably short space. However there were problems, the first being that to achieve the essential attitude meant a long and low, nose-up approach. In this attitude the pilot's view was strictly limited at a time when forward visibility was essential. The judgement involved lay in a precise memory of the last view of the boundary from a distance, and the ability to judge height and position from a line of vision around the nose, and perhaps at 45° to the line of flight. This essentially unnatural process occurred on other occasions, as in the last stages of an ordinary landing, in time becoming second nature but obviously until it did the problem was a formidable one.

After an hour's dual instruction in low flying which included a couple of precautionary landings at Windrush, I was despatched to practise these solo. My instruction had probably been as good as any of its time, and was based on the idea that you positioned the aircraft well downwind of your chosen landing ground, got down low, and approached at just over stalling speed, dropping the aircraft to the ground in the three-point position immediately over the boundary. It was not in those days generally understood that the ideal control was by the inter-related effect of the elevator and throttles, using elevator to control speed and throttles the rate of descent. Certainly I had been given no knowledge at all of this technique.

On my first solo precautionary-landing approach at Windrush, a sickening jolt instantly conveyed to me that I had struck the boundary wall of Cotswold stone. I whipped the throttles fully open in a desperate attempt to lift the aircraft away, but it was not to be, for the impact of the wheels had firstly forced the tail up and nose down, and secondly collapsed the undercarriage locks. With the engines roaring in desperation the aircraft drove into the ground in a flurry of shattered perspex and wood, as first the bomb-aimer's compartment in the nose and then the airscrews disintegrated. The shock was violent, and even as I slammed the throttles shut and whipped off the ignition switches, the tail of the aircraft rose into an almost vertical position and was for a second poised to overturn, before finally it fell back. To have ended upside down would have been nasty as fire so often followed, and getting out was problematical. By the time that the aircraft subsided I had the fuel control cocks off and then, there being no further business to attend to, released my safety and parachute harnesses and climbed out through the cabin door. There can be little so humiliating as standing beside the wreck of one's aircraft, but there was barely time to contemplate this, as with commendable efficiency the airfield fire tender and ambulance arrived. Beside the driver of the tender was my instructor.

In the rudimentary knowledge of flying instruction of the day was a pioneer fixation that a pilot involved in an accident should be pushed into the air again, with the minimum of delay, for fear that he should lose his nerve; and this is exactly what happened to me. After a twenty-minute dual check by my instructor, during which we only carried out an ordinary circuit and landing, I was again ordered off solo to practise precautionary landings. If anything this might well have caused me to lose not only my nerve but another aircraft; however, by luck rather than skill I survived. The ensuing enquiry found me guilty of an error of judgement, and led to my first interview with the Commanding Officer. He reprimanded me for damaging an aircraft and thereby detracting from the nation's war effort, but otherwise seemed surprisingly interested in meeting me. I did not then realise that the training accident rate was so high as to be causing major concern, and that it was indeed detracting considerably from the war effort. Neither did I realise what little opportunity the harried and harassed C.O. had of meeting the aircrew cadets under his command.

Out training continued in the cloudless brilliance of the summer sky, and as we sweltered we learned the intricacies of handling a twin-engined aircraft in varying conditions, gaining steadily in confidence and ability. A completely new experience for us was single-engined flying or, as it later came to be called, asymmetric flying which was in the case of a twin-engined aircraft flying on only one of these engines. There are, we were told, three categories of twin-engined aircraft: those that would climb on one engine, those that would maintain height on one engine and those that lost height on one engine. The Oxford, it was explained, belonged to the first of these categories, but in the event of failing to maintain height on one engine using maximum available power – land straight ahead! The truth was that the Oxford's performance on one engine was so variable for it to be impossible to lay down anything but the widest of guidance. An engine failure more often than not necessitated a fairly rapid and only partially controlled involuntary descent; but a great deal depended upon the skill of the pilot and this we strove to attain in the very limited time available.

Much of our flying was carried out from the satellite airfield of Windrush. This small and remote landing ground was used intensively by night and day, and in company with the parent airfield was the scene of constant major and minor flying accidents; to the extent that they were the rule rather than the exception. However, none equalled the incident of the Windrush Whitley, as it came to be called. There arrived in the Windrush circuit one day a very smart and fine-looking Whitley. This aircraft, built by Armstrong Whitworth, had a maximum speed of 222 m.p.h. and a ceiling of about 17,600 feet. It could carry between 3,000–7,000 lbs. of bombs, and was normally armed with five .303" air-cooled Browning machine guns. It was one of the heavy bombers of the time, which none of us had yet seen at close quarters, and was therefore the object of great interest and excitement to us. A fighting aircraft is in effect an armed, flying fuel tank; for the power required to lift the heaviest feasible armament to a strategic height and range at the greatest possible speed, needs copious fuel with a resulting high risk of fire.

The Whitley seemed to know its way about and began a well-planned and creditable approach from which it landed, without any apparent difficulty, in the far from adequate landing run. Taxiing into the dispersal point it was parked with its engines running, completely dwarfing the surrounding Oxfords which had loomed so large in our eyes; and the pilot left the aircraft for the Flight Offices. I was waiting in the sun for another flight and learned that the visitor was an ex-No. 6 F.T.S. pupil, now concluding his O.T.U. (Operational Training Unit) course, who had dropped into see his earlier F.T.S. instructor. They reappeared together and entered the aircraft followed by a stream of pupils, instructors and airmen groundcrew, bent on not missing so rare an opportunity of examining an operational aircraft in detail. After a while some of these left the aircraft and others entered, but during the resulting confusion, the engines opened up and the aircraft began to taxi. Whether the instructor or ex-pupil was at the controls was not known, but the Whitley taxied out, turned into the wind and began a take-off run. If I remember rightly there were twenty-two men on board and most of these, never imagining a take-off, had gravitated towards the tail with the intention of leaving the aircraft.

The outcome was inevitable, for hopelessly out of trim and grossly overloaded beyond its capacity for a short take-off, it lumbered across the field fast approaching the boundary wall without any sign of becoming airborne. At the last possible moment the pilot attempted to haul it off the ground to clear the wall. It rose heavily into the air with its tail weighed right down, climbed almost into a vertical position, stalled and cart-wheeled to starboard, hurtling into the ground behind the Flight dispersals, with engines screaming in an all-out attempt at recovery. The explosion on impact was horrible and there arose a great pulsating ball of black smoke and red flame. The resulting fire was ferocious and made hideous by exploding oxygen bottles, fuel tanks, ammunition and the cries of those trapped in the white-hot wreckage. Some escaped, but there was little if anything that even the fire tender could do for the remainder. It was my first experience of seeing men burning like torches, and of the phenomenon of such men breaking their way out to stagger from the aircraft, and then turn and stagger back into the inferno. This, it was believed, was caused by the shocking pain of the impact of comparatively cold air on deep burns. Worse perhaps, were the horrible agonies and ghastly screams of those who were caught or doused in the chemical foam pumped by the fire tender into the blaze. The heat of such a fire makes it impossible to approach the wreck; to overcome this difficulty the tenders carried long hooked poles (rather like giant window poles) and these were used for clearing burning wreckage and fishing bodies out of a fire from a distance. I could never see these later without visualising them hooked into blazing writhing bundles.

The whole incident was a succession of appalling examples of the ignoring of orders, regulations and the principles of airmanship; apart from misunderstandings and incompetence. We were not then sufficiently experienced to realise all of this, or in a position to know the facts, and the violent death of a number of men becomes paramount in any situation.

Six weeks after the course began, and with some forty flying hours on type to my credit, three major events occurred. The first and most momentous of these was the declaration of war upon Russia by Germany, which gave us another ally, even if it was a case of 'Misery acquaints a man with strange bedfellows.' The other two events were personal, the first being the elevation of about a third (ten) of our course, amongst whom I numbered, to the Officers' Mess. We lived in the Mess as Air Cadets, still wearing our airman's uniform (now with a white armband) and carrying on otherwise exactly as before. Sadly the pressure of work was so great that we had little opportunity for anything but eating and sleeping in the

Mess, and that pretty briefly. The third of these events was the beginning of our night flying training.

We could have absolutely no idea of what such flight would be like, and were most curious about it. To the human being night activity is fundamentally unnatural on account of the almost complete loss of a major sense, that of sight. In addition to this there was the oft-quoted adage: 'Only birds and fools fly – and birds don't fly at night', which did nothing to dispel any qualms. For night flying, in order not to interfere with the maximum external vision, the cockpit was unlit except for small shaded ultra-violet lights which caused the luminous dials of the instruments to glow. As most of these luminous calibrations were merely dots you had to memorise the instruments very well to know with which dots you were trying to align the indicator needles. As far as the controls went, one was literally in the dark and found and operated these entirely by the familiarity gained in daylight, augmented by much practice in blindfold cockpit drills and vital actions.

Take-off and landing was effected on a flarepath of flaming paraffin goose-neck flares as they were called. Little enough in the way of illumination, but for well-justified fear of enemy attack these flares were hooded. This, while partially concealing them from marauding enemy aircraft, equally concealed them from our own aircraft and made the flarepath extremely easy to lose. The flarepath consisted of flares laid on the airfield in the shape of a T, the cross-bar facing into wind. The flares were spaced in the main at 100-yard intervals, there being six along the leg, the third of which was doubled. Take-off and landing was made from the right-hand side of this leg, unless an accident obstructed it (which was a frequent occurrence) when changes were rapidly made to clear the left-hand side.

Our night flying was to be carried out at Windrush, and we were allocated to a different team of instructors for this second and advanced stage of our course. Arriving at Windrush before dark, which in mid-June was late, we whiled away the intervening time in helping with the unfamiliar preparations on the airfield as dusk gathered, the air cooled and the general threat of night settled over the silent countryside. Night is indeed a threat to the pilot, for it imposes a number of additional challenges, and considerably narrows the already slim safety margins in flight to which we were being trained. Of this we could not help being uneasily aware, and wondered with some apprehension how we would fare in these new circumstances. The arrival of our instructors almost too late for the scheduled time of first take-off and in an exaggerated party mood, rang hollow, and it rapidly became clear to us that they had somewhat reluctantly left the bar in the Little Rissington Mess for the occasion.

It is necessary here to take a look at the Service origins of these men. Most of the officers were ex-N.C.O.s of the peacetime R.A.F., who had been promoted in an attempt to meet the demand for flying knowledge and experience, at a premium in the huge training expansion then underway. Many were survivors from heavy bomber squadrons operating in the early and disastrous stages of the bomber offensive. In this both aircraft and training had proved inadequate to the task, and Bomber Command had suffered heavy casualties not only in the hands of the enemy, but as the result of faulty navigation, lack of experience and technical aids, in severe weather conditions. A number of them were very badly shaken and all had been posted to non-operational flying as a rest.

Flying instruction was in those days comparatively rough and ready, surprisingly little advance having been made since the First World War. Teaching was largely based on the imitation of the instructor, and the trial and error of solo experience in the air. That it should have been considered a rest was a prize misconception which persisted for a very long time. This was presumably based on the easy-going flying club atmosphere of pre-war instruction in unsophisticated aircraft, when the weather was rarely if ever challenged and night flying was strictly limited. The Oxford, however, was a sophisticated aircraft and instruction was being carried out at maximum intensity night and day, in all but the very worst of weather. These factors and the skill and intense concentration required in instruction (not to mention the strain of supervising and anticipating every move of the pupil) made it anything but a rest.

My own period of training at Little Rissington coincided with the nadir of despondency reached by Bomber Command in 1941, and while we had some inkling of this, we could not have understood its full meaning. Perhaps the air of muted disaster and despondency had become worse than the actual situation itself, as is so often the case. Be that as it may, we were thrilled to have as our instructors these men who had achieved our ambition of fighting in the air. They were to us the high priests of an order, initiation into which could only be by selection and ordeal – these were our heroes. They were a most varied collection, few having any instructional ability being only Screened Pilots (pilots resting from operations and not trained instructors) for in the desperate circumstances prevailing, the meanest of knowledge and experience had been pressed into service. For many of these men, flying instruction was neither of their choice nor to their liking. The instructor with whom I was detailed to fly that night appeared, smelling like a Christmas pudding and with an air of forced confidence and bonhomie. We went to our aircraft and I was treated to sporadic bursts of confused information, punctuated with intervals of complete preoccupation with the business of preparing the aircraft for take-off, during which I might just as well not have been there. It was not long before I realised that he was very frightened, and also realised my complete helplessness in the situation. This night flying business, I decided, promised to be most difficult.

In a night take-off, the visual aids of the flarepath and any vestige of horizon that there may be, however faint, are used until the moment of becoming airborne. At this point attention is transferred to the six instruments of the blind-flying panel, which are scanned in a continuous and rapid cycle of inspection; correlating their readings in an interpretation of the situation of the aircraft. At the point of transfer there is considerable danger, for unless the transition is smooth and accomplished, the aircraft may either sink to the ground or rise too steeply, and stall. My instructor seemed only aware of the risk of stalling, and grimly held the aircraft down on take-off building up an abnormal speed – but I knew that once past the boundary, out there in the pitch darkness was a stone wall, a barn and any number of other obstructions such as trees. By the grace of God we miraculously cleared them all, and began a circuit of the flarepath. Whatever else my instructor may have said was completely lost in the ceaseless repetition of: 'Keep your speed up – keep your speed up,' and to achieve this he continually dived the aircraft and then pulled it up to height and dived it again. We progressed, porpoise-like, in a perpetual switchback – and then on the downwind leg I distinctly heard one of the engines falter momentarily. This is not funny at any time, least of all at night, for a single-engine circuit and landing in the dark requires considerable skill. However, my instructor showed no sign of concern and I began to think that I had been mistaken.

The landing was quite horrible, being truly an 'arrival', but I did learn that you must keep your speed up on the approach and that if the aircraft has not touched down on the flarepath by the third flare, you abandon the landing, open up the engines to full power and go around the circuit for another attempt. The next take-off was petrifying, because halfway down the flarepath an engine faltered; as a result the aircraft swung badly in that direction, and we clambered off the ground and into the darkness at an angle to the flarepath. I knew then that my instructor (who was apparently completely unaware of any irregularity) was not only scared stiff, but was drunk. My situation was difficult because I could not leave the aircraft, as the judgement of an airman pupil could hardly be accepted against that of an officer instructor; neither could I impose my judgement on an instructor, and I realised with chill clarity that we were most unlikely to survive this flight. Once again we pitched and yawed around the circuit to make another breathtaking arrival on the flarepath. Undaunted, my instructor taxied round again to the take-off position and this time, it seemed, we were going through this performance together. At the take-off point (or taxiing post as the lighted marker was called) the door of the aircraft was suddenly opened from outside and my Flight Commander scrambled aboard. With the unbounded joy of the reprieved I realised that the situation was saved, for the Flight Commander must have witnessed these hair-raising take-offs and landings. There followed a long altercation, none of which I could hear above the engine noise, and then the Flight Commander left. To my horror we continued preparations for take-off, nominally with myself at the controls. As my instructor was huddled over these to retain them in an iron grip, chanting the while his litany of: 'Keep your speed up,' in between uncomfortable belches, I never had complete control of the aircraft at any time. At least the ailing engine did not cut, although it seemed to be surging, but this is hard to detect.

Back on the ground after no less a frantic circuit and landing, we taxied around once more and never had I so desperately longed for the feel of terra firma beneath my feet. At the taxiing post my instructor began to release his harness preparatory to leaving his seat, while at the same time asking if I would like to carry on solo. I had no illusions whatsoever about the inadequacy of my knowledge of night flying, or ability to fly the aircraft myself in night conditions, for my chances of getting away with it were negligible. My last chance of risking the breach of discipline in a desperate appeal to my Flight Commander was gone, and as he had not seen fit to stop the flight when he intervened, I concluded that I might just as well kill myself as suffer the same fate in the hands of my instructor.

Alone, I moved onto the flarepath and began my first night take-off. It was awful for the points of reference, just the line of flares in the pitch black, were so limited that detection of the aircraft swinging was a very fine judgement, and the necessary minor anticipatory movements of the controls became major corrections and inevitably over-corrections. I snaked off into the air and was just airborne when the rogue engine surged heavily. At that height there was only one course open in the event of an engine failure, and that was to cut both engines and land straight ahead, wheels up, in the dark, and mixing it with anything that happened to be in the way. There is little health in such a situation. Mercifully the engine did not fail, and I climbed away having decided to get the aircraft down and then to use my authority as pilot to place it unserviceable, which would mean a thorough inspection before it flew again. With flaps raised, undercarriage safely locked up, mixture returned to normal, engines throttled back to climbing boost and the aircraft retrimmed, at a height of 500 feet I began a climbing turn across wind. After the black void of the night ahead of me, it was a relief to see the flarepath appear as a series of pin-pricks of light in the form of a T; so small and remote a haven that it seemed impossible I should ever safely regain it from my tiny, suspended, dark-enveloped isolation. At 1,000 feet I levelled out, turned through 90° to fly downwind and parallel to the flarepath, at the same time signalling my identification letters in Morse code on the downward recognition light. The signal was picked up by a no doubt anxious Airfield Control Pilot (one of the instructors) at the head of the flarepath, who signalled the same letters to me on a green Aldis lamp constituting the clear to land signal. This contact with the ground was immensely reassuring, and I prepared to land by selecting the undercarriage down, returning the mixture to rich, pitch to fully fine, and the lowering the first stage of flap, retrimming the aircraft, all the while struggling to keep my height at exactly 1,000 feet.

So far my procedures had been perfect, but at this point I made a disastrous mistake. Having been given no guide as to the correct position for turning across wind again, I instinctively hugged the flarepath and turned far too soon; checking the undercarriage locked down, throttling back and lowering full flap as I gradually lost height. Turning into wind I began my approach to the flarepath. At night distance is deceptive owing to the lack of familiar points of reference, and a light can be a few feet away, or a star; it is often impossible to tell the difference. The judgement of one's height above, and distance from a flarepath takes a considerable time to acquire, and I did not realise that I was far too high until very late. I had to get down, being unwilling to tempt Providence again in relying on the faltering engine for a moment longer than was unavoidable, and had to get down by the third and double flare.

Throttled right back and dropping like a stone in a steep glide, the aircraft hurtled towards the flarepath in a type of approach demanding the greatest of landing skill, and which the most experienced of instructors would not attempt at night in a hurry. It was excessive speed which probably saved my life at this stage, for sensing the disturbing rate of descent I hauled back on the control column and as it happened, against all the rules of chance, rounded the aircraft out just above the ground. Had my speed been any less, or possibly any greater, I would have stalled straight into it. As it was, I whistled down the flarepath with the speed of an express train, leaving a horrified A.C.P. madly cranking his field telephone link with the Flight office. Before I realised what had happened, the flarepath had disappeared behind me and I was past the point of no return, hurtling into the dark and unseen obstructions ahead. There was little I could do but whip off the ignition switches and fuel cocks as a fire precaution, and had barely completed this when it happened. There was the most awful impact and everything seemed to fly to pieces in a violent explosion. I was aware of the numbing, consciousness-sapping drag of very rapid deceleration, in a long, jolting, ripping, tearing slither; and then all was suddenly quiet.

I do not know how I came to be standing in the grass, but I was – and instinctively I staggered away from the wreck for fear of the near 200 gallons of petrol the aircraft had been carrying, and almost inevitable fire. It was very dark, very cold, I was trembling violently and my legs (one of which had been severely wrenched) were about to give way. At my side was a dry-stone wall; I hauled myself on to it, sitting idly swinging my tingling legs, my mind a blank. Before long the lights of the fire tender, the ambulance, and a string of other vehicles appeared over the fields in the distance, and as they approached I could see in the glow a wide gap in the dry-stone boundary wall through which I had passed, the trail of wreckage – such small pieces – and where it had finally come to rest the shorn hulk of the battered fuselage. There did not seem to be anything left of the cockpit.

In no time the scene was brilliantly lit by the headlights of vehicles and the floodlights of the crash and recovery tenders. There seemed to be men everywhere, and I watched dispassionately as they systematically began searching the wreckage. Near to me was an airman with a pole turning over bits of aircraft, and it was only when he ceased momentarily, to self-consciously remove his cap and tuck it into his belt, that I realised they were looking for me and only expected to find a body. Lowering myself from the wall I approached the airman from behind and tapped him on the shoulder, having discovered a deep disinclination to speak. He spun around, went as white as a sheet, exclaimed, 'F——ing hell!' in rank disbelief and shot off into the dark. He had, in fact, gone to report his find, but it left me feeling unhappily ethereal in the interim period.

This accident led the next day to a limping and second appearance before the Commanding Officer who was seated at his desk, in his shirt-sleeves, and obviously under greater pressure than ever. He dealt with the matter brusquely, awarding me a further endorsement for an error of judgement, and this I received in stoic silence. I was reprimanded and very little was ever said about the whole incident; I never again saw my instructor of that night.

With a new instructor I continued my day flying training, which included pilot navigation in preparation for the cross-country flying test. A most likeable Flight Lieutenant took me for this test, sitting through two hours of cross-country flight in obvious boredom and with barely a comment, and then as we re-entered the local flying area he took over the controls and began teaching me to loop-the-loop. This was wonderful stuff and I thrilled to it; he demonstrated two loops and then I did one myself. Fired with enthusiasm, on my return I entered these exercises in my Flying Log-Book and thought no more of it. At the end of every month all log-books were submitted to the Flight Commander for checking and authentication, after which they were forwarded to the Squadron Commander for approval. No sooner had I handed in mine than I was run before the Flight Commander, who berated me furiously for entering in my log-book exercises that I had never done, and demanded that I erase the entry for aerobatics on the spot. As my instructor of the loop was in the office fixing me with a blank and unknowing stare, I did this. I did not then know that the Oxford was in no way stressed for aerobatics, was severely limited in maximum diving speed, and was so dangerous in an inverted stall that not only were aerobatics forbidden, but it was not thought that it could be looped without either breaking up or spinning in. To achieve a loop it had to be flown around the ellipse with an exactitude that was not normally possible, and for this reason I never chanced doing it again. I felt very badly indeed at having let down my instructor over this incident, and to my consternation he was almost immediately posted to an operational squadron. I last saw him at his farewell party in the Mess executing a war dance, minus his trousers, and firing a revolver into the ante-room fireplace – needless to say I kept well out of his way. He was later killed, but I doubt if I need have worried, for his posting may not have been unfortunate, as it is quite possible that he was trying for it in teaching me aerobatics without a word of caution on the need for absolute secrecy.

Back on night flying with my new instructor, I completed the syllabus without any difficulty and returned to instrument flying, formation flying, simulated bombing and cross-country flying; all by day. This last was a wonderful experience in such brilliant summer weather, for speeding from hill to plain, plain to wood, wood to meadow and so on provided a unique view of the English countryside at its very best. Particularly beautiful from above were the shady stretches of river and lakes, so inviting as to arouse an agony of longing to get down and revel in the cool water, away from the sweltering cockpit, noise vibration and unremitting concentration of flight.

The Cotswolds, which must surely be amongst the most beautiful country in Britain, lie fold upon fold of gentle dimpled hills, intersected by a jumble of unexpectedly steep, wooded valleys. In these nestle villages of the most delightful mellowed stone houses, crowned with beautifully hued lichen-covered stone roofs. Everywhere are dry-stone wall-confined lanes abruptly plunging, twisting, turning and climbing in the riot of intersecting valleys, or between the walled patchwork of tumbling farmland. The fast-running streams are often of great character and the frequent wayside springs, spouting into moss-lined stone troughs which in turn overflow into roadside runnels, are a most attractive feature of this endearing country. It is a stone country, with a stone peculiarly of its own reflecting the prevailing light through a large range of shades. None of these, however, approaches the most moving golden glow of Cotswold stone in the slanting rays of evening or autumn sunlight.

With the close of July, some nine months after enlisting in the R.A.F. and with fifty-five flying hours on an elementary and some eighty-five on an advance trainer, I paraded on the barrack square with what was left of my course to receive my wings from the Commanding Officer. Basic flying training to Wings standard had at this time been cut from two years to between six and nine months, and on the average during 1940–42 almost a third of all aircrew who passed selection for training were by this stage failed, killed, injured or discharged. At this particular time the percentage failing to complete training was considerably higher, the increase being chiefly attributable to deaths and injury in flying accidents. Immediately following the award for the flying badge I was required to sign my discharge as a Leading Aircraftsman, and to re-enlist as a Pilot Officer. My officer's uniform had been hanging in the bedroom cupboard for some days, after painstaking completion by the military tailor. It looked very smart indeed with its brand new pair of wings over the left breast pocket, and one very thin ring of braid on the sleeve denoting the rank of Pilot Officer. As it had never seemed possible that this achievement could be mine, when I shed my airman's heavy serge for this resplendent tailor's creation of the commissioned pilot, my feeling was one of complete astonishment – much as a butterfly must feel on emerging from something so prosaic as a chrysalis.

Throughout my R.A.F. training my mind had been fixed on achieving the captaincy, as a pilot, of a heavy bombing aircraft for this, my chosen rôle in war, had developed from experience in the Officer's Training Corps at school. It was there, as described earlier, that it had been borne in on me how easily and ineffectually a life could be extinguished in war, and I had determined only to surrender my own life in the greatest effort that the individual might ordinarily achieve against the enemy.

After qualifying for my wings at S.F.T.S., the next step would be a heavy bomber Operational Training Unit (O.T.U.) for training to join a squadron, and to this I confidently expected to be posted. It was therefore a considerable shock, and great disappointment, to receive a posting to No. 15A (War) Flying Instructors course, at No. 2 Central Flying School, R.A.F. Cranwell. This was an order and as such could not be questioned for the Air Ministry, in its wisdom, had apparently decided that I could be of greatest service to my country in this rôle, and I had to learn to accept it with good grace. The obvious first step was to understand why I should have been so chosen, and here I was at a considerable loss. Flying ability, character, personality and temperament are paramount requirements in teaching others to fly, and the facts were that I had barely learned to fly myself, and had in the process been involved in two accidents. The only explanation I later drew from my C.F.S. instructor was that I had the makings of a very smooth and steady pilot, had the essential analytical mind, was largely unshakable, and that my voice and casual matter-of-fact method of speech were ideally suited to instruction. Nowhere in this did I even remotely recognise myself, and protested at this obvious case of mistaken identity – but this availed me little, or in fact nothing at all. On reluctant consideration, I realised that in an unexpected way my desire to inflict the heaviest possible individual blow on the enemy, would perhaps be indirectly achieved through instructing (in which I too would certainly learn to fly to a high standard) and in this spirit I applied myself to my new task with great diligence. However, I never managed to stifle the fear that I might be unduly held back from operational flying, which would be both unfair and insufferable.

R.A.F. Cranwell, site of the Royal Air Force College, lies four or five miles to the north-east of Sleaford in the dead flat of the Lincolnshire Eastern Plain. There were two airfields, North and South, both of which were then all grass. Between

George R.I.

Tenable for the Duration of the Emergency

George VI *by the Grace of God,* OF GREAT BRITAIN, IRELAND AND THE BRITISH DOMINIONS BEYOND THE SEAS, KING, DEFENDER OF THE FAITH, EMPEROR OF INDIA, &c.

To Our Trusty and well beloved   **Denis Noel Shepherd**   Greeting:

WE *reposing especial Trust and Confidence in your Loyalty, Courage, and good Conduct, do by these Presents Constitute and Appoint you to be an Officer in Our Royal Air Force Volunteer Reserve from the Twenty-third day of July 1941. You are therefore carefully and diligently to discharge your Duty as such in the Rank of Pilot Officer or in such higher Rank as We may from time to time hereafter be pleased to promote or appoint you to and you are at all times to exercise and well discipline in their Duties both the inferior Officers and Airmen serving under you and use your best endeavours to keep them in good Order and Discipline. And We do hereby Command them to Obey you as their superior Officer and you to observe and follow such Orders and Directions as from time to time you shall receive from Us, or any your superior Officer, according to the Rules and Discipline of War, in pursuance of the Trust hereby reposed in you.*

GIVEN at Our Court, at Saint James's the Twenty-second day of August 1941, in the Fifth Year of Our Reign

By His Majesty's Command

P. Babington.

---

these the College lay uneasily, wearing the aura of aloof diffidence common to the one-time great; for its role as the heart of the R.A.F. in the training of officers for permanent commissions (the counterpart of Dartmouth for the Navy and Sandhurst for the Army) had been suspended for the duration of the war.

In the building of the R.A.F. as an independent Service, the need for a growing reserve of aircraft had soon become evident if Britain were to meet its defence commitments at home and overseas. To man these reserves the Auxiliary Air Force had been originated in 1924, with city and county associations, and based much on the lines of the Territorial Army. In 1937 there was formed in addition, to meet the need of wider expansion, the Royal Air Force Volunteer Reserve, to train non-commissioned pilots. In 1939 the R.A.F.V.R. had been extended to cover the whole range of aircrew and supporting branches. The regular or professional R.A.F. officer was identifiable by an unembellished uniform, for the A.A.F. wore a small brass A on each lapel, and the R.A.F.V.R. a similar VR, Of these three it was somewhat unkindly said that the R.A.F. consisted of officers trying to be gentlemen; the A.A.F. of gentlemen trying to be officers; while the R.A.F.V.R. was trying to be both! On the outbreak of the war the flood of volunteers was directed to the R.A.F.V.R., into which I had accordingly been commissioned. In war conditions the character of these reserves was becoming lost, particularly as in due course conscripts began incongruously appearing in the V.R. – and the distinguishing badges, if nothing else, were dropped.

On the 10th August 1941, following a short leave I arrived at Cranwell, by train from King's Cross London after a remarkably fast and easy journey for wartime travel. From the first I was impressed by the College in which the officers of my course were housed, for it is a vast and rather magnificent building. However, its cathedral-cum-museum atmosphere, and miles of dim passages and huge halls, made it neither very comfortable nor homely. It was not nearly so attractive or pleasant to live in as the Mess at Rissington, and to cap it all the food was the worst that I ever encountered in any R.A.F. Mess at any time. We were no longer pupil pilots, but dignified by the title of student instructors. I was surprised to find only myself and two N.C.O.s from Rissington, but I knew three others from I.T.W. in Newquay. The course had a strangely disembodied air about it and this was probably because the Flying Instructors' School at Cranwell, as an offshoot of the Central Flying School at Upavon, was a unit of detached flights or some such indeterminate status. It was also only one, and possibly the smallest, of a number of units stationed at Cranwell, and in this position of obscurity was largely unobserved by authority. The tempo of our course was totally different from that at Rissington, and retained something of the pre-war approach to flying which had been a largely sporting one, most suited to an enthusiastic extroversion, sometimes verging on arrested adolescence. We continued in our ground studies with an emphasis on airmanship and engines, beginning work at ten o'clock in the morning and finishing at tea time. On flying days we did not report until eight o'clock, and were finished by six or earlier every evening.

On the flying side, our first surprise was to find that we would be trained on the Avro Tutor during the early stages of the course, and the Airspeed Oxford at night and during the later stages. The standard elementary flying training aircraft of 1941 were the De Havilland Tiger Moth biplane (introduced in 1933) and the Miles Magister, a neat little monoplane. The Tutor of World War I lineage was presumably only retained by C.F.S. to make use of every available aircraft, but there appeared as well to be a considerable element of sentiment involved. To an outsider such as myself this was surprising, as was the general disapproval, amongst the older pre-war officers, of the modern monoplanes and retractable undercarriages. I was too young to have been involved in the conquest of the air or early aircraft development, and in consequence did not belong to the pioneer 'flying club' era. To me the efficiency of an aircraft as a fighting machine was paramount, and meeting the biplane mentality was always a shock. The Avro Tutor was a lovely aircraft to fly, with an extremely safe and versatile performance. It was fitted with brakes operated by a lever, which gave it considerable manoeuvrability on the ground. It was however an aircraft fundamentally of an earlier era, and in common with all aircraft of that time it was something of a ramshackle affair. I was very glad to fly it, as it was to be the only aircraft of its vintage that I ever had the opportunity to handle, but my first solo flight in the Avro Tutor was decidedly memorable.

My instructor, a Flight Lieutenant, and a pre-war officer of very considerable flying ability, decided after only one hour and fifteen minutes of dual familiarisation on type, to send me solo. It was not so long before that I had been flying the Tiger Moth, and I was perfectly confident in my ability to handle the Tutor. We were flying from the North Field and I took off, made a circuit and a comfortable landing back. At the end of my landing run I made for the edge of the field and taxied around to the upwind end, for another take-off. In taxiing a single-engined aircraft of that time, because the engine directly in front of the pilot obscured forward vision when on the ground, it was necessary to swing the aircraft from one side to another, progressing in a zig-zag. In this way, when swinging to the left the pilot could see ahead by looking down the right hand side of the engine, and vice versa. This was hard work, required continual vigilance, and was only possible when taxiing at no more than the safe speed of a fast walking pace, which was the invariable rule.

I had arrived in this way at the upwind boundary, turned across-wind and then parked the aircraft to prepare for take-off, all perfectly correct and in order. While carrying out the vital actions before take-off, to my astonishment there appeared, from below rising ground about two to three hundred yards away, a small single-engined cabin monoplane, the Percival Proctor. These were used at Cranwell for Wireless Operator training and this one, with its tail up, was heading directly towards me at such a speed that, although it was travelling across-wind, I at first thought that it was taking off. I soon realised it was not, but that it was taxiing dead straight on a head-on collision course with my Tutor. The question was, had the pilot seen me – and was he going to swing? There was very little time to consider anything, but it was incumbent upon him to detect me in his constant lookout and, as I was stationary, to avoid me. Should he have seen me and be about to alter course, then if I moved, and in whatever direction, there was a fifty-fifty chance that we would collide, and I would be largely responsible. It was inconceivable that he would continue at such a speed on a straight line for any longer, without swinging and looking ahead – but he did. Had I been able to abandon my aircraft I would have done so but, strapped in tightly, I was treated to the unique vision of the Proctor's five-foot metal propeller rotating at hundreds of revolutions a minute, closing head-on at a considerable speed.

It struck, and chewed its way along the nose of my Tutor, through the wings to the cockpit. The impact was considerable and the propeller passed less than six inches in front of my face before juddering to a stop on the framework of my metal seat, about four inches short of cutting through my legs above the knees. The cabin door of the Proctor flew open and out jumped a most dapper little Pole, quite beautifully turned out in the uniform of an R.A.F. Flight Lieutenant, unmistakably cursing most volubly in Polish. He tore off a pair of white gloves, flung them on the ground in front of me, stamped in fury, turned on his heel and walked off – I rather hoped to Poland, but probably he was heading for the dispersal buildings, in any case I never saw him again. Having watched this melodramatic performance of injured vanity with fascination, I was left in a bit of a fix, trapped in the cockpit of my Tutor on the wide open spaces of an airfield. In these circumstances attracting attention can be as fruitless and frustrating as trying to attract the attention of a waiter in a restaurant. Eventually I was disentangled, and

The first British jet aircraft, a Gloster Whittle E28/39
flying over R.A.F. College Cranwell in 1941.

went in search of another aircraft in which to complete the detail, this time without incident.

There had to be an official Court of Inquiry to investigate this accident but, as I was stationary in my aircraft at the time of the collision, the result was a foregone conclusion, and the Court found the Polish officer guilty of a breach of discipline in taxiing above the permitted speed, and of gross carelessness in failing to keep a proper look-out. I was exonerated from any blame by the Court, but even so I would have preferred to have taken off unmolested.

Perhaps not surprisingly, I kept an extremely sharp look-out when flying after that for any Proctor that might house my Polish prima donna. It was anyway necessary to keep a particularly good look-out on account of the variety of aircraft that were being flown from the North and South fields. Amongst these were Whitleys from the O.T.U., and of all surprising things, a solitary and aged Vickers Valentia in use as a flying classroom for wireless operator training.

Most fascinating of all was the secret operation from an isolated hangar on the South airfield, of the Gloster Whittle E 28/39, Britain's first jet aircraft; powered by the later famous gas-turbine engine invented by Air Commodore Sir Frank

Whittle, and of the existence of which very few were aware. It had first flown on 15th May 1941, and was flown regularly while I was at Cranwell, both airfields being cleared for the occasion amidst much secrecy. It was an astonishing and then uncanny sight to see this single-engined tricycle undercarriage monoplane, leaping into the air and whistling away with no apparent source of power. I would instinctively have assumed that the idea could never catch on, had I not realised that I should so be falling into the same category as those of the biplane mentality; which was as well for the jet engine in due course revolutionised flying. In spite of the secrecy over this Gloster experimental jet aircraft, I was taken aback one night in a pub to be drawn aside by a local, seeking the camaraderie of those 'in the know', and to be told in heavy beery confidence that there was a secret plane at the aerodrome – my informant had seen it in flight – and it went by suction. This was a most astute observation, although incorrect, for the experimental aircraft was not, as my informant imagined, an overgrown airborne vacuum cleaner that sucked itself along, but reaction-driven by the jet from the gas-turbine engine.

Once familiar with the Tutor we began to learn what was called the 'Patter', which my dictionary told me was, 'to repeat in a rapid mechanical way, or talk glibly'. This was exactly what it was, for the earliest patter had been evolved from the Notes on Teaching Flying For Instructors, drawn up at Gosport (the first R.A.F. School of Flying) in about 1917. This, with many embellishments, either passed on by word of mouth or sometimes typewritten sheets, became the famous 'Gosport Patter'. During the rapid expansion of the R.A.F. in the years before the Second World War, this patter was put into print in an effort to achieve standardisation and published in June 1939, more than twenty years later, as A.P. 1732. It was this Air Publication from which we worked, and the system was for the instructor to demonstrate each exercise with the patter, and then the student instructor did likewise, or at least tried to. The inception of this patter by Smith-Barry at Gosport was a remarkable achievement, and one upon which flying instruction throughout the world was later based. What was perhaps less remarkable was that after an enlightened beginning, throughout the twenty years of rapid aviation development which followed, the patter was so little improved. It seemed to have become one of the traditions of the R.A.F., and as such to be inviolate. It was outmoded as a system, totally inadequate for the needs of the time, and sadly out of date; belonging as it did, with the aircraft in which we were learning it, to a past era.

Although we could not fully realise this, we were partly aware of it by virtue of our experiences as pupil pilots, and also the obvious deficiencies of such a system in teaching what had become so technical and scientific a subject. It did however have one great value, and that was in teaching the co-ordination of executing in-flight exactly what you said you were executing, when you said it, and this is no easy matter for an experienced pilot, let alone absolute beginners. At this we slaved, sometimes with an instructor and sometimes with another student, and our flying improved and patter became near word-perfect. I particularly remember practising instruction in taxiing the Tutor because it demanded considerable dexterity, or a pilot endowed with a minimum of four arms and hands. If ever I had wondered at the early aircrew selection tests (which involved taking instructions to do several things at once over an inter-communication system loaded with a heavy background of engine noise) I realised then that the instigators of these tests were not the pure sadists I had imagined, but must simply have had the Avro Tutor in mind.

In the first place communication was by the 'Gosport' speaking tube system, which necessitated pattering into the mouthpiece against the noise of the engine, and one hand was really needed for this. Next, one's eyes were continually engaged in keeping a general look-out, and in particular scanning the ground ahead. Meanwhile a hand was required for operating the throttle through constantly varying settings. The control column had to be held hard back to prevent the tail rising and the propeller fouling the ground, and the ratchet locking brake lever had to be shifted into rapidly changing positions as one applied differential braking to the wheels through movements of the foot-operated rudder bar. Contrary to expectation, this was possible to a normally endowed human being by keeping one's mouth pressed to the speaking tube mouthpiece, following its vagaries by movements of the head; and holding the control column back in the crook of one arm, while using that respective hand for the throttle, the other hand being engaged with the brake. It was, however, difficult meanwhile to retain the dignity of the sage, in fact I know of no other calling in which one was expected to give a lecture, while one's faculties were all but totally engaged in a sort of one-man band exercise, on the execution of which one's safety and very life might at times depend.

My instructor was a good and very capable pilot. Just how good I realised one day when we were flying straight and level at little more than a thousand feet, and he began talking to me about fishing, with frequent references to a stream below us. As he talked the aircraft began very slowly to bank, and this bank continued in the first stages of a roll until the wings had very nearly reached the vertical. As his dissertation on fishing was entirely uninterrupted, it occurred to me that he might think I had control of the aircraft, and so I very gently tested the controls. There was no doubt that he had control, and so when the wings passed the vertical I clung on to anything within reach, as I fell first to one side of the cockpit and then into my shoulder straps when we became inverted, with legs flailing in an attempt to reach some sort of anchorage. All the time my instructor was chatting about fishing, as if we were sitting comfortably before the Mess fire in a couple of armchairs, with a tankard at our respective elbows. We seemed to remain inverted for an age, with ears drumming, eyes aching and the inevitable acute general discomfort; although we were slowly rolling and eventually came back to an even keel, with the peroration on fishing completely uninterrupted. My instructor's voice had not faltered, or at any time departed from a steady, easy, matter-of-fact tone, which never gave the slightest sign of realisation that the aircraft was flying anything but straight and level. A hesitation roll in extremis such as I had witnessed, is probably the most difficult manoeuvre to attempt in all flying and requires the most absolute skill. To talk at the same time so casually on a totally unrelated subject was superb – and I got the message that when I could fly and talk like that, then I could call myself an instructor.

I never forgot that demonstration, and practised it assiduously for years until I believe my mentor might have allowed my presumption in calling myself an instructor – unfortunately he had by then been lost in action, but I think that he would have approved. Apart from anything else, I found it both a wonderful test of an unsuspecting pupil's imperturbability, and also antidote to post-lunch somnolence in hot sleepy weather – the bane of any teacher's life.

The Cranwell Relief Landing Ground (R.L.G.) with which we were concerned was at Fulbeck, some seven miles to the west, situated in open Lincolnshire farming country dotted with little villages of which Stragglethorpe and Barnby-in-the-Willows have always remained in mind for sheer charm of nomenclature. This R.L.G. was of limited facilities, and possessed the same sense of isolation from higher authority that made flying from these fields particularly pleasant. On occasions we worked from Fulbeck by day, and spent the time between flights studying in the long grass at the airfield edge, or just basking in the sun. When the wheat was cut in the adjoining fields, we were surprised to see a team of Landgirls arrive following the reaper and binder to raise the sheaves into stooks for drying. The Landgirls' uniform was simple, eminently practical and particularly attractive for those girls who had a good reason (or maybe two good reasons!) for favouring a figure-hugging pullover; and yet another for shapely khaki breeches, which style was denied the members of the W.A.A.F. (Womens Auxiliary Air Force) and other womens' Services. We found these exciting, weather-tanned girls decidedly attractive and after admiring them for a day or two from a distance, struck on the idea of offering our help. By this time they were pitch-forking the sheaves onto tractor-drawn trailers, and willingly accepted our assistance. We were very fit and strong, but I do not think that I have ever been through such a gruelling experience; a sheaf is heavy on the end of a pitchfork, but this weight is greatly reduced by the rhythm and swing of the correct arc. We knew nothing of handling pitchforks or sheaves, and the work soon proved absolutely back-breaking, which in that heat was an agony. However, there was no letting-up for we could not possibly be put to shame by these girls and we laboured on valiantly, if not particularly effectively. The Landgirls undoubtedly scored over us and in spite of this, and the somewhat Rabelaisian style that rubbed off on many of them in their contact with the earth, we were left with a considerable respect for the Women's Land Army.

All our night flying was carried out at Fulbeck, and the nights being short in August it took some time to cover the ten hours' night flying required by the syllabus. This was made no easier by the regular bombing of the flarepath, with little or no warning, by German intruders. We all went for cover during these attacks, and remained there until it became unlikely that the intruder was standing off waiting for signs of activity before attacking again. In this way I came to know the local ditches quite well, but on one occasion, being out of reach of these when an attack started, I bolted for a group of vehicles, just discernible in the dark, and threw myself under the nearest of them. There I felt reasonably safe, until the flashes of the exploding bombs revealed that I was under a 2,000 gallon petrol bowser, and I must hold the all-time record for the petrified stomach crawl, achieved in an attempt to put the greatest possible distance between myself and that bowser.

On our return to the College for breakfast in the Mess, our accounts of these attacks aroused extraordinarily little interest amongst our fellow officers. Even less it seemed with authority, for we continued regularly to go out to Fulbeck without any precautions or change in the arrangements, and were equally regularly bombed. One morning on return to the College we were astonished to find the whole place in an uproar, and buzzing with excited conversation. We soon learned the cause of this, for an intruder had 'attacked' the College, or at least dropped a single incendiary bomb which had struck the College roof close to the Commandant's room, and from then on we were plagued with fire practices and other air-raid precautions.

R. de B. had regularly invited me to spend a long weekend leave with him at his grandmother's house, Synyards, in Otham near Maidstone. I had once managed to do this, and enormously enjoyed the beautifully timbered fifteenth-century house, with a carved crown adorning the kingpost supporting the centre of the building. Now another opportunity presented itself, but R. de B.'s grandmother, after a forty-year tenure, had been forced to make a strategic withdrawal from Synyards into a lovely but smaller old house nearby. It was to this that I was conveyed from Maidstone station one Friday evening by R. de B. in his Daimler (third of the line, his Armstrong having been destroyed by a bomb attack on R.A.F. Andover) – and so began a most enjoyable weekend. That night we paused for a moment in the turmoil of war, and before a glowing fire of three-foot logs in the dancing shadows of a great open stone fireplace, we sat and talked into the small hours of experiences shared, of individuals and incidents in our past, of hopes for the future and of all such things embraced in the warm comfort of great friendship – and it was good.

The next morning we were awakened by R. de B.'s sixteen-year-old sister Yvonne, who bounced into our room and insisted on cleaning our buttons for us. Somewhat ungratefully we raced down to the river for a swim, before breakfasting most leisurely. After passing the rest of the day walking in the Kent orchards and fields, we dined that night at Wardes (the gardener's cottage further down the lane was named After Wardes!) a dream of a sixteenth-century house, as guest of Angela's parents and delightful family – Angela being a close friend of R. de B. Sunday we spent in much the same way, lying that afternoon in the blazing sun on the stone flags by the lily pond at Wardes, with four friendly white doves frequently coming to talk to us, and the fish mouthing their superiority from the shade of the water-lily leaves. Wardes was not only a house of considerable attraction, but one with an atmosphere of deep calm and happiness, and the afternoon was a long moment of great contentment. War seemed inconceivable in the face of the potential loveliness in the whole span of life; I thought for a while of how insane mankind was to countenance it – and how doubly insane we must be to fly in it.

Journeying back to Cranwell that night, I pondered on a deepening realisation of the worthwhile things in life and their inestimable value. I was intensely grateful for the superb kindness and friendship just experienced, and to have known such people; such peace; such beauty; such freedom; such heavenly corners of England; and such sunlight. But in my gratitude I realised that a deepening understanding and appreciation of these things required matching by an equally deepening deter-mination to fight for the freedom essential to their survival. Otherwise I would not only no longer be true to myself, but fail in my duty both to society and to humanity. To fight so, I would need a ceaseless, single-minded, blind, ruthless self-persuasion. Here was an obvious risk, for what if I became all that I would increasingly need to force myself to be? Hell was surmised to be the loss of the sight of heaven – could I so be lost in such a hell? It was a horrifying thought – but, I decided, surely not in the face of the ultimate triumph of good over evil – and of this triumph time would tell. I had never before realised that death was not the only or necessarily the worst fate that might lie in store for me and many others in war, and in this I was deeply troubled.

September brought a deterioration in the weather, and flying began to be held up with the inevitable sense of personal frustration at our inability to get to grips with the enemy. An enemy now showing a fearsome potential, for since their invasion of Russia in June the Germans had made an almost uninterrupted advance, blockading Leningrad, taking Kiev and moving towards Moscow. This success, in the face of huge Russian armies and resources, emphasised most clearly the prodigious effort that would be required, firstly to halt and then to crush the Germans, and this massive effort could stem only from the unstinted contribution of the individual.

My last flight of the course was on 3rd October when, the ground examinations and C.F.I.'s. (Chief Flying Instructor) test being over, I found myself a Flying Instructor category C (probationary) with still almost everything to learn about flying. On 5th October 1941 I was posted as a Q.F.I. (Qualified Flying Instructor) to No. 3 F.T.S. South Cerney, almost incredibly again in my beloved Gloucestershire, and a year to the day from that on which I had been accepted at R.A.F. Uxbridge, for aircrew training. While this was an astonishing success in mobilisation, I had already witnessed something of the price in human life and limb of this achievement – and it remained to be seen if it could prevail in the face of German military professionalism.

CHAPTER 7

The Bearing of the Torch – Part 1

To hand on the torch – keep knowledge alive
Oxford English Dictionary.
The heraldic representation of a flaming torch appears in many R.A.F. Flying
Training School badges as a symbol of the dissemination of learning.

As a nation we must surely be unique in our attitude towards those who teach. There has never been any lack of appreciation of the importance or value of learning, yet the whole business of teaching and conception of education has been relegated to such a low position in the order of things, that its execution and development has been haphazard and largely accidental. So low was the status of the teacher that for decades the profession barely commanded a living wage. Qualification to teach was not generally considered to be necessary and the four-to-six-year-olds, a vital period in education, were taught by any well-meaning housewife or school-leaver who could find no better occupation. Such was our investment in the nation's future during the pre-war years and the lack of awareness of the importance of teaching, an attitude reflected to a surprising degree in the R.A.F., in spite of a number of men of vision who had struggled for the recognition of the importance of the teaching of flying.

The history of flying instruction in the R.A.F. dated back to 1916, when a Squadron Leader Smith-Barry's urgently pressed ideas on training methods were accepted by Trenchard, and the Gosport School came into being. Here the Gosport Instructional Patter was evolved, and speaking tubes (Gosport Tubes) were installed in aircraft to enable instructors to communicate with their pupils without using hand signals, passing notes, or even resorting to stopping the engine to make themselves heard. The Gosport School of Flying was established as the first flying

Oddentification

In Oxford's many seats of learning
Sits the u't aircrew, yearning
For that coveted, distant day
When each in his particular way
Applies his 'Varsity education
To Hitler's ultimate decimation.

[Aeroplane

instructors' school, and the system of instruction evolved was one of demonstration accompanied by a form of patter handed down by word of mouth, or sometimes typewritten sheets. After the 1914–18 war, the centre of instruction passed to the Central Flying School (C.F.S.) Upavon. As mentioned earlier, it was sobering to discover that following this enlightened beginning, the C.F.S. patter was only put into print in June 1939 (AP 1732) some twenty years after it was first evolved, by which time it was outmoded, inadequate and sadly out of date. I had entered the R.A.F. flying training system in early 1941, and experienced the 1939 'Principles of Flying Instruction' (AP 1732) Gosport Tubes and all. To me it was all new, exciting, and a major challenge to which I devoted myself entirely, and was not to realise many of its shortcomings until later.

Instruction in the air has several fundamental differences from instruction on the ground. In the first place, the pupil is in a strange, unnatural and hostile element, for an aircraft can only remain airborne in certain basic circumstances and if these circumstances are not met, then the aircraft plummets to the ground with obvious consequences to its occupants. Next, the pupil and his aircraft move in three dimensions as opposed to the two in which we normally move. In addition the pupil will be moving at speeds greatly above those to which he has been accustomed, and there can be no stopping to think or take stock, as below certain speeds the aircraft does not remain airborne but falls out of control. These unaccustomed high speeds bring many new experiences, the most disturbing of which is likely to be the loading imposed on aircraft and occupants alike, by acceleration or de-acceleration in changes of direction, speed and sometimes power. This loading is measured in terms of 'g' (gravity) on the weight of the body in question. Owing to the effect of inertia, violent control movements (such as may be made by a pupil in learning) can cause high loadings. Although the average pilot may momentarily be able to withstand a loading of up to 8g a sustained loading of from 3g to 5g will cause most pilots to black out, losing first sight and then consciousness until the loading is reduced, the dangers of which need no emphasising.

The pupil has as well to learn to divide his attention between the outside of his aircraft (where the main considerations are his attitude in the three planes in relation to the ground) with an all important never-ceasing lookout, and the inside of his aircraft. Inside the cockpit, he has to learn a cycle of survey and interpretation of a varying number of instruments, indicators and controls, without concentrating on any one of them for more than the minimum necessary time. All of this against a background of noise and vibration from the engines, the like of which the pupil has probably never experienced before, and which alone tends to be a major distraction. Meanwhile he has to listen for, hear and remember the words of his instructor, then think and act accordingly. Far from an overstatement of the pupil's problems this is the least of it, for the number of visual, oral and physical signals a pilot may be called upon to receive, consider and act on in a very short space of time can be great indeed; most particularly in action, or in an emergency, or more than likely both.

The De Havilland Tiger Moth and Miles Magister were the standard elementary training aircraft in 1939, and the Airspeed Oxford the advanced twin-engined trainer. Both the Tiger Moth and Magister were open cockpit aircraft, so belonging to a past era. The Tiger Moth, a biplane, although a wonderful little aircraft, was too easy to fly, and lacked many of the characteristics of the monoplanes that those trained on the Tiger were destined to meet. While the open cockpit reduced the sense of enclosure, it was pioneer flying in which it took time to become used to both the severe buffeting of the airflow and slipstream, as well as exposure to the weather, no longer an unavoidable experience. Open cockpit flying required the almost continual use of goggles, which not only considerably restricted vision, but were liable to mist up at critical moments – the alternative being to peer through almost closed, tear-streaming and wind-battered eyes.

In the early years of World War II, instructor and pupil communicated through a speaking tube. At the receiving end the tube divided below the pilot's head, a lesser tube running to each earpiece embedded in the flying helmet. In spite of the insulation of these earpieces with thick sponge-rubber pads, the outside interference from the buffeting airflow and engine noise was considerable, and this, coupled with similar noises picked up by the mouthpiece, made the interpretation of speech

The rapidly increasing costs of flying accidents in men and war production was only belatedly realised, and led to much publicity by an Accident Prevention organisation, later to be renamed Flight Safety.

difficult. Teaching is fundamentally a matter of communication, and while eventual familiarity with Gosport Tubes made their use easier, the pupil pilot was faced with the major hazard of frequently guessing at what his instructor was telling him, and this sometimes none too successfully.

Flying instruction at this time consisted of the instructor demonstrating the exercise in question, with patter, and then the pupil carrying out the exercise himself under the guidance of the instructor. There was no analysis in depth of what was being done, and little discussion of the many considerations involved. The limited and bald statements of the patter inevitably created an unavoidable impression in the pupil that, if after the demonstration he failed to master the exercise, then he must be considerably lacking. Frequently a high degree of visual judgement and co-ordination of the controls was required. I had found that I learned far more when flying solo, by experimenting and analysing cause and effect, than I did when flying dual. This was partially realised, but it was by no means understood at the time that it could be indicative of inadequate instruction. The system was accepted as the way in which flying had been taught since the beginning and, as all long-established systems, had become deeply entrenched.

The patter was comparatively easily learned, and this and its application in flight seemed to be almost the only qualification required of a flying instructor. Given the problems of shortage of skill in the huge war expansion of flying training, the growing complexity and sophistication of aircraft, and the obvious lack of glamour and direct action for the war effort in teaching flying, an enlightened plan was called for. The R.A.F. however, still subscribed to the popular idea that anyone could teach, and selection for this duty was obviously largely haphazard and of low priority. Amongst those detailed were many of the comparatively older entrants, presumably on the grounds of maturity, and the occasional natural teacher. One could look, largely in vain, for the qualities of enthusiasm, steadiness, flying ability, fighting spirit and potential to instruct, that would have created a pride in profession. The only comment or guidance I can remember receiving on our role as flying instructors was an introductory address to the C.F.S. course at Cranwell by the Chief Instructor, a Wing Commander. This consisted of a sombre, terse and far from inspiring warning that no requests for transfer from instructional duties would be considered, and that anyone who attempted to fail the course would be a marked man. So had begun our training for a fundamental and vital task in the R.A.F.

No. 3 F.T.S. South Cerney was equipped with the Airspeed Oxford aircraft, and on joining the staff on 5th October 1941, I found myself allocated to 'B' Flight of No. 2 Squadron in which a course had already begun its training. There I was introduced by my Flight Commander to my first four pupils, with two of whom I would fly in the morning and two in the afternoon. Two were Polish and two English, of which one by the name of Bodell greeted me with; 'How do you do, Sir – my father will be pleased about this.' I identified him at once, and was not at all so sure – for how fervently his father, Monsieur Bodell the French master of my school days, must have hoped that my flying was less incompetent than my French. Fortunately, it was. This meeting was an incredible coincidence (the odds against which were colossal) and I particularly enjoyed flying with Bodell junior, a good-looking, fair-haired boy with all the sensitivity of his French-teaching, musician father who had once given way to tears before us in his translation of the Valse Triste. Bodell, keen, intelligent and a joy to instruct, was later to provide me with my first instructional crisis. Instrument flying was practised in daylight by the pupil wearing an extended metal hood, after the fashion of an elongated tennis eyeshade, which limited his view to the cockpit. Bodell had settled down under this, and was flying so steadily on instruments that I progressed through increasingly steep turns with him, which amongst other things are an exacting exercise in accurately maintaining height.

In normal conditions the body is orientated by both vision and a sense of balance and turning given, oddly enough, by the mechanism of inner ear. Without external visual aids, the information given by the inner ear can become unreliable, giving rise to false sensations of attitude and turn, to the extent of a compelling belief that one is actually turning in the opposite direction to the fact – and this can rapidly lead to complete disorientation. In consequence, much of the training in instrument flying is learning an intense concentration on the instruments, and absolute faith in their indications to the exclusion of all bodily sensations. Bodell was holding a steep turn on instruments very well, when suddenly he became disorientated and without any warning applied sharp bank in the wrong direction. Before I could intervene, the Oxford rolled over and I found myself upside down in a non-aerobatic aircraft, at a height from which recovery without striking the ground was doubtful. I rolled it out, in a far from elegant scramble, just clearing the treetops and owing this recovery to the fact that I had most irregularly been upside down in an Oxford before, during the episode of the loops – otherwise I would never have made it. Bodell took all this as a matter of course and was completely unshaken, which was probably just as well – but he was to be killed after leaving South Cerney. When I heard of this it was all I could do to restrain bitter tears of sympathy for his gentle unassuming father, in the realisation of the cynicism, 'From those who have not – shall be taken'.

My other English pupil was an ex-R.A.F. engine fitter, who could hardly have been less suitable for training as a pilot. His slow reactions, lack of intelligence and frequently stupid behaviour taxed my abilities to the extreme, and I was greatly relieved when he was suspended from flying training and returned to his trade. By way of a replacement I acquired another Pole, which was certainly 'flinging me in at the deep end', for no amount of interest, enthusiasm and effort on the part of the three Poles could make up for the language difficulty. We got on very well, but in retrospect I blanch at the thought, for much of my instruction had to be conveyed by sign language and drawings, a situation before which a seasoned instructor might well have quailed. The rate at which we were flying was hard, inexperience and the language difficulties making it harder. I soon realised that while a normal flight only involved the intense concentration of one take-off and one landing, however long it might be; training flying could involve up to six take-offs and landings in an hour, and one seldom had the opportunity of a let-up in the diminished concentration of purely cruising flight. It was tough and tiring, but such was one's youth and involvement that I cannot remember ever being particularly conscious of the fact.

South Cerney airfield, one of the very fine permanent R.A.F. stations of 1937 vintage, was hard by the village of this name and only about three miles to the south of Cirencester. The Relief Landing Ground (R.L.G.) was above the beautiful old village of Bibury, some six miles to the north-east of Cirencester and seven miles from South Cerney as the Oxford flew. The station housed only No. 3 Service Flying Training School, which was organised on a three wing basis of a Flying Wing, Technical Wing and Administrative Wing.

The Flying Wing consisted of two Squadrons each of four Flights grouped, as an innovation, in twos. As each Flight was established with nine or ten aircraft, this created a total of eighty or so aircraft on the station, requiring sizeable technical and administrative support. The grass airfield, bounded on the north-east side by the Roman road connecting Cricklade and Cirencester, was not large enough to disperse these aircraft around the perimeter, and many of them were parked in the fields on the other side of the busy main road. Each Flight was staffed with a Flight Commander and six instructors, taking a course of 24–30 pupils through the whole S.F.T.S. syllabus, from arrival to 'Wings' standard. There were therefore eight courses on the station flying at different stages of progress and, even with the most careful of planning, this created an intense local air traffic pattern and crowded circuit.

The Airspeed Oxford had been designed in versions to provide training for all aircrew members, and some of the aircraft on the station were fitted with a manually operated turret mounting a single Vickers 'K' machine gun, intended for airgunnery training. Every day a number of these aircraft were put into the air, just before dawn, on what inevitably became called the dawn patrol. As part of the anti-invasion scheme, the task was to patrol a fixed line for the crucial hour following dawn, to detect and attack any possible invading airborne force. This was again the stuff of desperation, and smacked of the Tiger Moth and its bombs. As one of the most junior pilots on the station, my turn for this duty came around with remarkable frequency. With my wooden aircraft, manually operated turret and single machine gun in mind, I sought clarification of the *modus operandi* for the attack. I was informed somewhat vaguely by my Flight Commander that the idea was to shoot down the gliders carrying the airborne troops. To my polite inquiry of: 'What about the glider tugs and enemy fighter cover?' he encouragingly said, 'Oh don't bother about those – just concentrate on the gliders.' Candidly I had no intention of bothering about the tugs and fighters, but my concern was that they might not feel the same way about me. In the face of the multiple machine gun turrets of the tugs, and cannon and multiple machine gun armament of the fighters, it was hardly likely that I would ever get near enough to a glider for my single, obsolete, drum-fed machine gun to be of any effect. Fortunately the scheme died a gradual death.

The Prime Minister, Mr Churchill, rightly or wrongly incensed by the circumstances of the loss of Crete to German airborne assault during May 1941, urged the Secretary of State for Air to make every airfield a stronghold of fighting air-groundsmen, and not the abode of uniformed civilians, in the prime of life, protected by detachments of soldiers. This resulted at South Cerney in the introduction of a 'Fighting Day' which decreed that, in a contradiction of terms, every week there was to be no flying on Tuesday morning when the entire personnel of the station were involved in ground defence training for half a day! I had understood, to my pride, that every airman was trained first as a fighting man and then as a tradesman, and to this essential principle I was devoted. However, with the introduction of Fighting Day I discovered that in this belief I was completely and hopelessly wrong. It became abundantly clear with few exceptions the airmen considered that as tradesmen their task was solely to keep the aircraft in flying condition, and thereby in the air. The aircrew in general considered their task solely to fly, the business of fighting in the air being apparently largely incidental. The idea of fighting on the ground, and certainly training for fighting on the ground, was obviously repugnant to officers and men alike and every stratagem was used to avoid taking part in this training. As a result, Fighting Day was a less than half-hearted effort which lent great moment to the contention that the whole thing was ridiculous, and it too gradually faded away into complete obscurity.

It is inconceivable that a fighting Service should accept the limitation of its fighting rôle and spirit to one small section, such as R.A.F. aircrew, and that purely to involvement in the air. This however seemed to be the case, and perhaps even more inconceivable was that the fighting spirit of the aircrew was in no way that I ever experienced inculcated, but was almost entirely assumed. These things concerned me greatly, and my concern was not dispelled by the formation of the R.A.F. Regiment for ground defence, a move which seemed to completely negate Churchill's intention.

About a fortnight after joining 3 F.T.S., a new course (No. 57) arrived in B Flight of No. 1 Squadron, and to this I was transferred for the experience of taking my pupils through the complete syllabus to wings standard, from start to finish. It was to be a great and enthralling experience, but also extremely hard work. My four pupils were mercifully English-speaking, one of them being a New Zealander of Maori extraction.

Sooner or later in teaching military flying there occurs the problem of Lack of Moral Fibre (L.M.F.) as it was termed, arising from stress and taking many forms, these being generally and colloquially termed 'going yellow'. This I was to meet almost at once. The fundamental factor in flying stress is that from the moment of take-off the individual is in a strange and hostile element, in which the potential dangers are held at bay by ceaseless application and effort, ending only on the completion of a safe landing. Such application and effort is tiring enough in normal circumstances but if, for instance, there is added flying blind by instruments in cloud or at night, and combating the problems of weather conditions such as fog, snow or ice (the last of which can be encountered frequently) then the stress and fatigue is greatly increased. This is not the whole of it, for there must be added the not infrequent possibility of mechanical or technical failure in flight. Such failure in civil passenger or freight-carrying aircraft is always serious enough, but a large safety margin is allowed for these eventualities. A war plane however, is designed for maximum efficiency as a weapon which allows for little or no safety margin. Technical failure in these circumstances can impose a very great strain on the pilot and possibly crew as well. All of this is stress involved in the problems of flight, but superimposed upon it may be the additional and very considerable stress in the execution of the function of the flight, be it for training, operating in war or any other purpose.

Regarding training, for the instructor there is a position in every developing dangerous flight situation, beyond which recovery is impossible and disaster is inevitable. Halting the situation just short of this point of no return, to obtain maximum teaching value, is the skill of the expert flying instructor, but such a nicety of judgement involves great stress. The stresses of aerial operations in war are numerous, but are principally the tension of continual search for the detection of approaching fighter attack, often through hours of flight, and the considerable periods during which the aircraft may be under anti-aircraft fire. In either of these cases it is impossible to be unaware of the fact that in the air there is absolutely no cover or protection and that one is, so to speak, suspended in space and a completely exposed target. Human nature does not normally seek either hardship or danger, and the complete contrast between normality in the comfort, comparative peace and security of a United Kingdom base was no encouragement to get into the air in all possible circumstances. For this was needed a strong motivation, great determination and an unwavering enthusiasm for flying.

There has always been a considerable glamour in flying, and this was greatly accentuated in the extensive publicity given to the R.A.F. by the Battle of Britain when the nation was in desperate need of a victory. It led to a great influx of applications to the R.A.F. for training as aircrew, amongst whom was inevitably a number of individuals motivated by an astonishing conceit, the apparent prospect of a cushy war, and the enjoyment of reflected glory. These were almost without exception lacking in the moral fibre required to fly, let alone to fight in the air, a deficiency unlikely to be detected before much valuable time, effort and resources had been expended on their training. Such were clear-cut 'Lack of Moral Fibre' (L.M.F.) cases, of which the R.A.F. discharged some 300 a year, throughout the war. A very much more complex problem were those individuals who for one reason or another were unable, or later became unable, to face the stress of flying or fighting in the air, and who consequently suffered a nervous breakdown; of which the R.A.F. experienced some 3,000 such cases a year throughout the war, all but a small proportion of whom never flew again.

Knowledge and understanding of these things were very limited at the outbreak of World War II. As the flying instructor had both the earliest and the greatest opportunity of observing the individual, immediately before and after flight as well as under flying stress, it fell largely to the instructor to detect L.M.F., or temperamental unsuitability to flying. This detection was obviously of the greatest importance, in preventing suspect individuals injuring or killing themselves, possibly killing a crew, destroying or damaging aircraft; and for the erosion of morale that they could cause. In addition an important consideration was the saving of desperately needed time, money, materials and effort that would be lost in training such cases. Nevertheless this aspect of flying training was all but ignored in the most amazing ignorance, within the generally accepted idea that anyone who could fly could teach flying. I for one had suffered grievously from this fallacy, and was as a result particularly conscious of the vital role of the flying instructor, from the very start of my involvement. Our rudimentary training as instructors had not included any mention of the psychological aspects of flying, and so the detection of L.M.F. and temperamental unsuitability to flying was, at this time, left to the instructors' intelligence and experience; both of which could be conspicuously lacking. In later years I came to realise what a very large contributory factor this must have been to the appalling accident rate, and losses in killed and injured, during training in the early war years.

Teaching flying inevitably gave rise to hair-raising incidents. This was particularly so in working with a suspected case of temperamental unsuitability, as these characters could in their fear partially or completely cease to react to instructions, and impede the instructor's efforts to regain control of the aircraft. Having heard of many incidents from my fellow instructors, I realised that eventually I was bound to meet the problem myself, and had no intention of figuring in an unexplained fatal accident.

A continual difficulty in teaching pupils to land the Airspeed Oxford was that while it was necessary to move the control column steadily back during the landing, only one hand (the left) was available for this, as it was essential to retain the right hand on the engine throttles for the immediate application of power, should the aircraft begin to swing on the landing run. Unchecked this swing could develop into a ground-loop in which one or both legs of the undercarriage would probably collapse, shattering the airscrews and causing extensive damage. Because the backward pressure needed on the control column was considerable, pupils tended to relinquish the throttles in order to use both hands and it was extremely hard to break some pupils of what could become a most dangerous habit. A fellow instructor, one Flying Officer Palmer, had equipped himself with a nine-inch length of rubber hosepipe with which he had taken to rapping the knuckles of the pupil's errant right hand, as soon as it grasped the control column. This instrument became known as the 'Palmer Persuader', and many of us used it in some form or another. I obtained, for this purpose, a ten-inch solid rubber truncheon, which I quite unofficially carried stowed in a special pocket in the leg of my flying overalls.

My pupil of Maori extraction had from the start proved to be an extremely slow learner and dangerously slow in his reactions. I should not have persevered but on account of sympathy, inexperience, or most inexcusable of all, an unwillingness to accept failure in a misplaced personal pride, I continued to try to bring him to an acceptable standard. We had, on the occasion in question, been airborne for the better part of an hour when I decided that we would finish the detail with a glide landing. The Oxford's gliding angle was very steep, frighteningly so to the uninitiated, and this was one of the reasons why it was practised. By the grace of God my pupil accidentally climbed on the circuit and positioned himself for the approach higher than he should have been; but then passed the point to begin his approach. Several times I instructed him to close the throttles and begin the glide, but there was no reaction, and finally I closed the throttles and put the aircraft into a glide myself, before handing back control. Our attitude gradually steepened and the speed began to build up alarmingly, which first alerted me to an abnormal situation. There was no reaction at all to my corrective instructions and, taking my eyes off the rapidly approaching ground, I was horrified to see that my pupil was staring wide-eyed and fixedly ahead of him with a completely expressionless face. There was no response to my immediate instruction to hand over the controls, and I was quite unable to overcome the physical lock that he had on them. We were in what seemed to be a near-vertical dive, and the ground was rushing up at nearly one hundred miles an hour.

With no time for deliberation, I reached for my Palmer Persuader and dealt him a frightful blow on the back of his leather-helmeted head. He released the controls at once, and I began to haul back on the control column as hard as I dared. At first the only possibilities seemed either hitting the ground because I had not levelled out quickly enough, or going into a high-speed stall and hitting the ground because I had levelled out too fast. In either case we would have been most unlikely to survive the impact. As it happened, I managed to pull the aircraft out of the dive just above the ground without an inch to spare, and we streaked across the airfield at a speed far too high for landing, before climbing back thankfully into the air. My pupil never showed any resentment for the blow that I dealt him, which I rather unkindly attributed to an amazingly thick skull, and he was as relieved as myself when he was later suspended from further flying training. I do not know how I would have fared had he made an issue of it, as for an officer to strike an airman is an exceedingly grave crime.

L.M.F. was largely a problem of the conquest of fear, and could occur not only during training but at any time in a flying career. It was around one all the time and I remember the distaste that I felt for a fellow instructor who was withdrawn from flying as he not only suddenly refused to instruct at night, but refused to fly at all in the dark. Another of our instructors came from a fighter squadron, where he had been shot down into the sea and drifted for a long time in his dinghy before being picked up. We all carried a whistle on a shoulder lanyard for this emergency, as in a rough sea searching boats are more likely to hear the survivor than to see him. This fellow was forever blowing his whistle and eventually took to sitting on his bed in the Mess, blowing his whistle incessantly. He too was withdrawn from flying. The ultimate test of manliness is the ability to overcome fear in facing danger and possible death, and those who prove unequal to this requirement have for all time been derided as 'yellow-bellies'. It was only possible to regard examples of Lack of Moral Fibre in this way, but this judgement on those who suffered nervous breakdown, sometimes after very considerable stress, was much more difficult to accept. Nevertheless, somehow the 'yellow' stigma was inseparable from any failure to stand up and fight, and many undoubtedly went to their deaths struggling under the burden of a nervous breakdown, to which they were not willing to admit. These must surely have been the bravest of all men.

With four Flights to administer and supervise, our Squadron Commander was rarely seen, but the two-Flight sub-division to which I belonged in No. 1 Squadron was under the control of a truly amazing character, Arthur Bickerstaff Woods. Woods, the most restless of personalities, held the rank of Flight Lieutenant which in those days was still something of a comparative rarity, and seemed to us a state of considerable seniority and accompanying senility – he would, I suppose, have been in his early thirties. An ex-film producer of some note, being denied the acclaim of this status in his new role, his current bid for fame lay in outrageous behaviour and eccentricity to a point some might have considered akin to insanity. This, although entertaining, was almost completely without any form of subtlety or wit, and reminded me of an uncle of mine who, at a tender age, is reputed in a burst of frustrated fury to have bellowed every dreadful and wicked word he knew: 'Pee, po, belly, pot, bum!'

Woods' unpredictable zaniness and blatant disregard for authority and discipline relied upon shock for effect. It was a behaviour so outlandish as to achieve a strange immunity from authority, which simply did not know how to cope with it; he might well have been the first to provoke the comment, 'Master of the art of doing f—k-all, with a flourish!' He carried his scatty outlook and ebullient behaviour into flying, and I was never happy with him in the air. On one occasion he hitched a lift from Bibury in my aircraft, took over the controls and made the most fearful landing at South Cerney to the accompaniment of a whooping: 'Oops! bouncy bouncy!' which sounded unprofessional to say the least of it. He was, in his own parlance, ill-cast for his role and was seemingly selected for his appointment on age and a 'savoir-faire' largely acquired in the theatre and film world.

Woods always treated me with a kindness and consideration which I much appreciated, but I was not then wise enough to understand or tolerate his divided interest, as he was frequently absent on mysterious business in equally mysterious locations. It seemed to me that our work was of such import as to be all-engrossing, and I felt his absences not only to be an overt criticism of all in which we were involved, but also to be a lack of personal support for his juniors. He was much favoured by the beer-swilling fraternity as one imagined to be after their own image, although in his true sphere his abilities were such as to made them exceedingly small fry, outside their value as a claque. Before long, Woods was promoted and posted to Kidlington near Oxford, as Chief Instructor of a glider school, but I was sorry to hear later that he was killed flying a De Havilland Mosquito, the twin-engined fighter/bomber.

'B' Flight of No. 1 Squadron was commanded by an ex-Halton apprentice, Bill Sly, an excellent Flight Commander endowed with a considerable if unpolished charm, and whose laughing, devil-may-care attitude disguised a comprehensive competence and ability. He was a very fine pilot, and succeeded in landing an Oxford with most of one wing removed, after a pupil had collided with him during a formation flying practice. For this he was awarded a well-earned Air Force Medal. I was to serve under Bill Sly for most of my time at South Cerney and I owed much to his kindness and guidance. He was a most unassuming but effective leader.

Another of the Flight Commanders was Butch Baker, tall, slim, baby-faced, mischievous in the extreme and an excellent pilot and instructor. If I remember rightly he was a regular officer and this superior status, with a natural gravity, made him a seemingly distant individual. It was then all the more surprising when he indulged in little short of lunatic pranks. I was several times a victim of these, and in particular remember on one occasion taking off together in our respective Oxfords for Bibury. Baker closed on me and I gathered that he intended to use the flight for formation practice and unsuspectingly co-operated by acting as leader, settling down to steady flight at a little below cruising speed to give him the necessary margin for manoeuvring.

Formation flying requires intense concentration, instant reaction and continual anticipatory movement of the engine and flying controls. It is an advanced exercise in which pupils were usually positioned with their wingtip outside that of the leader, and level with the leader's tailplane in a close, but safe, formation. Instructors flying together would move in with wingtips inside that of the leader, and level with a point about halfway down the fuselage in a tight and much more hazardous formation. Baker moved into this position on my port side and then to my astonishment, steadily and with great precision, closed in until his wingtip was all but touching my fuselage. He then inched up, bringing his starboard propeller closer and closer to my port aileron, which is hinged in the trailing edge near to the wingtip. I was 'sweating blood' because the slightest unsteadiness on my part would have brought us in a flaming mass to the ground, and I had not a half of his experience. Still he edged forward, and I could envisage his airscrew slicing my trailing edge and aileron to pieces at any moment. By then there was no margin for any unexpected occurrence such as a 'bump' (a common disturbance in the air) which would rock the aircraft.

The ailerons control the movement of the aircraft in the rolling plane, and Baker can have been no more than six inches from my aileron when that wing began to drop. To hold it up, I found myself first applying steadily increasing opposite bank until the control was hard over on the stops, and then in desperation using opposite rudder – on the verge of losing control. Although I had never heard of such a thing, I knew what was happening. The proximity of the propeller behind my aileron was breaking the airflow, stalling the wing and making the aileron increasingly ineffective. This was dicing with death in no mean manner, and I could see Butch Baker absolutely convulsed with laughter. Just before I would have lost control, the wing dropping and my aircraft slewing into Baker's, he fell away and peeled off to land at Bibury. He can only have judged this point to a hair's breadth on the extreme position of my 'dead' aileron; an incredible performance.

A most interesting character was O.C. Chave, a thoughtful, humorous and sensitive man with a considerable knowledge of flying and flying instruction. He had published a number of poems, many with a flying theme, under the pseudonym of Ariel. These I was moved to collect assiduously while we worked together for some time in C Flight, and came to admire and understand something of him; I would dearly have liked to have known him much better. He was later given command of C Flight, but I think that this may have had little meaning for him other than in amusement at being able to sign himself, in the jargon of Service abbreviation, as O.C.C. O. C. Flt....! I find difficulty in selecting one item of Chave's writing, it being rich in understanding, knowledge, humour and the trials, horrors and wonders of flight, but one of my favourites is 'Dawn'.

> He who would see the dawn break bright
> Must first climb lonely through the night
> Till twenty thousand feet of space
> Hang between him and earth's embrace;
> Fearful but unafraid must he
> Dare all night's malignancy.

But then how splendid is the glow
That tints the wide horizon's bow,
How comforting a moral then
Dawn's fingers point for weary men!

Chave was later lost flying a four-engined Short Stirling heavy bomber in an attack on an Italian target.

Amongst the other instructors with whom I came into contact and flew at some time were the morose and hard-working Sergeant Lyon, who was killed in a Whitley while on a brief attachment to an Operational Training Unit for experience; the delightfully vague J. P. Kennedy with whom I was to work again later; Chico Robertson, afterwards killed in action; and Billy Benton. Benton had the misfortune, while parked at the taxiing post prior to take-off one night, to have a pupil taxi straight into the tail of his aircraft. Somewhat incensed, he leapt out into the dark and in the process of telling the pupil what he thought of him, bellowed, 'Look what you have done to my aircraft, you moron!' and threw out his arm in a dramatic gesture – unfortunately into a revolving propeller, which mangled his arm very thoroughly too.

These were flying personnel of our own Wing with whom we were living and working; we came into contact with the ground personnel of the Technical and Administrative Wings less frequently. They were known generically as penguins, being unkindly attributed with no wings and cold feet. There was a greater understanding between the aircrew and Technical Wing, than between the aircrew and Administrative Wing. While the Technical Wing did an excellent job, the relationship was on occasions strained by the continual pressure of aircrew for the working of wonders by Technical Wing, in servicing and repairing the very hard-worked and roughly treated training aircraft. Notices in technical crew rooms and offices such as: 'The difficult achieved immediately – the impossible takes a little longer' were common and clearly illustrated this situation. To the aircrew the technical officers were all 'plumbers'. To the plumbers, the aircrew were in turn unreasonable ignoramuses, which led to frequent good-natured trials of strength over the pilots' authority to ground an aircraft, by placing it unserviceable (u/s), and the technicians' authority to place it serviceable again. An example was the pilot who placed an aircraft u/s with the note: 'Something loose in the tail section', and later found it placed serviceable again with the recorded action: 'Something tightened in the tail section!'

To aircrew, administrators and their hair-splitting bureaucracy were anathema, and to administrators aircrew were many things including over-privileged, ill-disciplined, arrested adolescents. This lack of mutual understanding was not total, but emerged sporadically and had been, in some degree, forever so. It was rooted in the totally different task and perspective of the two groups, in which it is understandable that men continually facing danger, difficulty and the recurring possibility of imminent death, are involved with fundamentals, and are likely to view pettifogging demands and restrictions as inconsequential. I can well remember an occasion at South Cerney when we had been flying for most of the day in atrocious weather. There had been an accident, a number of difficulties and mishaps, and we were probably on edge when a senior officer of the Administrative Wing staff came into our crew-room on some errand. In the course of this he unwisely commented strongly on the very untidy, and possibly dirty state of the crew room, provoking a barrage of near insubordination under which he speedily retreated. We were of course quite wrong to behave so, and owed much greater support to the essential administration of the station than our prejudice and youthful intolerance would allow. However, the administrative penguin was typified for us at South Cerney by the Squadron Leader who was to be seen cycling behind cars on the station, checking against his specially fitted speedometer for any breach of the internal speed limit.

Meanwhile, No. 57 Course progressed apace and my first months of instructional experience closed on my twenty-first birthday, an event which I later realised the pressure of work had made it all but impossible to remember. With November began a steady deterioration in the weather, bringing recurring poor visibility, rain and cold. The poor visibility was perhaps the greatest problem, for we were flying in conditions which perpetually verged upon the unsafe, the dividing line being narrow and frequently debatable. This placed a great strain upon the instructor, particularly when flying below cloud, who was called upon not only to teach in conditions devoid of a horizon (an essential point of reference to a pupil) but also to be both continually identifying and tracking the aircraft's position, and keeping a hawk-like search for other aircraft. The collision risk in the limited and crowded airspace below cloud was very great, and the time available for avoiding-action after a sighting, almost negligible.

Inevitably there were occasions when one realised with chill horror that one was lost. This could most easily happen on descending from height and breaking cloud, after some disorientating exercise such as aerobatics; or after inaccurate flying below cloud by a pupil. To be lost in poor visibility without radio created a choice of flying below cloud into possible obstructions such as high ground, aerial masts, balloon barrages or crowded airfield circuits, until an identifiable pin-point was stumbled upon. Or climbing into the clear above cloud, and flying possibly long distance looking for a clearance through which to identify the ground and safely descend. If no such clearing was to be found before the fuel was exhausted, one could either bale out in the hope that the aircraft was not over the sea, or descend through the cloud into totally unknown conditions of cloud-base, visibility and the obstructions that these could mask. Either way it was not very good entertainment, and one could easily think of better things to do.

The longer one was lost the more dangerous the situation became, for while at first there was an approximate position on which to calculate, this would become increasingly vague and soon be lost. Climbing above cloud was usually the last resort, unless there were local obstructions such as mountains and so on – but however lost or apprehensive one might be it was a matter of pride never to disclose this to a pupil if it could be avoided and many a pupil, in the blind trust of those under instruction, must have had no idea of the dire peril in which they had been. To combat this problem, it was necessary to develop a strong sense of direction and locality; learn the ground detail of whole areas by heart; use carefully gridded and marked maps; devise plans of action leading to identifiable 'catchment' features, such as stretches of railway line, hills or river in each point of the compass – and in time come to know the major features of Britain from the air.

There is always more light looking upward into the sky than looking downward at the ground. So it was that in spite of every aid, it could often happen that the visibility would close in to the extent that insufficient detail was visible to identify almost anything from an aircraft. In these circumstances it was possible to fly over large well-known landmarks at low level, and fall to recognise them. Then only one course remained open; somehow to land at the earliest. On just such an occasion I found an R.L.G. (which turned out later to be Bishop's Cleve) and circled it very tightly while studying the landing run, and even then could see little in the mist. It was a superb example of the camouflage artist's work, patterned with the most genuine-looking hedges, painted on the grass. Having weighed this up I began the approach for a precautionary landing, which turned out to be the most desperate such landing that I had ever made, for what I had taken in the mist as a boundary hedge turned out to be a painting very well into the field, and what I had taken as a painting ahead, was a substantial boundary hedge with goodness knows what behind it. This left an incredibly short landing run, and it was too late to overshoot and climb away without losing the field in the mist. I dumped the aircraft onto the ground, braking so hard that the tail came up; knocking off the ignition switches to stop the propellers idling, and thereby use their drag as an air brake. The aircraft came to a halt with the propellers literally in the hedge. I could not have felt more crassly stupid, and turned to my pupil framing an abject apology, only to meet the most admiring gaze that I have ever known – and decided the least said the better!

It was in these conditions that the course reached the Pilot Navigation stage, covering cross-country flights of up to two hours duration, in which if concentration on the pupil's actions was eased for an instant, one ran the risk of becoming lost with all the ensuing difficulties. Later the Gosport Tubes in our aircraft were to be replaced with the TR9D, an outdated radio set which gave electrical inter-com-munication with one's pupil, but precious little else. This in turn was replaced with an efficient VHF (Very High Frequency) set, with which it was possible to use the R.D.F.* system, and to be lost then became a matter of injured pride rather than danger. I always considered myself fortunate to have flown and instructed without radio, for it required an ability which later pilots were never called upon to acquire.

At South Cerney we lived a life contrasting strangely between the dangers, intensity and pressures of flying, and the comparative comfort and security of a pre-war permanent station. The Officers' Mess remained well-ordered and run with traditional discipline which amounted to a calculated refusal to admit that death was literally at the Mess door. As no such standard of Mess life has been seen since, and never will be seen again, it is worth a digression in an attempt to recapture some little of it. At about the time of my arrival, batmen were replaced by batwomen and many of the stewards by stewardesses most carefully chosen

---

* R.D.F. – Radio Direction Finding.

from the W.A.A.F. for this innovation. I was, as a Pilot Officer, not only allotted a large, centrally-heated and modern bed-sitting room to myself, but was also allocated my own batwoman in one Leading Aircraftswoman Heaney. Heaney was a short, not unattractive and extremely correct Scot, who had before the war been a lady's maid. Heaney kept my room, uniform, clothing and belongings in spotless order, ran my bath, turned my bed back, called me with early morning tea and generally saw that I was a properly ordered officer.

Heaney was perfect, and although we rarely communicated, her presence was always evident and for this I was more grateful than she could ever know, as this support was invaluable to me. One strange thing was that when night flying, she would uncharacteristically leave my room exactly as I had left it until I returned. My commanding officer had, with great insight, ordered that after night flying every effort was to be made not to disturb us, and that we were to be served breakfast in bed. This privilege was hugely enjoyed and Heaney would appear to call me, in some magical way always in time for my next duty, and with a beautifully arranged tray of breakfast. She would then start putting my room in order while I surveyed my mail. It was arranged on my tray by Heaney in an invariable order – first any letter in my mother's handwriting, then any letter in a girl's handwriting, followed by other private letters and then at the back business letters and bills – Heaney was indeed perfect.

Meals in the Mess were excellent and of amazing variety and choice, considering the problem of rationing. These were served on gold-lined and blue-monogrammed white china in the large and attractive modern dining room, complete with musicians' gallery, and staffed with W.A.A.F. stewardesses. Breakfast was taken to the accompaniment of the rustle of newspapers laid out in readiness on a sideboard nearby, with collapsible table-top stands. Luncheon was taken to the accompaniment of a string quartet, which seemed always to be playing Strauss's Skaters' Waltz when I arrived, and this music has unfortunately since been irrevocably linked in my mind with soup. Tea was taken in sedate tranquillity, a W.A.A.F. stewardess materialising at one's elbow and softly enquiring, 'Indian or China, sir?' This was immediately followed by an individual pot of tea of one's choice, a rack of toast, dish of butter, plate of sandwiches and so on.

I witnessed a delightful incident one day at just such a tea. A Short Stirling, our latest and largest four-engined heavy bomber, force-landed at South Cerney owing to the dinghy stowed in the mainplane bursting through the upper surface of the wing in flight. The landing was masterly, for South Cerney, a comparatively small grass airfield, was littered with parked aircraft and was the centre of an intense flight pattern in which many of the aircraft were in the hands of inexperienced pupils. The pilot of the Stirling turned out to be a six-foot Sikh officer of the Royal Indian Air Force. The men of this fierce mountain warrior tribe do not cut their hair or beard, but comb and dress it beautifully, looking absolutely magnificent in R.A.F. blue uniforms, with pale blue turbans which were never removed in public. The Sikh stalked into the Mess for tea, seated himself at a table and was immediately attended by a W.A.A.F. waitress who cooed the query, 'Indian or China, sir?' The Sikh slowly turned his head and fixed her with a penetrating stare of ferocious and haughty disbelief – at which point the W.A.A.F. fled into the kitchen, closely followed by fellow stewardesses, and the poor man was left in splendid isolation. After some delay a reluctant chef was pushed into the dining room, carrying a tray on which reposed two pots of tea, both of which he placed in silence before the Sikh, who must have wondered anew at the unfathomable mysteries of the English tea ritual.

There was a curious inconstancy, in that although the Mess was largely staffed with W.A.A.F., the W.A.A.F. officers lived in their own Mess and as far as I can remember did not take their meals with us. In the R.A.F. hierarchy there was amongst the regular and older officers a bitter opposition to the idea of women in the Mess, and this was very strong at South Cerney. The W.A.A.F staff had been admitted as a necessary evil, but there it stopped. As a result, when a smartly uniformed visiting girl pilot of the A.T.A. (Air Transport Auxiliary), who ferried aircraft within the U.K., walked into the dining room for lunch one day, she was promptly escorted to the Ladies' Room followed by her lunch, where she ate in solitary state while our senior officers humphed and hawed in outrage. For a while this Ladies' Room sported a curious notice which read :

Ladies and W.A.A.F. officers are asked to leave the Ladies' Room by 22.00 hrs.

In spite of the W.A.A.F. officers' protests, it was some time before this unfortunate wording was changed, but the ban on all women in the Mess after 22.00 hrs. remained. Ladies could use only this room, and it was here for instance that E.N.S.A. parties were entertained. The initial letters E.N.S.A. stood for the Entertainment National Service Association, but was popularly held to more appropriately stand for 'Every Night Something Awful'. Entertainment given by this organisation varied enormously, but was nevertheless a much-appreciated service. To some extent the quality of the show given varied with the facilities available, and in this respect the permanent R.A.F. stations, with large complements and usually almost professional facilities, scored well. The small Service units in emergency or field accommodation fared less well, but none were neglected by E.N.S.A. which did its best to bring entertainment to all, whatever the conditions. At South Cerney it was customary for E.N.S.A. parties to be entertained after the show alternately by the Sergeants' and Officers' Messes.

Although at this time the Mess was still very well disciplined there was much tomfoolery, and I was taken aback one night on coming down from my room to stumble upon absolute pandemonium in the long ground-floor corridor joining the wings through the hall. A group of senior officers on all fours, each balancing a tankard of beer on his head, was racing pet 'dingbats' down the corridor with outrageous boring and barging! The dingbat figured frequently in R.A.F. slang, but as to the best of my knowledge it was a mythical winged creature attributed with immense speed ('going like a dingbat') the race was uproarious, and the endearments and exhortations to their faithful pets even more so.

Not unreasonably, it was held that in the interests of all the Mess rules were to be strictly observed, and to us some of the senior officers seemed over-zealous in their persecution of erring juniors. Imagine then our delight when an aged Squadron Leader appeared in our midst, who quite unconcernedly broke every rule that suited him, including wearing carpet slippers in the ante-room and spats with his uniform, and no one, not even the Air Vice Marshal commanding the group (who astonishingly addressed the Squadron Leader as Sir) would so much as suggest anything was not in order. This was the renowned R.R. Smith-Barry, who had learned to fly in 1911 and later evolved the first flying training system at Gosport; still determined to be at the forefront of the action and still as eccentric, wilful, daring and outrageous as ever. Such was his standing and seniority that the Air Ministry had given way to his insistent demands, and agreed to a flying 'refresher' course for him at South Cerney. In the Mess I remember him either as the almost perpetual centre of a group of fascinated but uncomfortable-looking senior officers, or wreathed in cigar smoke behind the *Financial Times*.

There was then in the Mess no such 'vulgar or dissolute' thing as a bar. If one required a drink it was ordered through a microphone in the wall of the ante-room and delivered promptly to one's chair by a steward. In later years shortage of staff was to make this impossible, but having once experienced this system I have never taken to the increasing crudity of bars in Officers' Messes. In replacing the batmen and stewards the W.A.A.F. Mess staff had been very carefully selected and trained, not only to combat the ill-disguised opposition to women in the Mess, but because they had anyway to be a success. Many of them were decidedly pretty, which went a long way towards their acceptance; but they had much to overcome including an understandable lack of confidence in the face of two to three hundred officers of all ranks, and the very fact that they were not only continually assessed as batwomen or stewardesses, but also as women. Telephone messages for Mess members were taken by a stewardess in the hall, who had been carefully schooled to then page the officer required by standing inside the ante-room door, calling his name, and should he be present informing him that he was wanted on the telephone. This led to a tall, blue-eyed blonde beauty standing inside the door of a very crowded ante-room one evening, visibly wilting, then with great courage loudly calling, 'Flying Officer – oh, Flying Officer – ' and in overwhelmed desperation, 'Oh dear, I have forgotten his name, but he is wanted on the telephone anyway!'

From the start there had been loudly voiced fears of impropriety, and such was in the circumstances inevitable, but during the early years it was very little in evidence and what undoubtedly occurred was discreet. In later years, with the wider acceptance of women in Messes and rapid decline in Mess standards, it was sadly often most evident and far from discreet. I remember only one incident in my time at South Cerney, and that was when on returning from friends I came into a deserted and darkened Mess at about midnight. The corridors and stairs were at that time lit only by dim blue lamps, to meet the blackout regulations, and as I entered the stairwell I could see another officer, great-coated and wearing an S.D. (Service Dress) cap, climbing the stairs ahead of me. Officers did not wear head-dress in the Mess, and this aroused my interest. Owing to the carpeted floors and stairs, the figure ahead of me was unaware of my presence and we climbed in unison to my destination of the top floor. There it hurried silently down the passage to stop in front of a bedroom door, remove the S.D. cap, shake out a tumble of long blond hair, and then step inside closing the door behind it.

As the year moved to a close there was added to the poor November visibility and heavy rain, difficulties in the rapidly deteriorating surface of the airfield. The grass could not stand the intensive ploughing and pounding that it was getting, particularly in the dispersals where aircraft movement was concentrated. Large areas of the airfield turned to a sea of mud and attempts were made to create a new surface with Somerfeld Tracking, which consisted of coconut matting held down by a heavy-gauge wire mesh, pinned into the ground with metal pins. This did enable flying to continue in a welter of mud and water, but it played havoc with the aircraft tyres; an added contribution to the continual toll of accidents and incidents.

A recurring shortage of instructors led to chronic overwork, but fully committed to our part in the struggle of getting a mighty armed force into the air, we knew the sense of urgency in the tenuous position of the Allies and satisfaction of extended effort to combat it. By day the course had reached the formation flying stage, and the aircraft being still equipped with Gosport Tubes, this complicated exercise was controlled entirely by hand signals from the leader. A hazardous and Heath Robinson system which nonetheless worked, although it was difficult in later days of advanced radio-communication to even imagine such a procedure. At about the same time the course started night flying in which, to limit the number of the staff flying each night, instructors were no longer confined to flying with their own pupils. So I found myself flying with a Polish officer on one of my first night flying flights as an instructor.

The Poles were something of a tight-knit little community within the R.A.F., banded together in their exile and a common inability to come to grips with the English language. Imbued with an intense national pride and pride in their own air force, they just wanted to be given an aircraft with which to fight the Germans – considering any training as a ridiculous and bureaucratic intervention in this obvious task. Abounding in initiative and bravery, it was difficult to keep them in check, and amongst other exploits they took to vying with each other in flying under the Severn Bridge, until one of them miscalculated and went under the Severn too – about which loss they were completely philosophical. The Poles had a twofold interest: women, and the destruction of Germany, and contrary to the indications the second of these was always uppermost in their minds; however, they managed this without in anyway neglecting the first. Taxing around the perimeter track with a Polish officer I realised that he was not attending to what I was telling him, but was fascinated by a W.A.A.F. who was walking nearby. Without shifting his gaze he suddenly stated in admiration: 'What a woman!' Indulgently I agreed with typical British reserve: 'Yes, a nice girl.' 'Nice? Nice?' he said. 'Not nice – bloody marvellous! A goddess! Too good for bed that one – outside in the summer grass.' Which first led me to realise that as a nation not only was our classification of women apparently sadly limited, but our enjoyment of them was, it would seem, equally unimaginative.

The major problem in teaching the Poles was not the language difficulty, although that was bad enough, but that many of them were experienced pilots who had fought the Germans before escaping to England. The least suggestion that they had anything to learn was liable to be considered an insult to their personal ability and their own Air Force. This led to a superb incident when an irate Polish officer, whose pronouncements on flying had met with a diffident reception from his English listeners, burst out in frustration: 'You think I know f—k nothing about flying, when actually I know f—k all!' The truth sadly being that he was unfortunately as ignorant of the technicalities of British flying, as of British slang!

My Polish officer was no exception, and to all my explanations and instruction on night flying he answered with the impatient, 'Yes . . . Yes . . .' that leaves one in the certain knowledge that little or nothing has been understood at all; but with no immediate means of establishing the fact. So it was when we arrived back at the take-off point after my demonstration, for the Pole's first attempt of his course at a night take-off, circuit and landing. We raced down the flarepath in good order and rose neatly off the ground, the twin engines roaring at full throttle. Here, however we remained, for instead of climbing steadily away we flew level with the ground, rapidly gathering speed. My warnings of obstacles with instructions to climb went unheeded; the leading lights, placed well ahead of the flarepath, had already been left behind and yet we remained perilously close to the ground in the black void of a completely horizonless night.

At this point I made a mistake I was never to repeat, for to avoid the implied lack of confidence in taking over the controls, I placed my open palms behind the spectacles of the control column, and applied a gentle back pressure to raise the aircraft nose. We began a shallow climb – and I awaited my pupil's reaction to this forceful hint – but there was none, and if I reduced the pressure on the control column, the nose of the aircraft sank again. We were boring into the sky within reach of the ground, still at full throttle, and somewhat sharply I instructed my pupil to assume climbing conditions – but there was no response. Or at least there was no immediate response, and then without the slightest warning he hauled sharply back on the control column, snatching it away from my open palms, and we shot upward into the night sky almost vertically. Even before I could taken control the engines were labouring, the aircraft was standing on its tail, losing speed rapidly, and falling away to starboard in what amounted to a stall-turn. I had to let it go over in a cartwheel motion, and then keep the nose down in a steep and suicidal dive to the ground, impossibly close in the unbroken dark beneath us, in order to build up enough speed to regain control. Every split second could have been our last, and vividly in my mind was the smoking, wreckage-filled crater to which that split second would reduce us.

We ended up hurtling miraculously, if completely desperately, back down the flarepath in the direction from which we had just come. We roared over an aircraft taking off after us, and an astonished and horrified Airfield Control Pilot (who must have wondered if he was suffering from a hallucination) before we were able to climb away and eventually rejoin the circuit. What had happened was that the Pole had managed well, as long as the flarepath remained in view as a guide, but then had been totally unable to make the vital transfer on take-off from visual indications to instruments. He lost track of his situation and very tardily becoming aware of the proximity of the ground, over-reacted on suddenly realising this danger to such an extent that he was not fully aware of what he had done. My Polish pupil, ignoring the enormity of the event (for we had involuntarily performed an aerobatic from off the ground and in the dark) with the disarming charm of

his breed announced penitently: 'That wasn't no f—king good – yes?' which left
me with a limited choice of answers, and which was probably just as well for I
was so shaken as to be all but speechless. After this we began our night flying
instruction all over again, but thankfully to better effect.

It was during the night flying period that an incident occurred, while we were
flying from Bibury, which I wished in retrospect I had been able to study more
carefully. A strange aircraft entered the circuit and requested permission to land.
To our surprise it turned out to be a Hawker Hurricane, the single-engine eight-gun
fighter. These aircraft were difficult to fly at night owing to the length of engine
obscuring forward vision, and the distraction of the exhaust flames down each
side of the aircraft nose, over which the pilot had to look ahead. The Hurricane
was marshalled into our dispersal, and almost before the engine had stopped the
pilot was out and accosting me as the nearest officer, demanding refuelling. He
was wearing white flying overalls carrying no badges of rank and I, being understandably suspicious, directed him to the Flight Commander's office. This was
apparently far from acceptable and I was told so in no mean manner – I instructed
an airman to fetch the Flight Commander, while our visitor fumed like a sporadically erupting volcano.

He was, we were to learn, Air Vice Marshal Park, Dowding's right-hand support
in the winning of the Battle of Britain. At this particular moment he was flying,
entirely unofficially, after German intruders in the area, and was furious at the
enforced delay of refuelling. We knew that the climax of the Battle of Britain had
been reached on 15th September 1940, and we also knew that in November
Dowding had been relieved of his command, and Park had been sent to Training
Command as Air Officer Commanding No. 23 Group, to which No. 3 F.T.S.
belonged. He was then, at this time, my A.O.C., but in the hurly-burly of the
tremendous training expansion it was not surprising that we had never before seen
him. Park's understandable bitterness caused us considerable unease, and if we
paused to wonder then at the character of the Service to which we were dedicated,
we were to have much greater cause when fuller information became known, and
although this was only to be much later it is included here for continuity.

The glorious victory of the R.A.F. in the Battle of Britain acquired a considerable
inglorious taint when the treatment meted out to the architects of this victory
became known. It was then realised that Dowding had achieved this stupendous
feat against the efforts of the enemy and a considerable opposition to his policies
from the British Government, the R.A.F. hierarchy, and even a number of his
subordinates. Churchill was to comment, 'The foresight of Air Marshal Dowding
in his direction of Fighter Command deserves high praise, but even more remarkable
had been the restraint and exact measurement of formidable stresses which had
reserved a fighter force in the North through all those long weeks of mortal conflict
in the South. We must regard the generalship here shown as an example of genius
in the art of war.' The intrigue which brought about the removal of Dowding and
Park from their Commands as soon as they had won the Battle of Britain later
became common knowledge, but it would seem that in his relations with the R.A.F.
Dowding felt most keenly the brutality, lack of consideration and lack of manners
in his treatment. Dowding was undoubtedly a gentleman, and he had believed not

only his superiors but his subordinates to be the same. It was a nasty story of disloyalty, the distortion of facts, personal ambition and internal intrigue. I was amazed at the ready acceptance by the average R.A.F. officer of this as the usual way of things, and an example of the perpetual state of affairs amongst the senior ranks. This I could not believe or accept and was greatly angered by the oft-quoted maxim, 'As crooked as an Air Vice Marshal', which I felt strongly to be disloyal, scandalous and dangerously destructive. As might be imagined it was not my opinion that prevailed, and throughout my career in the R.A.F. I was to be confronted both by this comment and with the opinion that promotion to Air rank was 'political'.

A rapidly growing confidence in my night flying ability was rudely shattered shortly afterwards in an unfortunate demonstration landing. The first and only Oxford on the station to be fitted with metal airscrews (R6017) had been allocated to 'B' Flight, and it was in this aircraft that I was carrying out most of my flying. The aircraft was new, contained all the latest modifications, and the metal propellers gave it an increased performance. It was in consequence most pleasant to fly. The night in question was one of scattered mist patches in generally very poor visibility, a worrying situation in which it was debatable as to whether the conditions were fit for flying at all. At night it is impossible to see the visibility deteriorating from the air, and if the home flarepath became blotted out the chance, without radio, of finding another in the area was remote. There was as well the hazard of Q sites, which were electrically lit dummy flarepaths situated on waste ground, and designed to mislead raiding German aircraft. These sites had at first been successful in attracting enemy bombs, but in time were to become increasingly ineffective. The dummy flarepath, on broken ground, was operated from an underground shelter by two airmen, who were supposed to warn off friendly aircraft which mistook the site for an airfield. However, perhaps understandably, with an aircraft showing interest in the flarepath they often preferred the security of the shelter and failed to acknowledge the signals of the visitor, however dire its distress. Whatever the circumstances, had one survived a landing on a Q site it is highly unlikely that one would have survived the ensuing ignominy – and so these things were a haunting concern.

I took off with my pupil, exuding an essential confidence which I certainly did not feel, and left the flarepath to make my point that in spite of the popular misgivings about night flying, nothing could be easier. After a brief cruise around, we returned to the flarepath and, I made a masterly demonstration circuit and approach, rounding out beautifully as we neared the flares and holding off for a perfectly judged landing. It was then that I realised the light of the flares had an ethereal, haloed look, which I had never before seen. As this occurred to me the aircraft stalled, not gently onto the ground as it should have done, but into space, and in spite of my immediate recovery action we fell for some twelve to fifteen feet before hitting the ground with a most terrible crash. My pupil was badly shaken, having knocked his head on the side of the cockpit; I had split a tooth, and later the aircraft, after an undercarriage and general check, was found to have two buckled airscrews. I had judged my landing on the refracted image of the line of flares showing on the top of a fifteen-foot layer of mist which had rolled across the airfield in our absence. That we had never been taught about this illusion was simply because the R.A.F. had little or no experience of flying in such conditions and, while it was no consolation, many instructors and pupils were to be caught in the same way, often with far more disastrous results. Accidents continued to occur at a startling rate, and hardly had my Oxford R6017 been fitted with new airscrews than another instructor's pupil crashed in it at night. He stalled on an overshoot by raising the flaps in mistake for the undercarriage; the fuel tanks exploding on impact and the aircraft burning out in a few minutes. When I saw it the next morning, little recognisable was left but the engines and metal airscrews.

The year 1941 was fast drawing to a close, and since the German advance on Moscow in October much had occurred. The government of the U.S.S.R. had transferred to Kubishev, and by the end of the month the first German offensive against Moscow had failed. A second offensive was begun by mid-November, but at the end of November the Russians launched a counter-offensive in the Moscow sector. Meanwhile in mid-November British forces had begun an attack in the Western Desert which was by mid-December to force Rommel into retreat, and at the end of December to bring the reoccupation of Benghazi. At home, on the 9th December, the National Service Bill lowered the age of call-up in Britain to 18½ years, and rendered single women of 20–30 years liable to military service; a measure which brought the war sharply home to all – hitherto however remotely involved.

All of this was suddenly overshadowed by the crippling Japanese air attack on the U.S.A. fleet in Pearl Harbour, made without any sort of warning. The following day, 8th December, Great Britain and the United States of America declared war on Japan. Within two days of this declaration, Japan had sunk the British battle-ships H.M.S. *Prince of Wales* and H.M.S. *Repulse* by aerial attack; proving beyond doubt the vulnerability of such ships, and bringing the era of the battleship to a close. The loss was appalling but was swept aside the next day, 11th December, by the momentous event of the declaration of war on Germany and Italy by the U.S.A. – sixteen months after the outbreak of the war in Europe; for the last six months of which Britain had been facing Germany alone. Britain was however then to suffer an even more bitter defeat at the hands of the Japanese, in the surrender of Hong Kong on Christmas Day.

For us flying ceased early on Christmas Eve and the unaccustomed quiet was impressive, the sky being for once briefly empty of both friend and foe. It had been a lovely winter's day, and I remember as I walked through the fields, in the late afternoon, how sweet the hay smelled in the barns. That night I stumbled upon a Midnight Mass sung in a hangar. There, in a cleared area surrounded by aircraft, was a large gathering including officers and airmen of many nationalities; in all of whose thoughts was uppermost the yearning for peace and home – thoughts poignantly epitomized in the singing of a most beautiful solo Polish tenor voice, echoing wistfully into the vaulted darkness of the hangar roof.

January 1942 brought for me unexpected promotion from Pilot Officer to Acting Flying Officer, only six months after the date of my commission and on account of a much-appreciated privilege achieved for flying instructors – for which we could certainly feel we worked. At much the same time we learned with relief of a new directive, permitting flying instructors to apply for posting to operational flying after completing twelve months of instructional work; until when flying instructors were screened from posting. If a positive sentence to instructing this was also good news, and needless to say I had my application ready for October 1942.

January also brought the onset of bitterly cold conditions, with the addition ofm snow and ice to the hazards of the winter weather. The frost created a rock-hard air-field surface, which while temporarily solving many of the problems of soft ground with which we had been beset, created another, for there was no give in the frozen earth and the aircraft tyres and undercarriages took an increased pounding. The temperatures were often very low with freezing winds, and one's heart went out to the ground crews whose duties were almost entirely outside. How work continued on the aircraft, and particularly engines, night and day during the most appalling weather, it was difficult to understand; it was continued, and carried out to the high standards essential for safe flight. Here indeed responsibility lay heavily upon the individual, for as in the maxim: 'A little neglect may breed mischief . . .for want of a nail, the shoe was lost; for want of a shoe the horse was lost; and for want of a horse the rider was lost . . .' and pilots' lives have been lost on account of so minute an item as a missing split-pin. The rarely failing reliability of the aircraft servicing was a great achievement, for which no appreciation could be adequate, and an achievement only occasionally given due recognition in the successes of aerial warfare. We were fortunate in that on the ground our flying clothing was some protection against the cold, and when airborne the aircraft cabin heating came into play and, at least at the lower altitudes, some sort of warmth could be maintained.

Flying over frost was invigorating, for the cold air usually brought a crisp clear visibility and the countryside lay below icebound and etched sharp, sometimes shadowless in the winter overcast, at others brilliant in the watery sun, and scintillating like cut crystal. The Airspeed Oxford was not fitted with any sort of de-icing equipment, and owing to the aircraft's extreme aerodynamic sensitivity, ice-accretion on the mainplane was deadly dangerous. This type of ice-accretion could build up whenever supercooled water droplets were met in air temperatures below freezing. These might be encountered in cloud or in some levels of precipi-tation such as rain, sleet or snow, and as the ice formed is clear it is difficult to detect, especially at night. Apart from airframe icing, there was too an ever-present possibility of engine icing in both the impact and carburettor varieties. Impact icing led to a gradual blocking of the air intakes, and resulted in partial loss of power. Carburettor icing was far more serious and in an unheated carburettor, such as was fitted to the Oxford's Armstrong Siddeley Cheetah X engines, this icing could cause a gradual loss of power to the point where the aircraft could not remain airborne, and would be forced to the ground.

In spite of these limitations, and the sharp rise in stalling speed with as little as an eighth of an inch of ice on the leading edge of the mainplane, we flew continually in icing conditions, in a desperate attempt to keep course progress near schedule. This was tricky enough by day, but by night it was 'dicing'* in no mean manner.

---

* Dicing – i.e with death

The system introduced was clever, if somewhat ruthless, in that all night flying was limited to circuit work at South Cerney itself, and each aircraft after completing three circuits and landings was taxied into a hangar where electric heaters were placed under the wings to melt off the ice. It was nothing if not exciting, for the most marked characteristic of an Oxford carrying ice on the leading edge was that it simply did not become airborne in time to clear the boundary of the airfield. The next characteristic was that it would suddenly stall way above its normal stalling speed on landing, which too could be disconcerting to say the least of it. For the second and third take-off and landing after de-icing in the hangar, one had one's heart in one's mouth, and could feel the Grim Reaper sitting on the tail. I have to admit that when detailed for this sort of night flying I found it very difficult to leave the brightly lit, centrally-heated, cosy security and familiarity of my room in the Mess.

For all of this, ice was probably the lesser of the twin evils of ice and snow. Falling snow enveloped an aircraft, with very little warning, in an impenetrable mantle of white – horizontal visibility was at once reduced to nothing, and vertical visibility to a matter of about 100 feet restricted to a very small area directly below. These were impossible conditions, and yet to attempt to climb above this weather was courting disaster either from engine and airframe icing, or the unlikelihood of ever getting down again without radio. There was one escape; having entered an area of falling snow the quickest way out was almost certainly to turn on to the reciprocal course (the opposite direction) and once clear, to make for home. The Meteorological Office gave warning of extended snowfalls, and these could be avoided; but the problem was the long periods in which scattered snow showers were possible, and might turn out to be heavy and protracted. To avoid these, flying would have had to be suspended for days on end which was not acceptable in the face of the desperate need for trained aircrew. I had several close calls in conditions of this sort, and of these, one was after a series of exercises with a pupil above the cloud. By ill fortune we descended into a heavy snow shower with no idea of our position within it, its extent, or in what direction it was moving. We were down to 200' without a sight of the ground, and in the knowledge that the Cotswolds rose to 600' and more around us. There we were, drifting into certain disaster, totally isolated from reality by an impenetrable blanket of white, which with a soft hypnotic quality obscured the hard and harsh reality of what lay ahead. The engine boost pressure gauges continued to fluctuate and fall – the chance of climbing being long gone and the chance of holding what little height I had in hand fast going, as the ice choking the carburettors gradually built up and the power fell off. The only remaining possibility, that of breaking out of the snowfall before lack of power forced the aircraft into the ground, was soon almost gone and too much to hope for. So the processes of the familiar life-or-death situation ran their course, and with the last chance gone I could only bow to fate. But had the last chance gone? The white mass below me suddenly thinned and greyed into a whirling vortex of snowflakes, through which I could dimly see a tiny patch of ground, far too small to be identifiable – but then a cluster of snowbound beehives – and immediately it was all gone again in the enveloping opaque white mass of falling snow.

Those beehives were but a tiny item in the infinite detail that made the Gloucestershire countryside, but I who (like Winnie-the-Pooh) had enjoyed a lifelong interest in honey, had earlier noticed the beehives and knew exactly where they were. I also knew the distance and lie of the land between that point and South Cerney. Turning steeply onto course, I timed the run to the vicinity of the airfield, in every minute of which my heart was in my mouth, for so near and yet so far – if obstructions or loss of power had felled me at this stage it would have been hard indeed. Losing height to about tree-top level, there appeared below in the swirling snow the station parade ground, and I swung the aircraft round in a desperately tight approach onto the airfield. I had not dared to lower the undercarriage, for fear that the considerable drag it caused would be too much for the remaining engine power. I knocked the undercarriage down during the hold-off for the landing, and prayed that it would lock down before touching the ground. It did, and I taxied into dispersal wondering for how many more minutes I might have remained airborne, and of the mathematical odds against the momentary let-up in the snowfall revealing anything as distinctive as that tiny cluster of beehives.

However hard we struggled against the frozen grip of the winter weather, flying had to be limited. As a result there were long periods during which we were grounded, and whiling away the hours in our crew rooms amongst a motley of semi-discarded flying kit, awaiting the slightest chance of getting airborne. In the lengthy crew-room discussions of these periods was a rare opportunity of getting to know one's fellows. To realise too something of current thought, feeling, ideas, problems and developments, in all of which was much of deep interest. Of this nothing was of such concern to me as indications of the undermining of discipline and Service legislation, with the purchase of cheap popularity, by many of those in authority; and the deliberate cultivation of what later became known as the cult of the personality. So it was borne in on me by degrees how totally undesirable and extremely dangerous these activities were. Consequently I believed that this growing cult merited every attention, and gave much thought to it. At risk of tedium I have tried to record some of these thoughts, as they were to develop by stages, because these selfsame thoughts were to prove fundamental to my entire service in the R.A.F.

It was necessary to establish what all of us were doing in our lives at that time. Our nation was at war with a most formidable enemy, and by common consent or public decree we were enlisted in one of the nation's armed Services, the Royal Air Force. The task of the armed forces is defined as: 'To destroy the enemy, be it in defence or attack'. It follows that there is no other organisation in which the fulfilment of its task offers certain death to a high number of its members – and at a pittance by the way of inducement. This being so, it is clear that as this task is abnormal and all-demanding, it will require abnormal and all-demanding methods of control, organisation and training. Just how this task can best be achieved has been a subject of constant study. In the fulfilment of the task, valour, which is defined as 'Personal courage, especially as shown in fighting prowess', had proved to be an essential ingredient. Valour can be seen to be either the outcome of intense self-discipline, moral strength and determination in a cause (wherein lies the greatest courage) or more commonly a modicum of these qualities, trained, augmented, nourished and strengthened by a military system designed to use such qualities to achieve victory in the face of all adversity. However, valour alone will not destroy the enemy, and the system must embrace many supporting ingredients, amongst which will be a unity of aim and an appropriate discipline; for to be effective, a community, military or otherwise, must accept 'rules' to ensure that the general conduct of the community contributes to its aim. In a military system this aim has to be clearly and continually defined with the object of maintaining the maximum united effort; but as all armed forces are faced with long periods of inaction between every brief period of action, this essential maintenance and dissemination of the aim is extremely difficult to achieve.

Nowhere else in life is a powerfully motivating spirit of service unity, intelligent discipline and legislation more necessary. In 1939 this motivation was canalised by the Nazi threat to the freedom of the individual, by all standards powerful enough a motivation for the task. I was to discover however that not only was it by no means as general or deep a motivation in my fellows as I had assumed, but the individual extent of such motivation could be highly variable, and was frequently subjugated in some degree to personal benefit or gain.

Of unity, and thereby unity of purpose, for every one hundred individuals there can be one hundred different opinions and one hundred different ways of approaching a task. However gratifying this may seem to the individual, it is a fragmentation of effort which must inevitably result in chaos. The maximum combined effort, essential to a fighting Service if it is to defeat the enemy, requires the greatest unity of purpose, and this can only by achieved in a disciplined organisation. The Nelsons whose genius warrants the turning of a blind eye to an order, can occur but very rarely in the history of a nation. It is unlikely that even the best motivated of inexperienced individuals will be blessed with the infallible intuition that would allow for legislation to be set aside to advantage; let alone those individuals whose motives may well be suspect.

In the R.A.F. at war, many factors contributed to the easy undermining of its basic discipline and legislation. In the first place, flying is fundamentally a sport and when operating from bases far removed from the front line, it was very easy to demilitarise the life, and thereby largely or all but completely lose sight of the aim. Secondly, the unavoidable lack of professionalism in the wartime mass of enlisted civilians gave them common cause to band together in the ignorance of their subject; and to react against all forms of militarism, be it discipline or regulations and so on, largely as an antidote to their inadequacy. This attitude was aided by the enormous dilution of the regular Service, and hence in the lower echelons the large number of over-promoted 'old soldiers', on whom the erstwhile civilians unfortunately based their opinion of the limitations and inadequacies of the professional officer.

The adage that, 'Rules are made for fools, and for the guidance of wise men,' is a profound thought. It was, however, seized upon by the 'extemporisers' who reduced it to a meaningless half-thought by acting on the first observation in this statement; thereby considering themselves qualified to ignore any inconvenient rule or regulation; and ignoring the second and uncomfortably demanding admonition.

Every ignoramus was liable to use this maxim as a licence to disobey to his own ends. There is too, an apparent intellectual superiority to be gained by deriding the establishment, which is after all simply the accepted and established way of doing things in the pursuit of law and order, evolved by experience. The achievement of this pseudo-superiority obviously has, on the one hand, much appeal to those of limited intelligence who can so indulge in an orgy of purely destructive action. On the other hand, it is bound to have a similar appeal to those who benefit illegally from such an action, as it gives them an entirely free advantage over their law-abiding fellows. In 'doing one's own thing', as it later came succinctly to be expressed, common sense dictates that such stolen advantage can only be gained by a minority, for obviously the advantage is at the cost of the majority who contribute to the system, and when there is no longer a majority, the system which provided the advantage is destroyed. The perpetuators of stolen advantage must either be lacking in common sense, or if not, knowingly embarking upon what is criminal behaviour, in engineering the destruction of the constitutionally established system for their own petty advantage.

Any intelligent thought on this subject would bring the realisation that finally the fundamentals of law and order are dependent upon discipline, and when discipline is flouted so is law and order, with its attendant ever-increasing dishonesty and general malpractice. A realisation too that it must not only be nonsense, but ignorant, foolish and downright subversive to suggest that for many, the rules and regulations or legislation of military discipline can, or should be, ignored. Ignored, on the assumption that they are in irrelevant bumbledom, and that when the time comes, in some miraculous way, those involved will so be better fitted to acquit themselves adequately in the strains of war.

At I.T.W. in Newquay, I had been concerned by the band of pseudo-intellectuals who had indulged in 'knocking the system', but they had then been of little significance. Now a disturbing factor in the continual undermining of R.A.F. discipline and legislation, was the widespread encouragement and support (if only by default) that this type of activity received at all levels. There was no noticeable stand made against it, or standards invoked. It boded ill for the R.A.F., and although apparently only local at the time, was amongst the first indications of what was later to become a national malaise.

So I pondered at length on the many indications of what amounted to an unofficial and unauthorised air force, existing within the confines of my Service. There was no escaping the realisation that this was in truth a parasite air force, living within and upon the Air Force proper, to all outward appearances indistinguishable − and yet living largely or completely to its own ends. A parasite air force, the members of which were bound together loosely, but with unfailing cohesion by the obvious and not so obvious ramifications of self-interest. The questions would be what was the extent of this parasitic influence; how large might it be, and how damaging its presence? Who would stand against it, and who would capitulate to his own self-interest by hypocrisy and evasion? If I had ever doubted the wisdom of standing against so insidious a subversion, there was etched in my mind both my uncle's and my guardian's magnificent example; and my guardian's admonition to me as a teenager to 'Serve without fear or favour, as a true English gentleman,' – so deep an insight into the responsibilities and problems of service. Even in my insignificant sphere, I could not fail such men and their selfless integrity.

Plainly evident was the number of officers and N.C.O.s at South Cerney who had no intention whatsoever of getting any closer to the fighting, and many of them did succeed in avoiding it completely. Of these I well remember one officer, who was indulging in considerable dealing in local property then in little demand and at depressed prices. He was later to make a very considerable 'killing' on the property market. However much all of this may have concerned me, it then seemed to have little bearing on the furthering of my own avowed intention, and from this I was determined not to be distracted.

Although the weather was rarely fit for flying instruction, it was possible to get airborne at times to keep one's hand in, and early in January I seized such an opportunity to fly to Ansty, visit my E.F.T.S. instructors and to spend a night with my friends, the Dicks. I took off into a sunlit world of white for the ground was deep in snow, a huge and beautiful scene of absolute perfection, but for the ugly black smear on the edge of Cirencester Wood where a Canadian pupil had spun-in the day before. The tragedy of his death was overborne by the vulgar besmirching of this otherwise unsullied picture, and as I winged my way through the cold clear air I was struck by how very small people look in such a world of white. Little black things – so very earthbound, and seemingly lost in the face of such superb immensity – scared to live and scared to die – yet with gifts of such knowledge and ability, and yet again with a propensity for such ready vulgarity and destruction.

At Ansty, where I had trained as an airman, I now found myself dining in the Officers' Mess with my one-time instructors, who could not have been kinder or more interested in my rapid progress. Although it was only some eight months since I had left No. 9 E.F.T.S. I already found it extremely difficult to appreciate this, having travelled so far in experience. In conversation I heard news of many of my fellows and learned that Woodhouse, the ex-schoolmaster from Babbacombe and Ansty days, was now instructing at Carlisle on the monoplane elementary trainer the Miles Magister. Brockman, also of Babbacombe and Ansty days, was ferrying aircraft in the Middle East. Mortimer, the ex-medical student/bricklayer whose companionship and ornithological knowledge I had so enjoyed at Newquay and Ansty, I was sad to hear had been lost over south-east France. Allan D.C.B., another ex-schoolmaster and perpetrator of an astonishing exhibition of nerve in marching out of a parade at Newquay, whom I had last seen as a fellow student on the Instructors' course at Cranwell, had since been killed with a pupil.

After dinner I was collected by Major Dick, who bore me off to the happy comfort and seclusion of Street Ashton Lodge, where the kindness and attention I received was touching in the extreme. When last thing at night the Major came into my room, on the incongruous pretext of ensuring I was in no need of pipe tobacco, he talked in his light-hearted and extremely entertaining way of many inconsequential things; but his troubled eyes worried me, and I realised something of the agony of a parent whose only child was overseas and at risk. Ian Dick was then in the Middle East theatre of war, flying as a trained navigator, and I hoped that somehow he could be benefitting from some form of the kindness I was experiencing. Of all cruel happenings, he was to be killed in May 1944, a victim of a desert flying accident. While Richard and Dorothy Dick never changed in their quiet, kind attitude to life, their lonely, private, unspoken agony of sorrow was appalling to witness undiminished through the years.

January gave way to February with little let-up in the frost or snow, and the battle to achieve flying time for the pupils continued under great pressure. Meanwhile, in the autumn of 1941, some of the first courses of pilots trained in the United States and also under the Empire Air Training Scheme in Canada arrived back in this country as qualified pilots in the ranks of Sergeant and Pilot Officer. These were composed of such drafts as had left Newquay for overseas training at the end of my I.T.W. course, and it had been felt that they were doubly fortunate in experiencing another country, and receiving training unrestricted by British weather and the limitations of active service conditions. On return to this country they were sent to an S.F.T.S. for a brief refresher training after the disruption of their journey, and at South Cerney a Squadron had been allocated to this work under the title of Advanced Training Squadron. As might be imagined, the staff of this Squadron was far from inspired by the tedious role of acting as safety-pilot to trained pilots carrying out flying practice.

It was a shock to the staff, and no doubt the authorities, to find that in the main the ability of these pilots was so low that many of them would never have qualified in this country. Their shortcomings were surprising and legion, but undoubtedly their major deficiency was that they had never flown in bad visibility or without a horizon, had never flown in bad weather, and were totally incapable of simple pilot navigation in the prevailing poor visibility and the superfluity of ground detail in Great Britain. In addition they had certainly not been inculcated with any sense of determination in the face of difficulty or danger. It was quickly realised that the requirement was not a brief flying refresher course, but a complete retraining in the entire S.F.T.S course from start to finish. With the passing-out in mid-February 1942 of the S.F.T.S. course with which I had been working, partially no doubt to mask the predicament that had arisen, No. 3 F.T.S. was renamed No. 3 (P) A.F.U. (Pilot Advanced Flying Unit) and we continued with the same syllabus as before. There then arose some ridiculous situations, in which we found ourselves suspending from flying training (as incapable of reaching the required standards) qualified pilots who had been made N.C.O.s or commissioned on the strength of their qualification. In terms of wasted effort this situation was appalling, and the authorities must have been in a painfully delicate predicament. Fortunately this was not our concern – but the professional ability of the Royal Canadian Air Force, and particularly our new allies the United States Army Air Force, was very much our concern, and we could only wonder at such shortcomings.

Early in March I found in the Mess letter-rack a note from Bill Sly welcoming me to the Night Flying Flight, which he was then commanding, and to which I had apparently been posted (as he said) 'For a short while'. This obviously contrived happening turned out to be two months of intensive night flying, during which time I was to become something of a specialist in the art, and this was of course the intention of these flights. The night flying syllabus had previously been covered by each instructor flying with his own pupils. As these pupils did not all reach the night flying stage together, it amounted to the instructor flying through the day to six o'clock, snatching a hurried dinner, beginning night flying at eight o'clock and flying through to the next morning. The instructor then slept until lunchtime, flying from lunchtime until six o'clock and so on. Apart from the murderous intensity of this flying, there were comparatively long intervals between the night flying period of each course, in which the instructors could fall out of practice; both of which factors stood to increase rather than decrease the night flying accident rate. The introduction of a Night Flying Flight was a break in the traditional, personal relationship between instructor and pupil, but at the rate at which it was now necessary to train a course, this was an inevitable and progressive step. The new system was that as soon as pupils reached night flying standard, they were handed over to the Night Flying Flight, where both the instructors and pupils then flew only at night.

Although I was to move into a curious, largely nocturnal existence, and to become extremely familiar with night flying, for me it never lost its atmosphere of mystery and restrained excitement. As the evening light waned, there developed that period of tension that always precedes venturing into the unknown. The tension was heightened by the purposeful movement of the ground crews amongst the aircraft, as they completed their final inspections and preparations, which as darkness fell became only partially visible in the swinging beams and dancing bubbles of electric torchlight. Then followed the shouted instructions and spluttering roar of starting engines, reverberating in the cold night silence, with the will-o'-the-wisp blue flicker of engine exhausts as the aircraft were run-up and taxied out. Meanwhile the flarepath lights winked and twinkled in the near distance, a seductive gateway into the night and the void of darkness beyond. There was a strong sense of isolation, of moving in a world from which human life had largely withdrawn and abandoned to the ancient mysteries and forces of the night. Over all an atmosphere of enhanced perception and added awareness that the loss of any of the senses of sight, sound, touch or smell creates – with a feeling of unreality, never completely dispelled as a growing familiarity advanced with the night.

By mid-March the winter was breaking, and with the astonishing reversal of English weather, spring was soon well on its way. I had so far been able to visit on occasions the Rivers sisters and Mrs Nevis, but now that I had the afternoons to myself, I was able to include a number of other friends. On reflection, I realise how very kind and accommodating these friends were with a warm and ever-ready welcome that cannot always have been convenient, as the problems of rationing made hospitality a feat of ingenuity. I realise too what a vital influence they and their homes were in the life that I was living, without which I might so easily have become warped in the ways of war.

Charles and Jeanne Renshaw had, a few years before the outbreak of war, purchased a little Cotswold-stone property in the dream situation of the Duntisbourne Rous valley. It was an old rectory beside a diminutive but complete stone church of great charm, which dated back to Saxon days. They proceeded to invest this group of buildings not only with their affection for each other, but their great love and understanding of the beauty of life and its embodiment in all things natural. There, in a house and garden of much loveliness, they created a considerable self-sufficiency, accommodating a pony and trap in the stone stable – an invaluable counter to petrol rationing. In this I was met in Cirencester and transported through miles of glorious country lanes, to the clip of the pony's hooves and rumble of the trap wheels, in a manner which can have no equal. I best remember the Old Rectory as Jeanne herself once wrote of it to me when I was immersed in the height of the war, knowing how deeply it would stir my heart. 'Coming up the lane one sees the giant elm tree* standing on high ground, keeping guard over the house of many windows and little grey stone church nearby. The iron gate opens, there is a wild rush of spaniels – the door opens, and once more is welcomed a very dear friend.' I have never known a house that so completely embodied English county living, and there was delight in it at every turn. There I spent many a happy day, in a world so divorced from war as to make it seem impossible; enthralled by it all, and no less by Jeanne herself.

Of my parents' generation, Jeanne was a petite woman of great character and charm with an ever-present sense of humour. Never idle, she was possessed of a great and sometimes disconcerting competence. To overcome a stammer she had developed a voluble, fascinating and melodious singing method of speech, the lilting whimsy of which could be entrancing. She approached everything with a refreshing zest and confidence. This included frequently airing a positively atrocious French accent, of which she seemed to be blissfully unconscious, breaking into the most awful Franglais with a breathtaking verve, aplomb, and admiration-seeking winsomeness of the little girl. Charles was very much the ex-cavalry officer, and too gentle and kind to have sought success in the world of finance or commerce; I was very fond of him. Now retired, he busied himself with the work of the property and other country pursuits.

Once, when bidden to join a dinner party at the Old Rectory, I found on arrival that amongst the guests was General Campbell V.C. He was known as the 'Hunting horn V.C.' for an amazing display of bravery in the trench warfare of 1914–18. He had rallied his men in an attack over no-man's land by striding towards the German trenches blowing a hunting horn. The General, now ageing and with failing eyesight, was excellent if somewhat obstreperous company and chatted to me at length. The occasion was most completely and perfectly organised to the last detail by Jeanne, who ordained a conducted tour of the garden before dinner. In this she excelled herself and the party progressed from one carefully pre-selected view, shrub, fruit, vegetable or flower to another, each one revealed by Jeanne in an uninterrupted flood of whimsical joy, for all the world as though we were witnessing the first creation. It was an uninterrupted flood until she stopped in her tracks, apparently struck silent by the General, who blatantly not attending at the back of the entourage, had plucked several spring carrots from the ground, swilled them in an adjacent butt, and was chewing them happily. The silence was short-lived, for the lilting voice asked, 'De-e-a-r General, do-you-love *les petites carottes de printemps?*'

---

* Since lost in the decimation of the English elm by Dutch Elm Disease.

'Why yes, Jeanne, nothing better,' he replied impenitently.

But the gentle punishment for lack of attention was yet to come, for smiling with bland sweetness Jeanne cooed, 'Me-tooo-oo-General, but-I-must-confess-to-preferring-them-less-*piquant*. That-was-the-liquid-manure-tub-you-washed-them-in!'

I particularly remember General Campbell as when later that night he followed me out of the house, ostensibly to see me off, he suddenly expressed his admiration for the R.A.F. and all it was achieving, adding sadly how greatly he wished he was able to be with us. From so distinguished an old soldier this was encouragement indeed, and of the many who were to express such feelings to me during the course of the war, he was the only one who I felt sincerely meant all he had said – and I was much humbled.

I also received the most generous of hospitality in a lovely house standing in a small estate to the west of Cirencester. There I was welcome at any time, which was perhaps unsurprising, as partly through youthful exuberance and partly to thrill Diana, Yolande, Richard and baby Nicola, all of whose company I greatly enjoyed, I used to fly very low over the house by way of a warning that I was planning to make a visit later in the day. On one such occasion the cook fainted, which cannot have eased the household administration.

These delightful children, who were convinced that I lived in my aeroplane – a sort of caravan in the sky – held a deep fascination for me. Perhaps this was partly because of their natural innocence and total ignorance of war, and partly because they were the inheritors of the life so many of my generation were relinquishing in their favour. I remember once on my arrival in the drive, spotting them with their ponies beside a stream below the house. I was struck so strongly by the idyllic remoteness of this scene, that I vaulted the low stone wall, and ran down to arrive before them breathless but exultant.

'Hullo,' said Diana. 'Why have you run all the way from the house?'

'Why, to see you of course,' I replied with avuncular affection.

'Oh,' said Diana. 'You are an idiot,' – and I could only ponder on the unencumbered clarity of a child's mind. If an idiot, I was a very naive one, for it was Yolande, I think, who was forever clamouring to be picked up and, of all things, to be held upside down. Once while obliging Yolande in this way her father laughingly commented, 'Well, I don't suppose that you have ever had a fortune by the heels before?' I was so shaken by this material discovery, that to her great disappointment I don't think I ever swung Yolande upside down again.

Richard, a quiet and thoughtful child, was destined for Eton. I happened to be staying with the family when the housemaster, who it was fervently hoped would accept him, had been invited to lunch. This turned out not only to be a cautionary experience of pride going before a fall, but also of the trying frailty of man's physical nature.

The extensive household preparations for everything to be at its wartime best went ahead in a strained atmosphere of suppressed anxiety. An anxiety which was dispelled only slowly after the arrival of the guest who, if accomplished and charming, was very conscious of his status and role in the upholding of ancient standards. The lunch was perfection, faultlessly served in the superb dining room by the parlourmaid. My hostess, as elegant and lovely as ever, presided over a table of beautiful silver and crystal, and the conversation warmed with the superb food and excellent wines. By the end of lunch the nervous diffidence of strangers out to impress one another was dispelled, all was demonstrably well and the men rose to take coffee in the drawing room. The select furnishings of this room included a number of glass cabinets displaying a collection of exquisite jade. This was my host's particular pride and one was honoured indeed to be invited to the ceremonial opening of these cabinets, with appropriately delicate handling of the antique pieces, accompanied by awe-hushed descriptions and comments. Our learned guest was lost in admiration, and there was no doubt that he was deeply impressed. However, into this hallowed atmosphere there suddenly erupted with horrifying reality, a freak of flatulence so startling as to evoke astonished, if reluctant admiration; roaring and ripping around the room in an outrageous, vulgar and lewd intrusion into so aesthetic a moment. The very jade figures seemed to jump on their heavy glass shelves, and the panes of the elegant glass cases to rattle.

In the brittle silence with followed this remarkably robust performance, it would have been interesting to know what were the innermost thoughts of those two oh-so-imperturbably-English minds. For my host at least, I could imagine his bitter realisation that in the years to come, whenever his son crossed his housemaster's path in the environs of Eton, the housemaster would recall not memories of the elegance of a stone-mullioned Cotswold house, the father's *savoir-faire*, scholarly inclinations and fine collections of superb jade – but only his anal prowess. Although outwardly all remained seemingly unchanged, in that brief moment his reputation lay in splinters on the thick moss-green carpet.

If the friendship and thoughtful consideration that I experienced in this elegant home exceeded my youthful understanding, it was nonetheless deeply appreciated. To this day I remember with particular gratitude the many extreme kindnesses, amongst which were breakfasts in bed, a huge bowl of snowdrops or other woodland flowers in my room, and the fetching from the cellar of cherished bottles of wine to mark my visits.

The first months of 1942 had brought news of a German retreat from Moscow, but otherwise only an unmitigated series of defeats and disasters for the Allies. The German battleships *Gneisnau* and *Scharnhorst* had run unhindered through the English Channel, and this failure of British arms was obvious to the whole nation. In the Middle East, Rommel had launched a new offensive in the Western Desert before which British forces were making the all-too-familiar withdrawal. The Japanese had invaded Malaya and Burma in the Far East, the British forces in Malaya withdrawing to Singapore, only to surrender on 5th April, in one of the greatest disasters in British military history. By mid-April Rangoon had fallen to the Japanese, heralding the conquest of Burma and a British withdrawal to India. The humiliation and frustration of our failures rankled desperately in every British heart. While it was possible for the R.A.F. in the United Kingdom to feel actively engaged in the struggle, the only land battles were far removed from Great Britain in the Middle and Far East; leaving the U.K.-based army seething under a sense of discreditable inactivity in the face of the Allies' most desperate plight.

My older brothers Neville and Allan (who had both visited me at South Cerney in January) had independently volunteered for service in the Far East, where it seemed that the vital action was now centred. In March, my younger brother Gerald had been called up for service with the Royal Navy; Neville came down from Edinburgh with his Regiment to Blandford in Dorset, and Allan, now an officer cadet, was stationed in Sudbury, Suffolk. In mid-April, within a very short time of each other, Neville and Allan were granted immediate overseas leave; prior to embarkation for an unknown destination. They at once telegraphed Gerald and myself, suggesting that we should meet at home where my youngest brother was still living with my mother. I applied forthwith for forty-eight hours leave, and this was agreed on condition that I found somebody to flight-test my aircraft that afternoon, and to undertake my night flying. Having inveigled one of my fellow instructors into carrying out this duty for me, I sped hot-foot for Surrey. The five of us met at home for the last time that we were to be together during the course of the war, and it was a most enjoyable and light-hearted, if brief, reunion. Neville and Allan were later not only to find themselves sailing from the same port in the same convoy, but of all unlikely coincidences in the same troopship, and bound for a destination that turned out to be India. There my brother Allan was commissioned in the Indian Army, and Neville crossed India to join the 5th Indian Division of the XIVth Army. An army that came to be known as the 'forgotten army' during the long campaign fought for the recovery of Burma from the Japanese, in the most appalling of jungle conditions.

My return by rail through London took me to Kemble Junction, where one changed into a delightful one- or two-coach train, whose diminutive tank steam-locomotive pushed or pulled it over the four miles of picturesque single track to the end of the line at Cirencester station. There, if in luck, one found a Service transport for the journey to South Cerney, but if not the only alternative was a three-mile walk. My arrival at South Cerney was not brightened by learning that the instructor who had agreed to flight-test my aircraft and fly for me had been killed during the test. This test was of a standard procedure, and apparently when he put the aircraft into a steep turn to check the limits of bank (before the giro instruments toppled and ceased to register) a loose panel flew off the upper engine cowling and sheared up the wing like a giant woodplane, tearing it to pieces and causing the aircraft to stall and flick into a spin. I realised that I had cheated the Grim Reaper at the cost of a friend, and in spite of the fact that I could never even have guessed at such a happening, could only feel strangely guilty.

Although the instructors of the Night Flying Flight rapidly became something of an elite, gaining considerable familiarity with the night and competence in flying in often difficult and always unnatural circumstances, accidents continued to occur by day and night. In consequence I hope never again to hear the magnificent and plaintive lament of the Dead March in Saul, for almost day after day it resounded from the middle of the camp, at precisely the same hour after lunch, as each funeral cortège left the station. One could visualise all too clearly the lines of airmen on the route, resting on arms reversed, the slow-marching escort; the poor blighter's cap on his coffin, and the solemn music subtly destroying any carefully nurtured imperturbability. Then later at the graveside the fighting

The Accident Prevention organisation became very aware of the importance of flying safely on instruments, and its economic ground simulation in the Link Trainer.

man's farewell from his comrades, in the rifle volleys and Last Post blown by the traditional R.A.F. trumpeters. Afterwards, one's fellows laughing and drinking themselves sick in the Mess, for fear of being unable to forget and being faced with trying to understand it.

Fortunately the majority of accidents were not fatal. We were strangely enheartened when the Chief Instructor, the Wing Commander commanding Flying Wing, experienced an engine failure on take-off and managed to make a very competent forced landing in a nearby field – at least there was no social distinction in the matter! Then there was the pupil who stood-off from the Bibury flarepath, which was temporarily obstructed by an accident. He was instructed to circle the Pundit* at a predetermined height, in order that he should not become lost. On a totally dark night it is difficult to tell whether a light is a few yards or many miles away. This pupil, anxiously watching the beacon as he circled for fear of losing his position, mothlike became half mesmerised and without realising it slowly lost height until, to his complete mystification, he suddenly struck the ground. Incredibly he walked away from a totally wrecked aircraft, explaining with injured innocence that he had been orbiting the Pundit as instructed, but the ground came up and hit him!

In the R.A.F. we were spared the widely separated but sometimes massive losses of land battles, or the similar heavy losses in big ships, which blunted the understanding and feelings. Our losses at South Cerney were light but continual, in which way each loss was likely to be acutely personal, and I never managed to isolate myself from the individuality of these deaths. I can clearly remember being first on the scene of many a crash, and the sense of absolute helplessness in the destruction with which one was faced, for the dying victims were often little more than ghastly, burst and burned bags of shattered and twisted bones. One such pilot began clawing at his chest on my arrival, with what was left of a burned hand, and I had to put my ear almost to his lips to hear his urgent whispers. He was worried about his Post Office Savings Bank book, which had been in his tunic breast pocket. It was all gone; and if I lied, he died happy having apparently no other care than the safety of this book for his wife and child. Another pilot, almost incapable of any movement at all, conveyed to me that he was urgently distressed about something. Fortunately I pieced together his halting, whispered words before anyone else arrived, as he was imploring me to cover his feet, exposed to full view, the shoes on which had a large hole worn through each sole.

In the early summer I was one of a number of us at Bibury toiling through the night, to lift an engine off a badly mauled pupil. He looked absurdly childlike in the blood and floodlight, and in spite of injuries was quite magnificent in his faith that we would rescue him. We had no heavy lifting gear, and were trying for some hours to extemporise something that would do the job, but just failed at each attempt. When a Coles crane at last arrived at dawn from South Cerney we lifted the engine, but the pupil then died. The night's work was over and we flew back

---

* Pundit – an aerial beacon flashing in Morse code, and placed at a safe distance from the airfield in open country.

to South Cerney for breakfast. As we entered the Mess through the east wing door in the early morning sun, my companion halted, cradled in his hand a rose flowering on the climber around the door, and after studying it for some time said: 'You know – it's difficult to understand how these things still grow,' and I knew exactly what was in his heart.

The most remarkable accident at South Cerney must have been that involving one of the medical officers, always affectionately known as 'Doc'. A medical officer was on duty during all night flying, and the one in question often elected to spend the night with us in the Flight, where he was good company and a considerable consolation. In all the hours that he spent in the bustle of night flying, he never flew with us, and amongst others I several times tried to coax him into the air, without success. I was not there the night that Doc suddenly decided to fly for the first time. He was duly briefed and installed in an aircraft, which taxied out for take-off. What went wrong I do not now recall, but the aircraft roared off and becoming airborne failed to climb, ploughing through a married quarter on the edge of the airfield, totally demolishing it and killing the occupants of the aircraft.

This was unbelievable enough, but there was more to the story, for the married quarter was that occupied by the W.A.A.F. officers as their Mess. On the night of the accident there was mercifully, and most unusually, only one W.A.A.F. officer in the house, who was unwell and confined to bed – and yet she escaped unhurt. Her astonishing explanation was that all night aircraft had been taking off and passing just over the roof, as indeed they would – but suddenly she heard one that sounded wrong, and she was convinced that it was going to come through the window. Leaping out of bed in this very short time she jumped from a window opposite, and so undoubtedly saved her life.

I was sorry to leave the Night Flying Flight, after the maximum time of two months allowed on this duty, as I had reached a stage where I could take some considerable pride in my familiarity with the dark and my night flying ability. With the lengthening days a new system of working hours was introduced, in a bid to reduce flying accidents by increasing the quality of instruction as well as the output of trained pilots. This was to decree that no instructor should work for more than an eight-hour period without rest, and usually a sixteen-hour break. With the growing complexity of flying instruction, and the conditions in which for much of the year we were trying to fly, this change was considerably overdue. There were now three working shifts, 06.00–14.00 hours, 14.00–22.00 hours and 22.00–06.00 hours, of which the individual instructor worked only one, and either of the day shifts left much of the day at one's disposal, which was particularly pleasant in the summer months.

On leaving the night flying flight I was posted to 'C' Flight of No. 2 Squadron, commanded by a tall, fair-haired, laconic individual by the name of French. The second-in-command was then O.C. Chave, whose poetry (about which he was very reticent) had captivated me. Early on, perhaps to increase our acquaintance, French, who was fuming about the delivery to the Flight of a quantity of seed potatoes with instructions for planting, lighted on me one sunny afternoon to give him a hand with the job, in what looked like a lull in the hurly-burly of the Flight operation. The idea was due to the wholly misplaced enthusiasm of the Administrative Wing for the national 'Dig for Victory' campaign. If we were able to find time to plant things, we were most unlikely ever to have the time to look after them, and the seed potatoes would have been far better employed elsewhere. However, the Flight having been ordered to grow them, French handed me the bag of potatoes and looked around for something to use as a dibber with which to make holes for planting. Dibbers not being a Service issue, he seized upon a complete small-bore cannon round consisting of live cartridge and shell. With this he led the way to a previously prepared plot in front of the Flight offices. I cannot imagine that French rated his chances of ultimate survival in the war very highly, and neither for that matter did I. As he said, indicating the cannon round, 'I don't suppose that this thing will go off,' but having been a devout coward all my life, I was not so sure – and followed his dibbing activities in a cold sweat and at as great a distance as I could, consistent with placing the seed potatoes in his 'dibber' holes.

The situation was, at least for me, fortunately resolved by a fearful rending, tearing, crashing thud, as two Oxfords (one of which was from C Flight) collided low over the airfield, quite close to the control tower and where we were working. The heavier pieces fell first, to be followed by a prolonged shower of fragments to form a dreadful, widespread, blood-and-oil-spattered litter on the grass. As the last of the fragments fluttered to the ground, French was still on his knees, face upturned, arms held away from his sides, cannon round clutched in one hand, in an unconscious pose of youthful supplication. 'Christ – ' he said, and I was struck most forcibly by how strangely appropriate was the all-embracing nature of this one agonized comment. Those potatoes were never planted.

After unrelieved night work flying by day seemed all too easy, but nonetheless it was a hard task putting the A.F.S. pupils through the syllabus, as one could never be sure of the pupils' actual, rather than supposed ability. Their previous experience did, however, allow one to indulge in the great confidence we were acquiring in the air, both in the Oxford as an aircraft and our ability to fly it. Amongst my accomplishments was a take-off on one engine which I had perfected; completely irregular, but most impressive. Also I would frequently stun my pupils by practising, in cloud, engine failure and the resultant single-engine flying. All unnecessary, and perhaps highly dangerous, but it could be done and I needed to prove this for I was above all aiming to fit myself for the limitless eventualities of fighting in the air. During this period my unsuspecting pupils forfeited a steady stream of beer, on lost bets that I could not achieve the apparently impossible, in taxiing an Oxford backwards.

On other irregularities, I look back somewhat thoughtfully, for to encourage promising pupils who solely lacked confidence, there was a series of carefully contrived circumstances which could be most effective. One of these was to feign total disinterest in what the pupil was doing, especially when landing, by virtually turning one's back on him and the controls, peering intently out of a window. Another was quite illegally not to bother to use one's safety harness; and yet another, to which I resorted on occasions, was to abandon one's seat in flight and stand casually preparing to leave, while the pupil landed the aircraft. All of these actions were in keeping with the policy I assiduously taught, of only taking calculated risks. Many were the turning-points for pupils between success and failure, and success was its own reward. Of course, I could have made a mistake, and for this I might well have paid with my life – but mercifully I didn't.

R. de B. had written to me with the news that Angela, whom I had met in Otham, was working with the M.T.C. at Fieldside House in the village of Blewbury. The M.T.C. (Mechanised Transport Corps) was a small and select body of girl drivers, usually employed in staff-car driving. This I could imagine, but I could not imagine Angela in uniform, however smart, on account of her irrepressible sense of fun. On a number of occasions we arranged to meet in Oxford, or the delightful village of Blewbury, which I achieved by persuading a fellow instructor to fly me to either R.A.F. Kidlington or R.A.F. Harwell. For the return journey I relied on Arthur Woods, ex-South Cerney and now a Squadron Leader in the glider training school housed at Kidlington.

Arthur Woods smiled benignly on my imagined philandering, and several times lent me a Tiger Moth for my return to South Cerney late in the evening. Better than that, he arranged for it to be picked up by his own pilots the next day. There are few supremely high moments in life, as most of them are the contradiction of a vast statistical unlikelihood. When such coincidence of rare circumstances does occur, then one is indeed of the chosen few and transported to the realm of the gods, where time stands still and all is perfection. So it was during those flights in a Tiger Moth, unencumbered by parachute or flying kit, and flying, at tree-top height, over an English summer countryside dappled by the long shadows and golden sunlight of a mellowing evening sun. I was suffused with the beauty spread beneath my wings, the glow of innocent friendship, the joy of unbridled youth, the freedom of flight – and in an ecstasy I sang, roaring unintelligible hymns of triumph, praise and thanksgiving, to the warm buffeting airflow that streamed my hair as I sped godlike for home, at the close of a perfect day.

Back at work, three things occurred rapidly. The first was that the Chief Instructor (the Wing Commander commanding Flying Wing) singled me out for a flying test, and in the days preceding the fateful moment I was in some apprehension of this unsolicited 'honour'. I need not have worried, because throughout the flight he was absolutely charming, and I actually enjoyed it. Afterwards I was left wondering what it was all about, until later awarded an 'Above the Average' assessment as a flying instructor. This came as a pleasant surprise which I found hard to believe and which was to have two direct results. One, a warning that I would shortly be required to fly with the legendary Squadron Leader Smith-Barry as a safety pilot; a euphemism as nobody dared say as an instructor!

Once crippled by an aircraft accident, Smith-Barry was then living in the Mess while incessantly badgering the Air Ministry in an attempt to obtain command of an operational squadron; there being a vague suggestion that he might join a squadron flying the Bristol Blenheim. At his age this was most creditable and in keeping with his aggressive courage, but it could only arouse the gravest of doubts as to the wisdom of the idea. From his home he produced an ancient and battered high-wing cabin monoplane, named *Annabella*. This wreck he happily flew to South Cerney, landed it there to the consternation of all and suggested that it might be overhauled a little. The whole thing was completely irregular but, being Smith-

Barry, *Annabella* was promptly almost completely rebuilt, and the A.O.C. commanding the group offered him the considerable courtesy of a parking space in the hangar housing the Group Communications Flight, at South Cerney.

Smith-Barry's style of flying still had all the abandon and dash for which he was renowned. He would, for instance, take off in *Annabella* in whatever direction suited him, regardless of the mandatory signals displayed, the wind direction, or the stream of pupils taking off and landing. If this was petrifying, even worse were his landings, for he would arrive over the airfield from any direction, execute an aerobatic or two above the control tower, side-slip off height and land straight into the Communications Flight hangar. The A.O.C. having once witnessed such an exhibition, thereafter had all the Communications Flight aircraft picketed out around the hangar, leaving Smith-Barry in sole occupation. Undoubtedly he enjoyed scaring and scandalizing, but this had become a way of life for him, and being fearless and quite unpredictable it was difficult to know if he still retained the skills that had earlier justified such behaviour.

I quailed at the thought of flying with Smith-Barry, the doyen of all instructors, who was with some justification credited with teaching the world to fly through the medium of his brainchild, the famous Gosport system of instruction. I wondered how to conceal my lack of experience, and general inadequacy, from this formidable man. It turned out that he was fascinating to fly with, but perhaps the most exhausting pupil I have ever experienced. This was because the bulk of his flying had been in a period devoid of any theory of flight, and all but the most primitive of instruments, in which aircraft had been flown by the feel of the controls and 'seat of one's pants'. Through these could be detected the onset of the stall from which it was possible, in early aircraft, to recover with barely any loss of height. In the far more advanced aircraft with which we were concerned, and perhaps the Oxford in particular, there could in some conditions be no warning whatsoever of the onset of the stall, and at the best recovery required considerable height. Each approach to the airfield made by Smith-Barry was completely hair-raising, as he was feeling for the stall all the way down, with a total disregard for the airspeed indicator which all lesser mortals used as a guard against this vicious condition. His landings however were then impeccable, and he would say, 'Well, what was wrong with that?' – to which I had no reply other than a silent but mighty sigh of relief. I only flew with him once, for it was finally decided to dissuade him from the idea of operational flying, and this amazing character left South Cerney.

The second direct result of all this was that soon after, I was posted from South Cerney to No. 2 C.F.S. Montrose. The selfsame school at which I had been trained as a flying instructor at Cranwell, now removed to Montrose in Scotland. It was a considerable shock to find myself selected to instruct flying instructors, only eight or nine months after I had myself qualified. Although I could perhaps feel some pride in my contribution to the war effort, I feared that I was becoming deeper enmeshed in the training system, and it was not 'the heaviest possible blow against the enemy that any ordinary man might achieve', on which I was determined. I dreaded that one day I might have to face the inevitable question, a question to which my answer could only seem less than convincing :

'What did you do in the war daddy?'
How did you help us to win?'
'Circuits and bumps and turns, laddie,
And how to get out of a spin!'

SUMMER RAIN

Fall soft, fall sweet,
Come cleanly down,
Smoothe, smoothe away
The tired earth's frown
Who, stirring, smiles
And glad receives
From heaven the balm
Her lover gives.

Wash from my eyes
As from a screen
The ugliness
That they have seen
Of broken men
And twisted steel
And hands that clutched
A burning wheel.

I bare my head
And cool-dropped peace
Runs from my hair
And bathes my face
Until, when done,
The summer rain
Sends me refreshed
To war again.

O.C. Chave

CHAPTER 8

The Bearing of the Torch – Part 2

'Go thou and do likewise'
To hand on the torch – keep knowledge alive
Oxford English Dictionary
The heraldic representation of a flaming torch appears in many R.A.F. Flying
Training School badges as a symbol of the dissemination of learning. That of
No. 2 Flying Instructors School Montrose, bearing in addition the Rose of
Montrose.

During the first two years of the war it was not authoritatively known within
the R.A.F. that a heavy four-engined bomber, capable of carrying a 12,000
lb. bomb load at speeds in excess of 150 m.p.h., was under development. There
were, however, so many rumours and fragments of evidence that it became obvious
this was the case. A specification for such an aircraft had been drawn up in strict
secrecy by late 1936, and from this specification were developed the Short Stirling,
the Handley Page Halifax and the Avro Lancaster. The earliest of these heavy
bombers was the Stirling, which proved disappointing in performance and complexity. The Halifax was initially disappointing in both performance and development problems; but the last on the scene, the Lancaster, was to become the
outstanding heavy bomber of the war. The first Lancasters went into squadron
service amidst much secrecy on Christmas Eve 1941, but by mid-1942 (when I was
posted from South Cerney to Montrose) the existence of these bombers in general,
and the Lancaster in particular, had become widely known within the Service.

These then mighty aircraft were the obvious weapon for realising my avowed
intention. Yet I was barred from operating in them by the rule dictating a minimum
of twelve months duty as a flying instructor, for those so selected. This realisation

was very hard to bear, and I could only console myself with the thought of my release from this obligation in October 1942. It was particularly hard to bear in the knowledge that as I journeyed north on my way to Montrose, I was travelling away from the 'front line', which now lay along the English Channel. Whatever my ordained duty, there was no avoiding the inglorious fact that with my back to the enemy, I was rapidly putting some 300 miles between us; or worse, 500 miles as I was posted direct to the detached flights of No. 2 C.F.S. situated at Dalcross, near Inverness.

The journey by rail from London to Inverness was a tedious and hectic experience in those days when, for economy, trains had been extended to the maximum weight that the engine could pull (sometimes twenty or more coaches, as against a pre-war ten or twelve) and were therefore very slow. In spite of, or perhaps because of, this, these trains were invariably packed, and I was often to stand or sit in the corridor for the entire journey of some eighteen hours. Traffic difficulties and troop and supply movements caused interminable stops and delays, but somehow one managed to accept it, in spite of the repeated failure of the steam heating and very poor, if any, restaurant-car facilities.

That first journey from London to Inverness provided endless time for reflection. Apart from my plight as an instructor screened from operations of any sort, there was the general war situation upon which to ponder, with the ever-present fear that it would develop leaving one completely 'out of it', and surpassed by the experiences and achievements of one's fellows. In the war situation there was little cause for comfort and much for apprehension. At home the steady move towards the conservation of resources had led first to shortages, with the disappearance of many familiar articles, and then to food rationing in 1940, followed by clothes rationing in June 1941. There was now developing the limited production of 'Utility' ranges in such items as clothes, furniture and crockery, all of which were of unaccustomed simplicity and restricted variety. April 1942 had seen the introduction of the National Loaf, using a much coarser and less refined greyish flour, to replace white bread which was not to be seen again until some considerable time after the close of the war. Against the background of continual threat of invasion the Germans began a series of air attacks on open towns and cities in England, which targets being of historical rather than military importance these attacks became known as Baedeker raids. The raids were widely scattered including Bath, Exeter, York and Norwich, causing some heavy damage which served as a reminder of our vulnerability.

Our own attack on Cologne by 1,000 bombers on 30th May was the first of such immensity, and was (unbeknown to us at the time) by way of research into the possibilities of saturation bombing and other aspects of the developing area bombing policy. Up to this time the largest force despatched against a single target by Bomber Command had been 228 aircraft. The direction of 1,000 bombers in a single attack could only be achieved by mobilising all suitable aircraft (including operational training aircraft) within the Command, and calling upon other commands for assistance. The attack was a demonstration of what could be done by a large bomber force, and to this end it was convincing. Over 600 acres of the built-up area of Cologne were completely destroyed, the overall damage and disruption being immense. Four hundred and eighty-six people were killed, 5,027 injured and 59,100 rendered homeless. These details were not known to us at the time, or we might have wondered at the nature of such an attack, for we were still naively imagining that it had been aimed at strictly military objectives.

Overseas Malta was suffering continuous air attack, mounted to cover enemy movements of supplies and reinforcements from Italy to North Africa. All were wondering for just how long this tiny island, vital to our Mediterranean operations, could withstand such an onslaught. In late May, Rommel had resumed the offensive in North Africa with massive tank support, which lead to a steady British withdrawal. Tobruk at long last fell to Rommel and the British retreat continued to El Alamein, endangering Cairo. Meanwhile the German offensive in Russia had been making spectacular gains, and the Allied cause was at so low an ebb that on 1st July a vote of censure on the direction of the war was debated in the House of Commons. In the unfolding, massive scale of the Russian campaign, the might of the German armed forces was becoming increasingly obvious. The public traditionally believed that 'Ivan', the Russian soldier, was a reluctant, ill-disciplined, ill-clothed, ill-equipped and inadequately trained fighting man; and there was ample evidence that our official intelligence was permeated by the same completely uninformed view. The Russians, it was generally thought, could only rely on sheer numbers (and the German's supposed inability to massacre such hordes) for domination. No one then expected the Russians to last long – and there was the uncomfortable realisation that once Russia was conquered, the Germans would return to invade England. With such thoughts passed the journey from London to Inverness.

No. 2 Central Flying School (later to become No. 2 Flying Instructors' School) had been created when the famous C.F.S. at R.A.F. Upavon was called upon to double its output of flying instructors. The new unit was first set up at Cranwell (where I had myself been trained in it as an instructor) and then moved to the Great War airfield of Montrose. There it had again expanded, to the extent that two of its flights were detached to a new airfield at Dalcross, on the Moray Firth just to the east of Inverness. At the time the main unit at Dalcross was an air gunnery school, where potential air gunners were trained on an another obsolete aircraft, the Bouton Paul Defiant.

Immediately after breakfast the next morning, I telephoned the adjutant to report my arrival and ask for instructions. He made an appointment for me to see the O.C. of the Detached Flights, later in the morning. Thoughtfully I climbed into my best uniform, polished myself up and duly reported at the detailed hour. I was apprehensive not only at meeting my C.O. for the first time, but in taking up an appointment as an instructor of flying instructors, at the tender age of twenty-one and with only six hundred flying hours to my credit, of which but half were hours as an instructor. In the face of this it was important, I felt, that I should convey the appropriate impression of reliability, steadiness and mature competence.

I opened the interview with a very smart salute and my C.O., a Squadron Leader, greeted me and talked for some time of my experience and the responsibilities of my new post. As befitted the solemnity of the occasion, I listened with earnest attentiveness. My C.O. too was solemn, but seemed all the time to be preoccupied with something with which he was struggling under the top of his desk. This puzzled me a little, but who was I to understand the burden of cares born by those in authority? Finally my C.O. intimated that the interview was over, and I rose to my feet, again saluted smartly and set out for the door. Barely had I reached it when there was a loud crack from behind me, and something hit the seat of my trousers with a stinging thud. I spun round to find myself looking down the barrel of a Webley air pistol, rock steady in the hand of an impassive C.O. Neither of us said anything, and then deciding discretion to be the better part of valour, I swallowed my dignity and sped through the door. The adjutant's conciliatory comment to think nothing of it, and matter-of-fact assurance that the C.O. was always doing this, did little to restore my injured pride. Such was my introduction to the elite of the flying training world, and so began my work as a C.F.S. instructor. I was to learn that the C.O. was notorious for his activities with the Webley, and as a practical joker was only run a close second by his adjutant, a lively fair-haired and florid Secretarial Officer.

Later, after I had left Dalcross, I returned on a visit and was entertained to lunch in the Mess. There, I noticed my earlier C.O. seated at a table with an escort of another Squadron Leader, and obviously under open arrest pending court martial. Whether it was a propensity for winging Service Policemen, or his un-bounded practical joking that had caught up with him I do not now remember, but my idol had fallen and perhaps I at least was, as a result, older and wiser.

The Moray Firth was a most beautiful place in which to be situated. Dalcross, an almost copybook airfield, was neatly rectangular and as flat as the proverbial billiard table; lying as it did in the narrow strip of plainland between the Firth and the hills. To the south, the Nairnshire hills rose abruptly behind us giving way to the rugged masses of the Monadhliath mountains, the Cairngorms, and the Grampians in the distance. In front of us to the north lay the Firth, across which only four or five miles away was the low-lying hulk of the Black Isle; behind which in turn, lay the great mass of the mountains of Ross and Cromarty. To our west lay Inverness at the head of Loch Ness and the Caledonian Canal; that great gash cleft through some of Scotland's wildest mountain scenery. To the east lay the Firth and open sea. Here, I lost my heart completely and irrevocably to Scotland, which was not so precipitate an action as it might appear, for this scene is adjudged amongst the most perfect in Britain.

Ever since my early youth I had been able to find a degree of relaxation and pure happiness in the solitude of open country, and to this I had been drawn increasingly. During those early days in Surrey I did not know why this should be, but when eleven or twelve years old, in one never-to-be-forgotten moment, there began for me the realisation of beauty. I had been watching rainbow-hued newts in a little stream running through wooded scrubland until, tiring of this, I rolled over onto my back and lay in the sun, head pillowed in my hands. White clouds drifted lazily in a brilliant blue sky; the warm air was laden with summer scents; grasshoppers clicked and rasped above the murmur of the stream, and there rose into the blue a lark trilling its excited, joyous song. Of a sudden, I too was born aloft in a great surge of delight and happiness in the beauty of nature; a beauty too great to be purely physical, and my spirit soared and sang with the lark, in urgent exultation. As this knowledge of life had developed and deepened through the years it had brought with its addicting joy first a sense of wistfulness, and later an increasing loneliness and longing for the completion of this wonder by experiencing it both with, and in another. But who could be trusted with so priceless a knowledge, which perhaps I could not even explain? Certainly nobody that I had yet encountered – and my soul yearned for a companion who would know without words all that was in my heart.

At Dalcross, the beauty of the panorama was breathtaking and was always a wondrous sight. Rarely were the mountains not capped with patches of snow, or brooding under a drifting mantle of clinging cloud; but in bright sunlight these self same hills would assume an incredible Atlantic blue. I never ceased to wonder at this ageless yet ever-changing scene, for every light, every wind and every season presented another aspect of its rugged beauty. I could not absorb enough of it; it was a joy to be going about one's everyday duties in such surroundings. At any opportunity I slipped off alone over the few brief miles into the foothills below the Cairngorms. There, I would look across the Firth into the distant hills of Cromarty and Dornoch and, more remote still, the highlands of Sutherland. Below, lay the narrow coastal plain, the pine woods, the rock-strewn slopes, the tumbling rivulets, the sands and the airfield, laid out like some great demonstration model of a giant landscape.

For the airman, the beauty was fraught with danger and the sudden changes in weather could be murderous. Bad visibility or low cloud is a problem to a pilot, as in it flight must be partially or wholly carried out on instruments. There then comes a point at which it is impossible to know or determine the exact position of the aircraft. Once cut off from the ground reliance has to be placed on dead reckoning, or a mental log of the aircraft's position calculated on a speed and time basis, with corrections for drift caused by wind. This can only be approximate, and the longer such conditions last the more inaccurate it is, as time rapidly increases any error in dead reckoning calculations.

Normally, an aircraft flying blind can fix its position every so often by radio or other navigational aid, but in those days our radio communication was very limited, and navigational aids in Scotland few and far between. Flying in these conditions depended largely on skill and a detailed knowledge of the country. Oddly enough, desolate areas of mountainous country, far from being devoid of ground detail, are so packed with it that even an encyclopedic mind could not possibly identify any isolated item with certainty. High ground is the pilot's greatest danger, and once visibility becomes too bad to see it ahead the only courses are to turn about, or alternatively climb to a height that will clear the highest point within range. There is always the possibility of striking a cloud-obscured slope in the process of such a climb. This however is the lesser problem for once above the cloud, at some time or other (ultimately determined by the exhaustion of the fuel) the aircraft will have to come down again, blind and into the same high ground. There was, for us, always the threat of Ben Nevis at 4,406′ above sea level, and uncomfortably close to base.

Dalcross was virtually hemmed in on every side by mountains, and the weather was capable of playing every trick, from the astonishingly rapid formation of ground mist (Haar) to gale-force winds in the region of 100 m.p.h. In the winter, snow and ice were with us all the time in between bouts of clear but wintry sunshine. In spite of heavy falls on the surrounding hills, I do not remember snow settling to any extent on the coastline around the Moray Firth, and believe it is for this reason that the Black Isle was given its name. We flew at every opportunity whatever the weather, and in conditions which would not normally have been considered safe for such flying. Flying in this way was tough but exhilarating, and was very much a matter of the survival of the fittest. One gained a great deal of experience, usually the hard way, and developed a seventh sense for impending danger. It also easily led to over-confidence, but much more often to rashness springing from the determination not to be beaten – but of such stuff must fighting men be made.

Overall the weather was not often bad, between times the crystal clear air of the Highlands being a delight. Visibility was frequently exceptional and in the summer, when the countryside if not at its most beautiful was at its best, we revelled in long, brilliantly sunny days which though cool compared to the South of England, were warm enough to be most enjoyable. Being so far north the winter days were short indeed, and summer days very long. At certain times of the year it never seemed to get dark at all. In those conditions one could read a newspaper by moonlight and several times I did to prove the point. Once or twice we witnessed the most magnificent display of northern lights (Aurora Borealis) which I found moving beyond belief. These huge curtains of tinted light, hanging in swaying folds above the shadowy purple of the mountain were, in the utter still of the night, a fantastic experience. The silence and awful grandeur of this vast scene, seemed to offer some message more tremendous than can any other moment of beauty, and I knew once again the uplifting surge of elation, and yearning desire to touch and be one with such infinite joy.

We flew very hard at Dalcross, preparing our Tutor and Oxford aircraft (self-same Tutors that I had flown at Cranwell) for flight as soon as it was light enough, and only ceasing day flying when the light failed. Then more often than not, night flying began and usually lasted until dawn. One was not conscious of the days of the week, as we flew on all days alike. Every instructor had one day off in seven, often at short notice, and which might fall on any day. It was a beautiful place in which to fly, and I loved the work. Our students were qualified pilots, which made the flying easier. Our task was to polish their flying and accustom them to the wrong (passenger) seat, as their pupils would occupy the pilot's seat, which is placed in the best vantage point. This change does not sound significant, but is, especially in single-engined aircraft where the instructor sits behind the pupil, and is subjected to a very poor visibility – for one thing, the pupil's head directly obstructs the forward view from the rear cockpit. When controlling the movement of an aircraft in three dimensions, the relative position of the machine to the ground, or horizon, is vital and the development of an instinctive knowledge, or feel, of that position is essential; a position which is different viewed from each seat or cockpit. In addition, we were teaching the principles of instruction in the air, the training methods evolved through experience, and a certain amount of instructional technique. It is interesting that even in those days instructional technique had not progressed far, and certainly had not assumed the prominence that it was later to be given. It was possible at this stage to select the comparatively few pilots who showed a natural ability to instruct. Later, when demand outstripped the supply of natural instructors, it became necessary to train pilots of far less instructional ability, and consequently the teaching of instructional technique assumed a much greater importance.

The work interested me greatly, and I took it all very seriously. One was always learning, and there was great satisfaction to be found in an increasing ability as a pilot and instructor. There were sobering moments, as the occasion when I was in our Nissen-hut crew-room, adjusting my parachute harness between flights. Sitting on the other side of the room watching me was a great favourite of us all, commonly known as Daddy Grout on account of his greying hairs and long service. An ex-N.C.O. of the old school, he was an excellent pilot and instructor, with kindly twinkling eyes and an outsize in moustaches. Grout was watching me, nodding his head in disbelief and smiling. After a while I asked, 'What is the trouble, Grout?' But Daddy Grout only continued to shake his head, smiling. I tried a little more positively with: 'Grout, whatever is the matter?' There was still no reply, and so with a touch of impatience I demanded: 'Come on Grout, out with it, what is the trouble?'

'Just to think of it,' he said, smiling.

'To think of what?' I queried.

'To think that when I started flying, you were only four years old,' mused Grout. To this indisputable fact I had no answer!

One of Daddy Grout's chief pastimes was to practise landing a Tutor in the shortest possible distance. In its time the Tutor had been an advanced aircraft as it was fitted with primitive brakes, an innovation in those days. With a touchdown speed of about forty miles an hour, and brakes, it was possible to land it in a very short distance. The trick with the brakes was to avoid using them so enthusiastically as to tip the aircraft onto its nose. Daddy Grout was always returning to the crew-room with yet another improvement on his last landing run, and in this he was helped by the strong wind that would sweep down on us unexpectedly from the mountains. In landing an aircraft (which whenever possible is effected into wind) every mile per hour of the wind speed reduces the speed of the aircraft relative to the ground; the landing speed of the aircraft remaining constant relative to the air mass through which it is moving. In this way, with a landing speed of 40 m.p.h. into a wind of 35 m.p.h., the speed of the aircraft on touchdown relative to the ground would only be about 5 m.p.h. This at times enable Grout to land in literally a few paces, and in no time he had us all trying to do the same thing.

These high wind speeds enabled us to indulge in a unique practice. Normally, an aircraft after take-off into wind must make a wide circuit of the airfield to position itself for an approach and landing, also into wind. However, in certain circumstances of suitable windspeed it was possible in the Tutor to take off in a very short distance, to throttle back a little, and while perfectly safely airborne to be carried backwards over the airfield the necessary distance to make an extremely short approach and landing. This practice was quite amazing to watch, and gave us a lot of fun. In the same way, it was possible to take off in a few yards, and then throttle back sufficiently to remain airborne but suspended stationary over the airfield. Both of these practices were for the pilot curious sensations, because remaining stationary or flying backwards are almost unheard-of experiences in a conventional aircraft, and are therefore very disturbing. This game, not surprisingly, became known as 'doing a Grout'.

A little thought discloses the ever-possible danger in these high wind speeds. The maximum speed of this diminutive aeroplane lay between 90–100 m.p.h. Should the wind speed exceed this, there was the choice of two alternatives; either to fly backwards over the ground headed into wind, or to fly with the wind at the rather alarming ground speed for such an aircraft of between 150–200 m.p.h., neither of which course was likely to convey the aircraft to an area where a landing would be possible. Remaining airborne until the fuel ran out was no answer either as once the engine stopped the aircraft would be tossed, like a leaf entirely at the mercy of the wind, into the first obstruction. We did not fly when winds of this sort were forecast, but these winds were not altogether predictable. As a result, if such conditions were likely one kept upwind of the airfield so that at least one would be blown down onto it.

The procedure then was that every available officer and man would be mustered on the airfield, where they would be placed in two long lines, forming a wide lane into wind. The pilot would try to make an approach for a landing into the lane, probably at full throttle in order to make any headway at all. There was no hope of a conventional landing, for the windspeed was well above the landing speed of the aircraft, but it was possible (usually after a number of attempts) to fly the aircraft into the lane just above the heads of the men. They would then jump and catch the aircraft in mid-air, dragging it to the ground, at which point the pilot cut the engine. This procedure was very dangerous for the men on the airfield, as the pilot had little control over the aircraft which was being buffeted about by the gale. Jumping in a raging and frozen wind at an airborne aircraft which is bucketing around, and in close proximity to a fast-revolving propeller, is not a thing that one would do by choice. However, airmen and aircrew alike always willingly undertook this duty; not finished once the aircraft was down, for they had to lie on the wings to prevent the wind lifting it off the ground again. Then began the task of pushing it gingerly, tail first, off the airfield and into the safety of a hangar.

In 1942 flying was still something of a sport in which the success of any flight depended almost completely on the knowledge and ability of the pilot. The pilot was captain of his aircraft, and once authorised for a flight all decisions were his; rules and regulations were few, and ground or airborne aids to flying were even fewer. Looking back on those halcyon days, it is now amazing to think that on a July day I could stand outside the Flight Office at Dalcross, and after a study of the sparse weather forecast of the time, look into the sky and decide to ferry an Oxford, due for a maker's overhaul, to Portsmouth.

Preparations were scanty; I was away early and made good progress. Some two-and-a-half hours later I had passed over York on my way south, and was idly looking over my shoulder at the Minster, when the port engine of my aircraft began to surge. An instinctive search of the instruments showed a steadily falling oil pressure, which left only one course of action. To close down the engine, cutting the fuel and ignition switches as quickly as possible, so eliminating the likelihood of seizure, or fire; and concentrating on keeping the aircraft airborne with the minimum loss of height. In the Oxford, with its unfeatherable wooden airscrews, the drag of a dead engine was very great, and created a toss-up as to whether it would be possible to stay airborne on the remaining engine. At the same time, I had to find somewhere to put the aircraft down at the very earliest, and in such conditions the pleasant green English countryside can look remarkably inhospitable. There had been a civil flying club at York, and the club must have operated from some sort of airfield. This I had never seen, let alone landed upon, which did not improve the situation. Somehow I coaxed the aircraft round and back to York, losing height steadily, and was fortunate enough to spot the airfield almost at once – but it lay on the north side of the city, which I would have to cross. At my rate of descent there could be no circuit, or positioned approach; if I made it at all I would have to land straight in.

With full power on one engine only, the thrust is considerably offset from the centre-line of the aircraft, producing a strong turning moment or swing in the direction of the dead engine. The drag of the dead engine greatly increases this tendency to swing, and the physical effort required to counteract it with rudder and bank is very considerable. In the Oxford it means holding one's leg fully extended, with a locked knee joint, against a fearsome pressure on the rudder bar. To hold this it was more than likely that the pilot would have to turn sideways, and jam his back into the bucket seat – altogether uncomfortable to say the least of it. All else being well, the length of time for which anyone could remain airborne in these conditions depended upon how long they could stand the physical strain. Some of this pressure could be trimmed out by operating a low-geared rudder bias, but this took time, was not wholly effective, and left a dangerous opposite loading that would again take time to trim out in the critical moments of the landing, as the live engine was throttled back. Before I managed to coax the aircraft over the airfield boundary, and down, my leg had begun to tremble involuntarily, accompanied by that sickening feeling of tiring muscles that will not answer to what is required of them for very much longer, and are on the verge of collapse.

Once down, I could only cut the live engine and roll to a stop. Still shaking like a leaf, with what I liked to think was physical exertion, I jumped from the aircraft and limped a few stumbling paces. In the relief of survival, I felt much the coolly dexterous pilot shrugging off the longest of odds, and was therefore somewhat taken aback to be met by a very young and enthusiastic Plumber (Engineer Officer) with the fatuous query, 'Is everything alright?' I considered asking him if aircraft usually arrived at York on one engine, weaving in and out of the chimney pots and scraping the boundary fence on the way in – but I thought better of it, and loftily said, 'Yes.' Then experiencing the momentary weakness that so often follows great physical and mental effort, I subsided casually on the mainplane – but glissaded off it again, to fall face forward on the ground and suffer the ignominy of being assisted most shakily to my feet. The entire mainplane behind the engine nacelle was running in a thick black coating of oil from the dead engine – which I had not seen behind me, although the Plumber had been studying it thoughtfully since he had arrived on the scene. In all fairness, I have to admit that he did an excellent job on the engine, carrying out some of the work himself as he was very short-handed; and I was on my way to Portsmouth again by early afternoon.

Ferrying an Oxford was one thing, but ferrying a Tutor long-distance quite another, which is probably why shortly after my arrival I, as a newly arrived junior, found myself detailed to ferry a Tutor from Dalcross to Upavon, on Salisbury Plain, and then to fly back in another Tutor. The open cockpit and low cruising speed of the Tutor decreed a long cold buffeting, in this case some five to six hours. There was too the major consideration of a mountain crossing over the Grampians (on one venerable engine) where an aircraft could disappear and not be found for a long time, if ever – and the Tutor carried no R/T (radio). The absence of R/T, and thereby complete lack of radio aids, meant that the pilot navigation had to be more than good to avoid high ground, danger areas, and other obstructions such as balloon barrages and so on. To assist in this, a complicated navigational calculator (the Course Setting Calculator) was used strapped to one knee, with maps attached to a small board. Refolding or changing these maps within the confines of the cockpit, without losing them in the slipstream, was an exercise in itself. All of this had to be achieved through goggles, and with hands gauntleted against the cold. It was real flying; the last of the near pioneer flying; and I was proud to have been privileged in this way to touch on it in that lonely, cold flight from Dalcross to Upavon and back.

In the afternoon of 25th August 1942 I was ordered into the air to search for a crashed Sunderland aircraft, across the Firth in the Langwell Forest area of Caithness. This, we were informed, was of especial importance and every effort was to be made to find it. However the weather was dreadful, with low cloud lying on the mountains, and even the most desperate of low flying failed to penetrate the area. We suspected that the aircraft was carrying highly secret equipment, or the search would never have been pressed so desperately in such poor conditions. I was again ordered into the air the next morning to continue the search, with no greater success. That afternoon, when off duty and waiting beside the road at the main gate for a bus to Inverness, I was surprised when a convey of the special Daimlers used as royal cars raced past heading north. There was a momentous purposefulness about that convoy, but I did not then connect it with my search. What had occurred was that the Duke of Kent (the King's younger brother) had taken off from Invergordon at about 13.00 hours on 25th August, as a passenger in a Sunderland flying-boat bound for Iceland. The aircraft crashed into the hills in the Langwell Forest area some 30 minutes afterwards, but owing to bad weather the wreckage was only found at about 13.00 hours the next day, some 24 hours later. The only survivor of a crew of ten, and four passengers, was the tail gunner. This grievous loss to the royal family and the nation was the first son of an English sovereign to be killed on active service for more than 500 years. The cause of the Sunderland flying off track and letting down into high ground has remained a mystery.

Dalcross was a wartime hutted camp and consisted largely of Nissen huts of several standard sizes, often cleverly amalgamated. The Officers' Mess was built close to the main gate in this way, lying on one side of the main camp road, and the officers' rooms lying on the other. My batwoman was a vivacious little Scot, whom I can now only remember as Jeannie. On my arrival I found it extremely difficult to understand her, or indeed any of the true Scots, and it was some weeks before I could hold more than the briefest of conversations with them. I found their style of speech quite charming, and have never forgotten my batwoman once hailed by a friend down the corridor with: 'Jeannie – arr'ye awaitin on t'boos – f'rrits awa the noo!'

A magnificent stone fireplace, open on all sides to the fire in the centre, had been build in the middle of the Mess ante-room from the remains of an old cottage. In this we burned tons of sawmill strippings brought down from the surrounding hills. A sad feature of the countryside was the number of forests and timber plantations, marked on our aviation maps, which had completely disappeared in the ravages of wartime economy. The large areas of sawmill scrap strewn over the hillsides were the only sign that they had existed. That roaring wood fire was a great comfort to us in the bitter cold of the approaching winter, and we crowded around it of an evening in the most friendly and happy atmosphere that I have known in an Officers' Mess. The only disadvantage was that a round of drinks was a sizeable proposition, on account of the dimensions of the fireside circle! This most enjoyable atmosphere sprang from what, to us, was the near outpost nature of the station. Inverness, the capital of the Highlands, was then by virtue of its situation something of a remote oasis of a city, with little to offer the visitor by way of entertainment but a romantic fascination and the superb beauty of its setting. I once heard a local defensively explain that there was, 'T'fushing – t'whusky – and t'other thing.' Knowing the Scots, I believe that these were probably the considered priorities. When pressed about the long winter months, the local pointed out that there was always t'whusky and t'other thing!

The Mess housed the officers of the station and Air Gunnery School with those of the detached C.F.S. Flights which it supported. These were widely assorted types, and there were some amazing members of that Mess, pride of place going to the senior W.A.A.F. officer, as the representative of the fair sex. She was a typical married Scotswoman of great propriety who, not altogether unnecessarily, took the care of her charges most seriously. For all of this she was extremely kind, full of quiet fun, and much liked and respected in the Mess.

It truly takes all sorts to make a world, and amongst the W.A.A.F. officers was a very gay and happy girl, who was much spoiled by the R.A.F. officers. I never saw very much of her, or learned anything about her until apparently one night she got her dates muddled, and an officer and a sergeant met in the dead of night in her room. I happened to hear about this because I knew the officer concerned. It was not the complete impropriety of this incident that concerned anyone who learned of it, so much as the apparent social gaffe that was involved. Even more difficult to understand was the flaxen-haired air gunner who, at every opportunity, quite openly dashed off to London on assignments with his men friends, who were obviously very generous to him.

In quite another category was Bregan, an armament officer of the A.G.S., who while talking casually at table would put three twists into the handle of a spoon or fork, which is no mean feat of strength. It was only a matter of time before we had a rather Baroque set of twirly cutlery, but nobody seemed to mind. Another of Bregan's attributes was that of an excellent mimic, and I witnessed an astonishing exhibition of this on my way to breakfast one morning. Bregan was ahead of me, walking from the sleeping quarters to the Mess, and in front of him were two W.A.A.F. officers as deep in conversation as only girls can be. They began to cross the road that separated us from the Mess, when Bregan hooted urgently from behind them. The two girls leapt back off the road with squeals of alarm, and then stood on the kerb in confusion, searching for the car.

There were many contenders for the role of local Lothario, but a fellow instructor of the C.F.S. Detached Flights probably led the field. He was a dapper little mustachioed individual, with all the hallmarks of the commercial traveller. He tried valiantly to inflate this somewhat inadequate image into that of the popular conception of the R.A.F. officer. However, being woefully lacking in material this largely consisted of punctuating his speech at increasingly brief intervals with the exclamation, 'Jolly good show!' Eventually he was exclaiming this believedly essential formula apropos of absolutely nothing, and at every turn, even on opening his flying clothing locker to put his kit away. Of course this unbelievable individual was wide open to perpetual ragging, and this he willingly accepted as proof of his imagined status and popularity. He owned a diminutive and aged seven-horsepower Baby Austin, which he attempted to drive in the manner of the racy and high-powered sports cars associated with pilots of the R.A.F. Once, with this in mind, while he was absent flying we raised the Baby Austin imperceptibly clear of the ground, on four blocks. When, on his return, he leapt in to make a screech start for the Mess, nothing could have looked more farcical than this ridiculous individual, crouched in his ridiculous car, engine racing madly, wheels spinning, but completely immobile – and no doubt murmuring: 'Jolly good show!' On another occasion, we attached a rope to the Austin and hauled it up on top of a large Nissen hut. There we left it, silhouetted strangely against the sky. Its owner spent a long time looking for it before he chanced to look upward, and must have spent even longer getting the car down again.

As is so often the case, this pantomime character was peculiarly successful with the girls. I was travelling with him one day in the canvas-covered back of a truck that served as a crew bus. This ran continually on a large circuit, connecting the main sections of the camp to the airfield dispersals. As we passed the parachute section, a W.A.A.F. left it to walk down the road.

'Look at that little parachute section W.A.A.F., isn't she a smasher?' enthused my companion in the appropriate fruity voice. I glanced at her, and using the current expression of complete disinterest replied, 'Oh – you can have her.' To this he replied somewhat aggrieved, 'I have, actually,' – and I have every reason to believe that he had. I once took a telephone call for him in his absence, which turned out to be from a distraught nurse, the gist of which was that she wanted her panties back. I assumed the shortage of clothing coupons had overcome her modesty – or perhaps she suffered from a shortage of both.

Whether it was his unsuitability for the C.F.S. task, his precarious life of self-deception, or the strain of keeping a wife of lesser days at bay that eventually got the better of him, I don't know. He was abruptly withdrawn from out midst and grounded as a case of flying fatigue, most of which cases never flew again.

Totally different was a fair-haired Scots officer of the C.F.S. Detached Flights. He was remarkable for the lock of hair that stood upright on the back of his head, as it must have done ever since he was a little boy. Wee Mac was a most likeable character and sported a surprising party piece. Surprising because it was not in keeping with his appearance of extreme youthful innocence. He would hang by his toes from a roof truss of our Nissen-hutted bar, and drink a pint of beer in this upside-down position. Anyone who imagines this to be easy should try it.

At the time in question, Wee Mac was due for leave and was becoming rather excited about it. It seemed that a wee girlfriend was coming to stay with him at his parents' home, and he was a wee bit fond of her. Part of his preparations took the form of amassing a dozen fresh eggs, which in days of rationed dried egg substitute were all but worth their weight in gold and would as a gift be a welcome, if somewhat prosaic, expression of affection to anyone. Wee Mac unwisely made the mistake of leaving his box of eggs on the crew-room table, while away on a last flight before his leave began. It was too much for us, we had the eggs out and inscribed on each one a message, 'With love to Wee Mac from Fifi', or 'Lulu', and ten other such variations. They were then carefully replaced. As we had expected, Wee Mac came dashing back, grabbed his eggs and disappeared on leave. To our horror two days later he was back again, in the depths of depression – his friend had thrown him over for another and our guilt and remorse knew no bounds. We tackled him indirectly about the eggs and discovered that he had not presented them to the girl, but had in the end given them to his mother. In a flood of relief we explained the whole plot. Wee Mac was vaguely amused because, he said, this explained his mother's parting words. 'You do seem to have a lot of girlfriends dear – I do hope that they are all *quite nice!*'

Not long afterwards, I heard that Wee Mac was lost over Germany having by then joined a Whitley medium bomber squadron, an aircraft whose performance and shape had earned it the name of the Flying Coffin. I was deeply sorry. Imagine my amazement when some time later on my way down the long Piccadilly (London) Underground escalator, Wee Mac flashed past me in the opposite direction on his way up on the adjacent escalator. 'Mac!' I shouted with wild enthusiasm, and then added happily as the distance widened between us, 'I thought you were dead!'

'I don't think so,' he shouted back, and with this matter-of-fact statement was swept into the jostling crowd at the top of the moving staircase. The wartime throng although inured to most things did, I remember, seem slightly taken aback at this ready topic of conversation between two pilots on a chance encounter. Mac had, I believe, escaped or evaded capture and walked to freedom, but I was never to see or hear of him again.

Eric Cooper, the Detached Flights Navigation Officer, was not a flying instructor but a rare instance of a pilot who had specialised in navigation. He was good company and we spent many hours together, becoming considerable friends. An apparently dry and austere individual, he was in fact most human, intelligent, interesting and the possessor of a great sense of humour. His home was in Chile but he had been educated in England, leaving him with that slightly mysterious personality imparted by an intimate knowledge of a remote country and its language. Eric had soon found the disclosure of his home country to be a continual source of irritation to him, for invariably on mentioning Chile, his interrogator would be struck by an awkward silence, eventually broken by a dawning smile of embarrassed relief and the astonishing statement, 'Oh yes – where the nuts come from.' Of course they don't, but Brazil seemed to be the furthest to which anyone could stretch their imagination. Poor Eric suffered continually in this way, as throughout the war the opening conversational gambit was inevitably; 'Where do you come from?'

Somewhere Eric had acquired what was left of a 1934 250 c.c. B.S.A. motor bicycle, and on this he explored the locality to the extent of a meagre petrol ration. It was a perilous procedure as I have never seen so dilapidated a machine, and riding pillion, as was my lot, was an act of insanity rather than faith. We were once stopped by a policeman on the outskirts of Inverness, who in walking around the machine recounted a string of obvious deficiencies (most of which put it outside the law) and ended with: 'I think you two had better go home!' Nevertheless, we ranged far and wide, even visiting some friends of Eric's at the fairytale-style Aldowrie Castle, beautifully situated on the Southern bank of Loch Ness. There, our bone-shaking arrival in a horrifying clangour seemed vulgarly inappropriate.

Eric was a great thinker, and would frequently withdraw from the hurly-burly of the Mess to the seclusion of his room to read or write. More than once I found him there lying on his bed in deep contemplation, and on each occasion he commented that he knew he would not survive the war. Indeed he did not, and in 1944 was lost over Germany in the night fighter intruder role (flying the de Havilland Mosquito) while based at Little Snoring in Norfolk, up to which time we had kept in close touch.

Amongst any recollections of the members of the Dalcross Mess, it would be impossible to omit the Polish officers. In their marked reluctance to learn anything but basic English, their dedication to the destruction of Germany, their loyalty, and ferocious independence, in some ways they probably found more in common with the Scots than the English. I was certainly astonished to hear one of them, who had married a Scots girl, refer in conversation to 'We Scots'! They were likeable, but an unruly and wilful bunch who contrived after long and secret planning, without authorization, to fly an armed Mustang (single-engined fighter) to Norway and there to shoot up German troops before returning. This was a brave and most creditable feat of airmanship, as the range of the Mustang had been calculated to be inadequate to reach the English coast on return from such a flight.

Looking back, it seems hard to believe that in those days we were still flying in a uniform officially designated as No. 1 Home Dress.[*] This was the expensively tailored airforce-blue barathea officer's tunic and trousers, complete with polished brass buttons and fittings. What was later to become No. 2 Home Dress, an airforce-blue working (battle) dress, had not then been wholly adopted by the R.A.F. Over our No. 1 we had to wear the heavy, one-piece canvas Sidcot of open cockpit flying clothing, or no protection at all. Inevitably, privately purchased cotton

---

[*] Or Service Dress – known as S.D.

overalls appeared and were worn as protection, to which authority sensibly turned a blind eye. This gave scope for limited individuality, and some weird and wonderful rigs were to be seen. For some reason I chose a black cotton overall, and with this used to wear an orange scarf, by which I became well known. What became of this in the end I cannot remember, but first No. 2 Home Dress was made available to us, and later especially designed and fire-resistant airforce-blue overalls.

Although both we, as instructors, and our students were more experienced than most at other flying training schools, this brought no great reduction in the accident rate; perhaps because of the difficult conditions in which we were flying. There were too, the continuing accidents in the A.G.S. of which we could hardly be unaware. I was on one occasion approaching to land behind a Defiant (the Boulton Paul fighter, fitted with a power-operated gun turret behind the cockpit) and saw it stall ahead of me on the turn-in to land, and spin into the ground in a horrible explosion. These aircraft had not proved a lasting success as a fighter, and were used in the A.G.S. for training in air-to-air firing. The turret was very heavy which made the wing loading high, and to avoid a stall the minimum speed on the approach had to be watched most carefully.

To the east of Dalcross, a mile or so inland from the Firth, lay our relief landing ground, Brakla. It was little more than a grass landing strip, set in a remote area of rock-strewn scrub and pine plantations. We used it all the year round, but in the summer weather worked there for several hours at a time; taking one or two students and sending these off from Brakla to complete their solo exercises, while we browsed, or clambered around in the sun. To the west of the landing ground a small river formed the boundary, its shallow sherry-brown waters from the moors and peat bogs above, racing through a bed of tumbled water-washed rock. Standing back from the far bank was a large plantation of spruce and pine; tangled, dark and mysterious.

One bright summer's afternoon I was walking down the side of the R.L.G., thrilled by its remote loveliness, when I heard the roar of an Oxford's engines on take-off suddenly stilled in a prolonged, rending crash. From the other side of the river and in the edge of the pine plantation, a billowing cloud of oily black smoke told its own tale. I began running, but was soon overhauled by the stand-by ambulance which, with a W.A.A.F. driver at the wheel, was bouncing across the airfield. It stopped just long enough for me to scramble aboard, and then lurched on its way again. We were halted by the riverbed, but the R.A.F. medical orderly, myself and the W.A.A.F. driver were out and running almost before the ambulance had come to rest. The wreckage lay on the far side of the river, and was burning fiercely, shrouded in a drifting cloud of black smoke. We could intermittently see the pilot trapped inside, and judging by the screams he was not enjoying it – there was a nauseating smell of burning flesh. The three of us splashed into the river with the medical orderly well in the lead, when the W.A.A.F. driver stumbled and fell at my side. I took no notice until I realised that she was not following and looking over my shoulder saw her lying inert in the racing water. I turned back and grabbing her under the arms, dragged her unceremoniously to the bank, where I left her recovering from a dead faint – in which I would very much have like to have joined. We never did discover what caused that crash.

There was an astonishing sequel to the disappearance one night of an Oxford flown by two students. It was eventually found totally destroyed in a remote pine forest, but curiously fairly close to the sole road in the area. As there had been no distress call or any indication of developing trouble, extensive enquiries were made locally, as well as a minute examination of the wreckage. These enquiries revealed that a young man and his girl had been on the road awaiting the bus at the time of the accident. Questioned about this, they said that they had heard the aircraft over the wood and very close, but could not say whether there was anything unusual about it. Questioned further the girl said that they had seen a red light, then a green light, then a red light, then a green light. These were the port and starboard navigation lights, and quite obviously what they had witnessed was the Oxford spinning in. Pressed for further details, they agreed that there had been the most terrible and prolonged crash. Asked what they then did, the young man said the bus came and they boarded it and left the scene. To the suggestion that their help might have been desperately needed, he made the point that there was only one bus a week to the cinema!

Of all the endless hazards to flying at Dalcross, the weather was undoubtedly the greatest, and I remember well the day in a period of prolonged snow showers that my C.O. sent for me. Why he chose me I never discovered but he wanted, he said, a ten-gallon drum of green paint collected at the earliest from Invergordon. This had apparently been arranged by telephone, and my part in the transaction was simply to fly across at once and bring it back. The visibility was bad, and the weather conditions worse, but Invergordon was only the other side of the Firth, a matter of comparatively few miles by air, although a very long journey by road, and I decided I could do it. For this flight I chose a twin-engined Oxford aircraft, and was into my flying kit, parachute and lifejacket in record time. I got into the air without any trouble, but had considerable difficulty in finding Invergordon, and greater difficulty in landing on its tiny airfield in such bad visibility.

Once there, as I might have expected, no one seemed to know anything about the green paint. I fretted and fumed with one eye on the darkening sky and rapidly increasing snow flurries, while the necessary enquiries were made. At long last the paint arrived; I stowed it hurriedly on board and took off rapidly into the murk. As luck would have it I flew straight into approaching snow, and it was heavy, at once obliterating all downward vision. With the snow came the complete failure of my R/T due either to the blanketing effect of the snow, or heavy icing of the aerial, or more than likely, both. I was again aware of that terrifying sensation of being severed completely from any link with the ground just left, and all life that belonged to it. The snow was soft, silent, all-enveloping, and I was utterly alone in it, with only the roar of the engines for company. My first thought was for just how long I would have this as snow is synonymous with icing conditions, and the Armstrong Siddeley Cheetah X engines of my aircraft had only the most elementary of de-icing equipment. The weak spot was the carburettor throat, where ice and frozen fuel could build up in minutes to choke it, so creating a loss of power, or even stopping the engines.

With this happy thought in mind, I set course in the hope that at Dalcross they would use every possible means of indicating the airfield position to me, before I overflew it and ran into the surrounding mountains. How I would get down at Dalcross was another matter. By this time the snow was matting over the cockpit windows, and freezing there. I tried opening the little clear vision panels which faced forwards, but the blast of icy air was intolerable, and the cockpit filled with driven snow. It was possible to open the side sliding window with difficulty, and although the freezing blast was little less, I could catch glimpses of the mainplane which, as I had guessed, was rapidly collecting a frozen coat of snow on the leading edge. Large chunks of frozen snow were now breaking off the propeller blades and striking the sides of the aircraft with alarming crashes.

An aircraft relies for its lift or support on the smooth flow of air under and over its wings. If the flow is broken it loses much of this lift, and the Oxford was particularly susceptible to the disruption of the airflow over the mainplane – already the aircraft was becoming difficult to fly. One course which had been open to me, that of climbing above the weather, was impossible as there would no longer be sufficient lift. As things were going I would almost certainly soon lose the lift to maintain level flight, and would be forced willy-nilly to the ground. It was a toss-up as to whether I lost the lift or the engines first – perhaps the snowstorm would break.

But it did not, and snow in flight is a different proposition from snow on the ground. By virtue of the forward movement, perhaps at a hundred miles an hour or more, the snow does not fall vertically on the aircraft, but strikes it horizontally as if it was stationary in a blizzard of such a speed. As a result, the individual snowflakes lose their identity and in the cockpit one is conscious only of a brilliantly white, soft, cloying blanket streaking past the perspex panels. While tussling with the aircraft, I had been calculating that for the speed at which I was flying I should by then have been over, or very close to, Dalcross but although I was low there was not the slightest sign of the hoped-for ground or air flares. A minute or two would take me straight into the foothills behind Dalcross, and disaster. At this moment the power began failing on both engines, and one reason was not hard to see. The snow was caking into solid ice on the mesh screens over the air intakes, so preventing the large volume of air required from reaching the engines. The only possible remedy was to edge the twin throttles progressively further open, but this had little effect. With the loss of power and loss of lift from ice-caked wings, the aircraft was beginning to stagger and becoming a real handful – at full throttle it was barely maintaining height. On my present course it was now a question of whether first I struck the hills ahead, or the ground below – and still nothing but the white swirling blanket of snow.

I had to turn, but the question was whether my position was now to the north or south of Dalcross. If I turned to starboard and was north of Dalcross, then I would strike the hills in the region of the Caledonian Canal almost at once. If I turned to port and was south of Dalcross then goodness only knew where I would end up, probably in the North Sea. I could turn about and lose height into what I hoped was the unobstructed Firth, but one would only live for a few minutes in the water at that temperature, and I could never be found in time. I turned starboard into wind.

The snow was spasmodically lightening and for brief moments the visibility increased slightly, but still there was not a glimpse of the ground – and my attention was all but completely absorbed in keeping the aircraft in the air. Without any warning a string of amber lights appeared almost below me – it was a flarepath – and in a flash I knew where I was. To the east of Dalcross lay Brakla, the relief landing ground; there was only one flarepath of that type in that area of Scotland, and I had drifted onto it. It was a line of sodium electric floodlights, used in a new training system of synthetic night flying. This flarepath had, it turned out, been left on by accident; it was not then fully realised that in bad visibility sodium lights of this type had a much increased penetrating power over ordinary lights. Had they been ordinary lights, I very much doubt that I would have seen them, and in the existing conditions I would not even have seen the sodium lights had chance not brought me almost directly over them. I was to the east of Dalcross, as I had hoped, but a few minutes more on my existing heading would have taken me straight into the mountains. The only course was to stagger in as tight a circle as I dared around those lights, so at least holding my position, and this I did for what seemed an interminable period, until the snow slackened into fitful flurries and then finally stopped. In the still, clear air Dalcross was visible ahead of me; I made directly for it and banged the aircraft down from a straight run-in, before the snow could start again.

My experiences in the matter are unlikely to be any different from those of others, for whenever I had known acute fear (which was often) then far more difficult than concealing it from others, was the problem of concealing it from oneself. Immediately after the event this is comparatively easy, as the elation of survival and triumph over apparently hopeless odds goes rapidly to one's head in a surge of relief and exuberance. The great danger lies in looking back on the incident, thinking over the hard facts and dwelling on the obvious possibilities. There is a reaction to that first elation, the onslaught of which is an overwhelming physical and mental weariness beyond description, and with that weariness comes depression. In that depression there is no energy left to fight against reality, and it is on such occasions that one knows just how great a coward one is. The tremendous struggle against logical reflection, the battle not to think at all costs, probably leads to much of the unorthodox life and behaviour of men who live dangerously.

On landing at Dalcross it was easy for me to report smartly to my C.O. in his office, followed by two airmen carrying the priceless drum of green paint. He was thoughtful. 'Did you have a bad trip?' he asked. To that I answered, 'Yes,' but he wasn't listening, he had walked over to the paint drum and was standing looking at it intently. 'My God,' he suddenly said. 'You oaf, I distinctly told you YELLOW PAINT.' I had very little time to reflect on this gross injustice, as during my absence a signal had been received posting me at once to the main body of No. 2 C.F.S., at Montrose, and I had immediately to hurl myself into a flurry of packing and farewells.

My reactions on finding myself posted to Montrose could only be mixed, for I was leaving the close comradeship of a small, detached and somewhat isolated unit. I was too, leaving an airfield in the most beautiful setting from which I had ever flown. At Montrose the airfield was situated in the Lowland coastal belt of Angus and Kincardine, with the North Sea to the east, and to the west the stirring background of the eastern slopes of the Grampian Mountains. If no compensation for the Highland setting of Dalcross, here was the unit proper to which I belonged; a centre of growing awareness in the urgent need to study, develop and standardise the principles of flying instruction, in which I had become deeply interested.

There had been coming together in the Central Flying Schools of the R.A.F. largely by force of circumstance, but no doubt partially by design, a body of experienced and gifted instructors of many nations; and not only from Service aviation, but civil airlines, flying clubs and many other walks of life. These brought a drive, general knowledge and intellect, creating a wholly new approach to the entire far-reaching subject of flying instruction, which had stagnated for so long. From this, to meet the needs of the Empire Air Training Scheme (in which increasing numbers of pilots were training in Canada, Australia, New Zealand, South Africa and Rhodesia) the Empire Central Flying School was conceived and formed, to replace the now outmoded C.F.S. founded in 1912. In the newly formed E.C.F.S., representatives of the air forces of the British Commonwealth of Nations and their allies, formed a conference of experienced instructors in permanent session. In this development, Montrose was re-named – Flying Instructors School – without any change in role, and continued to contribute much, including the development and introduction of psychology in flying instruction. So it was that in 1943 the 'Patter' (AP 1732) at last disappeared, to be replaced by two volumes published by E.C.F.S. (AP 1732A and B) which established in considerable and reasoned detail the principles of teaching flying on the ground and in the air.

R.A.F. Montrose, situated on the estuary of the river South Esk, was an interesting station of Great War vintage, and credited with a ghost of this era in the form of a wandering and apparently disconsolate aviator. For a number of reasons this old airfield could hardly have been less suited to the operation of aircraft of the day. To begin with it was built on sand which caused many difficulties, including the need to fit desert filters to the engine air intakes, which oddity always caused a considerable stir wherever one landed. Sited hard against the north side of the town, and right in the coastal sand dunes, the grass-surfaced airfield was barely large enough for the safe take-off run of the Oxfords, Miles Master II (single engine fighter trainers) and Miles Magisters (elementary trainers) on which we were working. The situation of the airfield was such that in taking-off to the south, the flight path was directly over the town followed by the two-mile square, tidal Montrose basin; and in taking-off to the east, it was directly over the sea. Both of which flight paths would be highly undesirable in the event of an engine failure on take-off.

In spite of these and other difficulties we worked there happily and effectively, enjoying the obvious compensations of the town and sea. Perhaps on account of wartime restrictions, Montrose was something of a dour and humourless town. Typically, I once saw in the window of a stationery shop a card leaning against a booklet of prayers, on which was written, 'Four Minutes with God – 1/6 (15½)' – and felt that surely this was too akin to a telephone trunk-call tariff to have escaped the notice of most! To add to this I found a gem of unconscious humour in a local paper advertisement which read: 'Cottage to let, suitable for married couple, or R.A.F. officer and wife!'

Our choice of hotel in the town was The Star, in the bar of which we often gathered in attempts to ease the frustration of our sentence to non-operational instructional work. This led to the conception and design of an unofficial campaign medal – the Montrose Star, and bar for those on a second instructional tour! It was to have a yellow ribbon, on which would be mounted one silver replica white feather, for each year of instructional work completed. We all but produced and adopted this medal for wear on our overalls, by way of a protest to authority at our fate. Incidentally, perhaps in the same idiom, the D.F.C. (Distinguished Flying Cross) which was awarded in the R.A.F. for gallantry in action in the air, was reputed to actually stand for: 'Dithering with Funk Continually'. The A.F.C. (Air Force Cross) awarded for outstanding achievement in non-operational flying – to stand for: 'Avoiding Fighting Completely'! There was often more than a grain of truth in both of these cynical titles.

We traditionally resorted to the bar of the Star Hotel on our way back from Service funerals. These were held at a cemetery on the outskirts of Montrose which, if I remember aright, was known as Sleepy Hillock; and to this the cortège was piped at a slow march, by the R.A.F. Montrose Pipe Band. There is little so melancholy or wistful as such a lament, and these regular funerals were damnably moving and hard to bear. It is a Service tradition that once the committal is completed and honours and respects paid, the cortège moves off at a spanking pace and to the tune of some well-known quick march, in a return to duty. The officers of the cortège wore black armbands as a sign of mourning, and more than once we outraged the inhabitants of Montrose by repairing to the Star Hotel bar, there to indulge in exaggerated light-hearted drinking, completely forgetful of our black armbands. This was too much for the Scots, whose deep respect for their departed forbears was then even more of a national characteristic than it is now, and they were scandalised.

The full extent of the difference in national character became apparent on Christmas Day, when all shops in Montrose were open as usual, without the slightest trace of the Christmas holiday atmosphere which we take for granted – but a perfectly normal day. On the other hand the New Year festival of Hogmanay was a public holiday celebrated over several days, and with a zeal that outshone any Christmas celebration of which I had ever heard. Needless to say we found no difficulty in adapting, and did very well out of it for we had our own traditional Christmas celebrations, and then went on to Hogmanay!

Memories of the Montrose of wartime days would not be complete without mention of the distillery, as it was always called; the Lochside Brewery on the outskirts of the town. This was memorable for the double hazard that it presented to the aviator, firstly in its towering chimney, and secondly in the regular shipments of its beer by coastal steamer to Newcastle. These shipments had somehow achieved a priority of 'Essential War Production', and were as such protected by a barrage balloon flown from the steamer during its passage. This balloon was supposed to be raised and lowered clear of the Montrose local flying area but the crew, deeply distrustful of all aircraft, were inclined to stick to its doubtful protection for as long as possible, and we were always coming face to face with this incongruous menace.

Inevitably we assume that our elders and betters belong to an outdated era. This assumption can be largely unjustified, but in the case of our Commanding Officer it most certainly was not. While probably not a bad commander, he was a commander of earlier days and had an elegant and leisured style which, if enviable in its confidence and detachment from reality, often left us amazed to the point of stupefaction. A dapper little man, he had seen service in the Royal Flying Corps during the Great War 1914–18, and before its amalgamation into the newly formed R.A.F. in 1920. His command of Montrose was ideal for the continuation of peacetime interests of fly fishing and shooting. Into these sports he threw himself wholeheartedly and was, too, a great protagonist in the formation and administration of the Station Pipe Band, for which a most attractive tartan had been evolved from that of Montrose, on an R.A.F. blue field.

The C.O. was to us a distant individual and difficult to approach officially or unofficially. I for one made many a fruitless visit to the adjutant's office, to leave mollified by his explanation of the inhuman workload under which the C.O. was struggling. However I was less mollified on the occasion that the C.O.'s office door was ajar during the adjutant's impassioned defence of his master, and through the door could be heard the C.O. speaking on the telephone, after the following style:

'What? A Thunder and Lightning (type of salmon fly) in the pool on the bend below the willow? My word, I must try that one afternoon – I haven't got into a fish that size this season.' All of which made the inhuman workload sound little short of enviable! This remoteness from at least his junior officers must have stirred some pang of conscience, or half-forgotten study in leadership, because one evening without any warning he appeared in the Officers' Mess bar in which, unusually, there were only a few of us. The atmosphere was strained, and after lengthy cogitation he turned to the nearest officer (probably because he had little idea of who any of us were) and asked rather unexpectedly, 'Have you ever seen anyone drink a burning gin?'

'Why, no, Sir', said the unsuspecting victim dutifully. There then ensued another uncomfortable silence before the officer realised that he had been singled out for the privilege of buying his C.O. a gin. At length this was placed on the bar counter, and the C.O. producing a box of matches tried to set it afire.

It was becoming increasingly obvious that this demonstration was the C.O.'s party piece of his youth, but with the passage of many years much had changed. The first change being that the inflated price of gin now all but precluded it from a junior officer's budget. The second, that wartime gin proved extremely reluctant to burn. On this account a number of different gins were tried (at the cost of the victim) before one was set alight. The C.O. then took up a type of sword-swallower's stance and holding his head well back, paused for the maximum effect of his act, and then placed the flickering glass to his lips. The third change was that not only was he totally out of practice, but rusty on the method, and we were treated to the astonishing spectacle of his moustache going up in flames. This was good stuff – but even in an attempt to achieve popularity, no man can face the world with the singed remains of a moustache. As one, we leapt to the aid of the

C.O. in beating out the flames. I don't remember his attempting that sort of public relations exercise again.

He did however attempt one major public appearance, which if anything excelled the burning moustache incident, and misfired rather like a damp squib. There was at the time a growing concern on the part of authority, at the increasing flying accident rate. This, then largely unstudied problem, was taking a fearful toll of life, limb and the country's war effort in man-hours and material. All commanding officers of flying units had obviously been exhorted to tackle this problem positively, and our C.O. decided to address us on the subject. In view of our (in the aggregate) extensive knowledge of flying, we assumed that he had some new and valuable information to impart on a subject which much worried us. Flying was brought to a stop early one morning in order to allow for the lengthy process of our assembly. This eventually achieved, to our utter astonishment we were treated to a meandering waffle on the fact that accidents had got to cease. The hit line was enshrined in the statement; 'If, for instance, you are coming in to land and the aircraft stalls – do something about it.' This left us speechless, for the C.O. was obviously thinking of the earliest of aircraft, where so low was the aircraft's weight and landing speed that if a stall occurred on the approach it might have been possible to do something about it. For many years the weight and landing speeds of most aircraft were so high that if any pilot was incompetent enough to make such an elementary mistake as to stall on the approach, the situation was terminal, and there would be little avail in trying to do anything about it, even supposing there had been time for such action.

Our judgement of the C.O. in this incident was harsh, and possible justifiably so, but on the other hand we were unable fully to appreciate the unique experience of his generation, which in a lifetime had seen aviation begin with the first powered flight and advance at a breathtaking rate to a most astonishing complexity, beyond the wildest imaginings of the pioneer.

Our C.F.S. role of standardisation remained, and the unit had the task of monitoring a number of flying training schools in Scotland for instructional ability and efficiency. A team from Montrose would make an annual two-day visit, during which time it would study the selected unit's training organisation, and fly with a number of instructors. These standardisation visits were both hard work and good fun, for human nature being what it is, it was to the hoped-for advantage for the host unit to fête the visiting team. We, as the specialists, were of course regarded by our hosts with considerable awe and apprehension. This was too good an opportunity for our C.O. to miss, for what could be more impressive than that such a team should not only be headed by their C.O. in person, but actually flown in by this Great War veteran of Richthofen days who, it was reliably reported, had then been in aerial combat with Goering – now Reichsmarschall, Commander-in-Chief of the Luftwaffe. We dutifully boarded the twin-engined Avro Anson, a most docile and vice-free aircraft then relegated to the communication flying role, and were flown to R.A.F. 'Q' by our C.O. There, in spite of the patently delaying tactics of 'red carpet' treatment, we managed to get down to work almost at once.

That night, amongst the general festivities in the bar, the two C.O's. were swapping yarns and experiences in a mellowing atmosphere of comradeship and confidences which inevitably touched on the problems of command. Both stations had a W.A.A.F. complement, but R.A.F.'Q' had the longer experience of this new and then somewhat daunting situation. Montrose had only comparatively recently been given a W.A.A.F. establishment, in pursuit of the policy of releasing men for combatant duties wherever they could be replaced by women. 'This dashed pregnancy thing,' said our C.O. anxiously. 'Damnably unfair that it should be held as a black mark against the Station Commander, when he hasn't even had the compensations of responsibility for the situation!'

'Why?' asked his opposite number. 'Have you been landed with this problem on your station?'

'No, not yet, but I dread the inevitable.'

'Good Lord old boy, you don't want to lose any sleep over that – it's no problem at all – absolutely no problem at all,' said his opposite number patronisingly, basking in a superior knowledge.

'How come?' said our C.O., intrigued. 'You obviously *have* encountered this situation?'

'Well, yes and no,' explained his opposite number enigmatically, and then realising the tactical advantage of putting our C.O. in his debt, added in friendly confidence – 'Look, I'll tell you how to handle this one.'

Certainly, as he then explained it, the solution was simplicity itself. It seemed that the key to the problem was to keep in close contact with the station 'Queen Bee' (Officer Commanding W.A.A.F.) and to get her to drop a hint immediately she suspected a pregnancy, and before it was officially diagnosed by the Medical Officer. All the C.O. had then to do was rapidly to set the wheels in motion for the W.A.A.F. involved to be posted to another station, and so maintain an unblemished record. As men of the world and fellow conspirators, in the course of a most convivial evening the two C.O.s laughed themselves into an atmosphere of carefree bravado at this so simple duplicity.

Late the next day we took our farewell, boarded the Anson and with the C.O. ostentatiously at the controls the engines were started. The lengthy warming-up and running-up procedures completed under the admiring eyes of our hosts, the C.O. with an imperious gesture waved the chocks away. To a burst of engine we rolled forward – only to come to a juddering halt in a rending crunch – the aircraft had taxied over an airman's abandoned bicycle – although that was not what the C.O. called it at the time! Before taxiing, a pilot is responsible for ensuring that the area around his aircraft is clear of obstructions. Of all aircraft accidents, there is none held in greater ignomiy than a taxiing accident, for which the pilot is invariably to blame and for which there is no excuse. We, the peers *par excellence* in the art of correct flying, were then involved in the shameful anti-climax of disembarking from our aircraft, while the wheel and undercarriage was freed of wreckage, and inspected for damage.

Back at Montrose the following morning, an unsuspecting Officer Commanding the W.A.A.F. was admitted to the C.O.'s office by the adjutant. 'Bad news I'm afraid, Sir,' she chirruped brightly, with a winning smile to further sweeten the pill. If she had expected a difficult reception as the bearer of ill tidings, she was taken completely aback by the C.O's. ill-disguised, venomous humour.

THE AIRWOMEN, W.A.A.F.

The Aircraftwomen, or A.C.Ws.—generally speaking, the W.A.A.F.—are in great evidence at any Station and lend it considerable charm as well as doing a lot of hard work.

Sometimes they are going busily past on foot, looking very purposeful and efficient and giving random and unexpected salutes to chance R.A.F. officers. For though A.C. Plonk salutes officers because he darn well has to the W.A.A.F. don't have to, except as a matter of courtesy. As a result they are inclined only to salute those officers who resemble favourite film stars, or who have nice eyes, or just seem sad and lonely, or for other feminine reasons—you know what women are. The result, of course, is that the more self-conscious officers often go miles out of their way to avoid meeting an A.C.W., in case she salutes him winsomely; or maternally; or pityingly; or even hopefully.

Or, worse still, in case she doesn't salute him at all, but just goes past with a sniff and a lifted shoulder. This has been known to put a sensitive type wrong with himself for the rest of the day.

RAFF and Antony Armstrong.

'What do you mean 'bad news', woman?'

'Well I don't know quite how to tell you this, Sir, but the Medical Officer has confirmed that one of my girls is pregnant.' The C.O.'s fury was immediate, and exceeded by far anything that the O.C. W.A.A.F. might reasonably have expected – but then she had not taxied over an airman's bicycle. The tirade was only broken by the exasperated question: 'How long has this wretched girl been at Montrose?'

'Well, Sir – that's the strange thing,' faltered the O.C. W.A.A.F. 'She only arrived yesterday.'

'Yesterday? Yesterday?' thundered the C.O. 'Then where did she come from?'

'From R.A.F. 'Q', Sir.'

The extent to which this problem bore heavily on Station Commanders was further demonstrated at a course on the Psychology of Flying Instruction, which I was nominated to attend at R.A.F. Brize Norton in Oxfordshire. This course was a development of the work on the subject carried out by H.D. Wing, one of our medical officers at Montrose, and on which he had circulated three draft lectures in 1942. The war provided a rare opportunity for the study of flying training and teaching in the air, and many unforeseen aspects of this subject became apparent. The need for such study was at last becoming realised, and amongst other courses instituted for flying instructors was the Brize Norton course of fourteen days, on this important and deeply interesting subject. The first morning of this course, we were assembled in the station theatre for the Commanding Officer's introductory address. The build up to this address was considerable, as we undoubtedly felt some sense of moment in the study of so erudite a subject, and anyway the C.O. was late. His eventual arrival was heralded by the appearance of the Station Adjutant and Station Warrant Officer, the last of whom announced in a stentorian bellow: 'Gentlemen, the Station Commander.' Instinctively we rose to our feet as the C.O. appeared, to mount the stage an obviously worried and harassed man. He motioned impatiently to us to sit down, and when the theatre was silent again, addressed us most earnestly. 'Gentlemen,' he said, 'please, please don't f—k the W.A.A.F.' This entreaty delivered, he walked off and we began our studies, equally as intrigued by the C.O.'s plea as by the subject of the course.

The Officers' Mess at Montrose had earlier been destroyed in an air raid, and at the time of my arrival was pleasantly re-established in a requisitioned country house by the name of Rosemount, at Hillside, perhaps three miles from the airfield. As the bedroom accommodation was inadequate, a number of Nissen huts had been erected in a large area of rhododendrons below the house. Although possibly not unusual in Scotland, it was a completely new experience for me to see these shrubs flowering in deep snow; which was more than my Southern upbringing could assimilate, and I never ceased to wonder at it.

Owing to the conditions of active service, few married officers were able to obtain permission to live out with their wives, or wished to so subject them to the strain of the continual losses. As a result the Mess was the home of most of us, and the house gave it much of a family atmosphere. The War Emergency Order, designed to save transport and thereby fuel, zoned many foods to their area of production, and this had the most extraordinary result on the Mess catering. The luxury foods of venison, salmon and lobster appeared on our menu so frequently that some Mess members were moved to enter a request in the complaints book, asking for a change!

I have never known such cold as that we experienced in the winter at Montrose, and the east wind in particular could be murderous. My room was in the Nissen huts, alongside that of a fellow instructor, Dusty Miller. The huts and primitive ablution by which they were served were in no way proof against the penetrating cold. Our rooms were heated by little coke-fired iron stoves which either burned at maximum intensity, or not at all. As the coke ration was strictly limited, Dusty and I reached an arrangement which was something of a *'marriage de convenance'*, by pooling our resources. At the time we were both spending many evenings studying for our instructors' re-categorisation from A2 to A1, which involved an examination in instructional flying, and allied ground subjects. What we did was to run one stove flat out on our joint fuel, and in the resulting tropical atmosphere, tested each other, or occasionally played cards. Meanwhile there was heating on the stove a mess tin of whisky, for mixing with ginger wine, which 'Whisky Mac' we assured each other was essential to ward off the cold and to aid study! Dusty was a good friend, and we had considerable fun together. For instance during the continual impromptu or organised parties in the Mess, we used to leave together at intervals to fire my 22" rifle, in turn, at the weather-cock above the stable clock; when we could hit it no longer we judged it time for bed! Dusty lost consciousness in a prolonged and completely unexpected blackout one morning in that wretched ablution; a victim of flying and instructional fatigue, he was never to fly again.

The Mess was the scene of almost ceaseless parties, undoubtedly chiefly on account of the fitful attendance of the Grim Reaper. I well remember the crowded ante-room one lunch time when a W.A.A.F. stewardess stood in the door and called: 'Pilot Officer James?' There was an instant complete silence, in which she again called: 'Pilot Officer James, please.' A voice from the back called, 'He's dead, you fool.' The stewardess about-turned, went back into the hall and in the continuing silence could clearly be heard to say blandly over the telephone, 'I am afraid he's dead!'

Much as in Coleridge's Ancient Mariner, we turned our backs, for –

> . . . Like one that on a lonesome road
> Doth walk in fear and dread,
> And having once turn'd round, walks on
> And turns no more his head:
> Because he knows a frightful fiend
> Doth close behind him tread . . .

It was at a Mess dance that I was inveigled into leaving the ballroom by one of the W.A.A.F. officers; a lonely, little, almost spherical creature, with hair piled in profusion on the top of her head in a naive attempt to make good her missing inches. There was little evidence of brain in that head, but she was a very good-hearted girl and we all went out of our way for her. Outside the south front of the Mess it was cold, very cold and clear. With the undiminished sounds of virile revelry behind us, the silvery quiet of the moonlit Angus countryside had all the romantic mystery that one could wish. Here at last, for a few brief moments, there was no ceaseless strain, tension, no horror and no war – we could know something of what it would be, to be young in a world of peace. We walked arm in arm in a silence sharpened and intensified by the cold dark air. In a sudden confidence she said hesitantly, 'I heard about my fiancé today,' and then in a whisper after a long silence: 'His tank was hit and set on fire, and he was killed climbing out of the turret.'

'My God,' I said, 'that must have shaken him,' and directing her firmly towards the front door, we passed in again and I laughingly projected her back into the anonymity of the throng. Over a succession of whiskies, I considered how perfectly I had qualified for the ranks of the unspeakable – I had wanted to be kind, but the fear to which we all closed our minds had produced the carefully schooled reflex action of a complete nonchalance; but again, least of all had I fooled myself. I – the brave one – had turned tail and fled from a gentle lonely agony. I at least, could know what sort of coward I was.

The highly charged atmosphere led to many outbursts of horseplay in the Mess. Of these I particularly remember two. The first was when one of my fellow instructors in executing his party piece, an excruciatingly funny (if unprintable) song and dance routine, on the top of the bar, fell off and broke an ankle. This was duly encased in plaster and he was equipped with crutches, on which he very inexpertly hobbled around. As this made him quite useless to anyone, he was despatched home on sick leave, and joined the next London train at Montrose. Hobbling down the corridor in the hopeless search for a seat, a compartment door opened and a dear old lady, at least as unsteady on her feet as was he, grabbed him and insisted that this poor dear wounded boy should take her seat. In spite of his most violent protestations, she eventually had every passenger in the compartment assisting our wounded hero into her place – to his undying misery and embarrassment!

The most incredible outburst was one Christmas Day. Without any warning two factions appeared, one proclaiming its title of 'The up or offs', and the other, 'The down or outs'; the first party insisting that you rolled your trousers up above the knee, or had the garment forcibly removed. The second insisting that you wore them normally, or were thrown out of the nearest window. The battle raged furiously for hours throughout the entire ground floor of the Mess, and the Wing Commander C.F.I. (Chief Flying Instructor) who walked unsuspectingly into the middle of it, promptly had his trousers removed! Hostilities only ceased when the two factions were completely exhausted by the violent activity.

The selfsame C.F.I., an ex-airline pilot, was a man of considerable presence and ability. In her own sphere his wife was much the same, and therefore seemed somewhat formidable. Actually they were both charming, and did much to lighten the inevitable loneliness of the single and unaccompanied officers of the Wing. At one stage they arranged a games evening for us in their house, and this was a great success. As the evening wore on, and the conventional time for taking leave of one's host and hostess approached, we finished our various games and assembled near to the door. There remained only a Polish officer, deeply involved in a game of cards with the Wing Commander's wife. We politely coughed to draw his attention, and failing in this loudly exclaimed: 'What a shame, we must be off now,' all to no avail. Finally, in desperation we all but bellowed: 'WHAT A PITY – WE MUST GO NOW,' This massive hint penetrated, and the Pole laying down his cards reluctantly, stood up, clicked his heels and bowing graciously to his hostess announced, 'I am very sorry Mrs. — , but I must f—k off too now!'

Mrs. — the perfect hostess, only blinked, and we were left with the well-nigh impossible task of later explaining to our Polish brother, that while we had always used this expression in his presence – it was one that was never used!

In addition to flying we had a number of duties, one being that of Station Duty Officer in which we represented the C.O. at night. Our Mess, Rosemount at Hillside, was about three miles from the airfield. The Duty Officer was allowed to sleep in the Mess, and whenever his presence was necessary on the airfield, he was warned by telephone and a vehicle was sent to collect him. On one occasion when I was Duty Officer, I was awakened well after midnight with the warning that a priority signal in cipher had been received. This entailed the S.D.O. going down to the airfield, arranging for deciphering, and then acting on the resulting instructions, or information. While I was dressing, I gave orders for the duty W.A.A.F. Cipher Officer, who was one of a group of W.A.A.F. officers on the station, to be called and informed that transport would be ready in a few minutes. This was done, but it seemed an extraordinarily long time before she appeared, which time I spent kicking my heels in the hall, for warmth. Imagine my chagrin when a very pretty and beautifully turned-out W.A.A.F. officer wafted down the stairs looking fixedly ahead through sleepy eyes, ignored me completely, and swept through the door to clamber into the back seat of the little canvas-covered Tilt that had been sent to collect us. Brusquely taking my place in front of her and beside the driver, we moved off into the cloying dark of the blackout. I was wearing a Service Dress (flat-topped) cap, and we had not been driving for many minutes when to my utter astonishment it was stealthily pushed over my eyes. Indignantly I righted it, but before very long it was over my eyes again, and once more I firmly straightened it – to no avail however, because it was soon gently being pushed forward to cover my eyes yet again.

There I left it momentarily, and equal to the occasion slipped my arms behind me around either side of the bucket seat; felt very gently for the W.A.A.F. officer's shoes; with great care located the ends of each shoelace, and tied her shoes together. This, I felt, would very satisfactorily put her in her place as soon as we arrived and she tried to get out. After settling my hat in its proper position, I was still thinking that she just did not look even remotely the type to play games with a complete stranger, when we turned into the airfield at the Guardroom. Once through the identity check, we headed for the cipher office and – again my cap was tilted slowly over my eyes. This time in some irritation I clapped my hand to my head, and struck at the same moment a rod, or possibly bolt about three inches long, which was sticking out of a rib supporting the canvas side of the van, at exactly the level of my cap. At once I realised that this had been lodging under the flat top of my cap, and the natural sway as we drove had repeatedly pushed my cap forward. We were by then drawing up outside the cipher office, and I was rapidly considering how on earth I could turn to this W.A.A.F., introduce myself and (as far as she was concerned) out of the blue announce: 'Don't get out, I have tied your shoes together,' without her calling for help. She got up, subsided again with an unhappy yelp and exclaimed: 'Whatever have you been doing to my feet?' That did it, I could feel the driver recoiling from the lecherous officer with the surprising kink, and savouring the good value of this 'turn up' in the barrack room. I took the easiest course and metaphorically fled, although in fact I believe I stalked stonily into the cipher room, leaving a damsel in considerable distress.

Eventually disentangled, she arrived in her office and without a word began the complicated mystique of deciphering the offending signal. I sat in a steadily deepening agony of embarrassment, but even at the age of twenty-two I knew only too well the dangers of embarking on far-fetched explanations. They not only have a tendency increasingly to exceed the bounds of credulity, but also rapidly to infer complete imbecility in both the perpetrator of the explanation and the unfortunate recipient, who thus in no time could feel twice 'taken for a ride'. No, that would never do, and in a flurry of panic to my surprise I blurted: 'When did you arrive?' She raised two twinkling eyes as she sweetly said: 'Yesterday.' It could not have been worse, and I had plenty of time to reflect on the situation. It explained her aloof appearance, as it was a lonely and difficult enough an experience for a man to weather those first days of establishing himself in a strange Mess on a strange station; but many times more difficult for one of a comparatively small group of girls in a predominantly male preserve. I was left feeling a prize and extremely obnoxious oaf – it remains one of the longest nights in my memory.

The weather of the long Scottish winter was very severe, which exercised to the limit not only our airmanship, but also our patience. Frequently we were grounded, awaiting the slightest break in the weather which might offer a chance of getting airborne. We passed endless hours of thick mist, dragging cloud or high wind, gathered around the crew room stoves in our Nissen-hutted dispersal amongst the sand dunes. Much of the time we played cards, a variation of vingt-et-un if I remember, for nominal stakes. For the rest of the time we talked, on diverse subjects. At the forefront of such discussions was often the delightfully vague and amusing J.P.Kennedy, from South Cerney days. It was he who instigated a discussion on our enemy, the Germans, to state positively that while he would do his duty as a fighting man, he could not hate the Germans. This was quite unintelligible to the less intellectual of us, who pressed him strongly on the subject – but no, he could not hate the Germans. 'What,' demanded one of us resorting to the emotional, 'would you feel if you got back one evening to your little house in St. Cyrus, to find that a sneak raider had destroyed your defenceless home, wife and child?' To this Kennedy replied that he would know many emotions – but he would not be able to hate the Germans. 'Well,' said another of us, 'what would you feel if you got back one evening to your house in St. Cyrus, to find that a sneak raider had destroyed your little boat, in which you spend so many happy hours sailing?'

'Oh my God,' said Kennedy leaping up in horror, 'I would be after the bastards at once!'

The crew-room discussions were often informative, deeply interesting, and always amusing, for humour amongst men living and working together can be of a high order. The spontaneity and ready wit amazed me as my fellows never seemed short of a humorous, if not always flattering remark. Typical of the off-the-cuff comment was that made when I was preparing for a flight by pulling on heavy woollen, old school, 1st XV rugger stockings, for wear inside my fleece-lined boots. A fellow instructor whose attention had been attracted by these revered colours of black, white and yellow exclaimed: 'My God, who on earth do you play for – the Clapham Urinals?'

The classic comment of all time was surely that made by John Holland, a most likeable personality with a slow smile and quiet sense of humour. Someone reading a Lincoln local paper, received by post, quietened the bantering circle around the crew-room stove by an amazed call of: 'Hey, listen to this, fellows.' What he then read was a report of how a Turkish officer, attending a course at R.A.F. Cranwell, had befriended a nurse from the local hospital. All went well, and this laudable international friendship must have progressed rapidly, it would seem, until in a burst of affection the Turk bit through both of the poor girl's nipples; landing himself in the magistrates court, and the nurse in her own hospital, with a problem in accounting for her malaise.

This report drew forth much merriment in the crew-room, and John Holland commented that from all accounts these Turks must be quite something. He went on to recount to us how, when he was at Cranwell, one of the Turks, whom he claimed was known as Mustapha Phurk, was the subject of a series of complaints to the C.O. from the matron of the same hospital. These complaints were based on the fact that a nurse he had befriended came on duty completely tired out, and in each complaint the state of the nurse had worsened to a condition approaching absolute exhaustion. The last letter in this dreaded correspondence between the Matron and the C.O., stated that the situation had now changed somewhat, as the nurse had been admitted to the hospital with a septic bite on the buttock! The silence which followed while we pondered on the implications of all this, was finally broken by John Holland who with his slow smile said, 'You know – in this country I don't think we know what a good f—k is!'

It was during my days at Montrose that I encountered a personality which was to become a major influence in my life. Diane was one of a number of W.A.A.F. officers on the strength of the signals unit at nearby Craigo. This was a 'Y' Station, in the extensive network of listening posts feeding intercepted enemy signals to Station X, the highly secret signals intelligence centre in south-eastern England. I was first introduced to Diane at one of the two or three large-scale Officers' Mess parties held at Montrose, in the course of the year. Although by no means the first girl that I had met or worked alongside in the close contact of Service units and an Officers' Mess, I found myself instantly drawn to Diane. This was partially on account of her undoubted physical attractions, but mostly for her quiet, unassuming personality and air of suppressed vivacity apparent in a pair of the softest sparkling brown eyes. From the moment of our meeting we travelled together into an ever-deepening friendship, with a great delight in one another, and a sense of the fulfilment of an ordained destiny so natural that it never crossed either of our minds to wonder at it. This was the more surprising for the competing interest of a considerable number of my brother officers, who were not unaware of her charms. One by one as they ceased to persevere, I was fascinated by their observations of:

'Not interested'; 'Frigid'; 'Aloof'; 'Reserved'; 'Stand-offish', and I could not believe that they were talking of the Diane I knew.

For my part there grew in my understanding a slow realisation that there had arrived in my life a messenger. A messenger of whose tidings, although I had not before realised it, I was in most desperate need. In spite of my fierce independence, superb physical fitness, youthful adaptiveness, strength, resilience and mental agility – all of this was not enough. The air, like the sea, is completely unforgiving, and although I did not know it I was wearying under the incessant strain of the hazards of intensive flying, and teaching in the air. For the time being, like the swallows heralding the summer (which I had so often watched relaxing on arrival at their destination – and before embarking on the purpose of their journey) Diane my messenger, woman eternal, rested after her long flight from eternity – a mysterious, graceful and beauteous thing, demurely vibrant with the joy and purpose of life.

Time off-duty was scarce, limited, and of necessity largely given over to sleep, but at every opportunity I had been walking, usually on my own, deep into the foothills and mountains of Strathmore, behind Montrose. The little-frequented and often remote loveliness was inspiring, and there I found great peace and consolation. The sublime solitude provoked thought, and led me to a realisation that here was inanimate proof of the fact that the truth of beauty and beauty of truth, transcends all. There equally, was the realisation that for this truth I would live; and for this truth I would almost certainly be called upon to die. There were as well troubled thoughts, for to move always towards the one paramount objective I had set myself, in striking the heaviest blow normally possible to the individual in the defence of this my country, I was purposely inuring myself to a strictly proscribed life, to the exclusion of all else. It was only alone, here in the presence of the wonder of the foothills, that I dared to consider what I might so lose in the doing. Anywhere else, such wistful thinking might well have completely destroyed me, but there, the rugged beauty in time quelled the tumult of pent-up emotions, and left only a sweet melancholy.

I found that I was increasingly seeking Diane in my off-duty moments, and that we were contriving to be together. She began to accompany me on my long walks and excursions, where I discovered that far from obstructing my communion with the beauty of the wild, she was enhancing it. So I watched fascinated the gentle revelation of the supreme beauty of nature, in the dawning realisation that Diane's own superb loveliness was not an entity in itself, but inseparable from the whole glory of creation. Wherever she was, was loveliness, but the nearer to the unfettered simplicity of the wild, the greater was that loveliness as she blended and mingled so imperceptibly amongst the creations and very materials of nature. This experience was to me as intensely invigorating and exciting as Diane herself, and was the more enthralling as my perception of these great truths was only gradual. I could delight in the joy of every moment of Diane's hair streaming in the wind, Diane's breasts rising to the lilt of her walk, Diane in the fields, woods, hills, mists and mountains; and understand so well the artists who have sought urgently to express this revelation, in the symbolism of the naked nymph rising from the elemental life sources of earth, rock, skies or water. So I was privileged to see and wonder at Diane; to begin to fathom the exciting mystery of woman, and to decipher her message.

Other than creating time together, there never was anything contrived in our relationship, it flowed so naturally and so easily that we were hardly conscious of our growing intimacy. I do not even know when first we kissed, because it never seemed in any way strange, but rather something completely natural that must have happened before. It could well have been on the warm sunny day we spent wandering slowly through the lowlands towards the foothills, and then along the pine-wooded banks of the river Esk above Edzell. We climbed and scrambled over the rocky riverbed and its often perpendicular banks, cut through the stone in the passage of ages; as beautiful as anything in Scotland and at its best in the superb weather of that day. At one time we lay in the sun beside the flashing, tumbling, rushing water; held fast in the spell of its beauty, and kissed as the joy of 'being' lapped over us in great floods of mutual understanding. It was on another such occasion that Diane surprised and perplexed me by exclaiming, 'When I am lying in your arms and you are talking to me – sometimes I feel as a child, and sometimes as a woman. You are an artist – or a very wonderful person – no, you are both.' In my perplexity I knew my first vague fears for my messenger.

As the months slipped from spring through summer to autumn and then winter, there were many such 'Swallow days'; amongst them equally peaceful hours before a blazing log fire in a room at the back of an inn, near the remote hamlet of Marykirk. There, by telephoned request, in some mysterious way the most enormous and sumptuous teas of bacon and eggs, home-baked bread, drop scones, butter, jam and cakes appeared as though by magic, in spite of the ravages and shortages of rationing. We ate with the awful enjoyment of youth, talked and basked undisturbed in happy silence before the burning logs. I never remember seeing anyone there except for the reckoning, and have been forever grateful for the kindness of such great humanity by our unseen host and hostess. It was during such days that I came to know in some awe, one of the sweetest, kindest and most thoughtful dispositions that can have been, and the depth of quiet understanding and feeling that hid behind an endearing vitality, and soft brown eyes.

During this time there was, too, the incident of the hay-loft which seemed unfortunate then, particularly as I was entirely responsible for our involvement. Later, I realised that Diane, being a commander of women and also essentially human, was certainly as familiar with life in the raw as was I. In fact it was a thought-provoking experience shared, which did much to deepen our relationship and common understanding. It came about in a strange way, for hay has always had a romantic fascination for me, although sometimes I wonder if it can ever mean the same to later generations weaned on the tractor's roar, and conditioned to the symmetry of a baler's precision. Perhaps, most of all, it was the sweet sunburdened scent of hay, the picture it generated of drowsy fields, of lilting lark song and that torrid sense of timelessness that is the heart of pure joy. So it came about that on leaving the Officers' Mess autumn ball at the height of the festivities, for a breath of fresh air with Diane, and sauntering down the wooded drive, I was again bewitched by a delicious scent of hay drifting on the cold night air from the old stable. Perhaps it was the hay – but anyway the war seemed afar and Diane was close and warm at my side, giving me absolutely no excuse for not thinking of it before, but it occurred to me delightfully innocently that it would be fun to again kiss Diane.

Nature in its wisdom has endowed a girl with a seventh sense, which seems always to enable her to know when she is about to be kissed. Turning this thought over in my mind, and with a quickening heart, I decided that so delightful a moment would lack nothing for my part, and I directed our steps towards the stable door and that heavenly scent. At this point my plan was nearly thrown into confusion by the sight of Diane's lovely upturned face, patterned in the lacework of moonlight thrown by the trees. That fleetingly lit expression – was it quizzical? Was it thoughtful? Was it hesitant? There was no way of telling, but above all it was softly trusting, and I all but crushed her to me on the spot.

We passed into the shadows under the arch of the door, and as we began to climb the stair into the hayloft, Diane's wide skirt was flowing inches from my face, so prettily feminine, and the intermingled scent of hay and her perfume set my heart pounding like a kettle drum. Perhaps there was no mystique in that seventh sense at all, for the whole floor must have been shaking under my heartbeat! We picked our way over the hay to a patch of moonlight at the far end of the loft, and there I held her at arms' length to gaze upon her. She looked down shyly at her feet, and those lowered lashes swept me into the most thrilling of embraces, and a kiss that was delectably sweet. It is only for the truly great moments in life that time stands still, and so I do not know for how long that single kiss lasted, but we were eventually disturbed by furtive steps and heavy breathing from below.

Whoever it was started up the stairs, and anxious whispered queries parried by exhortations told their own story. We drew back into the dark as the couple reached the loft and flopped noisily into a deep mound of hay. Then ensued a slurred monologue, punctuated by the sounds of sliding zips, popping buttons and the rustle of silks and clumsily pulled materials. At first, the monologue was a tedious succession of variants of the theme, 'I am sorry about this, but I can't help it,' – and one could almost smell the beer and whisky chasers. I was completely mortified for with some idea of what was coming, had no desire whatsoever to eavesdrop on such a scene, particularly at close quarters, which could only be unchivalrous to say the least of it. And yet, if we moved we could be recognised by one of our fellow officers, and Diane would be compromised. On the other hand, if we stayed concealed we might have to witness in silence something every second of which could be acutely embarrassing to both of us. A horrible choice of alternatives, neither of them honourable. It was the memory of that softly trusting expression as we crossed the stable threshold that decided me to stay, in the hope that all would be over quickly and in a silence that would leave room for the benefit of the doubt. We stood side by side pressed into the shadow of the wall, not daring to touch each other.

There was to be no benefit of the doubt, for the monologue continued with a marked note of drunken excitement, and gave way suddenly to an inane repetition of; 'Luvely grub – luvely grub,' which was in turn followed by a steady succession of sucking and slobbering noises, each peculiarly penetrating decibel of which hurt more than the last. The monologue had begun again breathlessly, and sounds of the forcible removal of the last resistant shreds of diaphanous clothing, were emphasised by the urgent explanation: 'I don't want to do this – but I have to.' Quite whose conscience could be stilled by so facile a statement, remains a mystery. That sharp little muted cry of hurt and resignation is with me to this day, and was the only sound that I heard the girl make. It was all over very quickly, signified by a loud and raucous passing of wind that startled the sleeping rafters, and was accompanied by a besotted sigh of uninhibited relief. Oh my darling Eve, were you ever so outraged? I could have wept with mortification, for I felt all women raped.

The girl was dressing rapidly, and slipped down the stairs on her own into the dark. Diane sought my hand, pressed herself momentarily to me, gave me a kiss that brought back the scent of the hay and whispered, 'Can we go now?' We waited to follow silently our Don Juan's unsteady progress down the stairs, and then passed into the night unobserved behind him while he noisily pissed on the jamb of the wide stable door. You could almost hear the steam rising in the cold night air, as the stars looked silently down.

Not only do I not know when first Diane and I kissed, I do not know when first we made physical love. Although a later development, it was not a separable part of our relationship and just as it could never have any ending, it seemed to have no beginning. The actual experience I could never forget, as it was not only my first sexual experience, and an experience born of great mutual love and understanding, but it was too my first experience of an unexpected and agonizing anguish. Although this double experience is etched vividly in my heart and mind for all time, I write of it with reluctance; not only because of its intensely personal nature but because even a master artist in the use of words could well quail at the task of using such a medium for a subject all but beyond portrayal in human terms.

I knew that Diane was pretty, but in the moment that I gazed upon the gift of her glorious body, I was completely awestruck. Given the loveliness of any woman, and also the fact that she was Diane, there remained a beauty defying description. It was as if she had an innate ability to symbolize the glory of creation, and so inspire the deep exciting stirrings of man's primeval affinity with nature – to me the revelation of an infinite wonder, and I lay beside her overcome, and trembling in an anguished confusion. Through this confusion broke a haunting fear of tomorrow, with a turmoil of shrieking engines, twisted metal and broken bodies, all in a bizarre juxtaposition to such beauty as I had never before known; creating a realisation that I might well never know it again. It seemed cruel beyond understanding – men rarely cry, but they suffer the anguish of a silent rending agony, which is surely worse. Diane drew close to me, and instinctively I hid my face deep in her hair. Her soft limbs were pressed close to mine, and the warmth and pressure of her full firm breasts against my chest transmitted a wondrous gentleness, stilling my heaving soul.

We lay long in the golden silence, until my trembling ceased and Diane gently turning her head placed her warm lips to mine. Kissing Diane had always been a sweet experience, but this was different. The sweetness, tenderness and deep understanding that flooded through me from her kiss was supreme. I drank and drank from the beauty of that kiss, as though utterly parched at a long-sought stream – and all time ceased, as with the matchless and unconscious art of a child of nature, Diane passed unhesitatingly with me into the so closely guarded realm of unbounded intimacy; to begin the conveying of her message of love, beauty and peace. Gone were the horrors of war, gone was the agony of sorrow, gone was everything but the discovery that only woman can satisfy and delight all the senses, and of the loveliness and sweet fragrance that was Diane. I knew for the first time a world of such beauteous joy as I had never imagined existed, and embarked on the realisation that I must know, and never forget, the life of strain, intense violence, death and destruction in which I was incessantly involved, was only a momentary and passing means to an end. Whatever damage or personal loss I might suffer, and however impossible it might come to seem, infinite beauty would remain inviolate, to be discovered again. Those first and carefree Swallow days were over. My messenger lay silent and cuddled happily in my arms oblivious, in a sleepy smile of dawning fulfilment, of the immensity of her eternal part in human life, and the dangers of her mission.

Although Diane is to appear again in this narrative, because of the intensely personal nature of our relationship she receives far less than her due. She was so very much always with me and so constantly in my thoughts, that in all justice I should record some of them, even at risk of duplication, for what are such thoughts of those closest to us if not the happiest of repetition? The wonder and beauty of Diane's simple womanhood, the understanding, wisdom and knowledge of ages in the intuition of a girl barely out of her teens – was all too fascinating and overpowering to be easily intelligible to me. Often I found myself gazing upon her at length in a mixture of the purest joy, admiration and considerable awe. Awe because of her largely unconscious ability to symbolise so much of all that is good, consequently surely of God. To me, it indeed seemed impossible that she could be any other than 'God-sent', for how else could she have arrived in my life, when unbeknown to me I had so desperate a need of her and the strength of her message? There was never any doubt in my mind, that without Diane I should not have survived whole, if at all, the long-term battering of teaching flying in war, or fighting in the air, and there were so very many who did not.

I saw her as the summer swallow, for I knew that like the swallow she must return from whence she came, and as a pilot in war my summer was likely to be of the shortest. For this reason time was precious, and time with Diane infinitely more so. I knew that I was often experiencing the greatly heightened appreciation allied to the proximity of death – that clearer-than-clear, realer-than-real insight, shorn of every artificiality and inconsequence – the ultimate gift in life to those called upon to face leaving it. Perhaps only this Diane could not know, and while she enjoyed the happiness I found in watching her, my long silent gaze occasionally disturbed her very deeply – and she would become strangely afraid. I loved watching her in movement or at rest, perfectly groomed or in disarray, clothed, partially clothed, or naked; for at all times she was the joy that is a lovely girl, and was a supreme happiness to me. I was too, strangely proud and humbled in her presence, the significance of which I enjoyed pondering over, but went to considerable pains to try to conceal from her, as she always utterly rejected the slightest hint of admiration. It was all of this and much more that was to be constantly in my mind . . .

To return to life in general at Montrose, for us this was inevitably dominated by the weather, in which we experienced many differing Scotlands during the long winter and short summer, all of them beautiful. Of the extremes of ice, snow, gales, calm, rain and sunshine, best remembered is the Scotland of blown mist and drizzle, the Scotland of clinging cloud streaming slowly down the gullies of gaunt mountains. There was, in this ever-changing meteorological repertoire, a phenomenon known as haar. Haar was the name given to a fog which would form without warning, and with great rapidity, when comparatively milder moisture-saturated air arrived from the sea, and drifted over cold land. All experiences of haar were frightening to the aviator, and I had many.

The ever-present risk in the eastward take-off from Montrose over the sea was in some degree mitigated by the presence of two high-speed R.A.F. rescue launches of the Air Sea Rescue Service, operating from Montrose harbour. These launches were able to make 35 knots or more, and would if necessary put to sea in almost any weather. We were encouraged to go out in these launches on their regular patrols, and I did this on several occasions. In rough weather it was a desperate business and crossing the bar, lying off Montrose harbour, it was all one could do to hang on to the safety rails fitted for the purpose. The very teeth seemed certain to be shaken out of one's head and the bottom of the launch stove in under the terrible pounding. The crews of these boats, being a particularly curious hybrid of airseaman, were justifiably proud of their efficiency. This was enormously enhanced one night when a Swordfish from the Royal Naval Air Station at Arbroath (H.M.S. *Condor*, south of Montrose) was in difficulties, and the pilot radioed his intention of ditching or force-landing his aircraft in the sea. It so happened that one of our launches was on patrol in the area and almost at once picked up the navigation lights of the Swordfish. The launch was able to follow the aircraft and as it ditched to come up alongside, to the utter astonishment of the sea-airman, who to his chagrin found himself extolling the efficiency of the junior service. Needless to say, the launch crew never let on that they were on the spot at the time anyway!

My own experience of engine failure off the coast was not so auspicious. It was during a night flying exercise in an Oxford north of Montrose that, without any warning, I experienced an almost total loss of power in the starboard engine at a height of no more than 1,000 feet, which allowed nothing whatever to play with. As the aircraft was unable to maintain height on the remaining engine, I decided to make for the coast and ditch the aircraft, rather than lose height in a forced descent into the first high ground in my path. This was a decision born of desperation, for at that time of the year the North Sea was so cold one was unlikely to survive more than five to ten minutes' immersion in it. However, there was a chance that the aircraft might float for a few minutes, and I hoped to put it down as near to the shore as was possible. As we approached the coast I transmitted a Mayday* call on an R/T frequency reserved specifically for such calls, and repeated my call sign and the message that I was ditching off the Stonehaven coast several

---

* The International Distress Call – from the French *M'aidez* – help me.

times before going off the air to attend to the ditching itself. This was done in the chill realisation that there had been no acknowledgement of my call from any of the many stations that maintained a listening watch on that frequency. I assumed that the aircraft was too low either for the transmission to have been picked up, or to receive any acknowledgement.

We were flying as close as I dared to the coast at about 300 feet above the sea, and losing height. My student was a hefty ex-policeman and I instructed him to fire a red distress signal, then arm himself with the signal pistol, as many cartridges as he could collect, and to jettison the escape hatch in the roof of the fuselage. He disappeared – and I awaited the rush of air that would indicated the hatch was safely gone. Nothing happened. We were down to nearly 200 feet and I was fully exercised in trying to get the very best out of the remaining engine, to drop the aircraft into the sea in a tail-down attitude. Glancing over my shoulder down the fuselage, I was momentarily treated to the comic vision of my pupil swinging his six-foot bulk like a child from the two handles of an immovable escape hatch, with an expression of pained astonishment. The answer to his predicament was that the escape hatch would only open if pulled on one side by one of the handles – but there was no time to enlighten him for suddenly the dead engine began to bang and fire in sporadic bursts. Frantically I nursed it into life again, edging the throttle slowly open until it was established that it would run at no more than about one-third of full power – but this was enough slowly to gain height. Heading towards Montrose we climbed laboriously in this way to some 2,000 feet, at which height the ailing engine cut suddenly and completely. From 2,000 feet it was possible to get into Montrose on the live engine and this I did, with the circuit and airfield cleared by Air Traffic Control.

I was more than glad to get down, and my immediate interest was how the dead engine had picked up at the last possible moment, only to fail again when we were within reach of safety. There was to be no answer to this, for the Plumbers found that a sizeable piece had broken away from a joint in the induction manifold, and there was no conceivable way in which the engine, in this state, could have picked up even temporarily. Only later did I remember my R/T distress call, which had failed to raise any response. It was possible that although it had been heard, the aircraft was too low to pick up an answer, and so I asked for a wide enquiry to determine what had happened, and whether the rescue services had immediately set in motion a search for us. The enquiry eventually revealed that my transmission had only been picked up by the Royal Naval Air Station at Arbroath. There, the Wren on radio watch had logged my call but had taken no action on it because, she explained, the transmission was so nonchalant that she decided it could not be anyone transmitting in a genuine emergency. This piece of feminine logic prevailed despite her instructions and the fact that the call was a correctly phrased Mayday call, broadcast on the emergency frequency. While I was flattered that my strangulated tones of stark horror had been considered nonchalant, I was shaken to realise that had we ditched we would have been so needlessly committed to certain death by exposure, however long we had struggled to survive.

While we exulted in our growing knowledge of flight and ability to do surprising things in the air, we were at this time considerably sobered by an instruction from the Empire Central Flying School. This argued that we had an inescapable responsibility, when teaching future instructors the stalling characteristics of the Oxford, to demonstrate the first half-turn of a spin and the recovery. An instruction no doubt prompted by the pressing need to diminish the number of Oxfords lost as the result of inadvertent spins. The aircraft had a wicked stall in which it would suddenly drop a wing, and if instant recovery action was not applied would flick straight into a spin. As it was widely known that once 'in', an Oxford was extremely reluctant to come 'out' of a spin, putting it deliberately into one did not have much appeal. Several of our aircraft were to be lost in executing this instruction, and I saw one of them go down myself.

We knew that in the best of circumstances it was not possible to abandon the Oxford quickly, and that in a spin getting out of the seats was difficult. The aircraft span nose down, and the greatest hazard was guarding against centrifugal force. This could grip like a giant fist and hurl the unwary up the fuselage, past the rear door emergency exit, to drive such hapless individuals like a cork into the confines of the tail. In the face of such difficulties, by the time recovery action had proved ineffective; the decision to abandon the aircraft had been taken; and one occupant had clawed his way to the exit; it was almost certain that the aircraft would be too low for a second escape. There were individual escapes, by parachute, from spinning Oxfords and amazingly by some of those jammed in the tail. This came about as the Oxford spinning nose down struck the ground nose first, killing instantly anyone at the controls – but on more than one occasion an individual jammed in the tail had survived in this, only piece of the fuselage to remain intact. As I never heard of a case in which both occupants of a spinning aircraft had escaped; a decision regarding one's own actions in these circumstances required considerable soul-searching, and left one only too willing to give way to any would-be hero. The Oxford I saw go down in this way, span nose down until it was too low for a parachute escape, and then suddenly changed into a tail-down attitude. What had probably occurred was all too apparent – only one had a chance of escape in the tail, but there had obviously been a difference of opinion as to whom this should be and both occupants had made for it, so changing the trim and the attitude of the aircraft. The tail struck the ground first and dashed them both to pieces.

Shortly before I arrived at Montrose there had been a multiple accident, some details of which are well worth the relating. There was always much inter-Flight and personal rivalry to be the first airborne of a morning, and while this undoubtedly contributed to the accident in question, the main cause was a lack of experience in the aerodynamic sensitivity of the Oxford aircraft. It was not then fully realised that even a slight coating of ice on the leading edge of the wings would considerably increase the stalling speed, and thereby the speed needed for take-off, so greatly extending the take-off run. What happened was that one cold and frosty morning, the aircraft flying the first detail were as rapidly prepared as the long airframe and engine checks allowed, and then the first three Oxfords moved out for take-off almost together. The take-off run was to the west over the railway branch-line and road that bordered the inland side of the airfield. The three aircraft began their take-off runs simultaneously but none of them lifted off at the normal speed, as would have been expected. They tore across the airfield accelerating rapidly, and having passed the point of no return (the last point at which they could have throttled back and pulled up safely) were committed to getting airborne at all costs. Not one of them did, as all crashed into the boundary. One, hauled off the ground in a semi-stalled state, sheared through the little signal box beside the railway line, totally destroying its wooden upper works and leaving the brick base and lever array open to the skies.

The first rescuers on the scene were treated to the astonishing spectacle of the signalman emerging from the wreckage, cranking his telephone set to raise Montrose station, and when Montrose came on the line, saying, 'D'ye ken t'boax a' Kinnebar Junction? – Weel, it's no here the noo!' This remarkable man gave evidence at the inquest on those killed – and was congratulated by the coroner on his miraculous escape. He explained however that he had always been convinced an aircraft would one day strike the signal box, and so every time that an aircraft began a take-off run in that direction, he set his signals safe and ran down to hide behind the brick-built base of the box. If ultimately rewarded, the courage of his convictions must have been sorely tried for hundreds of aircraft had taken off in that direction!

The most disturbing accidents were those for which there was no apparent explanation, and of these there were a number. On one occasion, for two whole days I took part in a low-level search of the mountains for one of our aircraft. This type of search is fraught with difficulties and dangers – which one willingly accepted in the knowledge that the missing pilot would have done the same for oneself. Our search was to no avail but, unlike other such incidents when pilot and aircraft were never found, an old shepherd inadvertently came upon the burned-out wreckage while rounding up some sheep. Knowing nothing of what a couple of hundred gallons of burning petrol can do, he informed us that fortunately no one was in it!

One particularly unfortunate accident involved a Master II on the Montrose circuit at night. This aircraft suddenly dived into the ground, killing the instructor and student. The cause of the accident was not then known, and this may have played some part in an inexcusable delay in the notification of the next of kin. The instructor was married and lived out in Montrose with his wife. She was shopping in Boots the next morning and on making a small purchase the assistant, much moved, said how very sorry she was to have heard the dreadful news. The wife totally unsuspecting queried, 'What news?' and the assistant equally unsuspecting replied, 'Your husband's terrible accident; we are all so sad for you.' By piecing clues from different accidents and incidents together, it was shortly afterwards discovered that this Master had been lost owing to a seepage of carbon monoxide contained in engine exhaust fumes. This escaped through a crack in the exhaust and into the heater jacket, from where it had been circulated through the cockpit by the heating system. In spite of immediate modifications to prevent such a happening, I think that many of us flew the Master with the cockpit hood slightly open after that, and happily froze!

A desperately unfortunate accident was the head-on collision of two Oxfords on the 'Beam' at Stracathro, in bright clear weather. The Standard Beam Approach was a blind flying radio approach aid that could lead an aircraft to the head of the runway on which it was in use, at the correct height for a landing. It was however necessary for the visibility at ground level to be adequate for a visual landing. In other words, although it was possible to make a blind approach on this system, it was not possible to make a blind landing. The S.B.A. system at the Montrose satellite of Stracathro was used extensively by us for blind approach training (there was a special B.A.T. Flight based there) but it should have been impossible for two aircraft using the beam to be flying at the same height, as the most stringent precautions were taken to avoid such a thing. I was one of the first over the site of the crash about four miles north-east of Edzell, picking up the smoke of a burning engine near Marykirk, and then detecting bits and pieces spread over a good square mile. In this collision two instructors and one student were killed, the other student escaping by parachute; an escape which would have been impossible at that height if he had not been thrown out of the disintegrating aircraft by the impact. Another fascinating escape by parachute was made at night by a fellow instructor, when thick fog closed one airfield after another, leaving him with no way of landing within range of his limited fuel. He remained with his aircraft until the engines stopped, and then abandoned it. On landing he struck the ground very hard, and decided for this reason and the limited visibility to stay where he was, wrapped in his parachute, for the remainder of the night. With daylight came an improvement in visibility and he soon concluded that he was in the mountains. He made slow progress by threading his way in a generally downhill direction, but it was some long time before the visibility cleared enough to see a valley below through which ran, to his delight, a railway line. He was more than exhausted when he at length reached this line and then, as he told me, came the agonizing decision as to in which direction he should follow it. His choice was an inspired one, for it was not very long before he came within sight of an isolated signal box, and marvelled that if anything was ever in the middle of nowhere, this must be it. Perhaps because of this, the wisp of smoke curling from the cabin chimney spoke more reassuringly of life than anything he could remember.

An aviator without an aircraft is shorn of all credibility, and being aware that announcing oneself a visitor from the skies can evoke a reaction at such a suggestion of gullibility, ranging from rank disbelief to outright hostility; he decided to proceed with care. When the door of the box was opened to his knock, by a quizzical signalman, there ensued this conversation:

'I am a pilot.'

'Aye.'

'My aircraft has crashed in the hills.'

'Aye.'

'I escaped by parachute.'

'Aye.'

'I have been walking through the hills for many hours.'

'Aye.'

'I saw the railway line early this morning.'

'Aye.'

For a long and utterly exhausted moment, our aviator thought that he had failed after all to get through – but the signalman suddenly announced, 'You'll be wanting a cup of tea then?' which if a considerable over-simplification of the situation, was at least a step on the road of return to all we call normality!

In a curious way, two widely varied minor truths coincided in my life at this time. One of these was to do with flying accidents, and the morbid fascination that they arouse. An accident is a sudden and unpredicted abnormal situation in which, amongst others, are to be found elements of disaster, destruction, violence, physical injury, horror and freaks of chance. Above all a flying accident is often of a cost in material, life and limb, which could never normally be experienced. For all of these reasons it becomes a scene or centre of intense activity, which has an undeniable fascination and engenders great general interest. Aircraft accidents are likely to be particularly spectacular and aircrew, who are cast to be the reluctant stars in any such event, understandably have always tended to adopt an apparently casual attitude towards the subject. This extended to the light-hearted aircrew term of 'prang', as an onomatopoeic substitute for accident (or more widely any sort of impact) and was a term adopted by most concerned with flying.

The other truth was to do with the unfailing and bizarre distortion of information passed by word of mouth. There is the classic story from the trench-warfare of 1914–18, in which at the height of a major Allied offensive a harassed company commander received a message, passed by word of mouth, from his leading platoon commander who was pinned down by enemy fire. The message received was: 'Send three and fourpence (three shillings and four pence – about 19p) we are going to a dance.' This astonishing request was too late discovered to have originated as; 'Send reinforcements, we are going to advance!'

The incident which brought these truths together sprang from an early-morning instructional flight made, on a very cold January Sunday with one of my students, a Sergeant Holden. For this flight I had chosen a Miles Magister, affectionately known as a Maggi; and walking out to the aircraft, announced to Holden that I was going to demonstrate how to teach the procedure for an engine failure on take-off, and embarked on the pre-flight instruction. The routine checks of the aircraft completed, we taxied out for take-off. All of this was slower than usual, because on account of the extreme cold we were wearing about everything that we could get on; I under my heavy Irvine jacket and trousers, and Holden under his Outer Sidcot. This gave us the appearance of being all but jammed into the little open cockpits, and consequently the clumsiness of our movements required considerable expertise to operate the controls smoothly and correctly.

The take-off was to the south and directly over Montrose, which called for an exacting demonstration and left little or no room for slow reactions or any error. With all of this in mind (and the knowledge that for safety extra height would be needed before simulating engine failure) I opened up on the take-off run, and began the demonstration and accompanying 'patter' with the ease and confidence of much practice. As I spoke, there was time for a last fleeting glance at the instruments, to satisfy myself that all was well before becoming airborne. It was, and I lifted the aircraft off the ground and began the climb away at full throttle, over the airfield boundary and town straight ahead of us. At barely 150′ above the ground, and without any warning, the Magister engine cut dead leaving me faced with the

The Miles Magister 1, known as 'The Maggi'.

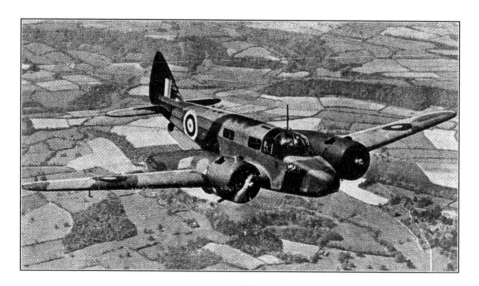

The Airspeed Oxford, known as 'The Ox Box'.

real thing – a forced landing on take-off – and in just about the worst possible circumstances. My brief, forceful and agonized comments at this moment were taken by Holden to be a superbly realistic demonstration, a belief he clung to until the last possible moment. However, that was yet to come, and I was briefly contemplating the possibility of our frequent boast that in these circumstances we would frighten the inhabitants out of their lives, by banging the aircraft down in the town square ahead of us (the possibility of which was highly debatable) and demand a drink at the Star bar as a *bona fide* traveller!*

Already frightened out of my life I decided against so hazardous, desperate and dangerous a course, particularly for the people of Montrose. It may be wondered why I should even have contemplated this briefly, but the correct action in an engine failure on take-off is to land straight ahead, and never, never to turn back to the airfield. The reason for this golden rule is that at the best the aircraft can have very little height and any turn would so increase the drag that the aircraft could only dive into the ground in the turn. But this very thing I decided to do, for behind me and to my left on the outskirts of the town was a small derelict clearance near to the sand dunes, perhaps a bomb-damage site, into which it might be possible to dump the aircraft. For an aircraft in the climbing attitude, one hundred and fifty feet above the ground is so little as to be a situation demanding an instant decision, and this I made by dropping the nose sharply and at the same time, turning to port onto the site. We sank like a stone, and had barely enough time to level out before the wheels struck the ground and we bucked and crashed over the rubble. The undercarriage was torn off as we lurched with a terrible crash on and into the side of a concrete pill-box (which I had not seen) and which impact knocked me unconscious.

I got the worst of this, flying in the front or pupil's cockpit. Holden as the instructor under training was flying in the rear or instructor's cockpit. When I came round, which can only have been minutes later, Sergeant Holden was bending over me but his face was as black as a nigger minstrel, with white-circled eyes where he had removed his goggles. In this black mask his teeth and eyes flashed white as he laughed uncontrollably, exclaiming between guffaws, 'You don't know how funny you look, sir – your face is black with oil!' In due course the crash and rescue parties reached the site, and we were carried off in an ambulance to Station Sick Quarters, for the compulsory medical examination. Apart from being extensively bruised and very badly shaken, neither of us was hurt. However Holden, who to my pride passed out very well at the end of the course, was later killed with his pupil in a Master II at Ternhill.

I was detained in the S.S.Q. for some time, and then released with orders to rest for forty-eight hours in the Mess; to which end I boarded the next routine bus to Rosemount. It rattled slowly on its way with a handful of passengers, and my mind was far from the two airmen sitting in front of me until I caught my name. What was being said turned out to be this: 'Ave yer 'eard the 'gen' abaht Flight Letenant Shepherd? – G'arn, yer must've, everyone bin talkin' abaht it all mornin', I 'eard it from Freddie in Workshops, when 'e come over to the b— Stores f'r spares.' Then with the patronising air of one imparting priceless and highly confidential information, he revealed: 'Flight Letenant Shepherd's bin gon' an' pranged a W.A.A.F. called Maggie in the bl—ing sand dune.' I was not sure if I cared for

---

* The licensing laws of Scotland at this time forbade the sale of alcohol on Sundays to anyone except a *bona fide* traveller. Sunday drinking was not introduced in Scotland until 1976.

being credited with rape, however daring, but particularly without the satisfaction which this airman's lyrical description seemed to offer. However rumours die very hard and as, no doubt, for its obviously rare scandal value, this one would die harder than most; I resigned myself to the less obvious perils of force-landing a Magister.

Regrettably Service funerals were a frequent occurrence and, for a brief period, it seemed that I was achieving recognition as on a number of occasions I was detailed to represent the Commanding Officer. In this role one was acting as chief Service mourner, following the coffin immediately behind the next of kin, should any be present, and from this privileged position it was possible to observe all that went on. Before long I was unhappily forced to the conclusion that my selection was either on account of the quality of my slow marching, or because my general appearance and demeanour was considered to be suitably lugubrious. Of these funerals several remain in mind, largely due to the inescapable fact that as civilians in uniform, our Service knowledge was limited to the job in hand, and we were woefully ignorant of much Service procedure and ceremonial. This easily led to incongruous incidents which could instantly tip the emotional tension from the sombre to the ludicrous; once the strain had been so broken the reaction was likely to be an unreasoned hilarity, which was an agony to suppress. For us funerals were particularly hard to bear, and our light-hearted view of them might easily have been misconstrued; a view which did not spring from any lack of sympathy or respect, but only from the fact that death was far too close to allow us to dwell on it in any but the most jocular of terms.

The coffin carried what could be found and identified of the victim, but this might sometimes be precious little and in these circumstances, unbeknown to the next of kin, the weight was made up with sand-bags. This sobering knowledge was the case for the funeral of a Sergeant at which I represented the C.O. The only family mourner was the Sergeant's sister, a newly commissioned W.A.A.F. officer who had travelled from Southern England. At the graveside service this girl conducted herself with surprising composure, other than that without warning (presumably when overcome by emotion) she would throw up a salute for her brother. The assembly being completely unsure of the procedure, one after another sheepishly followed suit; but no sooner had the forest of waving arms subsided than the girl having reached a further surge of emotion threw up another salute, and the whole thing started again. The service continued in what rapidly degenerated into sporadic cycles of uncontrolled saluting, which no one had the heart to stop; the situation verging on farce and becoming acutely embarrassing.

It was the custom for an Officer's S.D. (Service Dress) cap, with decorations and medals if any, to be borne on his coffin. This silently eloquent tradition was often difficult to fulfil as the cap could not necessarily be found. In these cases a brother officer would lend his, and as no one else would be aware of the substitution the force of the symbolism would not be lost. Or so it should have been, but on one such occasion at which I was again representing the C.O., all went well in this moving ceremony until the signal was given to lower the coffin into the grave. It began its descent with the cap (which should by then have been removed) still in position and I noticed this, mentally recording that it could be recovered with the minimum of disruption after the service was over. But this was not to be for suddenly, with all discipline cast to the winds, the owner of the cap burst violently through the ranks of the escort and firing party, to snatch the cap from the coffin as it was just about to disappear from sight into the grave. Whether it was concern for the safety of his property or he saw himself symbolically being buried, I do not know, but his fury was something to behold.

Perhaps a greater fury than this occurred at another funeral. There, owing to recent heavy rains and poor preparation of the grave, when the bearers came to lower the coffin it had hardly reached the bottom before the edge of the grave gave way, and one of the bearers fell in, landing with a soggy thump on the coffin. He was aghast, and stood with horror-filled eyes peering silently at us over the top of the grave, aware of the agony of the moment and his complete inability to get out unaided. Equally aghast, and completely nonplussed (there is nothing in the drill book about this sort of thing!) we returned his glassy stare with masterly inaction. It must have been the inaction of his so-called comrades, or perhaps an unbrotherly disinclination to share a grave, which triggered his fury, for abandoning all respect for the deceased he hissed; 'Get me out of this bloody hole, you morons!' This we proceeded to do, but in the undignified scramble that ensued, showers of dislodged soil ratted hollowly onto the coffin below, giving rise to yet another booming protest from the grave, which did nothing to alleviate the situation.

Next of kin were offered the choice of a Service or private funeral. Under private arrangements the funeral was usually held at the deceased's home town or village, and in these cases the Service responsibility ended when the coffin was seen onto the train at the start of its journey. The Aberdeen to London express stopped briefly at Montrose and would, at the request of R.A.F. Montrose, be stopped with a reserved luggage compartment at the end of a passenger coach, exactly opposite to the booking hall. This would enable the coffin to be lifted from the vehicle outside the station door, and carried through the booking hall, across the platform and into the luggage compartment, without haste and within the time for which the express would stop.

On one of these occasions I was detailed as officer in charge, and had halted the carrier outside the station booking hall only a minute or two before the train was due. As it came in with the roaring flurry of smoke and steam (so much part of the urgent excitement of the long-distance express in those days) the N.C.O. bearers unshipped their comrade's Union Jack-draped coffin, and waited in silence for the station master to signal that the van doors were open. On the signal, I gave the muted order to slow march and followed immediately behind the coffin, eyes downcast, at this slow, intensely dignified and solemn pace. In crossing the booking hall we found ourselves marching over confetti. Completely taken aback I looked up to find that we were moving onto the platform in the midst of a wedding party, which was milling around the very next compartment to that awaiting the coffin. Totally unsuspecting, this party was celebrating with an abandon that told of a highly successful reception. Our slow, deliberate and stately progress onto the platform threw the party into total disarray, as though unexpectedly caught in some sacrilegious orgy. The Best Man, clinging forlornly to the shattered remains of nuptial merrymaking, tried to ignore us attempting to rally his party with brandished bottle and glass; but as we slowly and silently advanced a completely distracted bride, eyes wide with horror at this unwelcome omen, stilled her befuddled husband, and the remaining shreds of revelry became totally and horribly inappropriate. It was a strange assembly that stood in the confetti as I stepped back on the platform and saluted the coffin before the doors of the van were closed; and one of those agonizing situations that can only be acted out to the bitter end.

As well as our training commitment, we had at Montrose a dual emergency-defence commitment in pursuance of the instructions on airfield defence, issued by Churchill while I was serving at South Cerney. One of these commitments was Operation Banquet, in which many of the flying instructors would, in the event of invasion, have joined fighter squadrons. The other was a ground defence commitment, for which the aircrew had to be equally prepared as the decision on their ultimate role would depend upon the local situation.

With a number of my fellow F.I.S. instructors, I was trained for Operation Banquet by an air-firing course on the Hawker Hurricane at R.A.F. Tealing, and familiarisation flying of the North American Mustang at R.A.F. Macmerry, which lay to the south of the Firth of Forth. At this time the Mustang (which was the aircraft we would fly in battle) was powered by an American Allison engine, the performance of which was disappointing. The engine was not fitted with the automatic boost control, then standard equipment in British engines, and it was very easy indeed to over-boost and 'explode' the Allison engine, with obvious consequences. For this reason it was known in the R.A.F. as the Allison time-bomb. It was not until later that the Rolls-Royce Merlin-engined version of the Mustang came into service, and proved to be one of the finest and most versatile fighters of the war. However, we were content with the Allison-engined version, and I believe that had we been called upon to do so we would have given a good account of ourselves, as a fair proportion of our instructional time on the Master II was given to air-to-air firing exercises in mock combat, using camera guns. I particularly enjoyed this, as in aerial combat much of the advantage goes to the pilot who can push his aircraft to its limits without exceeding them.

The ground defence commitment was perhaps as daunting, because the site of our stand in the event of invasion was to be amongst sand dunes lying in a narrow belt between the airfield and the sea. It was true that this position would command both the sea approach and the airfield, but as our defences were purely of sand, and our weapons small arms, revolvers, rifles, sten guns (a primitive sub-machine gun) and several Vickers K machine guns, designed for air-to-air firing, our chances of survival in a full-scale seaborne invasion seemed negligible. This thought was even more sobering when one realised the impossibility of withdrawal over the flat coverless expanse of the airfield behind us, and the ease with which our position could be isolated and destroyed. The great morale booster was supposed to be our solitary Smith gun, of which a number had been produced for the Home Guard. This horrific piece was capable of hurling a ten-pound projectile over one thousand yards, aided by primitive sights. It was a drain-pipe like unrifled barrel, mounted between two large disc wheels. To bring it into action it had to be tipped onto its side, the lower wheel providing a transversable firing platform, and the upper some sort of a splinter shield. If a masterpiece of improvisation, it was hardly likely to hold a seaborne invasion at bay. We entertained ourselves by betting on how many rounds it would fire before being put out of action, and the general opinion was one, if it and we survived the pre-assault bombardment. All in all, I think I favoured the Allison time-bomb!

At South Cerney I had been issued with a .45" Browning Colt Automatic pistol, which was then the standard personal weapon for pilots. This was a fascinating and sophisticated firearm which I much treasured, but it was perhaps of greater interest as a collectors' piece than for its efficiency, for it was heavy, when fired had a fearsome kick, and was prone to jamming. I must have been amongst the last R.A.F. officers to receive this issue, it being replaced with the smaller, simpler and basic .38" Smith and Wesson revolver. To my sorrow my automatic was withdrawn and exchanged at Montrose, for parachuting to the French Resistance movement I was told. This seemed an odd choice in view of its characteristics.

While the nation had been slow to grasp that the tradition of fine British craftsmanship was outmoded in production for total war (where basic practicality and volume of output were crucial) some of its essays into the bulk production of utility weapons were startling. In the same production category as the Smith gun was the Sten gun, with which a percentage of us were issued for ground defence. A crude 9mm sub-machine gun of utter simplicity, very cheap and easy to produce, it had a thirty-two-round box-magazine and range of 200 yards. The Sten gun was inaccurate at over 50 yards, but was effective at close range and could withstand dreadful punishment. However, it was far from safe and would, for instance, sometimes fire if knocked, making it almost as dangerous to friend as foe.

Defence-wise our geographical position at Montrose was not enviable, for in the early years of the war a German invasion from Norway could not be ruled out. Neither could raids, or a raid in force, for which an airfield on the coast (and within a stone's throw of a harbour) might have been tempting.

From our cloistered isolation in Scotland it was difficult to see affairs from anything other than a local viewpoint, which if anything emphasised our belief that the war was passing us by. It was – although for my part, at twenty-three years of age in October 1943, on looking back over the three years I had served in the R.A.F., it could be argued that by any standard this had hardly been stagnation. Of those three years I had worked for two as a flying instructor. Shortly after my arrival at Montrose I had been promoted to war substantive Flying Officer, and then little more than a year later promoted again to acting Flight Lieutenant, the equivalent of Captain in the army. In my two years instructional work I already held an above the average assessment as a flying instructor, and was well on my way to gaining the highest flying instructor's category of A1.

Our discontent may have seemed to be sorely lacking in appreciation, and outrageously impatient, but the tide of war was at last turning in the Allies' favour. As fighting men we could only feel some sense of shame that we had no part in the hardships and dangers so many of our companions were facing in the various theatres of war. At Montrose the war was perforce passing us by, and on the face of it I was not one whit nearer to achieving my avowed intention of 'serving by inflicting the heaviest possible blow against the enemy that an ordinary man might achieve'.

In Russia, the Germans after taking Sebastopol and Rostov were checked during August 1942, at Stalingrad. The Russians launched a counter-offensive from Stalingrad, which began a long series of German reverses, defeats and withdrawals. Similarly, in the Pacific at this time the Americans first checked the Japanese advance, and then began to drive them back. The indications in Burma were that the XIV Army of British and Indian troops was about to stem and challenge the Japanese successes. The British VIII Army under General Montgomery had, in July 1942, checked Rommel in North Africa and following the battle of El Alamein in October, soon had Rommel in full retreat. On 15th November 1942 the church bells, which had been silent to this date, were rung throughout Britain to celebrate General Montgomery's North African victories. November also brought an Allied landing in French North Africa, which was to lead to the defeat of the Germans and Italians in North Africa by May 1943. July 1943 saw an Allied landing in Sicily, to be followed in September by Allied landings in Italy, leading Italy to declare war on her former ally Germany.

At home, the conquest of Western Europe was now in every mind, for it had always been obvious that the decisive campaign of the war would be fought in Europe, and in this the R.A.F. had been involved since the very beginning of hostilities. Here would be the most colossal clash of arms, in which would be deployed in attack and defence endless and most fascinating instances of advanced technology. On 19th August 1942, in order to test both the German defences and Allied tactics, an ill-fated raid in force had been made on Dieppe, by some 5,000 Canadians and 1,000 British Commandos. The Canadians suffered terrible losses, three-quarters of them being killed, wounded or taken prisoner. While much had been learned, the awful cost left no doubt that in an Allied invasion of the French coast, the amphibious assault would be made at the expense of a horrifying loss of life.

However, my predicament was suddenly to change when a signal was received at Montrose posting me, on 8th February 1944, to No. 26 O.T.U. (Operational Training Unit) at Wing in Buckinghamshire. There I was to begin training to join a heavy bomber squadron, at last to undertake my share of the fighting, and almost certainly to take part in the invasion and struggle for Europe.

Whatever my exhilaration at this turn of events, I was sad to be leaving Scotland which now held many memories for me, and above all that of Diane. There could have been no more fitting a complement or guardian of this memory, than Scotland's great natural beauty. Of Scotland I would choose as my most unforgettable experience one afternoon when walking, deep in the foothills of Strathmore, for there grew from the wash of the heather-scented breeze in the pines, and tumbling splash of rock-bound streams, the skirl of the pipes. At first almost imperceptible, swelling, fading and then growing slowly in strength, until the mountain air was filled with this wild stirring music as there strode past a kilted figure, piping his solitary way from the hills to some business in a lowland town. The haunting sound then faded once more into the distance and the murmur of the wind. But for the sight of that figure, I could have believed that I had experienced a spontaneous, windborne expression of the ageless soul of Scotland, and its mysterious beauty – and I realised that I had been privileged by the perfect manner in which to hear the pipes.

If I left Flying Training Command for an operational squadron with few regrets, I left with much pride in its achievements. It was a Command which, in the U.K., was fighting its own unremitting battle, pitted against a perpetual challenge in the task of training desperately needed aircrew to the highest standards attainable. This not only in the pitifully short time available, but regardless of the difficulties and dangers of flying in the active service conditions of the European war zone. In this task the Command suffered steady losses in killed and injured,* but the British contempt for teaching is most deeply ingrained, and the fundamental and essential role played in the nation's war effort by Flying Training Command to this day remains unhonoured and unsung.*

---

* Training is not normally associated with casualties, but in all the R.A.F. was to suffer 7,554 killed and 4,204 aircrew injured in flying training accidents, 1939–1945.

Of the 3,000 cases of nervous breakdown and 300 of lack of confidence (L.M.F.) experienced, on the average, annually by the R.A.F. throughout the war, one third was in each of Flying Training and Bomber Commands, the remaining third arising in Coastal, Transport and Fighter Commands jointly.

TO A CITIZEN OF THE FUTURE

Son of my unborne son, it is for you
So many men so much so gladly give,
Think not they loved not life or dared not live
In this poor antic warring world, they too
Saw sunlight on their children's hair and knew
The many joys that God's impartial sieve
Scatters for all as Heaven's commemorative,
These and themselves they forfeited for you.
Keep faith, we pray you, let not our vision lie
That we have seen reflected in the deep
Of hostile seas, framed in a swarming sky,
Lighting the darkened rooms where women weep.
Yours is a dream – perfection set on high,
A dream to furnish our eternal sleep.

O.C. Chave.

CHAPTER 9

The Wings of Azrael

Azrael was appointed to separate the souls from bodies, hence becoming the
Angel of Death.

Mohammedan legend.

For the earthbound, 'To hear the wings of Azrael' heralded approaching death.

In early 1940, O.T.U.s were created to relieve the front-line squadrons of the
operational training role with which they had been occupied during times of
peace. The aim of the O.T.U. course was to raise crews to an operational standard
by both the perfecting of their individual aircrew skills, and the teamwork necessary
in an efficient crew. For the pilot, who in nearly every case acted as captain, it
meant perfecting his specialist knowledge as a pilot, and gaining a working knowledge of each crew member's skills.

After Scotland the gentle Buckinghamshire countryside was a heart-warming
contrast. However, the weather on arrival remained only too familiar for it was
very cold with a freezing north wind bringing occasional light snow. The village
of Wing lay some two miles to the south-west of Leighton Buzzard, and close to
the eastern boundary of Buckinghamshire. The airfield was a Bomber Command
station housing solely No. 26 O.T.U., some Flights of which were based at Little
Horwood, a satellite airfield seven or eight miles away.

The aircraft on which we were to train at this stage was the Vickers Wellington
X, one of the outstanding aircraft of the war. Designed as a medium bomber, it
had formed the bulk of the bomber force until replaced by the four-engined
Stirling, Halifax and Lancaster. The Wellington was powered by two 1585 h.p.
Bristol Hercules radial engines, had a wing span of 86 feet and fuselage length
of 64 feet. With a crew of six, it could carry 6,000 lbs of bombs, and was armed
with six .303" Browning machine guns. A mid-wing monoplane, the Wellington,
of the geodetic construction devised by Barnes Wallis, was capable of withstanding
extensive damage. However, it had several peculiarities, one being that the wings
flexed alarmingly in flight, to which it was difficult to become accustomed.
Another, the astonishing amount of hydraulic oil that seeped everywhere. This
was undoubtedly the main ingredient of the strong and unique Wellington smell,
which all 'Wimpey' aircrew would have instantly recognised blindfold.

The course was hard, working hours being from 06.30 hrs. in the morning until

18.00 hrs. in the evening. There was a sense of purpose about it and many worked on at night by studying on their own. The first fortnight of the course was devoted to intensive ground study, leading to 'crewing-up' or the selection of a crew by the pilots at the end of this time. The choice of a crew was all-important, for not only did the fighting efficiency of a crew depend upon the quality of its every member, but on its efficiency to a large extent depended the crew's survival. At that time the Bomber Command casualties were such that there were no histrionics in the thought that it was a choice of alongside whom one would fight, and possibly die – inescapably a matter of consequence.

The ground studies for the pilot were intensive and with an emphasis on airmanship. This, apart from normal piloting procedures and the learning of cockpit and emergency drills blindfold, included a detailed study of the Hercules sleeve-valved engine; the Rotol propeller with which it was fitted; and a general study of the Wellington airframe. At the same time there had to be achieved a working knowledge of Navigation, Armament (Bombing and Gunnery) and Signals. Once crewed-up we would begin training in crash, parachute and dinghy drills. Other crew training included escape, survival, and intelligence in which one was encouraged to learn as much as one could about the enemy and his doings. We were fortunate to have at Wing an outstanding museum and library on this subject.

An aspect of our training which came as a complete surprise was the increased rations served in the Messes. At the time the weekly civilian ration for each person consisted of the following:

Sugar	8 oz
Tea	2 oz
Meat	One shilling and two pence in value, perhaps 12 oz
Cheese	2 oz
Butter	2 oz
Margarine	4 oz
Cooking fat	2 oz
Eggs	1 per two weeks
Dried Eggs	¼ pkt
Milk	2½ pts
Sweets	3 oz

This ration called for great abstinence by the public and the most amazing ingenuity in feeding a family. It was therefore of some embarrassment to find that the rations for aircrew under operational training, or serving in front line squadrons, were greatly increased above the civilian level and in some items such as eggs, bacon, sausages, and sweets seemed almost unlimited. To cap it all we were regularly provided with oranges, which were by then unheard-of in civilian life.

We knew nothing of the arguments upon which this greatly enhanced ration was based, but it was a decision which in the Country's desperate privations cannot have been taken lightly. Undoubtedly such considerations as the physiological effects of flying must have been involved, as must the high incidence of physical failure and nervous breakdown, of which there were in the R.A.F. about 3,000 cases annually. Because aircrew operated in small isolated groups in which confidence and determination were essential, morale must too have been much in mind.

In the R.A.F. there were about 300 cases of 'lack of confidence'* every year, but this was probably realised to be only the tip of the iceberg, for it is not a state to which individuals will readily admit and connivance in crews could have concealed much. Whatever the considerations were, ours was a situation in which the surreptitious and close observation to which we were subjected did not bear contemplation, for there could be no profit in it. In consequence we took full advantage of all that was laid before us, even if it smacked much of the traditionally luxurious meal allowed to the condemned man before execution!

In Buckinghamshire one swiftly became aware of a phenomenon that had not occurred in Scotland – the advent of the Americans in large numbers, and their super imposition on local communities in southern England. One could not avoid becoming aware of the Americans owing to their sharply contrasting characteristics, and the nation was observing them in some astonishment, for the Americanization of the U.K. had not then reached the advanced degree to be experienced later. The mentality of the 'throwaway' society was completely new to us, as was the affluence that allowed it. The basic discipline, conservatism, modesty, reserve and restraint in the upbringing of the British was restricting, and placed us at a disadvantage in the confidently sweeping approach of the Americans to every problem, great or small. My initiation into the American presence was harsh and came about at a party organised for us by local residents. There I was introduced to a charming girl who in the course of the evening commented to me that she hardly noticed the R.A.F. in the district, and anyway those that she knew seemed to get killed† – but the Americans were wonderful.

The American G.I.s' generosity, naivety and charm was most endearing, as was much of their humour, but obviously we could not take kindly to hearing from these late arrivals that they had come to win the war for us – however decisive their latent strength and immense production was to prove to be. Socially the G.I.s were female-orientated, while our men were male-orientated. The G.I.s as a result, were most successful with our women and children, but not with our men. The G.I.s' eleventh commandment was (they held): Thou shalt not dip thy wick in the W.A.C.s (U.S. Womens Army Corps) an admonition certainly not extended to our W.R.N.S., W.A.A.F., A.T.S., and so on. The American lack of inhibition, the superior material of their uniform, higher pay, and access through their welfare services to many luxury goods which were unobtainable in the U.K., made them formidable competitors in the quest for female company. This, added to the British girl's ignorance of the superficialities of the American dating and petting system, enabled Americans wherever they were to make a clean sweep of the local girls. All of which deeply upset our own Servicemen and led to the bitter comment that the trouble with the Americans was that they were:

'Over-paid, Over-fed, Over-sexed, And over here!'

---

* A euphemism for what had once been broadly termed 'going yellow'.

† Perhaps she should be forgiven this statement as she had, I learned, been engaged to three R.A.F. aircrew members in succession, who had all been killed.

Once General Eisenhower had been appointed Supreme Commander of the Allied Expeditionary Force in Western Europe, the Americans neatly riposted that the trouble with the British was that they were:

'Under-paid, Under-fed, Under-sexed, And under Eisenhower!'

For all of this the relationship remained friendly, if critical, and created a prolific exchange of comment, amongst which were many gems such as the American term of 'blunderbuss' for a baby's perambulator! There was, too, the British wry criticism of the inadequacy of the new utility panties, all that was then obtainable – just one Yank and they were off!

Attitudes have changed so radically that it is, for instance, impossible to recreate the public view of flying at this time. Today flying is an everyday form of transport, and those who have not travelled in this way are a rapidly dwindling minority. However although the public considers itself to be familiar with flying, it knows little more about it than it ever did; other than the clinical process of passenger handling and encapsulation in a cabin. There in the greatest possible comfort, the passengers experience a few of the mildest sensations of flight, but are otherwise completely insulated from the complex procedures and problems of flying even a passenger aircraft of limited performance and large margins of safety. This experience has formed a restricted image of flying in the public mind which, understandably, the air transport industry has been at pains to instil and perpetuate. It has, however, totally obscured the realities of flying, particularly in the field of light aircraft where limited knowledge and facilities predominate, or equally in high-performance military aircraft with complex operating and physiological problems, as well as extremely narrow safety margins. This image has now produced so naive and knowing a conceit in the public understanding of those who crew aircraft, that it is difficult to imagine the admiration and respect with which the few connected with flying were regarded on the outbreak of war in 1939. The conquest of the air was then new, the depths of its difficulties and dangers were largely unplumbed, and the concept of flying was intensely exciting and exhilarating. Anyone who had actually flown was then a great rarity; vested in considerable mystery, and attributed with all but superhuman qualities.

The aerial engagements of the Battle of Britain, unlike a land or sea battle, had been fought in full view of millions of the nation's people. The 'knights of the air' concept was inescapable, and the R.A.F. as a whole acquired a considerable reflected glamour and glory. This was unfortunate in that it understandably engendered bitter feelings in the Army and Navy, who had suffered hideous losses in less spectacular battles, so often out of sight and largely out of mind. The Navy and Army held the R.A.F. to be an effete bunch of glamour-boys, who had it remarkably easy in the comfort of their bases behind the lines, and particularly in the U.K. with every comfort provided on permanent airfields. This image was not in the least improved by the advertising for a men's hair fixative, Brylcream. Cashing in on the euphoria surrounding the R.A.F. after the Battle of Britain, this company produced a more than life-size poster of a nauseatingly good-looking commissioned pilot, with a simpering smile and hair plastered down in glossy magnificence, presumably with Brylcream. This did it, and to the senior Services the R.A.F. aircrew were the Brylcream boys from then on.

Curiously, although the R.A.F. may have held a place in the forefront of the public mind by virtue of the novelty and glamour of flying, there was very little consciousness of what it was doing. In the fastness of the English countryside the contrast of large forces of heavy aircraft leaving every night over a land of comparative peace and quiet, for attacks on targets in Europe, was most marked. The populace had not the slightest idea of what it all meant, and consequently could feel little involvement. The endless publicity given to the American air operations by day, from southern England, caught the nation's imagination and completely swamped the night operations of the R.A.F. which was then delivering a far greater tonnage of bombs and suffering far greater losses. The Americans had arrived in Britain with an extensive public relations system, not only to smooth their integration into the U.K., but to tell the people there and in the U.S.A. what the American Servicemen were doing, albeit in a highly coloured account. Such a public relations system was then totally foreign to us and our ingrained characteristics of restraint and modesty. In truth, we just would not have known how to set about it had we so desired, which by no means was certain. Attempts were made to develop our P.R. but in the main we continued with such communiques as: 'Aircraft of Bomber Command last night attacked enemy targets – some of our aircraft failed to return,' which was certainly not giving anything away either to the enemy or ourselves! As a result the activities of Bomber Command were not only unpublicised but very ill recorded. The bulk of the photographic material available today was obtained with amateurs' illicit still or cine cameras; private cameras of any form being strictly forbidden on R.A.F. stations under the Official Secrets Act.

Returning to Wing, the time for crewing-up at the end of the first fortnight of the course was fast approaching and this would be a crucial moment. In the spring of 1942, some two years earlier, the decision was taken to fly heavy bombers with only one pilot instead of two. An automatic pilot was to be installed to assist. The decision created the need and opportunity to reshuffle aircrew duties and resulted in several new aircrew categories. In the place of the second pilot, a Flight Engineer was to be carried. To free the Navigator for the increasing complexity of navigation and its equipment, a Bomb Aimer/Gunner was introduced. Finally, one of the two Wireless Operator/Gunners was replaced with a straight Gunner. The comparison between the new and old heavy bomber crew was as follows:

pre-1942	1942 onwards
1st Pilot	Pilot
2nd Pilot	Flight Engineer
Observer/Gunner	Navigator
	Bomb Aimer/Gunner
1st Wireless Operator/Gunner	Wireless Operator/Gunner
2nd Wireless Operator/Gunner	Gunner
	Gunner

The new heavy bomber crew achieved a logical distribution of duties and a great training economy. Had the policy of two pilots prevailed, the essential expansion of Bomber Command would have been severely curtailed and limited to a very much smaller force.

A major problem in the reorganisation was that of morale. A crew could not be expected to commit itself to battle with the knowledge that in the likely event of the pilot being wounded or killed, they would be all but totally helpless and destined to a pointless death. This problem was recognised, but authority's solution was something of a sop. It was announced that one other member of the crew would be given some piloting experience, and in the main this consisted of a limited number of hours' instruction on a Tiger Moth. Sometimes, fortuitously, a member of the crew was a failed pilot and had more than the average of 'emergency pilot' knowledge and experience. However, he *was* a failed pilot, which can hardly have instilled confidence. To this I gave much thought, as it seemed fundamental to the efficiency of a crew as a fighting unit. However, it never appeared to be a significant consideration in my own crew. I had immense respect for such aircrew, who in carrying out their duties not only regularly put themselves in the hands of a sometimes none too skilled pilot, but stoically faced the likelihood of the loss of that pilot and the nightmare consequences – this as well as the conditions we all faced in going into battle.

At the time of our crewing-up the crew of a training Wellington numbered six and consisted of a Pilot, Navigator, Bomb Aimer, Wireless Operator and two Gunners. We then expected to add an Engineer and additional Gunner at the next stage of training, the Heavy Conversion Unit, where we would convert to four-engined aircraft. With some experience in judgement of character, I had formed an idea of the sort of men I hoped to gather as a crew. These would be 'six good men and true', primarily of specialist capability but secondarily men of a general capability that would surmount the emergencies of survival* and evasion.†

This would require men of self-discipline and stability which would be proof against the demoralising circumstances of, amongst other things, sudden, violent and perhaps disastrous happenings. These comfortable thoughts were all very well, but every other captain would be looking for the same qualities and I would have to make my choice rapidly, or be left without one. In the event it was surprising that for most the choice of a crew seemed a very hit-or-miss affair, and was frequently based on the strangest of qualifications and requirements, some of which were dubious in the extreme.

The evening before the crewing-up of our course, I was approached in the Mess by a Pilot Officer Bomb Aimer with a request to join my crew. This took me by surprise, and the ensuing conversation did little to dispel my initial misgivings. Ron Hitchcock had done some elementary flying at St Andrews University, and while he undoubtedly had the abilities required of an excellent Bomb Aimer, he

---

* Survival – the art of sustaining life on land or at sea when devoid of most or all artificial aids.

† Evasion – the art of living or moving in enemy, or enemy-occupied territory, without capture.

seemed a most unlikely fighting man. It was open to me to say that I would think about it, but to my astonishment I made a snap decision and accepted him as the first member of my crew. Ron was four years younger than myself, a charming and egocentrically inclined individual who took himself and his deep interest in the arts most seriously. He was what in those days might have been termed 'Very B.B.C.' (with which he had connections) and his cultured accent and interests might have seemed somewhat overpowering.

For crewing-up the next day we were assembled in a large hall in which the aircrew stood in groups of their own category, bringing to mind a Mop-Fair,* as each pilot moved from one category to another slowly collecting a crew. Almost at once I approached an Australian Wireless Operator and following a brief conversation he agreed to join my crew. Len Stretton turned out to be a tough but kind, thoughtful and gentle personality. He had a knowledgeable approach to life, a calm competence, and the easy-going self-confidence of the Australian. He abounded in initiative which he was as likely to exercise when entitled as when he was not. Len's native wildness led him into many strange situations, and he must have become well known to the police throughout the U.K. for his habit of celebrating somewhat incautiously, and finding himself lost in the British country-side. He would then telephone the police from the first telephone box he happened upon and was invariably offered overnight accommodation in a cell, always with early morning tea, and sometimes with a patrol car to collect and later to deliver him at a convenient point on his way.

Alec Mitchell, who joined the crew as Navigator, I judged studious and reliable – suitable navigator material. He had the semi-aloof attitude of the intellectual undertaking a task against his better judgement, and who did not approve of the crew's somewhat rumbustious goings on. Three years younger than myself he was sensitive, quiet, reserved and had, I believe, been reading classics at Cambridge before joining up. While I was doubtful about the general abilities he would need in an emergency, 'Mitch' proved a very capable navigator and never appeared the slightest rattled. I was concerned over his obvious incompatibility with war but, on the face of it at least, he seemed to overcome this by as complete an isolation from it as he could achieve.

The navigating team was now selected, but to complete the crew for that stage we needed two gunners. These appeared together and made it clear that they joined a crew together or not at all. This I liked, and liked even more what I saw and heard of them in a brief conversation. These two were to be our main defence and upon their conscientious and unceasing search of the night sky, through long hours of flight, would depend our survival and I considered them most important. Ormerod Suddall (Sue) was the elder, he came from what must have been a tough environment in Preston where I think he had been a butcher's assistant, and knew how to look after himself. He was confident, proficient and numbered amongst his major interests beer, girls and motorbikes, in an order seemingly dependent

---

* A gathering in the autumn at which, in old England, farm hands and servants were selected and hired.

upon which was occupying him at the time. He looked after his friend Sammy much as an elder brother. Samuel (Sammy) hailed from South Wales, had only just left school, displayed a big grin, was young, happy go-lucky and of course took his lead from Sue.

From this point began our training as a crew. Six extraordinarily dissimilar individuals, who had a remarkably short time to weld into an efficient fighting team. A team which from the moment it became airborne, until it landed again, would be totally isolated and self-reliant. Within that self-reliance entirely dependent upon each other, always in conditions of risk and frequently in periods of intense danger. In taking stock of each other the crew's initial reaction to Ron, the Bomb Aimer, was unfavourable. I had to admit to myself that his general characteristics and good looks did not promise at all well in assessing his likely performance in his crew role. In this matter the crew adopted the air of those suffering an injustice, imposed upon them by a discipline against which there was no redress, and I came in for considerable opprobrium. However, I was absolutely sure that Ron had the ability to become a most competent Bomb Aimer and he had the 'emergency pilot' experience we needed. For all of that, my faith was strained to the very limit when I observed Ron's distaste for his guns, the twin guns of the front turret for which he was responsible, and which he would man if we were attacked. I was utterly dismayed when, during our regular aircrew checks of the aircraft, I realised that he would delay checking these guns (which involved a certain amount of dismantling and reassembling) until the very last possible moment. Only then would he force himself to tackle this task and cover his hands with gun oil. In the event, Ron's outstanding ability as a Bomb Aimer and H2S* Operator, with his completely imperturbable coolness in directing the run-up on even the most heavily defended of targets, was later to earn the respect of us all. We were to become a crew devoid of any clashes of personality, and with a real respect and affection for each other. I could not possibly have wished for any better.

Our training as a crew began in the aircraft (or a training fuselage in the Airmanship Hall) with the endless practice of crash, parachute and dinghy drills. Once a certain proficiency had been achieved in these, we graduated to practising parachute landings in a hangar by jumping from an uncomfortably high staging in the roof, suspended in a harness which lowered one to the ground at the same speed as would a parachute. We also practised the wet end of dinghy drills in a local swimming pool, where we learned to inflate, right and board a dinghy from the water. This was far from pleasant and it was not difficult to imagine what it would be like at night, in the North Sea. In all of this we were becoming used to working together, learning our emergency duties, co-ordinating our actions and growing to rely upon each other. Above all we were gaining the essential proficiency that would enable us to get out of the aircraft in the few seconds which would be available to us in an emergency, and once clear, to survive.

At the end of February we transferred to the satellite airfield, leaving Mitch (the

---

* An airborne radar homing equipment code named Home Sweet Home and thereby H2S.

Navigator) behind to finish a course on the electronic navigation aid, Gee. The airfield lay between the villages of Little and Great Horwood, Little Horwood being seven or eight miles from Wing and six miles south-east of Buckingham. Little Horwood* was a quaint village complete with a lovely old church, village blacksmith, pond and public house. For all its charm it was not exactly pretty, but to me it was particularly attractive as it was wonderful to be back in the English countryside; and there was the added seduction that my sleeping quarters were in a Nissen hut across the road from the village pub, the Swan!

Although Little Horwood had a large R.A.F. airfield and camp superimposed upon it this was not particularly noticeable, except perhaps first thing every morning when it was for a while alive with men hurrying on duty. Even then, the clatter of feet in the still morning air seemed no more than a vulgar and unwarranted intrusion that could in no way detract from the age-old calm and peace of so typical an English country village. The brightly coloured curtains in the cottage windows remained closed to the morning sun, as no doubt they always had done; a farmer's boy led two old carthorses through the village at six-thirty every morning, as no doubt he always had done. Occasionally one would hear the clank of a pump as an anonymous early riser filled a water bucket; but strangely they were never to be observed; perhaps a gently closing cottage door the only clue to their identity. The birds sang in the thatch as though to shame us so-called early risers, and the little Swan Inn looked as though it never opened, no doubt as it always had done.

Here were based the detached Flights from Wing, in one of which we would make our conversion to the Wellington. Here too, I was to suffer a considerable shock at the ill-concealed hostility of the flying staff in which there was no vestige of mutual respect, fellowship or welcome as a brother officer. From the start I was made to feel most unwelcome and it might well have been that not only I belonged to, and was paid by an entirely separate organisation, but that the O.T.U. staff and myself were independent agents working to totally different ends. After so long in achieving an O.T.U. course I was enormously looking forward to it, and had sought as much information on the subject as could be obtained in the ever-prevailing atmosphere of wartime secrecy. I had learned that there were, at that time, very few Qualified Flying Instructors at the O.T.Us., and that the bulk of the staff were Screened Pilots – pilots who were resting from operational work and who had been pressed into the training role. While these were loosely termed 'Instructors', this was a misnomer which was later changed to Staff Pilots.

By the standards of those days I was a senior Flight Lieutenant, and not only a Q.F.I. of some experience, but had in addition the experience of instructing flying instructors. This I endeavoured to keep very much to myself as I was at O.T.U. to learn to fight in the air – and of this had little or no knowledge whatsoever. The bulk of the pilot students of my course were straight from the Service Flying

---

* The villages of Great and Little Horwood had many similarities and to us became synonymous as the airfield and its dispersal sites in both villages were collectively known as R.A.F. Little Horwood. It is in this sense that I refer to Little Horwood, although the inhabitants will be aware of the inevitable discrepancies.

Training Schools (S.F.T.S.) such as Rissington and South Cerney, which I had myself experienced, and they had as little knowledge of fighting in the air. I was then completely taken aback when no sooner had I arrived than I was summoned to the Flight Commander's office and there, before a number of his staff, was read a vicious and vindictive 'riot act'. Told that whatever I *might* think, I was a bloody student pilot, and as far as he was concerned any knowledge or experience I *might* think I had, meant f—k all – and that he wanted no C.F.S. (Central Flying School) shit in his Flight.

Here again was the comfortable, very loosely disciplined, airforce within an airforce. The parasite airforce that here held immediate sway, and the standards of which were solely those of convenience. I was undoubtedly seen as officialdom, a threat to their cosy, mutually supported mediocrity – and had been warned to conform or else! Any such behaviour as my Flight Commander obviously feared was not in my make-up and what he had to say was alright by me, and in different terms went without saying. What was not alright was that my Flight Commander should have demeaned himself by such a wild and fearful exhibition. An exhibition which had patently been prepared before my arrival, and which, having estranged me from my Flight Commander, left me without the proper channel of Service communication with authority which is every officer's right.

We began our conversion to type on the earlier Wellington Mark III, which was even heavier on the controls than the Mark X we were to fly later. It was not a pleasant aircraft to fly, and amongst others had the extraordinary characteristic of sharply rising some 300′ when flap was lowered in flight, unless a very heavy forward counter-pressure was applied to the control column. For me there were no problems, but hauling this aircraft about was most unrewarding and, as luck would have it, the situation almost immediately became fraught. There was no doubt in my mind that one of my first flying 'instructors' was incompetent, to the extent of being not only dangerous, but worse still was fully aware of this, and consequently was totally dogmatic.

I had not survived thus far to be killed, possibly with my crew, by furthering a collusion with incompetence. This was a situation I could well have done without, and had to make an awkward decision. I approached the Flight Commander privately to suggest that this instructor should be rested. His reaction was predictable, subjecting me to an outraged and lengthy tirade – but I was not detailed to fly with the instructor in question again. Some days later he lost control of his aircraft on take-off, swung and hit a petrol bowser* killing himself, the student pilot, the crew, and destroying not only the other aircraft refuelling at the bowser, but several vehicles. Having so forcibly discredited me, my Flight Commander was in a position which would never have occurred had he possessed any sense of responsibility and leadership, or the natural ability to command. He took the predictable way out, and let it be known to me that for someone in my position I had committed the heinous offence of being right, and for this I would not be forgiven or forgotten.

---

* Bowser – an aircraft refuelling tanker.

In spite of these difficulties we progressed rapidly, and after exercises in feathering the Rotol electric propeller, and landing the aircraft without flap, I was sent solo. From then on we flew detail after detail of circuits and landings, interspersed with dual checks. This was invaluable to me, but nothing short of tedious for the rest of the crew, and it was during this stage of the course that a particularly unfortunate accident was to occur in the Flight. The cockpit of the Wellington was situated between the propeller tips of the two engines, and for this reason was firstly very noisy (I was later to develop high-tone deafness caused by long hours of such engine noise) and secondly dangerous. Ice would, for instance, often be flung from the propellers in flight to batter the cockpit wall and perspex roof. The pilot's and instructor's seats were side by side in this cockpit, and when flying solo captains of aircraft would sometimes encourage other crew members to sit in the instructor's seat for experience. This was the case with one crew whose captain brought up the rear gunner during a detail of circuits and landings. On a subsequent take-off the starboard propeller began to overspeed (one of the less attractive habits of the Rotol propeller) and unless remedied very quickly the propeller would go out of control. Just this happened, the engine at once raced at an incredible speed and the propeller flew to pieces – one piece of which passed through the starboard cockpit wall and the rear gunner, killing him instantly.

Mitch had now rejoined us, and once proficient in day flying the aircraft we began practice bombing exercises at increasing heights. We were then flying about five hours a day in two details, for which we were up at six-thirty in the morning and were rarely finished by six at night. We worked a seven-day week, sometimes for four weeks at a stretch before being granted forty-eight hours leave – I remember being very tired. Bombing practice was a welcome exercise for this was the purpose of our entire training. To sight bombs accurately the aircraft had to be flown on a long run into the target, straight and level, at an exact speed. It was difficult enough in practice, but in action this run made the aircraft a perfect target for predicted anti-aircraft fire or enemy fighters, which knowledge was likely to raise the hair on the back of one's neck to say the least of it.

We were determined to obtain first-class bombing results, and never tired of practice in an endeavour to perfect the procedures. Again and again we ran up on that target, sometimes scoring better hits, sometimes worse, but always learning. In their bomber offensive the Germans had sown a wind and were now reaping a whirlwind. Of the many things which we then saw ourselves, primarily we saw ourselves as avengers. We did not see the target below as a white circle but as the warships, harbours, munition factories and so on which we would be briefed to attack. In all of this, I doubt that we ever saw ourselves as the 'angels of death', which we might well have done.

Day bombing training completed, we went over to night flying, and after the required number of hours on the circuit were once again practice bombing, but this time at night. Somehow I was at the same time cramming instruction on Gee[*]

---

[*] Trials had shown that Gee could place a bomber within five miles of a target, at the extreme range of 400 miles from the transmitters.

(the navigation aid) during the day. I particularly remember that one day in passing from the Mess through the village to the Gee Training Section, I met a truly venerable farmworker carrying two buckets on a yoke, on his way to feed the pigs. A happy old fellow who touched his cap and bade me good morning. Under my arm I was carrying a book of lettered co-ordinates, and was on my way to gaze into cathode ray tubes and other such equipment of which he could not even remotely dream. The utter contrast was mind-boggling, for we had not then started on the headlong rush of the spendthrift consumer-society, or the technological revolution promised to sweep all before it and create an earthly paradise. For a time in Little Horwood the very old and the very new were face to face. Unsuspecting Little Horwood had no conception of what might happen to it in this confrontation, or realisation that anything might happen to it at all.

The evening before, on the way to my quarters, I had been struck by the mellow loveliness of the sound of the church bells* in the soft light of the evening sun. It was Sunday and little groups of villagers in their best clothes, the day's work completed, were wandering towards the old church beside the Green for all the world as though time was not. With this in mind I felt strangely torn, for as a child of the new technological era I was in thrall to the fascination of the technical achievement that was a modern bombing aircraft, and inspired by all that would be developed from it in the future. But, I loved the timeless beauty, simplicity and humanity of life in Little Horwood, and wondered if its inevitable modernisation would improve any of these things, or in terms of true values would improve the quality of human life there at all. I had an uneasy feeling that they were then so very much nearer to God in Little Horwood, than was I in my world. When such changelessness had been swept away by the predicted torrent of progress, what god would Little Horwood worship, I wondered.

There was at this time, in the south of England, increasing evidence of the concentration of huge quantities of men, vehicles, guns and ammunition. With this went a mounting tension that, in spite of extreme security, clearly indicated the approach of the long-awaited invasion of France. We were determined to be involved from its very start, which much increased out sense of urgency in the course. Many of the training aircraft we were flying had a full 'short-range't bomb load permanently laid out beside the dispersal, for immediate bombing-up. This looked promising and led to much conjecture. In the absence of any information whatsoever on the subject we reduced the possibilities to two – either we would be called upon to take part in a pre-invasion bombardment of the French coast and rearward communications or, more likely, we would be called in if all did not go well and the landings were in danger of becoming bogged down. In either case

---

* Church bells had begun to be rung again in April/May 1943 and in many cases ringers absent on war service were for the first time replaced by women.

† The load of a bomber aircraft was made up of fuel and bombs in a variable ratio. The further the aircraft was required to travel, and therefore the more fuel it had to carry, the smaller would be the bomb load. Conversely, the less distance it had to travel the bigger would be the bomb load.

resistance was certain to be ferocious and we would begin our tour of operational work by being flung in at the deep end.

At the end of March we were sent on brief leave from Little Horwood, to return to Wing where we were scheduled to carry out navigation and gunnery training, the next phase of the course. On the way back I had arranged to meet Ron at Euston, and he turned up at the very moment all the station lights went out. In the hush that followed could be heard the wail of distant air raid warnings. While seeking our platform we were joined by a very young W.A.A.F. officer, who became extremely jumpy as anti-aircraft gunfire opened up and shell splinters started rattling around us. After two years in Scotland away from it all it was quite like old times, there was hardly a soul to be seen and the only light was from the flicker of the guns.

A cheery porter assured us that the train would leave on time, and indeed it did. In our compartment were an army officer-cadet, two soldiers, the W.A.A.F. officer and ourselves. It was dark, which was as well for the persistent piping of the W.A.A.F. was particularly irritating. By virtue of her uniform she considered herself an authority on all things aeronautical, and insisted upon giving a completely nonsensical running commentary on what she imagined was going on. What was actually happening was that as we crawled out of Euston, the German aircraft were putting down target-marker flares on London. Ron's professional interest was instantly aroused, and hanging out of the window he began making enthusiastic predictions as to what the bombers were aiming for. This he did by a somewhat Heath-Robinson calculation of the wind, the height of the attacking aircraft and his considerable knowledge of London. It was splendid stuff but suddenly, all enthusiasm gone, he pulled his head back into the carriage to the accompaniment of a horror-stricken, 'Oh my God – there are markers falling on Euston station!' I put my precious carton of eggs under the seat and attempted to sit on the floor, but the W.A.A.F. had got there first and by great good fortune I must have winded her, because instead of the hard floor it was delightfully comfortable, and she abruptly stopped prattling.

Sure enough, in a few seconds we were engulfed in the rending, tearing, rushing sound of a prolonged hail of tons of incendiaries. I discovered afterwards that the train was hit some eight times and on fire in several places, but it continued to crawl away from the station for which we were heartily thankful. Everything around us appeared to be burning and the station yards were swamped in the brilliant light of blazing incendiary bombs. Our own bombing tactics were to mix incendiaries with high explosive and I was tensed for just this but, while bombs were falling in the near and far distance, mercifully no high explosive fell around us. The train crawled on to stop suddenly, presumably for the fires to be extinguished after it had cleared the fallen incendiaries. The only noise was the noise of the raid, a spine-chilling orchestration to which, however often I had heard it before, it was impossible to become accustomed. With experience came only an increasing awareness of what was happening about one. There was comparatively little to be seen but much to be heard. The ominous pulsating drone of enemy aircraft in the night sky shot through and through one with a chill apprehension, while the wavering searchlights and melancholy sporadic crump of anti-aircraft fire seemed only to emphasise this malevolent presence. The enemy's intentions, although obviously lethal, were unknown to those below – not all could be at risk, but was one amongst those who were? With this thought uppermost, every nerve would be strained to catch the first sounds of the swelling, whistling, rushing, roar of bombs cleaving a downward path at terminal velocity. Once this was detected there remained only a split second in which to assess, by the increasing volume of sound, how close a strike was likely to be, and if necessary to dash for cover. This dash was of a nightmare quality for cover had to be reached before the tearing sound ceased in a blinding flash, earth-heaving explosion and searing, buffeting blast which left the senses shattered and numbed.

The duration of the eerie silence which would follow must have depended on the recovery of one's faculties, but always seemed surprisingly protracted. In reality it can only have lasted briefly, until there began the extended thud and patter of landing debris which had been hurled high into the air by the explosion. More likely than not this would be accompanied by the groans of the dying, shrieks of the trapped and mutilated, and perhaps the first shouts of would-be rescuers. Only then did one gradually become aware of being unharmed. I don't remember experiencing any particular feelings at the time of such an escape, but when the bombardment moved away and the noise of the gunfire and enemy aircraft faded into the distance, there undoubtedly arose in the hearts of the survivors a great and unashamedly selfish relief. Even if only a temporary reprieve, for the time being it was others who were at risk and were to die. With this realisation the light-hearted and jocular comment came discreditably easily in concealment of a barely departed gamut of emotions ranging from apprehension to gut-watering fear. It was such thoughts that were racing through my mind with the realisation that the train afforded not only the meanest of cover, but was raised into the danger zone well above ground level. The raid ebbed and flowed around us, however following the first cascade of incendiaries nothing fell particularly close, and after what seemed an absolute age the train began to move again gathering speed slowly on its way to Leighton Buzzard.

At Wing the next morning we reported to 'C' Flight, and began an intensive period of day and night cross-country exercises, between which were sandwiched a number of fighter affiliation practices. In these a Hurricane or Tomahawk fighter would make continuous attacks upon us, and under the direction of the gunners I took the most violent evasive action possible. The gunners were always confident that they had shot the attacker down – the rest of us ardently hoped that they were right, and didn't pursue the matter further! For experience I spent thirty-five minutes in the rear turret which more than confirmed my knowledge of its difficulties and discomforts. An attacking fighter presented a tiny head-on target, and swinging the hydraulically operated turret onto it with any accuracy demanded a considerable degree of practice and skill. Given this, I knew four .303" Browning machine guns to be inadequate in range and hitting power, in spite of their capacity to put 8,000 rounds a minute into the air. This could be very effective at close range, but I wondered if we welcomed the idea of a cannon-firing fighter at close range? I did not know how aware the crew might be of our limited capability for defence but to my knowledge, by intent or otherwise, the subject was never raised and I certainly would not have alluded to it. In my own mind I was sure that survival depended upon the cover of darkness, and that if we were attacked it would then depend upon the alertness of the gunners in spotting the fighter early enough for effective evasive action. Our guns I regarded as a last resort; we were not likely to get the better of a far more heavily armed and manoeuvrable fighter.

The flying programme was intensive and only broken briefly by bad weather or crew sickness. Ron at one time sprained an ankle and was grounded for a day or two. As an essential of the course was crew training, the whole crew was grounded; on these occasions we headed for Leighton Buzzard or Aylesbury, in what really amounted to a desperate search for a change of environment. It was in just such a way that one memorable evening I found myself in our favourite Leighton Buzzard haunt – The Plume of Feathers.

The Plume of Feathers was one of those small and simple country inns, that in happier days had provided the basic needs of the market throng and accommodated the occasional hardy traveller. It had a remarkable air of nondescript stability, as it was hard to see what changes may have taken place there in past decades, or to imagine any changes taking place in future decades – for it continued to serve its purpose. As in those happier days it rejoiced in a generally faded style of brown grained-oak paintwork, nicotine-smoke-stained ceilings and ageless, grubby plain-wood furniture. Here in the evenings of 1944, the Service men and women stationed in the area crammed its little bar rooms to the exclusion of all but the hardiest locals, seeking the warm friendliness of its smoky atmosphere and the few remaining vestiges of life in times of peace that it had to offer. Our visits to this little substitute for home were infrequent, as more often that not we were airborne at this time, clawing through the night on navigation, bombing or gunnery exercises, our minds preoccupied with perfecting our skills, and never able to forget that on these depended not only our effectiveness as an instrument of war, but our very survival.

On this particular evening I was spinning out a tankard of wartime bitter in the Plume of Feathers, idly staring into the flame of the bar counter gas-jet (a jet provided for smokers by a thoughtful proprietor, and where many a corn-cob, churchwarden and aged clay pipe must have been lighted) when I became aware of Sadie. Sadie was a W.A.A.F. Telegraphist, or so I deduced from her badges, and so was her friend, a sweet-looking little Irish girl with an attractive mop of unruly hair and a childishly innocent air. I became aware of Sadie because she intended me to and because Len, our Australian Wireless Operator, was engaging Sadie's friend in a rather one-sided conversation with his casual and shy Australian drawl. It was an aspect of Len that I had not seen before, and for all his tough Australian wiriness he was suddenly very young, very shy, very gentle and a long way from home.

The odds against Len appeared rather uneven (although as it happened I need not have worried) and I turned and joined the group to find that Sadie was an attractive but brash blonde, whose long hair was piled on her head in an attempt to add the inches she lacked to be completely stunning and, entirely inconsequentially, to meet the stringent regulations regarding the amount of hair that could be shown below a W.A.A.F. cap. Her greatcoat, worn with studied carelessness over her shoulders, hung open to show promise of an excellent figure. Sadie was eighteen, the possessor of fascinating dimples, and she knew all the answers. I was no match for her, as in my world there had been no such creatures; but I did my best. We drank, we talked and we laughed as the atmosphere became noisier and smokier, and the evening wore on.

The increasing hubbub in the packed bar room made conversation difficult, but Len was well away with the little Irish girl standing on her toes looking up to him in frank admiration, and he was enjoying her in his offhand, almost disinterested way. There was true beauty in the bright-eyed look of wondering bliss I saw that night in a little Irish girl, as she was lifted to the ceiling by a strange Australian aircrew wireless operator with the casual ease with which he had lifted many a bale back home. There in the thick atmosphere of a blacked-out bar room was a fleeting glimpse of a beauty that mankind has known from time immemorial, and which even the inhumanity of war could not suppress.

Someone was raising hell about his inability to get a room for the night, the problem apparently being that he wanted a double room and, as was nearly always the case in those days, no room of any sort was to be had for miles around. A very happy American airman with an English girl on his arm was trying in a fuddled, open-hearted generosity to offer his room in The Plume of Feathers for, as he explained to all and sundry, while he had two rooms they were only going to use one anyway. This rather complicated conversation dragged on. Time passed in the immaterial manner of a successful party, stray comments were made about last buses, but the effort of getting those concerned together seemed to be too great, and no one was very perturbed.

All too soon mine host called time and the crowd began good-naturedly to sort itself out and drift into the summer's night. I found myself on the pavement in the warm moonlight with Sadie. Sadie, it seemed, was stationed at Chicksands, an R.A.F. signals centre about which I vaguely knew, and Sadie was even vaguer about her bus. We walked to the little bus station, but not only was the entire place shut up and lifeless; there was a dreadful air of finality about it as if no bus would ever run from there again. One had a growing sense of disaster as the entire population settled down for the night. Blackouts were up, windows shut and doors barred. Uppermost in my mind was the fact that I was due to fly early the next morning – and as my instructor had once bluntly said, 'A tired pilot is like as not a dead pilot.'

There was nothing for it but to set out on foot, which we promptly did for after all, as I consoled myself, there are worse things than walking in the still, warm moonlight with an attractive girl. Sadie's hand was soft, warm and unre-sisting which was a surprise, and we walked through the night hand in hand, talking as the miles slipped by.

While Sadie was evasive about the exact distance to her billet, it became in-creasingly obvious that it was a very long way (twelve miles as the crow flew, and much further than that through the winding country lanes) and I began to feel that not only had I been taken for something of a sucker, but worse still was demonstrably so. However, there was nothing for it but to see her home. Something of my concern must have communicated itself to her because, when later we paused to rest against a gate in the shadows of a leafy lane, Sadie put her hand to her head and let a tumble of blond hair fall rippling over her shoulders, flickering silver in the dappled moonlight. She lent back on the gate and from her nonchalant stance and tilted head, I could sense the cool challenging look in her eyes. We walked on, the silent hours slipped past while we verbally sparred and duelled, and I mused as to what sort of creature it was that could be so beautiful and yet so steel-hard.

It was Sadie who suddenly drew me through a gate and subsided beside some stacked straw bales. While Sadie undoubtedly knew where she was, I did not. However, thankful for the rest I lay beside her, gazing in silent wonder at the stars in the peaceful immensity of the crystal-clear night sky. There flashed across the heavens a shooting star and with it the realisation that the night sky held my destiny, for to it I must inevitably return and there by all reckoning I should certainly die in a burst of flame, perhaps not so spectacularly as the shooting star, but no less finally; one moment there and the next moment gone. Such beautiful tranquillity would then never be for me to know again, which made all the more precious this moment to which fate, for some unfathomable purpose, had led us together in solitude and which I was acutely conscious could only pass never to return. Tomorrow would be another day but life, I conjectured, for all its agonies surely remained very lovely.

As if my silence was some reflection upon herself, Sadie bent over me. The touch of her lips, the flurry of blonde hair and soft warmth of her undulating shirt pressing through an open tunic, so startled me that I sat bolt upright. Sadie fell away at my side and lay looking at me in pained surprise. I rolled over to look down at her, never having known anything so wickedly tantalizing, and was confused by a surging flood of strange, powerful and conflicting feelings. I had absolutely no intention of taking on Sadie – and yet now some chivalrous streak refused to ignore that in her own way, and in her own language, she had paid me a great compliment. I could of course kiss her – in fact it seemed I should kiss her – or even must kiss her, although I well knew that likely to be as inevitable and masochistic a self-destruction as courting a female praying mantis. I lent slowly closer until our lips touched – it was cool and delightful – she lay perfectly still without the slightest response, seeming to wait as the young female animal waits having created a situation, without any show of interest or enthusiasm and in complete submission to the inevitable course of nature.

There can be nothing romantic in removing a uniform tie, it can only be businesslike. I knelt beside Sadie who was lying relaxed on the straw-scattered turf, eyes closed and arms outflung above her head in the instinctive pose of abandon which can be intensely stirring to the male; and yet for all the world appear the sweetest sleep of innocence. I knew that she felt the gentle unbuttoning of her airforce blue shirt, though she gave no sign of it, but it was as I drew the shirt back over her shoulders that I experienced a strange uneasiness. The silver moonlight poured down on her, adding to the flawless soft whiteness of her skin an indescribable translucent and marble-like sheen, yet with an amazing quality of soft roundness. My natural primeval urge deserted me, and I was left as awed and hesitant as in leaving heavy insensitive footmarks in virgin snow.

How coarse seemed those ill-stitched seams in the rough stuff of the Service issue brassière, stretched tight and living over her breasts; and fascinated by the wonder revealed, how incongruous were the clumsy fumblings in releasing the fastenings. At last it lay arresting, but now crumpled and inanimate, where I had cast it on the grass. It was then that my first strange sense of uneasiness (so like the bars of silence following the opening chords of some great paeon of triumph and joy) because meaningful, for as I turned to gaze in awe at the rising marble-white curves of her perfectly shaped breasts, it was indeed as if some vast choir and orchestra had burst into a crescendo of exultation that echoed and re-echoed into the starry infinity above us. Here was perfection in line upon line, curve upon curve of thrilling vibrant beauty as unashamed and unadorned Sadie arched her quivering breasts to me. Perfection in this girl, one of millions, Sadie, who did not know and would never understand the meaning and value of so priceless a possession.

While the heavens still seemed to echo with the fading sounds of that tumultuous introit, I was left crying the pitifully threadbare phrase, 'My god, you're beautiful'. It was a prayer and it was a thanksgiving, 'Beautiful – beautiful – beautiful,' and in the monotony of its repetition for me it became only the more sincere, but to Sadie this was unintelligible and she opened her eyes in puzzled bewilderment. Gently I touched this exquisite beauty as though for fear that it was unreal – or would disappear. Her dark, full, perfectly rounded nipples rose to my feather caress like some delectable flower unfolding from a bed of snow, and my fingertips ran back and forth slowly and ceaselessly savouring every inch of her soft warm loveliness, as some blind man desperately memorises a passing joy. Impulsively Sadie gently folded me into her arms drawing my head to her breasts and softly caressing the nape of my neck, for all the world as though I were a child hurt by some overwhelming emotion. In silence and stillness I lay lost in the joy of this revelation, this living proof of my faith in life, and fell gradually into the sweetest of sleep.

The shrug of Sadie's shoulders as she later dressed unmistakably proclaimed her disappointment in the occasion, and no doubt in herself for being so daftly soft. What went on in the blonde head I could not know, for she was strangely silent – but I remained without a care, born aloft in a glorious knowledge that would only die with me. We walked on in the first vague flush and rising scent of a summer's dawn, and the tower of the church whose clock we had heard striking across the fields at last came into view on the horizon. Once in the village Sadie's billet was soon reached, but my problems were by no means over, for naturally the billet was silent and locked. Fortunately it was an old country house and, unabashed, Sadie led me to the fire escape which, it appeared, was anyway the more usual method of entry. I recalled a reference to these Chicksands girls (overheard in The Plume of Feathers) categorizing them as 'Drainpipe Daisies', and wondered how many other unsuspecting escorts had trodden the long road to the foot of that escape. Once up the escape it occurred to me that contrary to popular opinion I was in no enviable position. For an officer to be found at about three in the morning in a W.A.A.F. Other Ranks' billet, would lead to a charge-sheet as long as my arm, and inevitably a court-martial – the outcome of which could never be in doubt – at the very least reduction to the ranks, if not dismissal from the Service, which meant an immediate call-up into the ranks of the army. However, thoughts of this sort seemed ungallant or even cowardly in the circumstances, and after that marathon walk I was looking forward to the intimacy of saying goodbye to Sadie. This turned out to be a strangely disappointing experience, a cool and indifferent kiss with Sadie in my arms soft and warm, but totally unresponsive.

I was dwelling on it when through the window came the unmistakable grating sounds of a foot on the bottom rungs of the fire escape. We froze in each other's arms as the climbing steps stealthily neared the window. Not only I, but Sadie too, was in a desperate plight. The most likely explanation was that the roving Service Police picket had spotted us climbing the escape, and was following us up in the knowledge that provided they used stealth we were inescapably trapped. In moments of danger one's mind anyway works fast, but in addition an unsuspecting Air Force had spent endless time and trouble in making mine work faster to master the successive rapid happenings of flying and war in the air, for which I have many times been deeply grateful. The darkness of the room was only relieved by the lighter patch of dawn sky showing through the window. It was ten to one that the intruder would follow the wall of the room in making a surreptitious search, and then move on into the building through the door. I recalled childhood games of hide-and-seek and sardines in the dark, remembering that the safest place for concealment was in the centre of a large room. There I drew Sadie, and we waited tense and immobile.

Although I could not see him the intruder came through the window and, as I had guessed, moved very slowly and with frequent pauses around the wall of the room. At times there seemed to be two of them, but of this I could not be certain. There was a silence in which he seemed to be listening. The critical moment was near, for once he was on the opposite side of the room to the window I intended to make a dash for the fire escape and the chance of getting away into the gloom before I was apprehended, always supposing that the rest of the picket were not below. Meanwhile Sadie, I hoped, would be able to slip away unnoticed to her room in the ensuing confusion. I was just gathering myself for the fateful dash, when I was astonished to hear a sigh of girlish content and a suffused giggle. The first thought that crossed my mind was that it could only be another W.A.A.F., and then in a flood of relief a sneaking suspicion occurred to me. My loud whisper, 'Len, is that you?' sounded a foolhardy bellow even as I murmured it, but an unmistakably Australian voice answered sheepishly, 'Yes, Skipper.'

This miraculous happening was completed on our reaching the foot of the escape where Len had parked a bicycle, which true to character he had procured in his travels. The bicycle was not fitted with any sort of a step or carrier and there was nothing for it but for me to perch myself on the handlebars, in the manner of some minor native potentate, and we set off. It was far from a dignified procedure, and I was in no doubt as to the propriety of a sergeant pedalling an officer home in this manner through the early hours of the morning. However, as we were shortly destined to enter battle and possibly die together, it seemed a little superfluous to quibble about the finer points of the matter. We arrived at Wing, in this somewhat feudal style, as the sun rose. I never did find out what became of that bicycle, and within a couple of hours we were flying out to sea with the rest of the crew on a cross-country exercise. I was more than busy at the controls and Len was seated angelically at his stuttering wireless sets. If either of us had time for any thoughts of our own, they bore the added sweetness of a mutual confidence between comrades-in-arms.

I was to see Sadie again in the most unexpected of circumstances. As the O.T.U. course wore on we were wrestling with a huge amount of information on a variety of subjects, all of which had to be mastered in a remarkably short time. This required constant study, and such was the intensity of the course that at one time we went without a day off for four weeks. The working hours were long and erratic involving much night flying, and the little time left to oneself had frequently to be devoted to private study. The only place suitable for such study was one's room, which was barely private as these rooms were packed into a Nissen hut, lying on either side of a central corridor. For speed and economy of material the rooms had been constructed with far-from-substantial timber-framed fibreboard walls which did not even reach the hut ceiling.

In these cubicles the proverbial pin could have been heard to drop anywhere in the hut, and although one learned to ignore intruding noise the fact was that it could clearly be heard. The Nissen huts were widely dispersed with other airfield buildings, over a considerable area, to minimise the effect of aerial attack. Such dispersal was particularly tedious to reach in the dark and bad weather, but we were usually so tired that it was very much a case of 'any port in a storm'.

Back at Wing some weeks after the Plume of Feathers incident, I was one evening seated in my utility bedroom lost in a detailed study of engine-handling procedures, when there came a knock at my door. As I did not hear anyone in the passage, the gentle knock was a sufficient surprise for me to wonder if I had imagined it. I listened for it again, but there was no sound, and yet I sensed that there was someone there. Rising from my desk I silently crossed the few feet to the door, alert and fully prepared for another of the practical jokes we were forever playing upon each other. What I was totally unprepared for was the vision revealed of Sadie, 'the steel-hard lovely one', beautifully groomed and standing in my door wearing the rank of Sergeant.

'Sadie,' I gasped, 'Whatever are you doing?'

'Looking for you,' she answered.

'But those stripes?'

'Oh, I borrowed those.'

'But you can't.'

'But I have.'

'But you can't come here.'

'But I am here – it was very difficult.'

'But it's most terribly dangerous.'

'Danger doesn't seem ever to have worried you.'

'But Sadie, I can't allow it.'

'You can.'

'No Sadie, as an officer I can't.'

'But as a human being you can.'

'No, it's too dangerous for you – I can't.'

Sadie looked down in silence, a silence that convicted me as positively as could any words, and she spoke no more.

It was an agonizing situation, and one which at any moment could become catastrophic should Sadie be discovered masquerading in a rank to which she was not entitled, and in an officer's bedroom. The long silence became increasingly difficult to break and I only managed it by blurting out with an unintended harshness, 'Sadie you must go quickly,' and then as she remained silent with eyes downcast, 'You must go – You Must Go – YOU MUST GO.' She left as silently as she had come, and with the fading of her superb almost vision-like presence I was left in some doubt as to whether the whole brief and astonishing incident had actually taken place at all. Grappling frantically with what had occurred, I subsided onto my bed.

Sadie must somehow have stowed away on the bus bringing the Chicksands W.A.A.F. senior N.C.O.s to the Sergeants' Mess dance at Wing that night. Once at Wing she had contrived to obtain a Sergeant's tunic, gain admittance to the Sergeants' Mess, and begun seeking information as to where my room was to be found. The enormity of it was positively stunning, and that she succeeded a masterpiece of intelligence, nerve and determination. For Sadie to enquire after my room alone was dynamite for both of us, she must have done it obliquely and by progressive questioning. The trail would have been a long one, as any N.C.O. encountered in the dance might or might not have known the location of the officers' sleeping quarters in the complex and scattered geography of the camp, but would certainly not know of my room. This information would be limited to a handful of officers and W.A.A.F. batwomen on the Officers' Mess staff, whom it would be almost impossible either to find or question. Even then, there was the critical problem to be overcome of actually finding the right officers' quarters and correct room, in the complete dark of the blackout. How Sadie had achieved it was beyond comprehension, but achieve it she did. Whatever, I wondered, had prompted this desperate venture? Could it have been because in Sadie's catch-as-catch-can world of practical fundamentals, 'boobs' or 'knockers' as they would be known, were only items of crude and smutty humour? Had I unwittingly penetrated the icy indifference of this girl, to touch a glimmer of understanding? What of my part in this incident? I did not want to think of it, or what might or might not have been – for perhaps that night I deftly killed both this physically lovely girl's first real feelings, and first understanding of beauty.

Some considerable time later, I passed a fellow pilot in the corridor of yet another Nissen-hutted Mess somewhere in the Midlands. He was on his way to bed, exhausted by a long flight and diversion to a northern airfield. The sight of me obviously reminded him of something, and he paused wearily.

'There was a W.A.A.F. up there who came to the Mess to see me,' he said. 'She wanted to know if I knew of you, and then whether you were still alive, uninjured and well – she sent her love.'

'Good God,' I said, 'Whoever was that?' for Diane was then in the south.

'Oh, I don't remember,' he answered. 'A very pretty little blonde, with superb dimples,' and with that he turned into his room. It could only have been Sadie. Was Sadie forlornly asking every pilot who passed her way for news of me – and from the sound of it at considerable personal risk and difficulty? I was very humbled, and recalled the deep insight and wisdom of the French airman and author, Antoine de Saint-Exupery, who caused his 'Little Prince' to learn from a fox he befriended that: 'You become responsible forever, for what you have tamed', – and I did not even know Sadie's full name, or an address that might have found her without it.

The climax of the course was the last cross-country exercise, a 'special' exercise or 'nickel', and this would be our first penetration into enemy territory (albeit a shallow one) where we would drop a cargo of leaflets on the unsuspecting French. I still have one of these, which was in the form of a booklet entitled *Chansons de la B.B.C.*, and contained parodies of popular French songs, aimed at ridiculing the Nazis and their French collaborators. This was part of a considerable operation in psychological warfare waged vigorously by both the Germans and ourselves. The booklet did not seem a very weighty blow for freedom, but perhaps it had a value. It carried the inscription, *Nous sont apportées par vos amis de la R.A.F!'* I regret that we were later to be involved in operations that were not nearly so friendly to the French.

All of us were very conscious of the risks, real or imagined, in our first sortie into enemy airspace; the gunners in particular whose task, unlike the rest of the crew, had no end product unless they fired their guns in defence of the aircraft. I had heard the most dreadful story of two crews on such an exercise which were attacked shortly after crossing the enemy coast, and sporadically attacked all the way to their target (dropping zone) and back again. As might be imagined, after so prolonged an engagement, the damage to the aircraft was awful and the crews suffered several dead and wounded. What never occurred to either of them as they slogged it out in the dark was that they were firing at each other.

Astonishing though this may seem at first thought, the fact is that a well-directed stream of tracer from the dark can hardly be interpreted as a friendly action. Even if the recipients were uncertain as to whether this attack was made by friend or foe, they were unlikely to 'turn the other cheek' by withholding their fire, so inviting destruction. Much of the bizarre nature of this incident was undoubtedly attributable to inexperience and the highly sensitive state of the crews, but there was more to it than that and therein lay a major problem. The air gunner's lot was not an enviable one, for with its superior armament the tactics of the Luftwaffe night-fighter in attacking a bomber were to destroy the rear turret while still out of range of the bomber's guns, and then to close in for an easy kill. In an aerial engagement at night the advantage undoubtedly went to him who identified and attacked his target first. There was much evidence to show that in spite of their superior manoeuvrability and armament, the Luftwaffe night-fighters were very wary of attacking a bomber the crew of which was alert and aggressive – the easy kill having obvious advantages. In these circumstances there was great appeal in the gunners firing a warning burst at any threatening shadow, and many captains instructed their gunners to open fire on the slightest suspicion. This inevitably bred a large following of trigger-happy morons operating on the basis of; 'F—k you Jack, at all costs I intend to be alright!'

I had thought about this a great deal, and realising that in the bomber stream there were many circumstances in which a friendly aircraft might be led to act abnormally and become a suspicious shadow, I opted for a positive policy and instructed my gunners that if they were in doubt, to allow the enemy to identify himself by opening fire. To hold fire in these circumstances was akin to allowing one's opponent in a duel to fire first, which needed a good man – but I had two in my gunners. In deciding this policy I had a secondary thought in mind as, having decided that the dark was our best protection, it seemed clear to me that in opening fire the source of the stream of tracer was obvious, and would give a fighter the perfect aiming point. Alternatively it could draw the attention of any marauding fighter which had previously been unaware of the bomber's presence. Against these thoughts I had to weigh the knowledge that the fighter's first burst of fire could be fatal and allow little or no response.

As it happened our Special Exercise from Wing was completed entirely uneventfully. We were left with the realisation that we had actually penetrated the enemy's airspace. A dubious jubilation akin to the childhood experience of having raided an orchard without being observed by the owner.

Our O.T.U. course was now finished and the group photograph of the course, pinned to the crew-room notice board, was adorned with an unfortunate number of carefully inked-in bowler hats or haloes, depending upon whether their owners had been failed the course, or killed in accidents. The enemies that I undoubtedly made had so far not prevailed against me, for I left with an above the average assessment. We had all of us made many friends and acquaintances during this course, but I was not alone in feeling it tempting providence to talk of meeting again when, judging from the Bomber Command losses of the time, so many of us would not live to see the day. In addition, I could not dismiss from mind the sentiment that R. de B. had expressed in a letter on hearing of my enlistment in the R.A.F. as aircrew: 'I hope that we shall meet somewhere – and I don't mean in the same grave!' On looking back, perhaps for these reasons, partings seem to have been of the briefest and frequently offhand to an extent that it is now difficult to believe such casualness. So often they consisted of only a passing shout or at best the briefest of spoken wishes for good luck, and handshakes in silence; concealing perhaps the many unspoken and unspeakable feelings of a common and crucial experience.

We learned we were posted to the No. 3 Group Escape School at Methwold, a clear indication that we were destined for a No. 3 Group Squadron. Rumour had it that this group was in the process of re-equipment with the Avro Lancaster, but that some of its squadrons were still operating on the four-engined Short Stirling aircraft of lower performance. We threw ourselves into the protracted business of Clearing the Station,* in the fervent hope that it would for us be a Lancaster Squadron. I was well pleased with our achievements as a crew but very tired, and it was bliss to know that Diane had contrived, against all odds, to come down from Scotland that I should know I was never alone. There were before me three incredibly precious days of relaxation, joy in Diane's company and the wonder of her love.

---

* One was required to obtain on a certificate, the signature of an authorised person for every section of the station with which one might have been involved, to prove no further liability or involvement.

The Escape School at Methwold provided a number of courses all of which centred around escape and evasion, with physical training activities designed to toughen aircrew before they passed on to squadrons. My crew was attending a Battle Course while I had been detailed to attend the Junior Commander's Course, and this proved extremely interesting – but to my surprise I was not to finish it. We were lectured extensively on International Law as it would affect us, but there was never any suggestion that the Germans might ignore it, as indeed we were later to learn they frequently did. Had we been warned that on capture our interrogation could be tough (to put it mildly) we would have been better prepared. A number of aircrew who had made amazing escapes from Germany, or occupied territory, addressed us at length and we could not have too much of this first-hand experience. Much time was given to training in escape and evasion, and also to toughening physical exercise, aimed largely at fitting us for the life of long-distance movement in the open that this would involve.

After only a week of the course (which ran for three weeks) I was posted to No. 1651 H.C.U. Wratting Common – a No. 3 Group Heavy Conversion Unit. This implied some urgent happening, which could only be the invasion of Europe. Although sorry to leave the Escape School prematurely, I was delighted that we were to take part in the invasion. United again as a crew we arrived at Wratting Common (roughly sixteen miles south of Cambridge) on 19th May, 1944. Here we were to fly the Short Stirling, one of the new heavy bombers, and after this conversion course would join either a Stirling or Lancaster squadron. As the Lancaster was known to be the better aircraft, we continued in our fervent hope that it would for us be a Lancaster squadron.

The Stirling was the earliest of the four-engined bombers to enter R.A.F. Service, having made the first 'heavy' raid on enemy occupied territory in February 1941, but a limited performance soon made it outdated. There were disturbing reports about the poor serviceability of the Stirling, and its inability to climb above 17,000 feet (or less) when fully laden. An astonishing aircraft, which seemed at every turn a reluctant departure from the flying boats for which Shorts were justifiably famous. It was a huge ungainly thing with a wing span of 99 feet, length of 87 feet, and perched upon what looked a complicated and ramshackle undercarriage. Extensive use was made of electrical systems throughout the aircraft, many of which were interesting innovations but as a result they suffered from continuing teething problems, which could be very trying. On account of these systems the aircraft contained a plethora of control panels, and with a massive fuel control system was a Flight Engineer's delight. Equally it was a pilot's nightmare, as owing to the spread and complexity of these controls, unlike the Lancaster it was impossible to fly the aircraft without an Engineer.

It was here that Eric Abbot joined the crew as Flight Engineer and our seventh crew member. Eric was a solemn personality, enlivened by flashes of dry humour and the capability of summing up a situation with ready wit. He proved an

The Vickers Wellington, known as 'The Wimpey'

The Short Stirling.

imperturbable, capable and reliable Engineer, but was later more disturbed and concerned by the implications of heavy bombing than were the rest of the crew.

No. 1651 H.C.U. was equipped in the main with the Stirling Mk III, and on this aircraft we were required to complete some forty hours' flying before passing on to a Stirling Squadron, or Lancaster Finishing School. There was the usual preliminary ground training on the aircraft, and not until 5th June (about a fortnight after our arrival) did we first fly a three-hour detail of familiarisation, circuits and landings. It was an amazing experience to be perched in the cockpit of this massive aircraft of the day, some twenty-three feet above the ground, and controlling with one hand the four Bristol Hercules XI radial engines which combined gave nearly 7,000 horsepower. I enjoyed flying the Stirling but it was a cumbersome thing, and it was here that I first met the strange blinkered attitude of many pilots who became sufficiently attached to an aircraft type to swear by it, regardless of its inadequacies.

The next day, 6th June, I was sent solo and it was while airborne on this detail that Len Stratton informed me he had picked up a B.B.C. broadcast announcing the day to be D-Day; the invasion of Europe by the Allies had begun. I think that we were all somewhat overawed by this momentous news, secretly fearful for the initial landings (which had gone so badly against us in the Dieppe Raid) and disappointed that after all we were not to take part in the initial assault. There were however, here as at Wing, full short-range bomb loads laid out beside each aircraft dispersal and we half hoped that we would be called upon to deliver them – although this would mean the landings were not going according to plan. For the rest of our course the invasion of France was uppermost in every mind, as we were conscious of its vast scale and that for the Allies it would be the crucial campaign of the war. News of its progress was scant and largely noncommittal, which experience had taught us to be indicative, at the best, of slow progress and, at the worst, of lack of success. The knowledge that such fierce fighting was taking place comparatively close by was frustrating, and deeply worrying in case all should not be going well. We concentrated as never before on the course, and following circuits and landings by day moved onto these at night.

It was at this time that the first Flying Bomb or, as it was termed by the Germans, V–1 (*Vergeltungswaffe* – Reprisal weapon) landed on London. The V–1 was a pulse-jet-powered unmanned flying bomb, twenty-five feet long with a sixteen-foot wingspan, flown at a height of between 1,000 and 7,000 feet. It carried a one ton explosive warhead at 400 m.p.h. for up to 152 miles. The German intention had been to mount a massive bombardment of London and southern England with this weapon, but a number of hold-ups (including R.A.F. intervention) delayed and much reduced the scale of the attack.* Nevertheless, by 15th June the Germans were launching 200 of these bombs in twenty-four hours, aimed in the main at

---

* Hitler had given orders for the V–1 attack on southern England to start on 15th December 1943, with a discharge rate of 5,000 Flying Bombs a month. At this rate some 50,000 V–1s would have been launched before the capture of the sites by the Allies, in September 1944.

The first R.A.F. attack on the sites was made on 25th December 1943, and these attacks continued in conjunction with the U.S.A.F., both delaying and reducing the bombardment. On the basis of actual experience some 15,000 bombs would have got through, compared to the 2,340 that actually arrived on target. The intended V–1 bombardment could have paralysed London or delayed or made impossible the assembly of men and material for the invasion of France. Either of which might well have altered the course of the war.

London. It was however an inaccurate weapon, and of the 8,617 bombs launched from sites in France mercifully only 2,340 reached the London region; the remainder being brought down or falling on the way. By the end of the bombardment in March 1945, the casualties caused in England amounted to 5,500 killed and 16,000 seriously injured.

At Wratting Common, when we had completed some twenty hours of day and night take-offs, circuits and landings, we graduated to five-hour cross-countries. The flying was hard and continuous which left us little time outside of sleep. This was probably just as well for the living conditions at Wratting Common were the most primitive and austere that I was ever to experience in the R.A.F. To offset this was some lovely June weather, and the most prolific flowering of the wild roses in the Cambridgeshire hedgerows that I had seen. They were beautiful, and seemed then most poignantly English. This time of the year also provided an extraordinary sight as the tall undercarriage of the Short Stirling raised the nose, and sometimes the mainplane, above the East Anglian morning mists which often collected in a shallow layer over the airfield and dispersals. These aircraft then looked uncannily like great prehistoric monsters lumbering through a primeval swamp, peering clumsily over the tattered veil of mist lying around their feet and tails.

Understandably, what little free time we had was spent in an almost desperate search for distraction from our concentrated training, in a change of environment. The climate of the time was one of general austerity in which movement was limited to save fuel and resources. As a result public transport had been drastically curtailed and at every turn one was likely to be confronted by the accusing poster enquiring: 'Is your journey really necessary?' For Servicemen away from home and frequently stationed in remote country districts, getting anywhere was a problem and getting back at night an even greater problem. This led to much bitter comment, and I once heard Len wryly state in answer to the question, 'But where is Wratting Common?' 'Five miles by camel from Six-Mile Bottom!'

It occurred to us as a crew that a possible answer would be to obtain a car. The idea had much to commend it, but there was the obvious limitation that a car would only accommodate four of a crew of seven. This threatened to be undesirably divisive but on the grounds that all seven of us would be unlikely to select to go to the same place at the same time, we went ahead with the idea. In the end Ron, Mitch, Len and myself agreed to split the purchase price between us, and we took the first opportunity to visit a large garage in Cambridge. There we became the proud possessors of a Hillman 10 h.p. saloon in very good second-hand condition, for which we parted with £120. Or at least, we would part with £120 as soon as we had raised it, meanwhile the car remained with the garage for final repairs and improvements. This car was to mean a great deal to us in enormously increased mobility, but the problem of petrol remained. Until 1942, there had been a basic ration for all car owners allowing for about 150 miles of driving a month. In March of 1942 this was abolished altogether and petrol could only be obtained for essential work, or health reasons. Petrol issued for commercial purposes was dyed red, but any trace of this dye in the engine of a privately owned vehicle could lead to a heavy fine or imprisonment for the owner. However, aircrew undergoing operational training or engaged in operational work were allowed petrol for about 150 miles (the old basic ration) when on leave. It was this petrol on which we had to rely, and were, for the time being, unwilling to think any further on the subject.

Our day and night cross-countries were followed by intensive fighter affiliation exercises, and in these I practised 'corkscrewing' the aircraft under the gunners' instructions. The corkscrew was a standardised manoeuvre of as violent an evasive action as the pilot and aircraft could manage. It was designed to throw a trailing fighter off the bomber's tail, but it was possible for an experienced fighter pilot to follow this twisting, diving movement. For the bomber pilot it was extremely heavy work, and combined sheer physical strength with an extensive knowledge of the aircraft. Evading a fighter would avail little if the pilot in so doing exceeded the aircraft's limitations and stripped the wings from the fuselage, which would not be particularly difficult to achieve.

This fighter affiliation completed our conversion course but for a cross-country exercise, delayed owing to bad weather. I was at this time offered the command of a Stirling Flight in the Middle East, which appointment carried immediate promotion to Squadron Leader. The rank of Squadron Leader was the first in the category of senior officer, then still a difficult and critical step to achieve, which made this offer tempting. However, it meant that we would be relegated to some comparative side-show in the Middle East, and I was determined to take part in the invasion of Europe, in which crucial clash of arms would undoubtedly be seen the most advanced technology of the time. I put it to the crew to find that only Eric and Sue were really with me, the others being either negative in their attitude, or for the posting. The situation was a difficult one, but I did not have any compunction in deciding for Europe where there was unfolding not only a colossal clash of arms, but what might well prove the final stages of the Strategic Bomber Offensive. Once this decision was taken the crew were unanimously behind me and the matter was never given another thought.

Our final cross-country at last completed, we left 1651 H.C.U. for No. 3 Lancaster Finishing School (3 L.F.S.), after logging 40 hours on type. We now knew, to our delight, that we were destined for a Lancaster Squadron. We left profoundly disturbed by the limited news of Operation Overlord, the invasion of France. The immense scale of the operation was obvious to us; Eisenhower had some 3,000,000 men under his command, with a vast assembly of stores, ammunition, vehicles and armour, in Southern England. Five landings had been made in the bay of the Seine on D-Day; two British, one Canadian and two American. This was the greatest amphibious operation of all time and the landings were made from, and supported by, the biggest armada of vessels ever known. The forecast of likely gains in the first fifty days of the operation proved extremely optimistic. Of the five beaches on which landings were made, in only one (in the U.S. sector) did the landings go badly. However, the British failed to capture Caen on the first day, owing to its unexpected garrison of a Panzer (Armoured) Division. The Normandy countryside consisted of 'bocage', small fields divided by thick hedges growing on banks of earth, ideal country for defence, and desperately difficult country for armoured attack. By D + 6 (12th June) the Allies had formed a continuous bridgehead 42 miles wide – but by D + 16, the day we left Wratting

Common for Feltwell, the territorial gains were only about half of that intended, and the Allies were still precariously situated in their bridgehead.

The intention of the No. 3 Group L.F.S. course at Feltwell, was to convert crews to the Lancaster before posting to an operational squadron in the Group. Our excited enthusiasm in at last experiencing this outstanding aircraft was for me tempered by the realisation that, in this scheme of things, we were destined to pit ourselves against the most formidable German defences with only some twelve to fifteen hours' experience on type. This was sobering enough a thought, but with our graduation to the 'real thing' came the inevitable awareness that the existing operational loss-rate made many of our fellow course members (and for that matter ourselves) already as good as dead men. For these the proverbial sands of time were indeed fast running out. I don't think that outwardly our light-hearted and sometimes ribald and rumbustious behaviour was in the slightest changed by this knowledge. However, whether or not an occasional hint of wistfulness was evident amongst us, we must certainly have felt it.

The average Bomber Command loss rate was at the time correctly believed to be about 4% of aircraft involved, per sortie. In even the most inexpert of arithmetic, this indicated to the individual crew undertaking a tour of 30 sorties that they could be facing an accumulated loss of well above 100%. The apparent anomaly was explained in the fact that over a period of 30 sorties, a squadron would be kept at full strength by the immediate replacement of lost crews. It followed that while some crews might survive in that period, others would have been replaced several times. In these circumstances the prospects of survival for any given crew could only seem remote, although it was then calculated at three chances in ten – or that for every ten men involved, three would survive. Hardly less sobering would have been the knowledge kept from us at the time, that the average operational life of the individual Lancaster aircraft was no more than some forty flying hours. This represented six or seven sorties, and each crew was scheduled to make thirty or more sorties in a tour.

Because of acute overcrowding in the Officers' Mess at Feltwell, I found myself allocated a billet in Hockwold Hall. This we considered a mixed blessing (if blessing at all) because the village of Hockwold-cum-Wilton was perhaps two miles from Feltwell. However, in the existing hustle to complete our training we were likely to finish the conversion course to Lancasters within a week, which made it hardly worth remonstrating. As it happened our brief acquaintance with Hockwold turned out decidedly memorable.

Of the village, especially notable was the church on account of a strange and moving incident there. I had become friendly with a fellow course pilot, a lanky individual with a casual sense of humour. He was interesting and good fun, but particularly interesting on his own subject as, of all surprising things, in civilian life he had been an organ builder. On this subject he was far from casual, becoming most animated and earnest. From him I learned much and became quite knowledgeable in such matters as spotted metal and thirty-two-foot diapazons! Naturally he could not resist the opportunity of inspecting any organ that came his way, and would enter every church with the most fervent of collector's zeal. So it was that very late one summer's night (or more correctly, very early one summer's morning!) on our way back to the billet from heaven know where, we walked into deeply slumbering Hockwold and found ourselves passing the church. This was too much for my companion who at once made for the door and finding it unlocked, led the way in. The interior was a contrast of forbidding dark, pierced by shafts of bright moonlight from the many elegantly long and narrow windows. It made one of those superb and moving pictures seemingly too perfect to be possible except perhaps in the imagination of a hopelessly romantic artist.

Unerringly my companion led the way down the aisle to the organ, and joy of joys it proved to be unlocked. Then began a detailed inspection accompanied by exclamations of surprise and delight. Finally seating himself at the keyboard, his hands wandered deftly in mock play. Suddenly, turning to me in almost childlike supplication he asked, 'Would you blow it for me if I showed you how to work the bellows?' Duly instructed I began heaving at the long wooden lever and was appalled by the clanking and moaning rush of air that my inexpert blowing produced. As this heinous noise echoed around the vaulted roof, it seemed in my guilty imagination to draw from behind every corner, pillar and dark recess, a startled rustle of protest from the myriad disturbed souls of the faithful departed. I might well have become badly scared, in this perfect setting for unlimited terror, if my companion had not at that moment begun to play. As the music trilled, rolled and thundered with an unearthly clarity in the still of the night, to my astonishment the mystery and terror dissolved. The moon no longer cast a chill eerie light, for in passing through the serried, leaded panes of the windows it was now a nebulous, pale, soft and wistful glow. Slowly I became aware that I was united and at peace with an ageless past; at peace with all time, past, present and future. Could this be, I wondered in utter absorbtion, a glimpse through a unique moment of great beauty of 'The peace that passeth all under-standing', enshrined in this remote place – and the peace that could conquer Richard Hilary's 'Last Enemy'* – death – with which we were shortly so con-tinually to be faced?

It might well have been an age before the enchantment faded with the last notes into the dark, and after carefully closing down the organ we left the church. In spite of this outrageous intrusion into its night's slumbers there was not a light to be seen, or a sound to be heard in the village. One could only imagine the inhabitants, in the face of such a nocturnal phenomenon, willingly leaving the church, the churchyard, the ancient cross on the green, the the village streets, to the mysterious doings of the disconsolate spirits departed – while they pulled the blankets closer around their heads!

Of our billet, the house, which stood in timbered parkland, was thought to have been built many centuries earlier (1497) and at the time of our billeting was owned

---

* 'The last enemy that shall be destroyed is death', 1 Corinthians XV. 26. *The Last Enemy* by Richard Hilary, 1942.

by Prince Duleep Singh, who normally used it as a shooting lodge. We were comfortably, if somewhat sparsely accommodated in the attic servants' quarters. For safety's sake these rooms were equipped with the Davy Fire Escape, which consisted of a small drum affixed near a window; through this drum passed a light but very strong fire-proof rope to each end of which was attached a sling. Escape was effected by arranging the sling under one's arms, climbing out of the window and then, with some considerable faith in the contraption, casting oneself into space on the end of the rope. The rope passed through a braking mechanism in the drum, which slowly lowered the sling to the ground while the second sling rose to the window. In this way an effective and fairly rapid escape could be made by a number of people.

I particularly remember this escape on account of what occurred when a party of us (who had been celebrating the final stage of our training, perhaps rather too enthusiastically, in several local hostelries) returned to our billet late one night. We were becoming conscious of the growing significance of time in our circumstances, and were ill disposed to the idea of spending it sleeping. Hockwold-cum-Wilton being not altogether surprisingly devoid of night life, we were happily indulging in the mixture of banter and foolery that can always be very enjoyable amongst men, but particularly when relieved of the cares and responsibilities of life by a convivial evening. On at last arriving in our attic, after a very noisy and eventful journey up the long back stairs, one of us spied the fire escape and began to cast doubts on its efficiency. The rest tumbling to its possibilities, variously described our dire predicament in the event of a fire in the house, and loudly demanded that it should be tested. Understandably there was a marked reluctance to do the testing as opposed to merely talking about it, until one of our number, Peter Lewis, volunteered to bale out of the window and let us know if it worked – thereby demonstrating the stuff of which Lewises were made. Flight Lieutenant Lewis, a popular member of the course, had celebrated even more enthusiastically than the rest of us, and being as a result in a fine mood of overconfident exuberance, failed entirely to see our amusement at this unfortunate double entendre! With something of the air of the daring young man on the flying trapeze, he prepared to undertake his public service.

The preparations were protracted by the need to keep Lewis's mind on the job in hand, while he flexed his muscles and postured before taking the plunge. Finally, amidst cheers, he cast himself into the darkness in the sling, but no sooner had he disappeared from sight than one of us seized a chair and as Lewis reached the windows of the floor below, jammed the chair leg into the braking mechanism so bringing Lewis's descent to halt. The intention had been merely to create an anti-climax to Lewis's exaggerated showmanship, by jamming the cable and leaving him suspended in mid-air and uncertainty, while we maintained that we could neither lower him to the ground, nor haul him up again.

Events, however, took a different turn for the bedroom window below us flew open and an irate pyjama-clad figure (whom we assumed to be Prince Duleep himself) angrily harangued our would-be hero as he swayed to and fro before him. Lewis, who was blissfully unaware that his interrogator was in far from a party mood, insisted that he was on night flying training, and to dispel any possible disbelief began appropriate sound effects as he continued to swing slowly back and forth. This was all great stuff, and up above we were convulsed with laughter, but in the ensuing storm of abuse Lewis began to realise that his suspension put him at a tactical disadvantage, and some of his alcoholically inspired confidence was evaporating. He was, by this time, being subjected to demands that he return to his billet forthwith, but as this was a course entirely beyond his control he was left looking insolently insubordinate. This both increased his interrogator's fury, and further reduced Lewis's flagging enthusiasm for what had once seemed a desirable and possibly heroic venture.

The incident then began to take a serious turn, for 'Prince Duleep' having failed to rid himself of this floating presence at his bedroom window, demanded the malefactor's name for reporting to our C.O. It was, we felt, time that we freed Lewis from his suspended pillory, and attempted to remove the chair leg jamming the escape mechanism. However, owing to the weight on the line it was well and truly stuck, and while wrestling with it we were surprised to hear Lewis, with an unexpected clarity of mind, identifying himself as Flight Lieutenant Peter Pan! Fortunately at this moment the chair leg came out and Lewis sank, with suitably theatrical effect, into the darkness below.

I was never to know if the Commanding Officer was presented with the whimsical complaint that Flight Lieutenant Peter Pan had been flying outside our host's window, as certainly we heard no more of the matter, and were anyway shortly swept from active service into action with No. 90 Squadron.

THE ROOM
(No Moment Lovelier)

If it be true the dead return
To haunt the place they loved the most,
Then surely I'll come back to learn
If you too have become a ghost.

After so many years have gone,
I shall come back again to know
And ever after gaze upon,
The room we loved in long ago.

For it was in that little room
That something looked at me through you;
Until the place was all abloom
With such a light I never knew.

Oh, such a bright, incredible wonder
Your loveliness about me made,
I felt, whatever time might sunder
This fleeting moment could not fade.

No moment lovelier than this
My hungry heart would ever see
Your lips were quivery to my kiss;
Your smile was flooding over me.

What if the house has long since been
Crumbled away from every eye,
That little room I loved you in –
My heart will never let it die!

Louis Ginsberg